Ma –

Christmas
1987

With much love
from Carolyn
x x

ASTAIRE

By the same author

McQueen
Royal Romance: Prince Andrew and Sarah Ferguson

ASTAIRE

The Biography

Tim Satchell

HUTCHINSON
LONDON   MELBOURNE   AUCKLAND   JOHANNESBURG

© Tim Satchell 1987

First published in 1987 by Hutchinson Ltd,
an imprint of Century Hutchinson Ltd, Brookmount House,
62–65 Chandos Place, London WC2N 4NW

Century Hutchinson Publishing Group (Australia) Pty Ltd,
PO Box 496, 16–22 Church Street, Hawthorn,
Melbourne, Victoria 3122

Century Hutchinson Group (NZ) Ltd,
PO Box 40–086, 32–34 View Road, Glenfield, Auckland 10

Century Hutchinson Group (SA) Pty Ltd,
PO Box 337, Bergvlei 2012, South Africa

British Library Cataloguing in Publication Data
Satchell, Tim
  Astaire: the biography.
  1. Astaire, Fred   2. Dancers—United
  States—Biography
  I. Title
  791.43′028′0924   GV1785.A83

  ISBN 0–09–173736–2

Typeset by Deltatype, Ellesmere Port
Printed and bound in Great Britain by
MacKays of Chatham Ltd, Chatham, Kent

For Amanda

Contents

	List of Illustrations	viii
1	The Astaires	1
2	Omaha	8
3	New York	17
4	Early days	27
5	Broadway	42
6	London	56
7	Adèle	73
8	Finding a partner	90
9	Keeping in the lines	104
10	Top Hat	122
11	Hollywood years	135
12	War	154
13	MGM	166
14	Laughter and Garland	177
15	Phyllis	191
16	Another last dance	203
17	Going straight	215
18	Ann	223
19	Melody and Robyn	233
20	Finale	248
	Appendix	257
	Chronology	260
	Key	262
	Bibliography	298
	Index	301

List of Illustrations

1. 2326 South 10th Street, Omaha, Nebraska – the house where Frederick Austerlitz Jnr was born in 1899. (Tim Satchell)
2. Fred, aged 5. (Bettmann Archive / BBC Hulton Picture Library)
3. Fred and Adèle, brother and sister dance team. Around 1910. (Bettmann Archive/BBC Hulton Picture Library)
3a. Fred aged 13, and Adèle aged 15½. (Culver Pictures Inc.)
3b. With Adèle in *Over the Top*, 1917. (Culver Pictures Inc.)
4. Adèle, aged 16. (Culver Pictures Inc.)
5. *The Bunch and Judy*, 1922. (Culver Pictures Inc.)
6. *Over the Top*, 1917. (Culver Pictures Inc.)
7. *Stop Flirting*, 1923. (Stage Photos Co.)
8. With Tilly Losch in *The Band Wagon*, 1931. (Culver Pictures Inc.)
9. Adèle on her wedding day, 1932. (From left) Mrs Astaire, Lord and Lady Charles Cavendish, Marquess of Hartington, Duke of Devonshire and attendants. The Duchess is conspicuously absent.
10. Lismore Castle, Adèle's new home. (Tim Satchell)
11. Adèle's premature daughter dies at birth. (Tim Satchell)
12. Fred married Phyllis Potter on 12 July, 1933. (Bettmann Archive/BBC Hulton Picture Library)
13. Together for the first time, Fred and Ginger Rogers in *Flying Down to Rio*, 1933. (Culver Pictures Inc.)
14. Fred, the image perfected, 1935. (Culver Pictures Inc.)
15. Top hat, white tie and tails, 1935. (Culver Pictures Inc.)
16. With Ginger in *Carefree*, 1938. (Culver Pictures Inc.)
17. With Hermes Pan and deceptive dance diagrams, 1936. (Culver Pictures Inc.)
18. With Ginger in *Swing Time*, 1936. (Bettmann Archive/BBC Hulton Picture Library)
19. With Ginger, forty years on at RKO lunch for donation of archives to University of California. (Bettmann Archive/BBC Hulton Picture Library)
20. With Fred Jr, and a 222lb marlin, 1953. (Bettmann Archive/BBC Hulton Picture Library)

21. With Anthony Quinn and his daughter, Christine, Fred escorts daughter, Ava, to a Beverly Hills debutante ball, 1959. (Bettmann Archive/BBC Hulton Picture Library)
22. Off set, and unshaven in *Let's Dance*, 1950. (Culver Pictures Inc.)
23. With Cyd Charisse, 1957. (Culver Pictures Inc.)
24. With his horse, Triplicate, Astaire won the San Juan Capistrano Handicap, 1946. (Bettmann Archive/BBC Hulton Picture Library)
25. With Rita Hayworth in *You Were Never Lovelier*, 1942. (Kobal Collection)
26. Up the wall in *Royal Wedding (Wedding Bells* in UK), 1951. (National Film Archive Stills Library)
27. With Judy Garland, a couple of swells, in *Easter Parade*, 1948. (National Film Archive Stills Library)
28. With Gene Kelly in *Ziegfeld Follies*, 1946. (National Film Archive Stills Library)
29. With Barrie Chase on TV dance spectacular, *Hollywood Palace*, 1960. (Associated Press)
30. On 27 June 1980, Fred Astaire and Robyn Smith were married. He was 81; she claimed to be 35. The two are shown here in January 1979. (UPI)
31. Exit, 'Puttin' on the Ritz', 1946. (Culver Pictures Inc.)

1
The Astaires

The story of Fred and Adèle Astaire is the story of the American dream.

Second and third generation Americans from humble mid-West beginnings, the brother and sister dancers became America's and then England's, favourite entertainers.

Adèle taught the Prince of Wales to tap dance and when she retired from the stage, by marrying into one of Europe's grandest families, she became Lady Charles Cavendish, a member of the British aristocracy, and lived in a fairy tale castle in Ireland. Fred went on to become a wealthy and hugely successful Hollywood film star, much admired and with a style emulated throughout the world.

Fred and Adèle Astaire are a fascinating pair. She was gifted with a natural talent as a comedienne and performer. Dark-haired and impish. Warm-hearted, impulsive and a libertine. His talent, on the other hand, was achieved by hard work and an obsessive perfectionism. On stage and screen he was a brilliant and warm character, yet underneath dispassionate and single-minded.

As youngsters there was nothing that marked them out for success yet together they became the most praised theatrical couple of their time. The tops, with an extraordinary lightness, empathy and yet, in the words of Sydney Carrol in *The Times* (London, 1923) 'as odd as golliwogs'.

When Adèle left the stage and Fred arrived in Hollywood, more by chance than planning, he found an apparently perfect partner in Ginger Rogers. To a generation Astaire and Rogers symbolised everything that was marvellous about the silver screen. On the studio sound stage sets he called her Miss Rogers or Miss R, she called him Mr Astaire or Mr A. Despite their practical coolness together, on screen they were magical. It seemed that theirs was a truly great romance in an age of innocence. 'I make love with my feet,' Astaire said, when asked why the couple did not kiss on screen in the first seven of their films.

[1]

In later years Fred Astaire claimed that he didn't know enough about dance to talk about it. That was no affectation, but his friend and dance director on many of his films, Hermes Pan, did give me an insider's explanation of the reasons for Fred's success: 'First of all he has a tremendous sense of rhythm. There are many beautiful dancers who can do more fabulous things than Fred, they can make fantastic leaps and so forth, but Fred has an uncanny quality of timing they don't have. Second, Fred can dance a very intricate routine and he makes it look so simple and easy. It gives the audience a sense of self-identification – kind of a feeling that they, too, can do it. Third, he has a wonderful personality with a definite impact on people. This comes through in his acting and singing, as well as his dancing. He can just sit on a stool and sing a song and captivate every single person in the audience. Fourth, and most important, is his creativity. He never liked to repeat anything he'd done and would constantly run movies of his old dance routines to make sure every step was fresh and new. The move on the golf course, a child skipping rope in the street, anything would give him ideas for dance routines.'

But there is more to his success than that. Dancing in its most basic form is a release for aggression, an energy which both Astaires had acquired as children and as youths. Brilliance in dance is achieved through competition.

In the early years Fred's competition was with Adèle. After his ideal partnership with her, he competed with himself. And, on film, it is while dancing alone that he displays his greatest talent and also appears to gain most pleasure: he can prove more to himself, all the credit is accrued to him and he is the star on his own. Those performances reveal a deadly competitive seriousness and in the perfection of the art the movie watcher does not usually notice that the amazing control does not make the dancing a fun activity. Fred Astaire did get it absolutely right, maybe too right, inhumanly so, the absolute obsession for perfection superseding the pleasure of dancing. Yet it is attractive because of that very perfectionism, with that beautiful, balletic grace.

Although there was nothing outwardly personally objectionable to Astaire about Ginger Rogers – despite her occasional attempts to upstage him, a potentially dangerous thing to do – there is little doubt that Fred Astaire hated her.

He particularly disliked the 'Fred and Ginger' thing. 'People talk of us as a team, we sound like horses,' he complained more than once. By himself he was determined to outshine any team that the devil himself could put up against him – never mind if he was a member of that team himself.

As Dr Charlotte Fienmann, a senior consultant psychiatrist at London's Middlesex Hospital, who studied the life of the Astaires and the still available film clips, explains: 'His attitude is understandable – having had the perfect partnership with Adèle he didn't want a partnership with anyone else – he was caught in the dilemma of needing a partner, yet wanting to do it alone.' In some ways he achieved that by rehearsing with his male collaborator, Hermes Pan, taking Ginger Rogers' role. Pan would teach the steps to Ginger, and only then would Astaire and Rogers dance together. After all that, it would be Astaire and Pan who would add the tap dancing to the soundtracks.

Astaire see-sawed between aiming for an unrealistic peak of perfection and deciding that he would follow Adèle, with her easy-come, easy-go attitude, into retirement. Adèle found contentment in her life once she had overcome her disappointment at not having children. But with Fred's first five, short-lived, retirements, his ambivalent attitude caused him even more angst: he thought he could make the decision to stop dancing and then couldn't.

Away from the bright lights, Astaire was a complex and often troubled man. His childhood was peripatetic, disrupted when his mother's ambitions took him and Adèle away from their small-town background on an extraordinary journey which cut them off from any paternal influence – even the loquacious Adèle rarely mentioned their father in later life. Fred would sometimes attempt to justify the relationship, but his father remained an uncle figure in their life, visiting them occasionally at holiday times. Johanna Astaire was left to raise the children, and her influence on them was profound; both children sought to compensate for that lack of male influence as they made their progress. It was certainly more of a loss for the six-year-old Fred than for the older Adèle, and in the early years the only strong, masculine influence came from their stage school teachers, the theatre managers, the train drivers of their travels and the ever-knowledgeable bell-hops.

Ann, as Johanna became known, took over the father's rôle completely. Some analytical theory might suggest that this would affect the sexuality of the children, that children brought up too close to their mothers are more likely to become homosexual, yet Astaire was comparatively rare among male dancers in always being heterosexual.

[3]

What did happen was that Adèle became a libertine and Astaire developed into an obsessive, finding it difficult to show real affection. Throughout his life, his mother and his sister were the only ones with whom he dared show any true emotion.

Throughout his life, the most important influences on Fred Astaire were women. As far as his offspring were concerned, he had a deeply ambivalent feeling towards his son, and a deep love of his daughter. He took as his first wife a woman who had experience of a previous marriage and had a child of her own; she was responsible and emotionally in control – a steady mother figure who stayed close by his side. This low-key relationship satisfied him and relieved him of the need for the womanising expected of a Hollywood star.

Even with his own family's opposition, his second marriage was relatively successful. And in Fred Astaire, Robyn Smith found the father that she never knew. He found the affection of a young bride and a replacement daughter. It couldn't be an equal relationship despite her own considerable financial achievement.

Away from the screen Astaire attached great importance to promoting his private life in the same way as his public image – a healthy and flawless lifestyle. He tried to be as fastidiously perfect in his private life as in his dancing. He exorcised his insecurities by creating a very structured environment, while Adèle roared her way through life, taking risks and having fun.

Astaire's satisfaction in life came directly from his work, but with increasing age he had to accept lower standards. On film and in real life he was always self-deprecatory. He frequently said he owed his success to his mother, but rarely paid full tribute to some of the backstage people, like rehearsal pianist Hal Borne, or Hermes Pan, who for so long was almost literally his shadow. He survived in the complex world of Hollywood for a number of reasons. When he arrived there he was thirty-three years old, and somehow never seemed to age (the long-lived Nebraska stock?). He never followed the California diet of pill-popping, psychiatrists and paranoid vitamin consumption. While other top calibre performers fell from the summit, Astaire retained his sense of proportion, avoiding the pitfalls that trapped others. Where Buster Keaton took to the bottle and ultimately was sacked by Louis B. Mayer, Astaire stuck to his last, and assiduously remained friends with the studio top brass without undermining his own standards. Where Clark Gable succumbed to the obfuscations of drink and lost his regal good-looks, Astaire drank his one dry Martini and retained his ageless

[4]

appearance. Where Maurice Chevalier, having been accused of collaborating with the Nazis (he sang to them, he claimed, to save Jewish friends), ran into trouble with the US authorities and was refused re-entry into the States in 1951 for signing the Communist inspired anti-nuclear Stockholm Appeal (although he did eventually make films in the US), Astaire supported Uncle Sam's war effort but otherwise eschewed, both publicly and privately, any political involvement. Where Charlie Chaplin voraciously pursued, bedded and sometimes wedded young girls – and the younger the better – there was never the slightest whiff of scandal surrounding Fred Astaire, even though a number of ambitious young actresses and fans offered themselves. Astaire, despite his elegant, androgynous aloofness, retained a virility that was expressed in his private life and his supreme performances.

There were other dancers, Donald O'Connor, George Murphy, Dan Dailey, but Astaire off and on screen was always a class above them. The nearest to his achievement was Gene Kelly, also a brilliant choreographer. Where Kelly enjoyed choreographing for others, Astaire choreographed for Astaire. And where many performers sought ever more lucrative contracts until their egos or greed (or maybe need?) outgrew their box-office appeal, Astaire, while always keeping a weather eye on his income, sustained his $100,000-a-film plateau for many years. He thus ensured he remained a desirable business proposition. He was hired, and he would perform. He was not paid *per diem*. The studio might have a schedule and Astaire might sometimes set himself some form of timetable, but he would go on working until he personally was satisfied with his performance. That performance was not for the director, the film crew, his fellow performers, the money men or his peers. He discovered early in his career that they could all be fairly easily pleased. His performance and his dancing were for himself alone.

He might occasionally discuss ideas with Hermes Pan, but his innermost views were rarely vocalised. 'You had to translate, and work out what he wanted,' said Pan. Astaire hated to analyse himself or his dancing: 'I've said all I've got to say about myself. I don't know enough about dance to talk about it.'

When filming was over, the studio stills photographer would re-set the day's proceedings to take publicity shots. One day there was a call for photographs of Fred Astaire planning and writing out the dance steps for one of his routines. In vain Astaire explained that the choreography was never annotated. But the publicity department said they still wanted the photographs. So blackboard and chalk were found and Astaire and Pan drew a succession of lines, squiggles and arrows and posed obligingly for the session. At the last minute Astaire added a mess of chalk marks at the bottom of the 'plan'. The photographs were widely circulated and much reproduced as showing the great man at work. Photographs cannot speak, which is a pity. Because what Astaire said as he added his finishing touch was: 'And that's the bullshit this whole thing is all about.'

My interest in the Astaires started, as it did for many of my own generation, in the 1950s, after my father had died and I, not quite a teenager, and eager for sophistication, was left with warm memories, a pair of co-respondent shoes (too big then, too small later, and long since given to a church jumble sale), a black silk top hat, dated photographs of a young man enjoying himself in London and the South of France and a collection of 78 rpm gramophone records from the late twenties, thirties and forties. I played those records endlessly; by the age of thirteen I knew all the words to 'Funny Face', 'Top Hat', 'Cheek to Cheek', 'Pick Yourself Up' and 'Puttin' on the Ritz'.

I even had the London First Night programme from *Funny Face*. It was only later that I discovered from Dickie Fester, a fellow law student and co-conspirator with my father, that they had been unable to buy tickets, so, in white tie and tails, had calmly walked in, stood at the back of the stalls, and cheered themselved hoarse with the rest of the audience.

If Adèle Astaire is identified with her grand retirement then Fred Astaire is most identified with, and identified by, the Irving Berlin song he borrowed for his own from Harry Richman's 1930 movie, *Puttin' on the Ritz*.

Astaire heard Richman sing the song in a New York club, immediately added it to his repertoire, and recorded it in London in March 1930. With the aggressive staccato lilt, his high hat and coloured collar, Fred Astaire showed that anyone could be puttin' on the Ritz. He made it look as though it was possible for any ordinary-looking fellow to burst into song and dance with the same, seemingly effortless style.

Although the song, with its complex counter rhythms and compulsive drive, was virtually his theme tune whenever he appeared on stage or radio, Fred Astaire did not perform 'Puttin' on the Ritz' in a movie until his twentieth feature film, *Blue Skies*, in 1946 – it was intended to be his ultimate screen appearance.

The 'Puttin' on the Ritz' sequence, the last to be shot for the film, reveals much about Fred Astaire the man and Fred Astaire the performer. The vocals, both in style and words, are different from the light, 1930s version. Berlin wrote new lyrics, removing the references to 'Harlem', 'Lennox Avenue', 'darkies' and 'their Lulubelles', and moving the action to 'Park Avenue', where the Astaires lived in Manhattan.

From a low-key opening Astaire also sets a more desperate, driving pace. He appears alone, grim faced and elegant in top hat, black tail coat, grey cravat and white spats, as though dressed for Royal Ascot, a wedding or funeral rather than night-time dancing, hitting his brown day cane against the beat – it leaps from the floor to his hand when he throws it down (arranged by a hidden spring mechanism on the sound stage floor). He continuously looks off-camera, his feet push through the backdrop curtain and kick open a wall of mirrors where there is a chorus line of eight identical top-hatted images. By multi-exposure (hardly an exact science in 1946) the eight-strong, perfectly drilled chorus line is all Fred Astaire. As the deliberate, hard-jawed, swaggering routine reaches a machine-gun crescendo the perfect Astaire chorus suddenly divides into two different, alternate lines, walking towards, and away from, the camera.

Finally the solo singing and dancing Fred Astaire draws forward from the line and the camera closes. For the first time in the routine he faces it, as Fred Astaire, content in his hard-earned isolation, dances by himself.

2
Omaha

Wednesday 10 May 1899, towards the middle of a bright, sunshiny morning. In the bustling mid-Western railway town of Omaha, Nebraska, in the back room of a small whitewashed clapboard house standing at 2326 South 10th Street, Fred Astaire was born: Frederic Austerlitz, a son and heir for Frederic and Johanna Austerlitz.

It was just seven years since 'Fritz' Austerlitz, the twenty-three-year-old son of Stephen Austerlitz and his wife Lucy Heller, had left army service in Vienna, Austria, for the United States of America, land of opportunity and wealth – or so he, and many millions like him, hoped. He had taken the slow sea voyage to the New World at the behest of two young Austrian friends, Morris Karpeles and Huber Freund, who had left Vienna a few months earlier with an ambitious entrepreneurial scheme to set up business in Omaha, the fastest growing township in America. Karpeles and Freund had already worked out their plans and had a grandiloquent name for the business: The International Publishing and Portrait Company. Now they needed a salesman to assist them in their rise to riches.

Omaha, Nebraska, had started life as a suburb of Council Bluffs, Iowa – the terminus of the railroad from New York. To go farther west than Council Bluffs, one needed a horse and wagon to reach the easternmost point of the track that stretched to the California coast. With the advent of the Union Pacific railway and the Golden Spike ceremony at Promontory, Utah, in 1869, East and West were finally and firmly united. Omaha, ideally located on the Missouri River, attracted railroad workers and transcontinental trade. The town prospered mightily and became the trading centre of the whole United States, proudly boasting the world's largest stockyards. Farmers from North and South arrived daily to sell their cattle and produce. The livestock boom brought with it much peripheral business: the canning and leather industries prospered, as did everything imaginable in the

[8]

way of services. The aim of the International Publishing and Portrait Company was to tap this lucrative market twofold: as portrait photographers to the rising high society of tradespeople, and as a publishing rival to the existing Omaha Street Directory, which at an annual $5 a copy was an essential resource for the local merchants and hugely profitable for the businessmen who owned it.

Omaha was a logical choice for a couple of ambitious Austrians to set up shop, as it was already the centre for many German-speaking immigrants. Unhappily for the optimistic entrepreneurs, the dream of instant riches soon faded. As in many other areas, the massive railroad expansion was followed by a glut of labour when the tasks in hand were completed. The meat barons and leather merchants were badly hit by the trade downturn, known as the Panic of '93, and among the many schemes which foundered was that little minnow with the big name, The International Publishing and Portrait Company.

Fritz Austerlitz, without funds and with few friends in a strange country, set off along the dusty streets of Omaha in search of work. He had been lodging at a boarding house at 1418 Howard, but there too he found life collapsing around him. Mrs Starkey, his landlady, was in no mind to extend credit to a jobless young immigrant who could hardly speak English, and she gave him notice to leave. The new West was hard, but Fritz, always buoyed by enthusiasm and a sense of humour, went determinedly from place to place until he found himself a job as a cook at a saloon run by another immigrant, Fred Mittnacht, at 1112 Broadway.

Mittnacht, like Austerlitz, was a Lutheran Protestant, and it was through the church – which served as a notice board of local life – that Fritz had first heard of the saloon job.

Indeed it was not only employment that Fritz found through the Lutheran church and its community; he also met fifteen-year-old Johanna Geilus, a bright-eyed, slight, shy young girl with long, raven-black hair. She was a native of Omaha, born on 22 December 1878, shortly after her Lithuanian parents, David and Wilhelmina Klaatke Geilus, had arrived in the New World from Susemilken, in east Prussia (now part of Germany). Her father had originally worked for the Boyd Packing House, a canning company, but by the time Fritz and Johanna met he was a furnace man and moulder at the gigantic railway workshops of Omaha's largest employer, the Union Pacific Railroad Company. Johanna had already started to help out as a teacher at the Lutheran church school.

[9]

The happy-go-lucky young Fritz, sprightly, with a moustache and a pronounced Austrian accent that he never quite lost, assiduously courted young Johanna. To her he seemed terribly sophisticated, with his stories of Vienna and of life with his brothers Otto and Ernst in the Austrian army. One day, he claimed, he had been clapped in the guardhouse when he had failed to salute Ernst. That, he said, was why he had decided to come to America. There is not a shred of evidence for the stories, which were embellished differently at each telling, but they may as well have been true as false. Fritz made Johanna laugh, flattered her and told her: 'There are two kinds of Austrian – musicians and rascals. I, of course, am a musician.' And between the rascally stories, he did play the piano with gusto and sang Viennese ballads and drinking songs in a fine tenor whenever the occasion allowed.

Johanna became increasingly fond of the Austrian short order chef – she would sometimes sneak in to the Mittnacht bar to have a quick chat in the middle of the day – and their romance prospered. They talked of getting married when Johanna reached her sixteenth birthday at the end of December; but then, in the autumn of '84, she found that she was pregnant.

There was consternation in the Geilus household, but it was decided by Johanna's mother that the couple must marry as soon as possible. On Sunday 17 November 1894, after the morning service at the white-painted wooden First German Lutheran Church at 1005 South 20th Street, Johanna and Fritz were married by the pastor, Rev. Julius Frese. With the licence, on which Johanna had to add a few months to her age so she could pass for sixteen, they had managed, amid tantrums and rows, to get from her father the necessary letter of permission for the marriage of a minor. As witnesses they had the bride's elder sister Maria and her fiancé Wilhelm Wilke.

There was neither time nor money for a honeymoon, so the young couple simply started their married life at the inexpensive but clean Metropolitan Hotel at 820 Broadway, near the Mittnacht saloon. Johanna's relatives did their best to persuade them to move away from the centre of town, where the bride's pregnancy could cause a scandal. So, loading their few possessions into a buggy, they crossed the Missouri River to a boarding-house in Council Bluffs, near enough to keep in touch with the family but far enough away for them to start a new life. Fritz found a job as a salesman with Harle-Haas, who traded in glasses and fancy goods at 33 Main Street, and Johanna, now called 'Anna' by Fritz, rested at home.

A shadow of mystery surrounds the new Austerlitz family at this point. When the records have been examined, and every possible avenue explored, the only remaining feasible explanation is that Johanna's first child was stillborn. Infant mortality was all too common in those times and many a sad little body was buried in a tiny grave. There is no record or recollection of either Johanna or Fritz ever discussing the matter again – certainly not with the two children that were eventually born to them. Indeed, in later years Johanna used to say that she and Fritz were married in 1896, two years after they actually wed.

After a while they decided to return to Omaha township, and Fritz went to work for Walter Moise, who sold beer, wine and cigars in his store at 214–216 South 11th Street. Johanna found them a convenient little clapboard house to rent at 1112 South 11th Street, and within a few months she was once again pregnant. This pregnancy was calm and peaceful. On Friday 18 September 1896, with the assistance of midwife Louise Mohr, she gave birth at home to a healthy, noisy baby girl that the happy couple named Adèle Marie after Johanna's two sisters.

By the time the baby was two years old, Fritz, always eager to improve himself, had both a new job, as a travelling salesman for the Omaha Brewing Association, and a new home, on South 10th Street. Once more, Johanna was pregnant. The child, born on 10 May 1899, was called Frederic Austerlitz II. He was rather small and weak, so sickly that for a while it seemed he would not live long. Fritz did not even bother to register the birth – the walk to the other end of town seemed hardly worthwhile. It could always be done later, Fritz thought, but how much later he didn't imagine. In fact, it was Johanna who eventually registered the birth of Fred Astaire, as he would become, thirty-three years later, when she suddenly realised that her son had no birth certificate to prove his existence for a marriage licence.

According to his cousin, Freddie's first years were as uneventful, or eventful, as those of any quiet, well-behaved non-screaming child can be. He tottered at one, walked at two and – making a major move for mankind – also joined in his sister's dances around the little house. When he was a few days past his fourth birthday – on 16 May 1903 – he joined her at the local Kellom School. Adèle was a pert and pretty child, the apple of her father's eye, and Freddie, small, elfin, adored by his mother, did his best to please and keep up with his sister and all her activities, playing with her paper dolls, and trailing around behind her

– to her pleasure, when he ran her errands, and to her annoyance, when she wanted to be left alone with her friends. When Adèle was enrolled at the Chambers Dancing Academy, a popular little school run by Willard E. Chambers (a former First National Bank clerk) at 2424 Farnam, it wasn't long before Johanna decided that it would be a good idea to let Freddie go along with her. Freddie loved to try on Adèle's dancing pumps, imitating her little ballet steps on his pointed toes, and pestering his parents to let him go too. This certainly solved the problem of what to do with him while Adèle was in class, and also helped to build up his slight physique.

It was soon apparent to Willard Chambers and Johanna that Adèle really did have some talent. So no one was surprised when she announced, very seriously – as only a little girl going on seven can do to her doting father – that she was going to be a famous dancer when she grew up. 'And so am I,' insisted Freddie.

'Of course you are,' said Fritz Austerlitz reassuringly, ignoring the faces being pulled by Adèle. Sometimes he and Anna took the two tots to see the vaudeville theatre's singers, dancers and acrobats; to Fritz the happiest sight of all was the faces of his children, wide-eyed and open-mouthed at the sheer glamour and glitter of the spectacle.

It was a simple and healthy early childhood. There wasn't a lot of money around, but the family never went short of food, clothes, or treats – Johanna made their clothes, and Fritz their toys. Adèle did well in the classroom and, their teacher Adèle Gratoit reported, both were very bright, Freddie being somewhat more serious than his sister. Willard Chambers was increasingly pleased with Adèle's progress. He told Johanna that, if the child continued to improve at the same rate and worked hard, there really might be a future for her as a dancer: she had a natural flair that was quite unusual in one so young.

Between school and dancing class, brother and sister lived cheerful small town lives: they played ball on the streets with their friends and occasionally went in the small family buggy with their mother to visit their cousins the Prochnows, who had a truck farm a few miles outside the city limits complete with cows and ducks and chickens and pigs. The favourite game, particularly enjoyed by Freddie, was to ride on the wide, scratchy sow, who would set off around the yard, snorting wildly at the indignity of being taken for a pony – the excitement, as well as the frequent falls and squeals from both humans and pigs, were re-membered long afterwards by his cousins as Freddie grew and prospered. It was, they said, difficult to realise that the elegant chap

[12]

bounding across the movie screen was the same young Freddie who used to ride the old pig.

Two elements of those early days were to leave a lasting impression on Fred Astaire – one of these he acknowledged while the other he pushed right to the back of his sub-conscious. The first had to do with the location of the Austerlitz home. When Freddie was still a toddler, the family moved the mile or so from South 10th Street to 1426 North 19th Street, to be nearer the centre of town. This put them closer to the mighty railroad. Night and day they felt the powerful and regular beat of the mighty locomotives rumbling from coast to coast, each train creating its own syncopation as it gathered speed over the track plates with punctuating, ever-altering bursts of hissing steam. They heard the irregular and incessant clanging of engines and trucks being shunted and the noise of the vast couplings clattering together. In the daytime Adèle and Freddie would play at being trains, tapping their feet to the ch-ch-ch-ch-choo-choo sounds; at night the background battery would lull them into a deep and untroubled sleep.

The other relevant feature of that period was something that happened when Freddie was five years old. Turning a cartwheel on the sidewalk, something he had done safely many times before, he slipped, fell badly, and broke his arm. For two months his arm was firmly strapped to a wooden splint; playing in the street and dancing were forbidden. Later he claimed to have forgotten the incident, but Adèle recalled it well and remembered her brother being absolutely miserable about it and furious that dancing was not allowed. Astaire said that his only memory of that time was of having measles and, later, scarlet fever, when his mother put a note on the door of their house warning other children to stay away. But the episode of the broken arm perhaps explains why he was always so very wary of acrobatics in his dance routines. Although it was only when trying a skateboard many years later that he did suffer another fracture, he was constantly confronted with the need to come up with steps that were new and different yet which posed no risks. Of course, to achieve the effects he wanted he did sometimes have to take chances, but only after a considerable amount of persuasion by the few people he trusted. Then again, there could be another reason why Astaire couldn't remember breaking his arm: he said that he left Omaha when he was four years old – two years before he actually did – and the incident occurred in those 'missing' two years.

Fritz was well settled in his job. The company had been taken over in 1902 by Arthur Storz, member of a prominent and prosperous Omaha

[13]

family, and was now called the Storz Brewing Company. Sometimes Fritz would go out with his boss to shoot wild duck; other times they would stay late at the office and have a few drinks together when the day was finished. Johanna did not object very strenuously to his late nights and drinking and, as far as one can tell, did not even create many scenes over Fritz's other women; but she did find herself increasingly dissatisfied with her lot. She was almost twenty-six years old, and understandably, considering she had her first pregnancy at the age of fifteen, she decided that there must be more to life. She was to find her escape, but not at all in the way she expected.

The highlight of life in Omaha, and in Nebraska generally, was, and is, the Coronation of the King and Queen of Ak-Sar-Ben by the Knights of Ak-Sar-Ben. The Knights are no sinister secret society but merely represent an attempt by turn of the century Nebraskans to win back some of the prestige lost to the state of Washington when Seattle was chosen for the World's Fair, a direct result of the Gold Rush of 1897. The burghers founded a society that would not only promote their state but would also do charitable works; for a name they took the word Nebraska and simply spelt it backwards: Ak-Sar-Ben. It was an all-male organisation, as might be expected, and it quickly prospered. Enlightened self-interest bought land and created a major sports arena and racetrack, today both splendidly modern and profitable. But the social side of Ak-Sar-Ben is just as important to the locals. There is an annual Coronation of a King and Queen chosen by the Knights: the King is a worthy citizen, inevitably a prominent businessman, his Queen a teenage girl chosen, in theory, for personality, but the right social connections, a wealthy family, and good looks are no drawback. They are crowned at a big, back-slapping ceremony enlivened by dancing, singing, and a pageant performed by a troupe of attendant children.

In the Nebraska of 1904, as in any society with no previous formalised structure, the belief in stratification was intense. It was every mother's ambition that her daughter should be the Queen, or at least one of the attendants of the regal couple. A team of Ak-Sar-Ben Knights arrived at the Willard Chambers Academy to conduct auditions. Adèle, then seven and a half, and Freddie, five, rehearsed their routines till they knew the steps backwards, and they danced their hearts out. They might as well not have bothered. For while they were talented, able, and attractive, they lacked the fine clothes of the richer children and the prosperous well-connected parents who were so

[14]

important to the success of the Ak-Sar-Ben operation. Of course Johanna turned them out beautifully, but they didn't live in a smart house and move in chic circles. So others were chosen, and the Austerlitz children were passed over. Their mother tried to comfort them in their disappointment, but she couldn't tell them the real reason they hadn't been picked. Willard Chambers was sympathetic: they were certainly among the best performers to his eyes, but he knew that things were not that simple. It was a first bitter taste of failure and not one that Johanna intended her children to experience again.

Fritz was all for taking a sabre to the selection committee, but Johanna's better sense prevailed. 'Do you not think,' she asked him, 'that if Mr Chambers is telling us the truth about Adèle's talent, perhaps we have a duty to help it in any way we can?' And so they talked. Maybe Chambers was right, and Adèle should have further coaching. Surely, the doting parents agreed, if she had the right training there was a bright future for her as a professional dancer. She couldn't get that training in Omaha; she would have to go to New York, and Johanna would have to go with her. Why, Adèle might even do very well as a child vaudevillian: there was always a demand for talented youngsters. In the larger world she would be judged on her merit rather than her connections. Fritz, who could see himself ending his own days as a lowly brewery employee, was enthusiastic about his daughter's prospects, and Johanna was keen on the idea of getting away from the drudgery of life in Omaha. If they could work on the vaudeville circuits, she could be useful – making the children's clothes, acting as their tutor, and generally chaperoning them. She would, at last, be independent – just as long as they could survive financially. When Adèle was consulted, she was filled with enthusiasm for the project. 'Can we go now?' she begged. Freddie understood less, but he could hardly be left behind. If Adèle thought it was a good idea then so did he.

That winter was a time of furious economies in the Austerlitz house, with every possible cent being put away for the new adventure. The plan was that when Johanna and the children were settled and Fritz had managed to save some more money, he would join them in New York and find himself a job there. Later on, all agreed that it had been sheer folly to think they could go off into the unknown and expect to survive, but at the time everyone was too excited to assess the realities of the venture. Willard Chambers had recommended an establishment run by Claude Alvienne, a professional director with a good reputation,

[15]

whose card Fritz had seen in the *New York Clipper*, the theatrical trade paper. So it was decided: the children were booked into the school, and an advance on their fees was sent ahead.

It was no sad parting. At twenty-six, Johanna was making her first journey away from Omaha; for the children, it was an adventure. The January of 1905 was even colder than the usual Nebraska winter, but no one complained about that. Fritz drove them to the station in the buggy, and their few possessions were piled on the seats next to them. Adèle, aged eight, and Freddie, five years and eight months, chattered away, waving furiously to their Nebraska home as they set off for the two-day, two-night journey. 'I don't care if anybody else goes to New York, as long as I do,' said Freddie, as he was helped up into the train, wrapped in his scarf, hat, and winter coat. His parents bustled about, making sure that all was correctly loaded. Sister Adèle, her hat and scarf not quite covering her two beribboned pigtails, holding her purse tightly to herself, turned to her boisterous brother. 'Oh, shut up,' she said.

3
New York

It was a grey and blustery day when Johanna and her small charges arrived at Pennsylvania Station and for a few moments stood in a bemused group on the platform, surrounded by people, clouds of steam from the train, and the noise of the terminus. Then Johanna got directions from the porter and set off determinedly, with the children behind her, for the Herald Square Hotel, which had been recommended by Claude Alvienne as being comfortable, convenient, clean, and suitable for a woman with two children, as well as being, most importantly, inexpensive.

On the following Monday morning, Fred and Adèle, holding tight to their mother's hands, found their way to the Grand Opera House building on Eighth Avenue at 23rd Street. They climbed the worn, narrow wooden staircase up to the door announcing Claude Alvienne's School. Inside was one large room done up as a small ballroom, with three mirrored walls lined with cane chairs and a small stage at one end. The cream paint on the walls was flaking, the floor-length mirrors were showing signs of age, and some of the chairs looked unsafe; but to the Austerlitz family it was heaven. Fred was rather surprised to be left with his sister in the charge of the kindly, white-haired Alvienne, who beat time with his stick on the back of a wooden chair, but he was always happy to go along with whatever Adèle was doing. They were keen and bright, and straight away joined in with the crowd of youngsters at the school, all eager to shine. Alvienne was a gentle and patient instructor; when any of the children made a mistake, he would lay his stick on the chair and stop the pianist. 'Now we do it like so,' he would say, as he demonstrated the step. There was drama and dancing and music – theory and practice – throughout the day, either in big classes or the little cubby holes that were just big enough for a piano and a couple of people to squeeze in.

After class in the afternoon, they would rush up to Johanna when she

[17]

came to collect them, full of their stories of the day's activities. They would return to the hotel, where she would teach them their three R's, with Adèle and Fred scratching away earnestly with their chalk and slates. In any spare time Fred would also enthusiastically practise his piano scales. Adèle decided early on that she was happy just to dance.

They soon created a whole new world for themselves. There were other permanent residents at the Herald Square Hotel: businessmen, salespeople, and some old folks, all of whom the children, after an initial shyness, befriended. It wasn't long before they were taking the cosmopolitan city life for granted. Johanna even adopted a new identity: in future she would be called Anna Austerlitz. As time went on, even that sounded too informal; when the children eventually changed their last name for professional purposes, Johanna was transformed once more, to Ann. The kids, known at home and to their friends as Delly and Freddie, would always stick to the more formal Adèle and Fred in the outside world. When people inquired of the whereabouts of Mr Austerlitz, Ann would explain that he had business commitments in Nebraska and would be joining the family shortly: that unhappily for them all it had been necessary to find the best dancing teacher for her young daughter, so they had been compelled to set out for New York without him.

There was no master plan for Adèle and Fred and the future. They attended the school, their talents were honed, and they had the time of their lives. But always they talked of going back to Omaha one day. 'There was no idea of a career,' Ann told an Omaha newspaper many years later. 'We were just trying to give the children the best possible start. It was plain that Adèle had real ability. We just made sure she used it.'

Fred was gravely serious about every lesson, step, and routine; he told Adèle: 'Mr Alvienne is going to make a big star out of me.' Adèle was scathing: 'Don't be silly, that's me.' For extra-curricular treats, Ann took them to Broadway shows. They saw the good, the not so good, and the very good. Stars such as Lilly Langtry, Laurette Taylor and Ethel Barrymore, and each new singer and dancer added to their enthusiasm for their work. If they enjoyed a production, they went back again and again – their great favourite was the Danish ballerina Adeline Genée, whom they saw in *The Soul Kiss*. 'I reckon it was about twenty-eight times we saw the show,' said Fred, who was totally enamoured and for weeks couldn't stop talking of her.

Adèle and Fred made their New York début in a show for pupils and

[18]

parents held in Alvienne's ballroom. In a brief dramatised extract from Edmond Rostand's 1897 play *Cyrano de Bergerac*, Adèle, with a false nose made of putty, played the great duel-fighting lover and poet, and Fred, three inches shorter and dressed in a satin gown and blonde wig, played the beautiful Roxane, the object of Cyrano's adoration. Astaire remembered the incident with little more than a slight twinge of embarrassment. But Adèle claimed: 'Freddie was quite the most adorable thing.'

History of a sort was made at another performance a few months later when, for the very first time, Fred appeared in top hat and white tie, in a bride-and-groom sketch planned by Alvienne. Two large 'wedding cakes', each about three feet in diameter and eighteen inches high, were fitted with bells that could be played with the hands and feet, and electric light bulbs that could flash on and off. The costumes, made by Ann, were quite fancy: Adèle was in a white satin gown and Fred in black satin knickerbockers, top hat, and white tie – tails were too hard to make, so he made do with a rather oversized black overcoat. The bride and groom played 'Dreamland Waltz' on the bells as they danced on and around the cakes in a crazy routine. The lights lit up and the duo exited and returned to do solo spots – Fred's was a tap dance and Adèle's a short ballet routine. The finale featured Fred in a bright red costume as a lobster and Adèle in a billowing skirt as a glass of champagne. The lobster and the champagne glass danced an unlikely duet.

Now they were, by Ann's reckoning, achieving something. Alvienne himself said that they would soon be able to perform on real vaudeville bills; there was a continual demand for juvenile acts. There was just one thing that bothered Ann and Alvienne – the name Austerlitz. So the decision was made (with the approval of Fritz, still in Omaha) that the family name should go. They played around with all kinds of combinations and variations in search of the magical nomenclature which would suggest stardom even before anyone had actually seen the act. Auster was tried and rejected – not quite right. Astier was tried and briefly accepted: it was as The Astiers that Fred and Adèle first appeared in Alvienne's concerts. But that too was turned down. It almost sounded French, and they wanted to escape any suggestion of foreignness. A compromise was reached: they would try Astaire, which combined many favourable elements. It sounded like the fabulously wealthy Astors; it gave some idea of the ladder of success. And for Alvienne, it had a happy overtone of Astarte, the goddess of productive energy. If Astaire didn't work, said their wise mother with the final word, they could always change it again later.

Fred Astaire could never remember his name as anything else. He had heard his mother talk of the change, but it did not really seem to involve him – it could have happened several generations earlier as far as he was concerned, and he was dismissive of queries about it. 'Astaire is the only name I've got,' he said. 'Austerlitz sounded too much like a battle.' And Adèle added: 'It was a clumsy name. We needed something simpler and shorter that would fit on the theatre programmes.'

By November funds were running low. Adèle already observed that when money was scarce her mother became worried; she also understood the relationship between performing on stage and money – young troupers learn fast. What she knew, Fred soon picked up. Adèle was eager to try out their routines on a proper audience. So, through Alvienne, they were booked downbill into the Pier Theatre at Keyport, New Jersey – a rickety establishment that seemed marvellous to the Austerlitz family. Nerves? 'No, of course not,' said Adèle, 'we were far too young to worry about things like nerves. I just wanted to get on stage.'

The Astaires: Juvenile Artists Presenting an Electrical Musical Tap Dancing Novelty, arrived on Monday morning, far too early for the theatre to be open. The kids went searching for coins dropped by weekenders on the beach while Ann organised their props and costumes. For their professional début Fred and Adèle Astaire, aged six and a half and nine respectively, went on first at the 3 p.m. matinée, bottom of the four acts on the bill.

Alvienne came out to inspect the performance and sat with Ann, who was nervously concerned for her children. She needn't have worried. They went through the routine, before a handful of people, with consummate ease. Alvienne announced: 'It's okay, kids, just some practice, just some work, and it'll be smooth and a real pro act.' Ann was delighted by his comments; when she next wrote to Fritz, her letter was full of the news. The two little Astaires well deserved the $30 they earned that week.

It would be a mistake to portray Ann as a typical pushy stage mother: she was not. But she was eager to learn and naturally she did everything she could think of to ensure that the act was a success. Shy and unversed in the ways of the world, her very innocence enabled her to get on. On the second day of the Keyport engagement, she visited the offices of the local newspaper and there, the nameless critic – perhaps also the editor, office-boy, and coffee maker? – obligingly printed what she told him: 'The Astaires are the greatest child act in vaudeville.'

Fritz, seeing signs of a return on his investment in his family, was wildly enthusiastic about his children's prospects, and with optimism born of ignorance he made a hasty visit to New York. For the kids, Fritz's visits were their favourite times. When Father was in town, it was treats all round: off they would go to Luchow's German restaurant on Fourteenth Street or to the Café Boulevard, with its Hungarian Orchestra, at 156 Second Avenue. There would be laughter and fun: Fritz would tell them how wonderful and talented they were and Ann would smile indulgently and remember how charmed she once had been by this man. It seemed perfectly natural to the kids that their father did not live with them: they could hardly remember their life in Omaha, and what memories they had were inspired by the stories told by their mother. Whether he was there or not, Fritz did his best to make himself useful, and whenever he did get to New York he would make it his business to bluster his way into the offices of producers and agents, to sing the praises of the infant stars.

Ann started an album with programmes, reviews (unless they were too awful), and other souvenirs of each engagement. Without these huge scrapbooks, it would be all but impossible to trace the route of the Astaires as they toured from Keyport to Perth Amboy, Passaic, Paterson, and onwards through a mass of small towns and even smaller clapboard theatres. [Some of those books Fred kept; Adèle, always less careful in keeping things, eventually gave hers to the Twentieth-Century Archive at the Mugar Memorial Library in Boston, Massachusetts.]

In Omaha, the Astaire act was promoted through the local newspaper. On Sunday, 1 February 1906 the *World-Herald* carried a glowing, if not quite accurate, progress report on the children. After their success on the New Jersey circuit, they had appeared at Keith's in New York, but the Gerry Society, self-appointed guardians of the child labour laws, had interrupted that engagement. The paper went on to say that they had been booked for the entire theatrical season on the Pennsylvania circuit, and were now 'booking in Europe and expect to leave some time in April, opening in Paris in May'. The international tour, reported by Fritz in a fit of enthusiasm, was hogwash. But, in the world of theatre, fantasy and fact wander hand in hand; programme notes and publicity handouts sometimes become more real to the

[21]

performer than the facts. There was a lot to remember, as Adèle said later, but also a lot to forget.

The ways of the vaudeville world were learned quickly by Ann. She was bright and adaptable. Her skills as a seamstress were useful to the other acts and the backstage staff. Her abilities as a cue card reader were freely offered and gratefully accepted. The great reward for this generosity was that other acts always spoke warmly of the Astaires and their 'so terribly nice mother'; a reputation that stood them well with booking agents and theatre managers in all but the darkest days.

Nonetheless, there was no dramatic launch into show business. Bookings were few and far between. For two years the youngsters struggled along with their dancing lessons, occasional local engagements, and schooling from their mother in the cramped hotel room with its three cots and small kitchen area. Fred took his studies seriously, but Adèle had developed a casual attitude to her lessons. As long as she was better, faster, and quicker than her brother she reckoned that she had done enough. It was fine for Fred to hit the books, but Adèle would much rather play with her paper dolls.

From Nebraska, Fritz continued to send them some money, but he faced new problems of his own. Threats of local ordinances, precursors of Prohibition (from Maine, in 1846, it finally reached Omaha in 1916), endangered his job with Storz Brewing. The early laws did not extend to the hops, barley, malt, yeast and sugar available at pharmacies, so the company continued to sell brewing supplies even when their manufactured product was taken off the market but wages were lowered for the retrenchment. Moreover, Fritz had adopted a rather expensive double life. He now, according to the Astaires' cousin Hélène Geilus, as well as local historian Harold Becker, shared his house at 43rd and Lafayette with an attractive young woman, known to his neighbours as 'Mrs Austerlitz', who gave birth to a child in 1908. It was all too easy for people to 'disappear' in those days, and there is no trace of the new 'Mrs Austerlitz' – or her child in the sketchy records; nor is there any evidence that Fritz ever divorced Ann or that he married again.

It was not an ideal situation, but Fritz was content with it, travelling once or twice a year to New York to see Ann and the children. They retained warm memories of him and Ann always managed to explain away his absence in a totally convincing manner. They managed to enjoy at least the semblance of a home life, celebrating Thanksgiving and Christmas in the hotel or with friends in an environment where everyone was determined to have a good time – and a present from Fritz was always the highlight of the day.

[22]

When things were looking particularly bad, Frank Vincent, head booker of the Orpheum Circuit, came to see the act in Paterson, New Jersey, and was sufficiently impressed to offer the kids $150 a week and travel expenses for a series of engagements. Now, trains and city signs flickered through their lives as the hopeful trio, gaining in confidence, travelled from Pittsburgh to Dayton, Sioux City to Des Moines, Butte to Denver, Seattle, San Francisco, Los Angeles, Salt Lake City, Lincoln, and Milwaukee. Everywhere they saw new sights: in Seattle the lumber ships loading, in Salt Lake City the vast Mormon Temple, in Los Angeles the vineyards and orange groves and the Angel's Flight funicular railway. They were snowbound for two days on a train between Butte and Denver; some of the passengers were panicky, but the young Astaires hoped the adventure would never end. It all looked so beautiful and seemed so exciting – the only dampener was their mother, anxious about being late for their Denver dates.

In December 1908, Adèle and Fred played their hometown at the Omaha Orpheum, where years before as tots they themselves had sat in the audience. Astaire's recollection in his 1959 autobiography, *Steps in Time*, was that the town gave them a memorable welcome, heaps of publicity, and bouquets that overflowed the stage at every performance. 'One huge basket of flowers for Adèle contained a live white poodle,' he said of one gift from the Geilus family. But his memory was more generous to Omaha than Omaha was to him. The advertisements in the three local newspapers were brief and the reviews briefer; the *World-Herald* even managed to get Fred's name wrong, calling him Harry. And they were upstaged by the National Corn Show at the City Auditorium.

Astaire's memory also recorded that at the time they were 'seasoned vaudevillians', 'although barely nine and seven years old', but mathematics never was his forte – in fact they were twelve and nine and a half when they played Omaha. The poodle was hastily given away to the Austerlitz and Geilus cousins who came to the shows often with free tickets, compliments of the ever-generous Fritz. Maybe, the cousins said, these kids will really go far. Maybe taking them to New York hadn't been such a crazy idea after all.

On this trip the Astaires gained a lot of stage experience, and they got the chance to work alongside other vaudevillians, from dog acts to ventriloquists, acrobats, and musicians. The veterans of the circuit were invariably friendly to the two youngsters and their practical mother, and helped to make them feel at home wherever they went,

[23]

suggesting the cheapest clean lodgings and restaurants in each town. 'What did we know? Nothing,' said Ann. 'But we were very lucky with the people we worked with.'

After the tour, the family vacationed in Asbury Park and discussed their plans with Fritz, who joined them from Omaha and re-auditioned them for his own pleasure. Together they decided to cut the clumsy, space-consuming wedding-cake props, but keep the costumes and songs; for, as they were beginning to realise, you don't need gimmicks if you've got a good act. There was one cloud on the horizon: while Fred had grown a few inches and was a pert little lad, Adèle had grown not only in height but also in sophistication. The kids themselves neither noticed nor cared, but Ann knew that it would not be long before the theatre managers would spot the increasing discrepancy. But the problem was solved in a most unexpected way, for as soon as the Astaires performed again disaster struck, thanks to the ubiquitous, well-meaning Gerry Society.

The Gerry Society, founded by New York lawyer Eldridge Thomas Gerry, was dedicated to the welfare of children, and to protecting them from exploitation. The Society's local branches had managed to get laws passed in many cities and some states forbidding children (in some cases under fourteen, in others under sixteen) to work. Of course the goal was to stop the abuses of the sweat-shop, the mine, the mill, and the farm. But the catch-all rules also included the stage, where the Astaires and other children were having the time of their lives.

The only alternative to coming off the road was to lie about their ages. So off-stage Fred was stuck into long pants – in an era when boys wore short pants until they started to shave – and Adèle would wear lipstick and a little rouge. When the local Gerry Society representative came to investigate (at the Orpheum in Los Angeles, for example), Ann, using a lot of sweet reason and a touch of duplicity, managed to talk him around. Fred was a very late developer, she explained, and she was surprised his high voice had not broken yet.

But it was a close thing, and the situation would become more uncomfortable. Adèle, picking up the mannerisms of the dancers she observed, was fast developing into a juvenile lead and increasingly looked an unsuitable partner for her kid brother. Inevitably, one day a theatre manager reported, in a phrase that was to haunt Fred for many years afterwards: 'The girl seems to have talent but the boy can do nothing.'

The promoter repeated this to Ann, a worried Ann told Adèle – on condition that she didn't let it get back to Fred. But Adèle, during some petty argument, did just that, and Fred reacted with shock and anger. 'What do they mean I can't do anything?' he demanded of his mother. 'I was dancing and singing.' Ann did her best to soothe him, but he would hardly be comforted. A few days later he seemed to have recovered from this blow to his pride, but Ann could see the trouble that lay ahead.

To all these problems, there seemed only one solution: to retire the act temporarily. They had earned enough money to allow them to live normally for a while, until the dark shadow of the Gerry Society no longer hung over them. But Adèle and Fred were convinced, with the sincerity and seriousness of the young, that vaudeville was the only life for them.

None of the family wanted to stray far from the Manhattan they knew, but, by enquiring among friends in the business, they found a house they could rent cheaply in Highwood Park, the residential part of Weehawken, New Jersey, a short ferry ride from midtown. For the next two years, the Astaires lived like ordinary children of their age, attending the Highwood Park School. Adèle had her doubts about this new life – it did seem awfully dull after the excitement of the road – but Fred settled down quickly and happily, enjoying the seventh grade and the baseball parties with ice cream and soda pop. They all made new friends and were introduced by their neighbours to the local community activities. The absence of a father was noted, as was the fact that the family was not at all well off. But there were plenty of admirers for Ann, a young and attractively vibrant woman: one in particular, a wealthy New Jersey widower, wanted to marry her, adopt the children, look after them all. Ann was flattered but not convinced, and anyway, she said, her husband still hoped to join them as soon as he could. She had no intention of sharing her children or losing her independence.

After two years, with the children growing up and funds running precariously low, something had to be done. Ann thought the children should go to a good vaudeville school to get back into the swing of things. Enquiries were made and after much discussion Adèle and Fred were enrolled at Ned Wayburn's dancing school on West 44th Street. Many school directors had long since retired from active careers, although they would never admit it, but Wayburn still functioned as a professional dance director, and his practical knowledge was particularly welcome. In later years Adèle and Fred credited him with teaching them more in six months than they learned at any other

[25]

formative stage in their career.

No one could guarantee the future, but Ann reckoned that Adèle, young though she was, really did have potential, although it was still too early for any long-term predictions about Fred. Wayburn was sure that Adèle would find bookings, so, with enthusiastic long-distance encouragement from Fritz, Ann decided to buy an act for her daughter. A good routine was a smart investment; it could last a lifetime in those days, when there was no voracious camera eye to devour each performance. Ann and Wayburn discussed the possibility of a solo spot for Fred, too, which would have made the future of the Astaires a very different affair: but Wayburn, thanks to his professional wisdom (or perhaps his desire to keep both pupils), persuaded Ann that the kids would be more novel as a double act, even though it meant casting Adèle as a young girl rather than as a juvenile romantic. He thought he could come up with something suitable for the two of them.

The price of the new act was $1,000 – a tremendous sum in those days, enough to buy a house or keep a family for a good long time. However, the money didn't have to be paid entirely in advance. The idea was that Wayburn would write the act, rehearse the couple, and then help them find work to pay for his services. It looked good in theory, but Wayburn had debts of his own: he enjoyed his whisky and he lived well, so he was easily sidetracked. It was only after much pressure from Ann that the script for *A Rainy Sunday* finally arrived.

Fred appeared in a baseball uniform, a grey pinstriped New York Giants outfit with a logo identifying The Little Giants, and Adèle wore a summer frock. Kept indoors by the rain, they while away the time imagining how her first beau will propose to her, and acting out the scene; then the scene shifts and Fred – who has donned a top hat – imitates 'Father' stumbling home late, worse the wear for drink, and suffering the scolding of his 'wife' Adèle. Although the top hat that Ann found for Fred never did fit him – she always thought he would quickly outgrow his wardrobe – with the twelve-minute *Baseball Act*, as it became known, the Astaires had their first fully professional routine.

[26]

4
Early days

The Astaires had played their kiddy routine everywhere and the theatre managers were not climbing over each other to re-book them, even though Ann maintained that they were now 'juveniles' rather than 'children'. Eventually it was Wayburn himself who helped them out – their $1,000 weighing heavily on his conscience – by putting them into a Sunday night benefit programme he was organizing at the Broadway Theatre. *The Baseball Act*, tucked low on the bill, went over well. They had officially made it: they had played Broadway! The *Morning Telegraph* reported: 'Fred and Adèle Astaire are a clever singing and dancing team.' Ann always reckoned that Wayburn had written the review himself, but it really didn't matter – they were back in business. Just a week later they opened at Proctor's Fifth Avenue, on the corner of Broadway and 28th Street, their first big-time booking.

Heading the bill was Douglas Fairbanks, who was – as was the custom for stars of the legitimate stage – making a short vaudeville tour between plays, in a cameo sketch called *A Regular Businessman*. Young Fred Astaire watched him in awe, eagerly soaking up every detail of his dress and manner. The Astaires went on first; as it was a long bill, they weren't even preceded by the flickering cinemascope newsreel, which had become the usual curtain-raiser. They were a bit concerned about this: as the openers they would have to compete with the sound of late arrivals, for few in the vaudeville audience minded missing part of the first act. 'Come on, Fred,' said Adèle, 'don't look so glum. If we do well in the matinée we might get a better spot in the evening show.' But the act went down like a lead balloon. The sparse audience hardly acknowledged them. Dashing back into their dressing rooms, Adèle burst into tears, unconsoled by Ann's attempts to comfort her. 'We just hadn't seen it coming,' said Adèle later. 'We had been a couple of cutesie kids and we were fine, but then we'd got bigger and we weren't so cute any more. That evening we went back to see the running order and, boy, had we been removed from the Number One spot – right off into nowhere.'

The 'cancelled' sign on their act was a bitter blow. Adèle and Fred chewed it over endlessly: as Adèle said, 'There wasn't much else for us to do at the time.' To add to their troubles, Fred's voice began to break. Adèle thought it sweet, but the thirteen-year-old lad was embarrassed and confused. They differed, too, in their feelings about the series of disastrous engagements that followed: Adèle thought some of their dates were not too bad; Fred, having tasted cordial audiences and warm applause, became increasingly angry and annoyed. (Later he was to blame the act itself for the tepid response, calling it 'unformed, dull, and awful'.) But they were both determined to give their friends in Weehawken the impression that they were prospering, so the Christmas edition of the *New Jersey Star* carried photographs of Fred and Adèle, 'The Youthful Brother and Sister', in a holly-trimmed advertisement reading 'Very Best Wishes For The Holidays'.

When they began their studies with Wayburn, Fred and Adèle commuted daily by ferry from Weehawken, but it was a long, tiring journey. Ann decided it would be better all round, and probably cheaper, to move back to Manhattan. There were a few regrets about leaving their young friends, and the Astaires promised to return regularly. Ann found an inexpensive boarding house on West 45th Street, a comfortable brownstone on the south side of the street between Times Square and Eighth Avenue – Astaire later placed his room somewhere around the third row of the balcony of the present Royale Theatre – but they did not stay long. As soon as a bit of money began to come in, they moved to the more comfortable Calumet Hotel on West 57th between Eighth and Ninth Avenue, next door to the Church of Zion and St Timothy, which was to play a big part in Fred's life.

It's hard to picture nowadays, but then the sight of kids actually playing ball on the sidewalks of midtown New York was not uncommon. During just such a ball game on 57th Street, Fred met Rev. Randolph Ray; or rather Ray, a young Episcopalian curate from Mississippi who was attached to the Church of Zion and St Timothy, would invariably meet the ball game as he crossed the street each day from the Hotel Grenoble, where he had a small studio. Most grownups gave the players a hard time, but Ray remembered getting into trouble for the same kind of thing as a boy, so he ducked and weaved to avoid stray balls without losing his temper. He was particularly intrigued by the playing technique of one slightly built boy in the regular group. Ray

loved vaudeville – he had asked for a posting to New York especially so
that he could see more shows and become involved in the theatre – and
he thought he could spot something special in the way the youngster
moved. As he wrote in his memoirs many years later: 'I had been in the
theatre often enough to know a tap dancer when I saw one. The young
lad called Fred was a nimble player and he would break into a primitive
war dance when he scored a hit. I spoke to the boy and with a grin he
said he was a professional, his sister and he toured in vaudeville in the
winter but in the summer lived at a nearby hotel. He said that they
didn't go to school as they had a private tutor.' It was some time before
he discovered that the 'tutor' was actually Mrs Astaire herself, but even
she did not quite put the record straight for the clergyman. He recalled:
'She was a handsome woman who told me she had once been on the
stage herself.' Well, she was an off-stage voice in the *The Baseball Act* and
she had always acted as assistant and helpmate to Adèle and Fred . . .
Good manners prohibited pointed questions, so Ray didn't learn much
more except that Fred's father lived far away and couldn't come to join
the family.

It was hardly surprising that Randolph Ray became a firm friend of
the Astaires. Like them, he had no family in the city, so he easily fitted
into the rôle of adviser and confidant. He found Adèle a bit of a tomboy
offstage, much more boisterous than her brother, and he was always
amazed to see the transformation when she performed on stage. 'She
had a way of turning on cue into the purest thistledown,' he said. He
was delighted when Ann told him that Fred, who had long been
fascinated by the quiet, the echoes, and the music of Ray's church, and
who with his mother and sister was a regular attendant on the Sunday
mornings when they were in town, wanted to be confirmed. Ray took
him through the catechism and the actual ceremony was held, at the
church to which Ray was about to transfer, the Church of the
Transfiguration, on East 29th Street.

The Church of the Transfiguration had had a long association with
the stage as headquarters of the Actors' Church Alliance, now known
as the Episcopal Actors' Guild of America. The Alliance had been
formed in 1870, after one Joseph Jefferson had been unable to find a
church that would conduct a funeral service for his actor friend George
Holland; eventually Jefferson was told that there was one church
around the corner that would not object to burying actors and, so the
story went, he exclaimed 'God bless the Little Church Around the
Corner!' – and so it has been known ever since. For Ray, who was to

[29]

become only the third rector of the church since 1848, Fred was the first of many performers he would confirm there over the years.

Fred had been baptized in the Lutheran Church, but the practical distinctions between Lutherans and Episcopalians were not great. Ray's opinion of the differences between Protestant sects was embodied in his story of the Presbyterian elder and the Episcopalian bishop who sat down to dinner together. The Presbyterian said 'I think I will take a little wine for the stomach's sake,' as he gingerly sipped at his glass; the Episcopalian drank his down without apology. It was one of Fred's favourite tales; on balance, he reckoned the Episcopalians were a better bet.

The Astaires returned to the small-time mid-Western vaudeville circuit and for two years played every two-bit theatre they could find. They were making up to $150 a week and life seemed sweet – even in Coffee Cup, Indiana, where they had to climb a ladder to get into their dressing room as the only downstairs space had been given to the other act on the bill: a troupe of performing seals who could do just about anything except climb a ladder.

They moved from flea-bag hotel to flea-bag hotel around the country. If times were good they had separate rooms, otherwise they all bunked down together. After breakfast, Ann administered their lessons. 'I was fifteen before I could tell the time,' Adèle said many years later. 'I couldn't tell my left from my right for ages. I do wish I'd concentrated a bit more, but there was so much else to do and Fred did enough for both of us.' Adèle also found that she had to wait less and less for her brother to catch up with her. With his pencil grasped firmly in one hand, his brow furrowed, and his other hand holding his writing book, he would determinedly press on, until they were released to dash off to the theatre for rehearsals. Their education was completed by the multifarious people they met on their travels. Fred acquired his early sophistication and knowledge of life by talking to the bell-hops, who always knew what was going on in town, and to the other youngsters on the vaudeville circuit. On the train, he would chat with the porters and the engineers, who were always happy to welcome the boy to their cabs.

No one could call this a regular home life, but Ann Astaire had managed to instil in her children a quality that set them apart from other performers on the circuit. For instance, she insisted that both on and off stage they enunciate their words in the manner of the English actors of the day – undoubtedly a bit affected by present-day standards, but it was clear and could be understood across the country and in the highest reaches of the balcony. She always saw to it that they were well-dressed, and she taught them that politeness, thoughtfulness, and good manners were important in their daily lives. Adèle, an increasingly pretty teenager, was keen on dressing well but not so convinced by all of her mother's other precepts. 'Look and learn,' Ann would say. 'You can learn from both the good and the not so good.' Backstage and in the booking offices it was not difficult to encounter a disproportionate number of scoundrels, chisellers, and perverts, but the kids somehow managed to avoid them. Adèle became somewhat flighty, but Fred, lacking her self-confidence, spent his time improving his routines and style lest one day he disgrace his older sister in public. He found that his dedication to work had another use, for it enabled him to disguise his off-stage shyness. He became fastidious about his clothes – shoes highly polished, garments neatly pressed – to complement the professional conscientiousness that was to become a second religion for him. Charming Adèle and serious Fred were both popular and admired among their fellow performers.

Then, as is the way of the world, when the work was coming in and things were going reasonably well, trouble cropped up in Omaha. Fritz feared – correctly – that he would soon find himself out of a job. He wrote to say that he was thinking of moving East to Detroit, where he had heard opportunities were better and where he might find work.

By careful husbanding of their resources, Ann did at least ensure that she and the children could escape from the summer heat of New York, when most of the theatres closed down anyway, and have a vacation at the Delaware Water Gap in Pennsylvania. This mountain resort was an ideal place to wind down from the strain of touring. Fred, ever eager for new experiences and new sensations, learned to ride, swim, and play golf. He had heard a lot about golf backstage, for many vaudevillians were keen players, and for Fred it became an instant passion, a suitable sport for a dancer who enjoyed both the elegance of movement and the technique involved. But he claimed that his dancing did not give him as great an advantage as he hoped: 'It was quite easy for me to make progress at the beginning, but to really improve my technique was tough.' He was happy to get around the nine-hole course in forty or under: quite respectable considering the large rocks that lay on the fairway. During Fred's second summer at Delaware Water Gap, when he was fifteen, the golf pro let him help out in the shop in exchange for old golf balls – a bargain which delighted the lad.

Adèle had grown into a gorgeous creature. Ann tried to keep an eye

[31]

on her, but Adèle, self-willed and enjoying the attention of men, often managed to sneak off by herself. 'I was a pretty mature seventeen-year-old,' she recalled many years later to a friend in Ireland. 'I'd been out on the road for quite a while then and although I'm not sure that in those days Fred was aware of what went on at some of those theatres, I'd already got quite used to people grabbing my fanny backstage – that is when they weren't all homos.'

In 1914 the movie star Mary Pickford and her sister Lottie and brother Jack came to the hotel to make a film called *Fanchon the Cricket*. And amid all the excitement generated by the actors, crew, and impedimenta of the production, in the most inconspicuous way possible, Fred and Adèle Astaire made their movie début.

Film-making was in its infancy, clumsy and awkward, and the big cameras and reflectors seemed to engulf the place. The Astaires were totally intrigued. They had heard – rumour travels fast in a hotel – that Mary Pickford was being paid the staggering sum of $1,000 a week by Adolph Zukor's Famous Players company. They made it their business to discover everything they could about her – they had heard that she had also started out as a child performer. Her father had been killed in a railroad accident when she was five years old, and shortly thereafter she had been 'discovered' by one of her mother's lodgers and put on stage as Baby Gladys – her real name was Gladys Smith. Baby Gladys became Mary Pickford in 1907 when, at the age of fourteen, the pushy and ambitious child talked her way into a starring rôle on Broadway in *The Warrens of Virginia*. Two years later she inveigled her way into the embryonic movie world – a hand-cranked camera and a sunny day made a movie set – and started to make films with D. W. Griffith. She quickly became America's biggest star, first as a nameless biograph feature player distinguished by a golden mop of curls and then, because she demanded and got star billing, in her own name. An astute business woman, she kept the operation very much a family business. In *Fanchon the Cricket*, she played Fanchon, 'The Little Wild Girl of the Woods', who falls for Landry (Jack Standing), whose sweetheart Madelon was played by Mary's nineteen-year-old sister Lottie. Brother Jack Pickford, just turned eighteen, was also roped into the film in a minor rôle, and it was Jack who spent his evenings dancing showily to the hotel's band, who recruited the Astaires.

Fanchon the Cricket was fairly typical for its time, a two-reeler film about a wild child who watches with a mixture of amusement and envy as the local youths dance and picnic. At first she pretends to be a ghost, to scare them, but later, when her beloved Landry is dying from some unspecified ailment – lovesickness? – she extracts a promise of kind treatment from his father and raises him from his sickbed. The director needed extras for the dancing scenes, and it is there, among the jumbled crowd of twenty or so youths on the village green, that in a scene so brief that a blink would make you miss it, Fred Astaire, along with Adèle, made his movie début. When they eventually got to see the film they couldn't even spot themselves; they assumed that their contribution had been cut. Even with the benefit of an editing machine, slow-motion, and stop-frame, the Astaires are almost lost in the mass of bodies.

Ann Astaire became friendly with the director, James Kirkwood, and talked with him about the prospects for her offspring in this new world. Kirkwood, then thirty-three, was Mary Pickford's regular director and had also acted with her. He was happy to be consulted, but he told Ann that the early vogue for dancing acts and vaudeville routines had been superseded by a modern demand for stories, and it could only be as dramatic performers that he could see any future for the Astaires in the movies. He could certainly get work for Adèle, but there was a glut of young men, and the fifteen-year-old Fred, for all his experience and serious demeanour, did not spring to mind as a romantic lead type. It was quite true, of course; Adèle was an attractive young woman, but Fred was still a boy.

The movies were on everyone's minds as the Astaires resumed their stage career in the autumn of 1914. More and more vaudeville houses were showing the grainy movies that had so captured the imagination of America, and even those managers who still believed that live entertainment would always be in demand would schedule a 'short' as a curtain-raiser. Every week *Variety* carried advertisements from exhibitors eager to acquire more theatres for the new craze.

Although the Astaires did seem to be increasingly mis-matched, with audiences expecting a far more adult routine from someone like Adèle, there was one major improvement in their act as far as Fred was concerned. Adèle was now fully grown at five foot three and Fred was at last noticeably, if only marginally, taller than her. 'She still carried me,' he said, although he admitted that the height gave him more confidence as a partner. Adèle had always played down her age, and now the kid-sister act became easier to carry off. When people asked the difference in their ages she would feign forgetfulness, adding to Fred's years and subtracting from her own. But Fred would reply, 'Oh, she's a year and

[33]

a half older than me,' thus neatly taking off one year from the actual figure.

They didn't do a bad round of theatres that autumn, but they knew it really wasn't a particularly good tour either. Fred would arrive early at the theatre each day, go through his routine, and wage what he called 'The Battle of the Rosin', surreptitiously spreading rosin chalk from the bottom of an old sock, to ensure that the stage had the right surface grip for his dancing. His colleagues didn't always appreciate performing on a super-smooth dance stage, though, and the managers were almost unanimously alarmed by the danger of Astaire's rosin messing up someone else's act. There were other setbacks, too – on one disastrous date their wardrobe trunk failed to arrive, and the printed bill advertised FRED and ADLEE ASTAIRE.

One thing was obvious: the baseball routine had had its day. When the weather warmed up and the bookings dried to nothing, the family decamped for the Delaware Water Gap to do some hard thinking, or rather rethinking, about the future. Fritz came up from Detroit, where he was now living (and where, as soon as he had heard about the possibility of war in 1914, he had hastily become an American citizen to avoid the possibility of being drafted into the Austrian army), and another family conference was called. Adèle said she was happy to go along with what everyone else decided, but she was bullied into having some views on the subject herself.

There was no need to force Fred – he was convinced that he was the weak link in the act and worried about it night and day. But Fritz summed up their situation most succinctly: the kids had outgrown their act, but Fred was now mature enough to make a realistic dancing partner for Adèle. So what to do? Where could this re-vamped team find an appropriate routine?

Fritz, ever the keen reader of theatrical papers, had a bright idea. He would get in touch with a man called Aurelia Coccia, who, with his wife Minnie Amato, had a successful dance act on the vaudeville circuit and who taught as well as performed. He might be able to help them create a proper act.

So back to New York they went, and for six months they studied with the Coccias, learning tangos, waltzes, and the finer points of an adult act. They had mixed feelings about this. Fred was glad of the change, but when he heard Coccia tell his mother, 'They'll have to forget all they know and start again,' he was less sure. He told Adèle what he had overheard and together they wandered around in despondency for a few days. It was only later that they realised that Coccia's 'start all over again' had just been a bit of a pep talk, designed to arouse their enthusiasm. In truth there was no need for a pep talk: both Adèle and Fred realised that progress was essential. The alternative was unthinkable – doing something else with their lives.

Astaire was never fond of pep talks, and never understood why people should knock you down in order to build you up again. But to Aurelia Coccia he acknowledged a great debt, for teaching him not only steps but showmanship. Fred thought he had been learning by watching other vaudevillians, but he began to realise, as Coccia put him and Adèle through their paces, just how little he really knew. The new routine, which was to be called 'New Songs and Smart Dances', featured numbers they had found by scouring the music publishers. It began with Fred shouting from off stage: 'Stop! Stop! Don't you dare to move; you're under arrest!' Adèle replied: 'What have I done to you!' He went on: 'Stop! Stop! I've got you covered; see that badge on my chest?' Then Fred would pull her into a spotlight and sing 'Love Made Me a Wonderful Detective', written by Ted Snyder, a business partner of Irving Berlin. This routine was followed by tap dances, a song sung by Adèle and played (on the piano) by Fred, and a spectacular adagio number.

Fred had put himself in charge of finding material for the act. He spent his days in the city trailing round from one publisher to another, listening to whatever they had – a thankless task, as no one would offer anything really good to a pair of unknowns. Fred had set his heart on a song from the hot new writer Irving Berlin, a one-time singing waiter who had already had a huge hit with 'Alexander's Ragtime Band', and he persisted until Snyder agreed to let him use 'I Love to Quarrel With You'. Unlike the present day, when any recorded song can be used with impunity, back then one needed permission from the publisher, who would take care to assign the material as exclusively as possible. 'I Love to Quarrel With You' had been given to a number of acts in different locales, and with luck the Astaires would not be using it on the same bill as anyone else. (Fred recorded it eventually in 1959 in a medley on an LP entitled 'Now'.)

They took their new act on the road, trying it out at various summer resorts before setting off on the East Coast circuit up to Boston. Reports were mostly favourable – when there was an audience. But things didn't always go well. On one occasion they rushed off stage after the awful silent sound of one hand clapping had greeted their best efforts.

[35]

Adèle stuck out her tongue at the recalcitrant audience from behind the curtain; unfortunately for her, the manager could just see this brave, if futile, gesture. He rushed backstage. 'What do you mean by sticking out your tongue at my audience? Don't ever do a thing like that again,' he stormed. 'I'm going to have to put that in my report.' But Adèle was not one to spare her favours. As he turned his back she stuck out her tongue at him, too. 'Stupid fucker,' she said.

This period also signalled a change in the relationship of the Astaires to one another. Fred had taken over the organization of the material and rehearsals; Ann looked after lodgings and train timetables; Adèle was in charge of . . . well, having a good time. She was pert, vivacious, and bright. She liked being taken out for a drive in an open car, she liked window-shopping, and she was content to leave most of the planning to Fred. He would tell her when he thought they should rehearse (every day, as far as he was concerned), she would complain that they had already rehearsed more than enough, and eventually a fairly good-natured compromise would be reached. And while Adèle was out playing, Fred extended his sophisticated on-stage persona into the rest of his life, admiring sports cars, studying menswear shop windows and the behaviour of the smooth young blades around Manhattan and the college towns. In New Haven and Boston, the situation was actually reversed: the Yalies and Harvard men, whose Mercer sports cars and raccoon coats were so admired by Fred, flocked to see the Astaires' smooth dancing and air of sophisticated ease. After every show the college boys hounded Fred for an introduction to his sister.

And so the Astaires adopted off-stage rôles that they played for many years. She invariably referred to him as 'my big brother', meaning 'taller', but before long this was interpreted as 'older'. As he sometimes called her 'my young sister', in a protective way, their relative ages became increasingly obscure. What began as friendly banter became part of their everyday life. And certainly Fred, with his perfectionism and sober air of concern for his mother and sister did have a demeanour that belied his years – particularly when compared to Adèle's impishness and sense of fun. One bonus for Fred in all this was that his position as the elder sibling brought him more respectful treatment from Adèle's suitors than they would have shown a 'kid brother'.

The Astaires had regained their confidence, thanks to their new well-to-do friends and to good reports from the managers. Their New York agent, a cheerful, if small-time, optimist called Lew Golder, managed to persuade the Orpheum circuit to take the new, grown-up act at the princely sum of $175 a week. The dates took them up to Canada and down again but in Detroit disaster struck.

For Fred and Adèle it was a bolt from the blue. There had been a lot of talk backstage, but no one thought there would be serious consequences when the vaudeville proprietors, increasingly concerned about the business they were losing to the cinemas, imposed wage reductions. But the 'White Rats', the showbusiness trade union set up in opposition to the National Vaudeville Association which ruled on the Keith Albee Circuit, went on strike, although it was doubtful if it had enough support to sustain any meaningful action. (Rats backwards spells star, and the union is now under the banner of the Four A's, the Associated Actors and Artistes of America.)

In Detroit, the audience for the non-union show, with every act given an extra long spot to fill up the shrunken programme, was filled with striking performers, union sympathisers, and their families, all prepared to vent their rage at the 'blacklegs'. Old tomatoes, eggs, flour, and insults were tossed at the Astaires as they struggled through their routine. The manager soon decided to close the show.

Suddenly the Astaires' contented existence came to an end. The strike stretched out and theatres were closed. They sat it out in Detroit, eating up their savings. They moved to a cheaper hotel, but within a few weeks they found themselves without even enough money to get back to New York. Even if they did return, the vaudeville theatres were closed there too, so they stayed put. Ann hocked her one piece of jewellery, the diamond ring given her by Fritz, and sold her fur coat. Fred spent his time pacing the floor: 'Don't worry, Mother,' he said, but he worried enough for all of them. He went to the offices of music publishers, trying his hand at songwriting – maybe, like some of his friends in New York, he could write a quick tune and sell it. He could not – he couldn't have sold a blanket to an Eskimo just then. Adèle and Ann went to the parks, walked the broad streets, watched the ships unloading, and invented ingenious new ways of passing the time and forgetting the ever-present need for money. They thought of trying to get jobs of some sort, but that too was a failure. 'I was pretty fit,' said Adèle. 'We walked everywhere.' She recalled a day when her mother boiled their only egg and gave each of her children half.

Details of the strike are lost in the mists of time, and even Frederick O'Neal, President of the Four A's, is unable to discover them. However, after a few months that seemed an eternity, the strike did break and the Astaires went thankfully back to work. Their agent, bolstered by more good reports, booked them for the first time on the Deep South circuit.

As their experience mounted, Fred became increasingly compulsive about checking the conditions at each venue. On the Monday mornings, at the first rehearsals with the musicians (anything from one piano and a drummer to a ten-piece band) he always had trouble getting them to play at just the right tempo – they thought he should consider himself lucky to have any music at all. But eventually, at most places, Fred would get his way. He and Adèle went on to play the whole Orpheum circuit except Los Angeles and San Francisco, which were reserved for the top acts only. At the Palace in Chicago, even given the dreaded first spot on the bill, they managed to stop the show, took six bows, and were called back by the stage manager to take yet another. They felt they had arrived at last.

The Astaires worked with many of the legendary vaudevillians of the time. The Spanish dancers Eduardo and Elisa Cansino, another brother and sister act, became particular friends and advisers. Fred greatly admired their style and flamboyance; Adèle developed a passion for the darkly handsome Eduardo. 'I thought he was quite marvellous,' she recalled. He thought she was quite marvellous too, as she gazed adoringly at his performance, but nothing, to Ann's relief and Adèle's frustration, came of it. (Many years later, Fred encountered the family again, in the person of Eduardo's daughter Margarita Carmen, who danced as Rita Hayworth.) In the Gus Edwards Song Revue, a travelling vaudeville show of child performers, they met Arthur Freed, a future MGM producer, and also Morris Brown, who later ran the wardrobe department at MGM. Each night they played they were unwittingly storing up experience and contacts that would be useful in later years, and Fred, always left to invent his own entertainment, added to his wide and varied education in life. With the great tap dancer Bill Robinson he polished up his pool and billiards, and everywhere he went he played golf. Meanwhile, behind the scenes, Ann cooked and cleaned and pressed.

When at last they returned to New York, in the late spring of 1916, Fred set out once more to scour the publishing houses for new songs. The indefatigable teenager became friendly with the youngsters in the publishers' front offices and they would sometimes find him something suitable. In this way he picked up 'They Didn't Believe Me' by Jerome Kern, from a short-lived show called *The Girl from Utah*, and some

[38]

material by Cole Porter, a wealthy twenty-four-year-old Harvard graduate who had studied law at Yale so lackadaisically that the Dean of Yale actually encouraged him to switch to his obvious first love, music. At Yale, with his fellow student T. Lawrason Riggs, Porter had written and composed a two-act show called *Paranoia* or *Chester of the YDA* (Yale Dramatic Association), the high point of which was the song 'I've a Shooting Box in Scotland'. A revised version of this number first appeared on Broadway in *See America First*, a fifteen-performance flop, but Fred liked the song and also its slim, elegant, somewhat effete composer. The song fitted perfectly both Fred's new plan to promote the Astaires as the epitome of sophistication and his private dream of an idealised lifestyle – as it was eventually recorded by Astaire, with Bing Crosby, in 1975:

> My favourite pastime is collecting country places.
> I've a shooting box in Scotland,
> I've a château in Touraine,
> I've a silly little chalet
> In the Interlaken valley
> I've a hacienda in Spain . . .
> In travelling, it's quite a comfort to know that you're never far from home.

Fred made another useful contact in the office of the Jerome H. Remick Music Publishing Company, where the front-office song plugger was a lad even younger than Astaire himself. Born Jacob Gershwine, he had only recently anglicised his name to George Gershwin – quite the opposite social extreme from Cole Porter, but Fred was knocked out by the songs he played secretly in the office. Gershwin was a large, gangly fellow who had given up his mother's dreams of his becoming an accountant when his father had died of leukæmia. The eldest son, at the age of fifteen he had gone out to work demonstrating the songs of Remick's writers for a much-needed $15 a week, which he supplemented in any way he could. His jazzy playing had been admired by a piano roll manufacturer who paid him to make some pianola rolls – $5 a piece or six rolls for $25. Like Fred, he was a great student. He taught himself to play the saxophone, on the grounds that if the European War dragged on and he was called up, he could at least join a military band. He taught himself to dance, and haunted the vaudeville houses to pick up the latest steps, so he knew the Astaire act well. His attempts to have his own songs published by Remick were futile, although he did store

[39]

up some of his compositions from that time to use later – 'Nobody But You', which he used in *La, La, Lucille*, for example. To earn extra money for the large and hungry Gershwine family he also used to play night clubs or in vaudeville pit orchestras, and Astaire got him assignments as a regular rehearsal pianist for new shows. Their friendship grew – Astaire would always call in, searching for new material and potential hit songs, and Gershwin would demonstrate some steps for him. 'It would be fair to say that George was an enthusiastic dancer,' said Fred diplomatically. But Gershwin got his own back when Fred sat down at the piano and tore into his popular stride technique, with plenty of rhythm but not a lot of harmony. 'We used to do a turn around,' said Gershwin. 'But we decided that I'd stick to writing and Fred would stick to dancing – we were that good.' They talked of their plans and dreams. Gershwin wanted to write musical comedies; 'You know,' said Fred, 'that's exactly the kind of show I want to do with my sister.'

Their travels around the country went well: their wages peaked at $350, and Astaire recalled that the reviews were so good that he intended to take a full back page ad in *Variety* to display them. In fact, he did not; the cost of $150 – including the 20% premium for special position – was a whole week's pay. Instead, he settled for the top of an inside page of the 1916 Christmas issue, with a photograph and an announcement saying that he and Adèle were represented by Max Hayes and would be playing Keith's Orpheum in Washington over the holiday period. They got a marvellous reception in the capital city, which was gripped by the fever of the European war. (President Wilson was mobilising the armed forces, and it seemed only a matter of time before the United States declared war on Germany.) Tension and troubled times always create a demand for entertainment and Keith's Orpheum, Washington, was packed to capacity. For escapism, people found nothing finer than the light-hearted wit and magical dancing of the Astaires.

The advertisement in *Variety* had not passed unnoticed. Several managements sent along talent scouts to catch the act, but the reports back were not all positive. Dorothy Dixon, a Broadway headline dancer, was one of those asked for her opinion. 'I came back and told my producer that the girl was very good, but that she needed another partner,' she said. 'I'm really quite ashamed of myself now, as I was very young and didn't know anything at all about dancing myself.' Happily, not everyone was so myopic. At least one unsung hero had a different opinion, and so one day they heard from impresario Lee

Shubert, who with his brother Jake had launched Al Jolson on Broadway. He was considering them for a small spot in his next show.

The words 'Lee Shubert wants to see you' sent the Astaires into a spin – whoops of joy from Adèle and even a brief grin from Fred. 'We're going to have to polish up the act,' he said. For once Adèle was not reluctant to rehearse. Ann went carefully through their wardrobe to pick out what they should wear for their meeting with Shubert, their potential saviour from the vaudeville grind. At last Broadway, the Great White Way, was calling, and the Astaires were ready.

5
Broadway

Broadway theatre productions were controlled in the main by just four men: New Yorker Abe Erlanger and the three entrepreneurs who hailed from Chicago, Florenz Ziegfeld and the brothers Lee and Jake Shubert (nés Semanski). Erlanger represented the old time tradition and the main theatre controlling consortium, Ziegfeld represented a new and up-market glamour and close behind came the Shuberts, the hungry pretenders to the Broadway crown. They conducted a lifelong feud with Ziegfeld, although in time they would fall out between themselves and start an equally bitter internecine feud. However, the Shuberts were still very much in business together in 1917, when they planned *The Nine O'Clock Revue*, a gimmick to catch theatregoers who either could not or did not want to make the traditional 8.30 curtain. They announced that the production would star the English comedian T. Roy Barnes, the beautiful former Ziegfeld girl, Justine Johnstone, and the dancing Astaires. No sooner had the announcement been made than the European conflict which had been rumbling along for the last three years became a reality for Americans – on 6 April, when President Wilson declared war on Germany. 'It won't affect us', was the general view. But by July, draft papers were being sent out to Uncle Sam's youth and by autumn, when *The Nine O'Clock Revue* after a six-week try-out in New Haven, was ready – or rather, not quite ready – to open in New York, the effects of the distant war were beginning to bite and a regular stream of soldiers was leaving for battle. Fred Astaire, eighteen years old and healthy, was not surprised to receive his draft card during the rehearsal period: to him it seemed perfectly natural to go and fight for his country, no matter that all the fuss seemed a long way away. What would happen to the act? They would have to reconsider that when the time came. However, as it turned out, the decisive American intervention brought the conflict to an end before he was called up.

The Nine O'Clock Revue was re-titled *Over the Top*. It was not as smart a vehicle as the Astaires would have liked for their Broadway début, and the constantly changing scenery and many numbers in the show made Fred uneasy. However, he had established from the start that it would be in everyone's best interests for the Astaires, meaning himself, to choreograph their own material, so he at least felt confident in their own performance. Backstage, Fred was entranced by the beauty and style of the gorgeous Justine Johnstone, although his adoration was never actually expressed, and certainly not reciprocated – she was very friendly to the boy, but she had bigger fish to fry.

Behind the scenes, short tempers flared. Adèle became increasingly tetchy as each new 'improvement' had to be rehearsed into the show. But if she went too far in her exasperation and turned on someone with an elegantly enunciated 'Get stuffed . . .', Fred would always be near at hand to rescue the situation: 'Hrmm . . . I think what my sister is trying to say is that maybe it would be better if we could find another way of doing this particular scene change. . . .'

Eventually, *Over the Top* did reach Broadway. The show opened at the intimate new Roof Theatre which the Shuberts had built onto their 44th Street Theatre, on Wednesday 28 November 1917, after an all-night dress rehearsal plagued by stage-moving equipment that stubbornly refused to operate. The Astaires, exhausted from the long rehearsals, looked on with pleasure and amazement as the theatre was transformed from a rather seedy hall into a flower-decked auditorium fit for a palace. Then the first-nighters arrived, a tide of men in white ties and tails, and glamorous women with floor-length furs, jewels sparkling at their throats. The Astaires had seen opening nights before, with the crowds pressing on the pavements, the lights and puffs of smoke as the press photographers took their celebrity shots, but their own first night was something else. Peering through the side of the stage curtain, seeing that swelling sea of people gossiping, laughing, and then, in a gigantic slow-moving ballet, placing themselves in the seats, Astaire knew that this was what they had been working for during those years on the road. Adèle loved the sight of the handsome men, the glittering diamonds, and the hubbub of the crowd. The Astaires knew they were better than the swells of the carriage trade: now all they had to do was to go out on stage and prove it.

For all the effort that had gone into the show, the Astaires, at least, were rewarded by the *New York Globe* review: 'One of the prettiest features of the show is the dancing of the two Astaires. The girl, a light sprite-like little creature, has really an exquisite style in her caperings, while the young man combines eccentric ability with humour.'

[43]

Over the Top soon reverted to the more normal 8.30 curtain time. Roy Barnes left the show in the midst of much shouting and was replaced by Ed Wynn, who proved not only easier to work with but also much better for business. Wynn, a runaway child and one-time hat salesman, was a headlining baggy-pants clown by the time he was eighteen; he was a relaxed and quick-witted performer, never happier than when he was heckled or encouraged by the audience. Offstage, he was a kind and considerate man who had the added advantage, as far as Fred Astaire was concerned, of being an enthusiastic golfer, always ready to play a round while dispensing the wisdom of his years. 'You see, young Freddie,' he would say, 'we do have an ideal kind of life. You get up in the morning, play a round of golf, and then entertain the people at night. What could be better?' Not everyone in show business is generous; in fact far from it. However there are those with a true generosity of spirit who, when they see something special, will try to nourish it, and in Ed Wynn the Astaires made a fast friend, admirer, and supporter who did much, in just mentioning the Astaires, to promote their career.

The show closed in New York and travelled down to Washington, DC, for a two-week stint. The capital was alive with excitement and tension. People were eager for escapism and *Over the Top* at last played to full and enthusiastic houses. The final version of the show was received so well that Lee Shubert immediately planned another, more lavish edition, provisionally titled *The Passing Show of 1918*. He booked this spectacle into the Winter Garden with a larger cast, a long chorus line and plenty of beautiful girls. One of the Astaires' numbers featured them dressed as bird aviators with a whole chorus of chicks behind them. '"Twit, twit, twit" . . . that was the song we sang. And that was what Freddie felt like, too,' said Adèle. 'I don't think he ever did like feathers.'

The Passing Show fared better than *Over the Top*, but was not without its own problems. The director, J. C. Huffman, believed in the screaming and ranting technique of direction, which Astaire did not appreciate one jot. During rehearsals in Atlantic City, when the spotlight was not following Fred and Adèle properly during a tango number, Astaire stopped the orchestra to point out the mistake. Huffman was not amused and bawled him out: 'If you want to direct the show, just step this way and do so. You won't last a second on Broadway unless you know how to take orders!' This time it was Adèle who stepped bravely into the firing line: 'Mr Huffman, you don't understand. We've been

[44]

doing this dance for years in vaudeville. My brother knows how it should look. This dance is sacred to us.' There was dead silence from the auditorium where Huffman was sitting. Seconds ticked by. Finally the director's voice, heavy with sarcasm, came out of the blackness: 'All right, young lady, may we now go ahead with the "Dance of The Sacred Cow"? Music please!'

When the show opened on 25 July, the Astaires had their just reward in some glowing reviews. 'It almost seems as though the two young people had been poured into the dance,' said one. They were kept busy by Shubert – for no extra pay – with Sunday charity concerts which showcased the cream of the talent playing Eastern cities, such as Al Jolson and Fanny Brice.

Although his mother still called him Sonny, Astaire at nineteen had developed into a fine young man, conscious of his clothes and style. The family still lived carefully, but at last there was reasonable money coming in. Even Fred's habitual worry that it wouldn't last, that the show would close the following week and they wouldn't be able to get any work – what Adèle referred to as his Moaning Minnie routine – did not prevent him from expanding his horizons. His colleagues always said that Astaire was careful with money in everything except his clothes. If there was a new fashion or trend, he wanted to be part of it, although he would justify it to himself and to his family by explaining that it was for his work – which indeed it was. It was in 1918 that he also discovered two other prospective drains on his cash and energy: girls and horses.

The first was a twenty-year-old dancer in *The Passing Show* called Jesse Reed, a lissome girl from Houston, Texas, who had already been through two husbands, the vaudevillian Ollie Drouper (whom she wed when she was fifteen) and then Louis Herzberg, who used the stage name Lew Reed. But the second marriage was already over, and the good-hearted girl was delighted to receive Fred's attentions, just as she was delighted to receive the flowers, furs, and baubles that her other admirers pressed on her. 'I would stand gaping at her like a dope,' said Astaire. 'She was always pleasant to me, but my crush got me absolutely nowhere.' She had plenty of other devotees, and although she told the other girls 'Freddie is so sweet,' his roses just filled one more vase in her dressing room. It was not long afterwards that she got married once again, this time to the dashing millionaire Dan Caswell, a godson of the late President McKinley.

Romance had played no part in Fred's life before he met Jesse; it was

[45]

as though the dominating influences of his sister and mother had fulfilled the rôle of the female for him. It wasn't that he was not interested – he certainly was, but his sexual energy was entirely taken up with the business of perfecting his craft and searching for new material. Also in vaudeville there had not been the same opportunities – none of the winsome chorus lines that he now found in the revues. Fred, naturally an introvert off stage, for a long time found himself awkward and embarrassed with these ambitious girls, and Adèle, who claimed it took little to make him blush, got no thanks from him for constantly trying to match him up with dates.

Fred made his other great discovery one beautiful and fateful autumn day when he was invited to join some fellow performers at the racetrack at Belmont Park. Astaire had never seen a horse race, but it seemed an amusing idea, so he jumped into a friend's Stutz Bearcat and set off for the track. The simplicities of betting were explained to him, he backed a horse called Tiger Rose, and, much to his delight and his companions' surprise, it romped home at 4 to 1. He ended the day in the black. Beginner's luck, he called it, but winning like that put the seal on his instant enthusiasm for the racetrack. Winning was not the only thing he enjoyed: there was the noise, the rumbling thunder of the horses racing for the post and the yells of encouragement from the stands; the colour, in the multi-hued silks of the jockeys; the sights, the gleaming flanks of the well-muscled horses, the minuscule gnarl-faced jockeys; and there was class, the owners in their vast cars with wives and girlfriends swathed in furs. He soon learned that horse racing was the Sport of Kings and the King of Sports. He also discovered the truth of the adage that all men are equal on the turf and under the turf. Backstage at the theatre he began to join in the daily track gossip, quickly picking up the slang, and there was always an illegal bookie or two hanging around the stage door who would take his bets, which were never large – a few cents here and there and an occasional one-dollar splurge.

The Passing Show played five months on Broadway before going on the road. The tour was memorable to Fred for the occasion in Detroit when he fell asleep at his hotel after a matinée, waking just fifteen minutes before the 8.30 curtain time. Down the fire escape from the eighteenth floor, into an elevator on the fourteenth, tipping the elevator boy to take him down non-stop, a six-block sprint to the theatre, and a dash on stage without costume, make-up, or much breath – but on time. After that, Fred's normal concern for everything being right became an

[46]

obsession: he always set his watch ahead and arranged with at least two people to make sure he had arrived at least an hour before any performance.

In Chicago, with Adèle's encouragement, Astaire bought his first motor car, a Mercer sports model much favoured by the young college swells. He sold it after a few weeks, deciding it would be too expensive to take back to New York.

When the tour was over, and after the usual family conference – Adèle enthusing, Fred cautioning restraint, and Ann acting as referee and buffer – they decided to improve their home base. They found an apartment overlooking the park at the Hotel Majestic on 72nd Street and Central Park West. Their plans for the new digs were grandiose, largely inspired by things British: London, with its royal family and elegant ladies and gentlemen symbolised that aura of class that Fred and Adèle were so keen to emulate. On and off stage, consciously and sub-consciously, they adopted the mannerisms of the English. They drank tea, Fred's suits were copies of the latest Savile Row designs, and Adèle bought him a signet ring – a traditional accoutrement of the upper-class Englishman. But whenever Fred adopted an element of style, he introduced some variation of his own, and thus it was with the signet ring, which is always worn by the English gentleman on the little finger of the left hand (where it will not impede his sword-play!): Fred always wore his on the little finger of his right hand – initially from ignorance, later from habit.

Work was at last flowing in. The Astaires were offered, and eagerly accepted, a contract for $350 a week to do a show called *Apple Blossoms* for producer C. B. Dillingham, like Ziegfeld and the Shuberts a Chicago entrepreneur now on Broadway. Charles Dillingham had arrived on a high with dancers Vernon and Irene Castle in the 1914 show *Watch Your Step*, which had featured a ragtime score by Irving Berlin: after teaming up with Ziegfeld for a disaster called *Miss 1917*, he was on his own again. The Astaires took an instant liking to Dillingham, who sent them home, after their first meeting, in his chauffeur-driven Rolls-Royce. They were suitably impressed. 'Say, I like these. We ought to get one,' said Adèle. 'Yes, I think that's a great idea,' said Fred – and he wasn't joking.

Before *Apple Blossoms* went into rehearsals, the family took a vacation at Galen Hall, a resort in Wernersville, Pennsylvania. It was a quiet place, totally lacking the social attractions of New York, but this suited Fred, then twenty years old, and even Adèle, twenty-two, just fine. Fred

[47]

played golf; Ann and Adèle simply relaxed. But they did make some friends who would play an important part in their lives – and vice versa: a sophisticated young brother and sister, Jimmy and Liz Altemus, children of Lemuel C. Altemus, a Philadelphia stockbroker who had lost much of his money and parted from his society wife, Bessie Dobson Altemus. Mrs Altemus befriended Ann, and the younger generation followed suit. Fred was particularly taken with Liz, only thirteen years old but blessed with a beautiful face, long blonde hair, perfect olive skin, and the easy manner of the comfortably brought up. Mary Elizabeth (to give her her full name) was crazy about animals, particularly horses, and she had arrived at Galen Hall accompanied by her pet racoon. Jimmy Altemus, a few years younger than Fred, had immediately attracted Adèle by arriving in a Hudson Super Six wire-wheeled roadster. Actually, the Altemus family had chosen Galen Hall because it was cheap, but the Astaires never realized that – they assumed quite wrongly that their new friends had plenty of money. Fred paid assiduous court to Liz, although he never did find out where she ran off to in the mornings – but Fred's rival was only Willy, the garbage man, or rather, Willy's horse.

It might seem strange, the Philadelphia society folk and the youthful vaudevillians teaming up. But in fact, as Liz told the author, 'We were the only young people at the hotel, so it was quite natural that we became friends. I never realized that there was anything unusual about being friends with them. We used to play golf together, dance in the evening, and then on Sunday nights there would be a kind of church service in the lower room of the hotel and we would all join in.' The two families balanced each other well. Fred and Liz were the well-behaved; Jimmy and Adèle were always fooling around. 'You never could tell what they would get up to,' said Liz, 'particularly in those Sunday services. We used to have the most terrible trouble trying not to laugh as we all sang along. Freddie could hardly sing at all – that came as quite a shock when he became known as a singer later. Sometimes we played "snitch" – dominoes – and in the evening there might be dancing. Freddie wasn't much good as a social dancer – he used to hate it. I find it difficult to realize that my first partner was Fred Astaire.'

Ann Astaire quite easily became friendly with Bessie Altemus, for by now Ann had acquired an air of such fine breeding that she could have passed, Pygmalion-like, at least as a duchess. Questions about the past, about her husband – Mrs Altemus had been deserted by hers, too, so that was no problem – could be dealt with either by avoiding direct

[48]

answers or else embellishing the facts somewhat. Adèle had heard all her mother's tales before and, if the mood took her, could elaborate still further. No one quite knew who made up the story of the family name being L'Astaire and coming from Alsace Lorraine, but suspicion did point to Adèle – or it could even have been Fritz, who always had a marvellous story for every occasion.

For her fourteenth birthday, Fred gave Liz a three-quarter-keyboard upright piano; she never did learn to play it, but in later years Astaire would make use of it when he visited her mother's Philadelphia home. But Fred's wooing was sabotaged by Adèle, who discovered that pretty Liz, knowledgeable enough about the animal world, did not really know the 'facts of life'. 'Adèle sat me down and told me all about it – it put me off men for some time, I can tell you,' Liz recalled. At the end of the vacation, the Astaires left Galen Hall with promises from the Altemus clan that they would come and see *Apple Blossoms* just as soon as it opened. This was the family's first real acceptance into high society, and they loved it.

When rehearsals started for *Apple Blossoms* in New York, Astaire began to think all his relationships with directors were doomed. During the first week, the British director Fred Latham, then in his sixties, shouted at him for being a couple of minutes late one morning. It was a rare lapse and Fred answered Latham, giving as good as he got – after all, the Astaires had arrived on Day One with their own two numbers completely ready and rehearsed. Even Adèle was impressed by his invective. After that, things calmed down and the Astaires, whose rehearsal pianists included the show's composer, the world famous violinist Fritz Kreisler and Fred's songwriter friend, George Gershwin, returned to everyone's good books with their dazzling performance on opening night. The reviews were good; the hugely influential critic Alexander Woolcott wrote in *The New York Times*: 'There should be half a dozen special words for the vastly entertaining dances by the two Adaires (sic), in particular for those by the incredibly nimble and lack-a-daisical Adaire named Fred. He is one of those extraordinary persons whose senses of rhythm and humour have all been mixed up, whose very muscles, of which he seems to have an extra supply, are downright facetious.'

In the gap between their spots 'the Adaire named Fred' – Woolcott soon spelt their name right – would go down to the basement under the stage to play stud poker with the crew. With a fifty cent limit there was no danger of blowing his salary.

Liz and Jimmy Altemus came to see the show and introduced the stars to more of their friends. The Astaires went out to night-clubs and parties, where they were always a popular couple: she, vivacious and funny; he, shy and charming. They were rarely persuaded to dance but Fred could sometimes be talked into playing the piano. He was determinedly happy with life: the audiences loved the act, the work was not too demanding, and he had plenty of time for the race track and gracious living. The show ran until the summer, when Dillingham decided to close it for the airless hot months and then take it on tour. The Astaires packed themselves off to Galen Hall, to meet up again with the Altemus family, for a summer of golf and tennis and laughter, then headed back to New York to begin six months on the road.

In Detroit, Fritz's business ventures had not been prospering. He talked of joining the family in New York, although no one imagined that there could be a complete reconciliation between him and Ann: they had grown too unlike for that. She was now an imperious New Yorker while he remained an Austrian mid-Westerner, delighted by the success of his offspring and particularly pleased that their new show was written by Fritz Kreisler, another Austrian. The family were proud of each other and that, particularly as far as Fred was concerned, was what was really important. *Apple Blossoms* was a hot ticket, and by the end of the run the Astaires' joint salary had risen to an astronomical $750. Now they could live like the Broadway stars they had fast become, with plenty left over for relaxation at Wernerville – just the three of them, Fritz was in Detroit – while Dillingham planned another show around them.

Dillingham found *The Love Letter*, adapted by William Le Barron from a story by the Hungarian Ferenc Molnar with music by Victor Jacobi. The Astaires, billed under the star comedian John Charles Thomas, realised that after their eight happy months in *Apple Blossoms* this would be no picnic, as the adaptation was heavy and the vehicle cumbersome. They were almost relieved by the notices, which included the *New York Herald*: 'The Astaires made the high score of the evening, getting four encores for their entertaining singing and nutty dancing.' The 'nutty dancing' was the one felicity of *The Love Letter*, for it was in this production that the British choreographer Teddy Royce hit upon a dance which became known as the 'Oompah Trot'. The Astaires positioned their arms as though they were gripping a bicycle's handlebars and trotted side by side in large circles around the stage to a continuous Germanic oompah oompah beat. It was simple then and

[50]

would be unsophisticated in the extreme today, but their lightness of touch guaranteed the success of this innocent exit-sequence. Encores were routinely demanded: the 'Oompah Trot' stopped the show on the first night, 4 October 1921, and was to prove itself time and time again.

Otherwise, as far as the Astaires were concerned, the skies were black. They had become accustomed to success, and their first encounter with the pall of disaster that hangs over a flop was as unexpected as it was unwelcome. They took to staying home at night and dropped out of the night-club circuit; for a time Fred even gave up his regular visits to the Fifth Avenue haberdasheries. After thirty-one performances, *The Love Letter* was history.

But life goes on and there's only so much room-pacing one can do, so before long Fred emerged from his room and resumed his rounds. Chance took him into Finchley's, just off Fifth Avenue, to look at ties. The young man who helped him, smartly dressed in the way that assistants are in men's shops, smarter than any of their customers, recognised Astaire. He said that he was a great fan and rather presumptuously offered his advice: the duo should be doing light musical comedy rather than revues. Astaire had been thinking the same, and in theory that was what *The Love Letter* was – it just happened to be a bad example of the genre. He was relieved to discover that his advisor was not just a pushy shop assistant but the son of producer Alfred A. Aarons of Klaw and Erlanger. His name was Alex A. Aarons, and he was actually a part-owner of Finchley's. He and Fred discovered a mutual acquaintance in George Gershwin; Aarons had produced Gershwin's none-too-successful first musical *La, La, Lucille*, which had run for 104 performances but barely recouped its expenses. They exchanged addresses, Fred took his ties, and he and Alex Aarons promised to keep in touch.

During the brief life of *The Love Letter* there had been many admiring backstage visitors, including the bright young thing of the London theatre Noël Coward, a former child actor and now, at twenty-one, a respected juvenile lead who had already adopted a particularly exotic and elegant style. 'What can I say?' Coward said to Fred. 'You two were *marvellous*, of course . . . but the show . . .'

The witty and wordly Coward, struck up an immediate and firm friendship with the Astaires. He told them of his plans to write and act in his own shows ('It's the only way you can make sure you get the good lines') and sang them his songs. He whisked them around the night clubs, explaining politely to each maître d' that the Astaires were the

[51]

most important people in New York, and encouraging Adèle to promote him as the most famous man in England, thus ensuring a constant supply of complimentary champagne and food. He was insistent that they come to London; 'You'll cause a riot,' he predicted. Britain seemed a long way off, but the thought was delicious.

Fred negotiated a release from Dillingham, so that he and Adèle could do a show for his new friend Alex Aarons. Unhappily, Aaron's plan to get George Gershwin to write a musical for the Astaires fell through, as the composer was tied up on *George White's Scandals of 1922*. Instead, he hired Billy Daly, the musical director of the ill-fated *Love Letter*, and Phil Lannin, who came up with a script called *For Goodness Sake*. The male lead was a well-to-do actor friend of Aarons, Vinton Freedley, who also invested some money in the show. Fred could hardly wait to get started, to obliterate the failure of *The Love Letter*; he was eager to try out new ideas and thought there might be a chance of rescuing some of the better ones from their earlier experiences. Daly and Lannin wrote a zany number called 'The Whichness of the Whatness and the Whereness of the Who', which Fred decided would be an ideal accompaniment for the runaround routine that had been such a showstopper in *The Love Letter* – good material should never be wasted.

When the show opened on 20 February 1922, the Astaires felt that they had regained some of their old confidence. Fred once said: 'I never did work out why, but I always did good first nights. Maybe sometimes the second nights weren't so hot, but the first nights were always just swell.' That night was no exception: in the *Morning American*, Alan Dale wrote: 'The two Astaires are the principle asset of *For Goodness Sake*. They can speak a little, act a little, and dance quarts. They are as nice a twain as you could wish to see.' And Robert Benchley wrote in *Life*: 'There isn't much to say about *For Goodness Sake* that you can't say about most musical comedies except that the Astaires (perhaps late of Astaires and Down) are in it. When they dance everything seems brighter and their comedy alone would be good enough to carry them through even if they were to stop dancing, which God forbid!' A dreadfully weak joke from a great wit who would in later days work as an actor with Fred (in a small rôle in *Dancing Lady*, as well as co-starring in *You'll Never Get Rich* and *The Sky's the Limit*). But these enthusiastic comments were a minority vote. The jeunesse dorée came to see the show, but not in enough numbers to take it through the summer. The heat gave Aarons an excuse to close *For Goodness Sake* at the end of May.

[52]

To gain their release from Dillingham, the Astaires had agreed to star in one more show for him, for $1,000 a week, this one the first created especially for them. After a summer of relaxation, they began rehearsing *The Bunch and Judy*, written by the Anglophile songwriter Jerome Kern. The fairytale plot could have been devised by a clever seer, for Adèle played a dancer who retires from the stage to marry an English lord. The climax of the first act featured Fred and Adèle dancing on top of a baronial banqueting table held high in the air by a troupe of chorus boys. The original comedy lead, Joe Cawton, had already broken his leg (his rôle was rewritten for a brother-and-sister team, Johnny and Ray Dooley) and the ever-cautious Fred was convinced that he and Adèle would slip off and suffer the same fate. And sure enough, slip they did, although fortunately no bones were broken. Adèle, dumped off the table in the final out-of-town dress rehearsal, sat disgruntled on the stage and complained, 'This is a hell of a way to become a star.' That rehearsal finally ended at 4 a.m. and the Astaires went miserably back to their hotel, where Adèle broke down in tears. Fred, assuming his guardian rôle, said: 'Come on, let's go put our head in the noose. At least the run around number will get 'em, if nothing else does.' Once more the oompah routine had been resurrected.

When *The Bunch and Judy* arrived at the freshly painted Globe Theatre on 28 November, the Astaires were no happier. On opening night, Fred felt that the Dooleys had been more of a hit than Adèle and himself, the nominal headliners. Although the reviews could have been worse ('There will be no other Globe show this year,' said one, which at least gave them four weeks to run), the show lasted just three and a half weeks in New York. Adèle said she would undoubtedly have died if Alex Aarons had not come to the rescue. Would they take *For Goodness Sake* to London? he asked. Would they? They would love to.

The wealthy London producer Alfred Butt, a former director of rationing at the Ministry of Food and since 1922 the Unionist Member of Parliament for Wandsworth (Balham and Tooting), had seen the show in New York and, if the terms were agreeable, was eager to put it on in the West End. The terms did in fact surprise him: the Astaires said they would be needing passage for three. For three? Yes, Adèle, Fred, and Ann. But I just want the dancing Astaires, Butt said. You can't expect Adèle to make a trip like that unaccompanied, surely? Ann went too. It was their very first ocean voyage, and they enjoyed every minute. They were even persuaded to take part in the traditional

[53]

charity concert given on board for the Seamen's Fund, although Fred was not too keen on the idea. What about the rolling of the boat? 'Oh, come on' said Adèle – but Fred's fears were well-justified. That night there was an impressive swell, and chairs and tables slipped and slid about as the Astaires bravely improvised comic turns to cover up disasters in their dancing. They must have succeeded, for passengers and crew alike promised to see their show in London.

They docked in Southampton, travelled by train to Waterloo Station, and checked into the Savoy. Fred sallied forth to reconnoitre the London theatreland. He was impressed by the musical comedy star Jack Buchanan, the British top-hat-and-tails dancer, in *Battling Butler*, but was somewhat alarmed by the demonstrativeness of the audiences at other theatres, who showed their displeasure with catcalls and by pelting the stage with pennies. During the Liverpool previews of *For Goodness Sake* (renamed *Stop Flirting*) the London première of a play with American actress Laurette Taylor was interrupted by stink bombs and snuff thrown at the stage and general pandemonium in the audience. So the Astaires were uncharacteristically nervous, particularly coming from what Fred called *The Bust and Judy*. But the out-of-town reviews were good, the audiences warm. Noël Coward, who had been among the first to welcome them to London, encouraged his friends and contacts to spread the word about the dancing darlings: he was determined to introduce this amusing, soigné couple to London society as the bright new talent of the year. He came to see them in Liverpool with the Earl of Lathom ('Ned' to his friends), and afterwards dined at the Midland Adelphi with them and the high-living, high-spending theatrical producer and playboy. It was the Astaires' first meeting with a real British blueblood.

For Fred the Liverpool previews had gone a shade too well: something was bound to go wrong at the Shaftesbury in London. 'It's old Moaning Minnie,' announced Adèle to Ann. 'He's always going on about something.' But on opening night, 30 May 1922, it was clear by the middle of the second act that the audience was with them, joining in with the chorus of 'Oompah, Oompah, Oompah' as 'The Whichness of the Whatness' worked its showstopping magic. Adèle, caught unawares, was pushed forward to make a speech. She looked around from side to side of the expectant house, and took a deep breath: 'My brother and I thank you from the bottom of our hearts and – we want you all to come and have tea with us tomorrow.' She confessed afterwards: 'It was the only British sort of thing I could think of saying.' She pulled

[54]

Fred forward. He was even more awkward than she; when the noise stopped, he muttered: 'She said it . . .'

What a relief to come off-stage and head for Claridges Hotel in Mayfair, where Sir Alfred Butt had arranged a suitably star-studded party with Tallulah Bankhead, Somerset Maugham, their friend Nöel Coward with Gertrude Lawrence, and a heavy sprinkling of tiaras and society types. 'Your success here is assured,' Coward told Adèle. 'You've got youth, energy, humour, looks and fun. That's exactly what the English like.'

First nights often give a fallacious impression – angels, friends, and hangers-on applaud absolutely anything. But the theatre critics, while not overly enthusiastic about the show as a whole, gave the Astaires a decent press. *The Times* wrote: 'They are as lithe as blades of grass, as light as gossamer; and as odd as golliwogs.' The *Evening Star* said of Adèle: 'She could dance the depression out of an undertaker.' Nonetheless, business was slow to take off. London was more interested in the events of the day – the resignation of Prime Minister Bonar Law and the death of Lord Chaplin, the statesman father of the famed society hostess Lady Londonderry – than they were in the two Americans appearing with the British headliner Jack Melford at the Shaftesbury. It looked as though Adèle might yet be required to dance for that undertaker when two weeks into the run Sir Alfred put up closing notices backstage. The Astaires had come, they had seen, but for all their efforts, they had obviously failed to conquer.

6
London

The invasion of Britain, which they had launched with such high
hopes, seemed about to end in disaster. Adèle was in tears and Fred was
. . . well, he admitted to kicking a few things. But even if it hadn't been a
triumph, they shouldn't worry, their mother told them. Fred had
celebrated his twenty-fourth birthday just before the première and
frankly, Ann said, he should not plan to go on working for too much
longer anyway – another decade in New York, where he was much in
demand, and then he could probably retire. 'You're entitled to it,' she
said. 'After all, most young people don't start to earn a living until they
get out of school when they're twenty-two or so. Here *you* are: at
twenty-five, you've already been working for twenty-one years. By ten
years from now, you'll have had thirty-one years of strenuous work.
Then you can do something that puts less of a strain on your heart, or
perhaps take it easy and not work at all.' Fred was none too impressed
by this vision. He wasn't the type to give up easily, and neither was
Adèle. They decided to give the last few shows everything they had; if
they still did not succeed, it wouldn't be for any lack of effort. Some
guardian angel must have seen their plight and taken pity on the two
newcomers, for to their total amazement and delight, the Royal Family
came to their rescue.

One night Prince George, the handsome twenty-year-old fourth son
of King George V, slipped fairly inconspicuously into the Shaftesbury
Theatre. His enthusiasm for the show and for the Americans who were
dancing and singing their hearts out was immediate and obvious. 'Oh
Gee! oh Gosh! oh Golly! I Love You' and the 'Oompah Trot', with its
instant singalong chorus, charmed the royal party utterly. Prince
George buttonholed the theatre manager and raved about the show;
the theatre manager told the Astaires, and Adèle quite shamelessly told
everyone. Next day the Prince's enthusiasm was noted in the newspapers, an endorsement worth more than any number of great reviews

– better than just 'good', the Astaires and *Stop Flirting* were now fashionable. This was indeed a blessing, but for Alfred Butt a mixed one, for he had to quit the Shaftesbury in two weeks' time. Fortunately, the nearby Queen's Theatre suddenly became vacant and he arranged to transfer the show there – it was smaller and thus better, he assured the Astaires, for fewer seats meant greater demand; they would soon be the hottest ticket in town.

Prince George returned, this time with his brother, the Yankee-loving David, The Prince of Wales. The heir to the throne was without doubt London's most influential arbiter of social taste and style, and he thought the Astaires were the best thing since checked suits. Success was now assured, and the Astaires quickly developed into social gadflies, in demand at late-night parties and smart luncheons around town. Not everyone was surprised by their instant social acceptance. 'I knew that you would be a riot,' Fred was told by Noël Coward, who was well aware of the long-standing love affair between the British aristocracy and the entertainment world: from King Charles II and Nell Gwyn to the Earl of Northesk, who had just married the former Ziegfeld chorus girl Jessica Brown. For Noël Coward the Astaires were complementary talents, both socially and professionally. Fred claimed he couldn't sing, Noël said he was an awful dancer. Preparing to star in the revue he himself had written, *London Calling* (which was to open, backed by Ned Lathom, in the autumn at the Duke of York's Theatre), Noël managed to acquire some extra talent and kudos by persuading Fred to choreograph and coach him and his co-star Gertrude Lawrence in three dance sequences. Together with Noël and Gertie, who were long-time friends, Fred and Adèle swanned from the Kit Kat Club to the Embassy, the Café de Paris, Ciro's, and Kate Meyrick's 43 Club, becoming regulars at all of them.

The friendship between Noël and Fred was natural and immediately close. There was much similarity in their early careers, and also an affinity of talents and tastes; furthermore, Coward was a welcome, unthreatening male influence in Fred's life. Coward was the very image of upward social mobility, and he was happy to guide Fred on the road. He complained that he had a much heavier cross to bear than the American Astaires – the stigma of having been born into a middle-class family in Teddington, Middlesex, which was neither poverty-stricken nor affluent. 'I didn't gnaw kippers' heads in the gutter as Gertie always quite untruthfully insists she did; nor was my first memory the crunch of carriage wheels in the drive – because we didn't have a drive,'

[57]

he said. Like the Astaires, as a child performer Noël had had problems with the authorities. All his stage appearances until he was fourteen years old necessitated a visit to London's Bow Street Magistrates Court, where the business manager of the theatre company, the little boy, and his mother would apply for a licence; if the magistrate was brave enough to query whether acting was really in the child's best interests, his splendidly tough mother would deliver a magnificently lachrymose speech explaining that if her son were not allowed to act he would undoubtedly go into a decline and have to be admitted to a sanatorium – a performance that always got little Noël his licence.

Apart from the dancing lessons, Astaire and Coward together decided they needed some musical education, so they enrolled at the Guildhall School of Music as students of harmony, under Orlando Morgan. The venture was not a great success. 'I have only had those two music lessons in my life,' said Coward in the preface to his 'Songbook'. 'They were the first steps of what was to have been a full course which Fred and I signed for, but they faltered and stopped when I was told by my instructor that I could not use consecutive fifths. He went on to explain that a gentleman called Ebenezer Prout had announced many years ago that consecutive fifths were wrong and in no circumstances should be employed. At the time Ebenezer Prout was merely a name to me – as a matter of fact he still is, and a very funny one at that – and I was unimpressed by his Victorian dicta. I argued back that Debussy and Ravel used consecutive fifths like mad. My instructor waved aside this triviality with a pudgy hand, and I left his presence for ever, with the parting shot that what was good enough for Debussy and Ravel was good enough for me. This outburst of rugged individualism deprived me of much valuable knowledge, and I have never deeply regretted it for a moment.'

The Astaires adored everything about London. The chic little shops in the Burlington Arcade, off Piccadilly, were like nothing Fred had seen before and the elegance of the Savile Row and Dover Street establishments, with their cross-legged tailors working away in the basements, utterly captivated him. He discovered where the smart people got their clothes, and he too went to order shirts from Beale and Inman and Hawes and Curtis, and added suits and shoes and ties from Jermyn Street and hats from St James's Street. Adèle became a regular browser in Bond Street. 'What are we going to do with all this stuff?' his mother asked. But Fred was having too good a time to worry about things like that.

He and Adèle saw the sights of London under the aegis of Alfred Butt, who was delighted to have this attractive couple share his Sybaritic pursuits, eating at the best hotels and restaurants, meeting the grandest people, and following the fortunes of his fine stable of racehorses. Fred had already had some guidance in the English racing scene from his dresser George Griffin, an authentic working-class Londoner and a great racing buff, who randomly dropped his aitches in speech and even in writing – one day Astaire was surprised to find a note in the dressing room announcing AT ERE, which turned out to be a reminder from George to himself that Astaire's hat had been left there. Earlier, during the Liverpool run of *Stop Flirting*, Fred had met another more professional source of racing information when the jockey Jack Leach came to see the show. Through Jack he met many of the top riders of the time: Charlie Smirke, Harry Wragg, Brownie Carslake, Charlie Elliott, and the other Leach brothers, Felix the eldest and Chubb the youngest. But no one could stay out later than Gentleman Jack, or have more fun or enjoy his champagne more heartily. Like other high-earning riders, Leach would sweat away some weight at the Jermyn Street Turkish Baths, then don white tie and tails and go out on the town. Fred found him and the other jockeys his natural friends; they were all slightly built, a bit pixieish, and physically fit – just as he was. Their unofficial drinking headquarters was the Piccadilly Hotel, where Astaire would meet Leach to go to the local London meetings: Windsor, the now-disappeared Alexandra Palace frying-pan course in North London, Kempton Park. Jack Leach recalled: 'It was prize-fighter Jimmy Carney who said: "There shouldn't be a last race – they ought to do away with it."' Well, for the racing folk, the 'swine' as Astaire sometimes called them, there often was no last race, for afterwards it would be run over and over in the bars of the race track and in the restaurants and night clubs around town.

Royal patronage showed no abatement; Prince George and the Prince of Wales came back yet again to see *Stop Flirting* – the former's third visit, the latter's second. This time Fred and Adèle reacted more calmly, at least up until the interval, when Major 'Fruity' Metcalfe, the Prince of Wales' tall Irish equerry, came round to ask if the Astaires would care to join His Highness for dinner at the Riviera Club after the show. Adèle had mixed feelings – she really wasn't sure that she would say or do the right thing. 'Do I curtsy? What do I call him? What should I wear? Oh, Freddie,' she said. 'Can't we just meet him and go home?' 'No, we can't,' said Fred, even though he later admitted that he was not sure either how you addressed the man who would be the next King of England. At the Riviera, all eyes were on the late and elegant arrivals. It was an intriguing group. With Edward Metcalfe – whose nickname 'Fruity' had no disparaging overtones then, and referred solely to his deep and much-imitated Irish brogue – were Lady Alexandra Curzon, known as Baba, daughter of former India Viceroy Lord Curzon of Kedleston, and his American heiress wife Mary Leiter, as well as the glamorous Mrs Dudley Coats. Audrey Coats, née James, heiress to yet another American fortune, had been engaged to Lord Louis Mountbatten before he jilted her – he always claimed that it was the other way about – when he had furthered his career by going on a round-the-world trip with the Prince of Wales. While Mountbatten was absent Audrey James had met and married the immensely rich Major Dudley Coats of the cotton family – society tittle-tattle was that she had preferred the arms of Coats to the coat of arms. Audrey Coats, an open, fun-loving girl of twenty-one, fitted perfectly the penchant of the twenty-six year old Prince for rich, worldly, beautiful American women – 'America is the only place where I actually feel at home,' as he said. Baba Curzon and Metcalfe would be married within two years; the tall, broad-shouldered Metcalfe, incidentally, showed scant respect for the Prince of Wales and behind his back invariably referred to the dapper Prince as 'The Little Man'.

At the table David, the Prince of Wales placed himself firmly next to Adèle. As they drank their cocktails and collected their breath, he asked her: 'Are you too tired to dance?' 'Sir, I'm exhausted,' she said, with which she jumped up and onto the dance floor, dragging the delighted Prince with her. Fred was fascinatedly studying the Prince's immaculate clothes: white tie and tails, beautifully cut, and an intriguing small white waistcoat with tiny lapels.

Next morning Adèle slept late, but Fred had an early morning call to make, to Hawes and Curtis, who, he had found, made the Prince's dress shirts and waistcoats. At their hands he got an object lesson in English reserve. 'I'm afraid I don't know what you mean, sir,' he was told when he asked for a waistcoat like that of the Prince of Wales. 'I'm afraid that we couldn't possibly discuss any clothes that we have made for other customers.' At first he was annoyed, then angry, finally deflated. 'Okay, okay,' he said. He trotted a few doors down, to Anderson and Shepherd. This time he knew just what to do. 'I want you to make me a white dress waistcoat with small lapels, small enough so that the waistcoat doesn't come below the front of the coat,' he said. 'Look, I'll draw what it should look like.' Anderson and Shepherd also made clothes for the Prince of Wales, but this time Fred's approach was entirely correct and the cutter was quite happy to carry out the instructions.

The Prince of Wales claimed to have seen *Stop Flirting* ten times before the end of its run. He came with his other brother, Bertie, the Duke of York, who had married Lady Elizabeth Bowes-Lyon a month before the show opened. He also came again with Audrey Coats, who encouraged these visits and admitted that she found the company of Astaire particularly delightful. Indeed, Fred was very taken with her, too. Although there were those who considered it shocking that the Prince of Wales should escort a married woman, Astaire decided that what was good enough for royalty was fine for him. He made several luncheon dates with Audrey, and they found themselves at the same late dinners on more than a few occasions.

For five weeks over the Christmas pantomime season *Stop Flirting* was transferred to Birmingham, where the royal connection was kept up. Prince George, then attending Dartmouth Naval College, came up with his roommate one weekend on leave and stayed at the Midland Hotel having fun with the Astaires. Another visitor to the show was the young *Vogue* photographer Cecil Beaton, who confessed to his biographer how he squirmed in his seat with pleasure. 'Delirious with happiness whenever they are on stage. She is so American and perfect and slim. I admire her ugly face and the pearls tight around her neck,' he told his diary. But it was not until the following year that he both collected their autographs and photographed them, after he had seen them dance again in London. 'I adored the Astaires so much I almost died in my stall.' Beaton had first met the Astaires in Palm Beach, along with Marjorie Oelricht who would, like Adèle, have the distinction of initiating him into the pleasures of heterosexual sex. In *Vogue* (May 1929) he wrote of Adèle as a 'rather too roguish but a delightfully brittle puppet'.

Back in London, the loyal royal fan club maintained its interest; on one occasion all three brothers, the Prince of Wales, the Duke of York, and Prince George, called together backstage. Their enthusiasm in itself was not so unusual – it was often done in those days to see a show more than once – but it put the definitive seal on the Astaires' London acceptance. Their mother Ann, making friends and playing bridge with the dowagers, seemed to become more grand and more English with every passing day. The list of famous visitors grew by the week. Lord

Mountbatten, whom they had met through Noël Coward, brought his new wife, Edwina Ashley, heiress to the Cassel banking fortune, as well as Douglas Fairbanks, star of the Astaires' unlucky one-performance-only Broadway début – ('I didn't even know you were on the bill,' he said to Fred afterwards), and his wife Mary Pickford, who said she remembered them from *Fanchon the Cricket* at the Delaware Water Gap – although Fred reckoned she was just being nice.

There were other experiences too: in October the Astaires had gone into a primitive sound studio – one huge microphone with musicians and singers gathered around it – to record 'The Whichness of the Whatness' and 'Oh Gee! oh Gosh!' Both numbers from the show were being played by hotel dance orchestras all over London, and Alfred Butt felt that the Astaires should be benefitting from some record sales.

In the first weeks of 1924, before the end of the year-long run, Ann travelled back to New York alone, when she learned that Fritz, who had not been well for a while, had fallen seriously ill; she did, after all, have her matrimonial duty to him. She collected her husband in Detroit and brought him to Pennsylvania for a rest. There was an immediate improvement in his condition when she told him of the success of his beloved Adèle and Fred; but just two weeks later, in London, Alfred Butt came to Fred's dressing room in a sombre mood – Fritz Austerlitz had died quietly in Wernersville. Fred was stunned; he knew his father had not been well, but his mother's letters had given him no particular cause for concern. Butt did what little he could to console Fred, offering to cancel the performance or even to close the show for a week or two. Fred, drying his eyes, broke the bad news to Adèle. Although Fritz had not been as close to them as their mother, he had always been a solid and important source of support, advice, and encouragement to his children, and even in his absence he had given them something to strive for – to bring some comfort to him by making his dreams for them come true. There were tears aplenty, but there really was nothing that they could do. Their initial reaction was to cancel the performance, but then after they talked it over Adèle announced that the show ought to go on – certainly that's what Fritz would have said. So they went out there and were better than ever. 'You know, that was the first really bad news I had ever had in my life,' Fred recalled, 'and it took some time to get over it.'

Ann returned to London – it took six weeks for her to settle things in Wernersville and make the slow Atlantic crossing – but in the frigid late British spring of 1924 she too became unwell and had to retire for a time to a London nursing home. Another inmate in the home was Sir James Barrie, author of *Peter Pan*, who, when he heard of his fellow patient, sent a note requesting the Astaires to drop by and see him. 'Miss Astaire,' he announced from his bed, when Adèle called, 'I have seen you dance and act and all I can say is I wish that you would play Peter Pan. I would very much like to see you in that.' Adèle was flattered and delighted by the old man's suggestion (Barrie was then sixty-three), and it is a shame that nothing ever came of that intriguing wish of his.

Barrie wasn't the only distinguished author who admired Adèle – George Bernard Shaw considered her one of the most beautiful women he had ever met. 'What do you think of actors, Mr Shaw?' she asked him. 'Nothing,' the old reprobate growled. 'If it weren't for authors there wouldn't be any.' 'I should have said dancers,' Adèle demurred, to Shaw's delight. After that they agreed that they would be friends.

The Astaires had been away from New York for eighteen months. Although it seemed that their royal patronage could still sustain them for a while in London, they felt that if they didn't go home soon, America might completely forget them, so reluctantly they brought the run to an end. The closing-night audience joined in the songs and sang 'Auld Lang Syne', and the Astaires both felt quite sentimental about the occasion. At the final curtain, to loud cheers and a standing ovation, they promised the audience that they would be back.

There were no dancing turns on the SS Homeric on the way to the United States, although Fred was happy to act as compère. When they reached New York the very real concern they felt about having been forgotten proved quite unfounded. Newsmen and photographers were out in force to greet them and quiz them about their friendship with the Prince of Wales, who was the darling of the American public. Adèle was ready for them: 'Now listen you boys, if you think you're going to get some of those dope headlines from me, you're crazy. The Prince of Wales and other members of the Royal Family were very kind to my brother and me and I'm not talking about it for publicity purposes.' There was nothing that Adèle needed to learn about publicity! The newspapers duly obliged with heavy headlines about the Prince and the Dancer, without actually saying anything that might upset her new-found friends and admirers. But Fred found he did have some defending to do, for a comment Adèle had made in London to the *Daily Sketch* newspaper had been picked up in New York: 'In America everyone is so rude. They say they have no time to say please and thank you. But here, although London is so big and bustling everyone is always saying thank you in the shops and the buses. So do the taxi drivers and the policemen and people in restaurants and the hotels. We feel that we shall not be able to stand the rudeness when we get back and I'm sure that we shall tell the Americans that they must come to London to learn politeness.' Fred had to do one of his 'What my sister really meant was . . .' routines, before taking her aside and telling her that, even if it was true, she must learn to keep her big mouth shut.

Alex Aarons had by now gone into full partnership with his former lead actor Vinton Freedley; together, they did at last have a George Gershwin show called *Black Eyed Susan* for the Astaires, whose joint salary would leap to $1,750 a week. Gershwin's elder brother Ira would write the song lyrics and the well-established team of Guy Bolton and Fred Thompson would write the book. Fred and Adèle would play an impoverished brother and sister, turned out of their home for non-payment of rent; unsurprisingly they would both end up with wealthy partners. By the time rehearsals started the show's title was changed to *Lady, Be Good!*, which did not immediately appeal to Fred – that is, until he heard the catchy title song. All the numbers were vintage Gershwin: 'Fascinatin' Rhythm', 'The Half of It, Dearie, Blues' (with lyrics by Desmond Carter and demonstrated by Gershwin with his own tap dance break in the middle), and the lightweight 'Swiss Miss', created for the traditional Astaire 'Oompah Trot'. After out-of-town runs and previews with few changes, the show opened on 1 December 1924 at the Liberty Theatre. It gave Gershwin, whom some people had considered arty-crafty and incapable of writing a musical, his first great popular success.

The management of the Trocadero asked the Astaires to do a late-night cabaret spot after their show. Adèle recalled: 'Fred thought it might be fun to pick up a big sum of money very quickly, so he said to me "How about if we asked for $5,000 a week for six weeks?" I said I didn't mind. How about doing it and getting a Rolls-Royce out of it? So Fred said "Okay: I'll ask $5,000 a week for six weeks and then if they say no we just drop it.' To their amazement, the demand didn't cause a blink from the club; the very fact of this astronomical fee would bring in the crowds. The Astaires were not ballroom or exhibition dancers, so they quickly had to assemble a new routine suitable for a club. For three weeks business was fine, but late-night work was tiring and neither Fred nor Adèle was very happy about the smoky, noisy night-club atmosphere or the noise of people eating and drinking during their performance. But it was fun and smart and, of course, hugely lucrative, for the Astaires if not for the Trocadero. They couldn't hope to get away with it for long, and Fred wisely decided to pre-empt the situation when the crowd thinned out after the first ultra-packed weeks. He presented a flashy silver cigarette case and a whisky flask to the owners of the Trocadero as a token of gratitude and suggested that as a further thank you he and Adèle would be happy to accept $3,000 for the last two weeks of the engagement. The management gratefully accepted both the presents and the offer, and Fred went happily on his way to tell his sister that they could indeed put that Rolls-Royce on their shopping list.

Lady, Be Good! ran at the Liberty on Broadway till the middle of September 1925 and then went on a tour of the East Coast, taking in Pittsburgh, Cleveland and Detroit, before an engagement in London. Now experienced trans-Atlantic travellers, Fred and Adèle returned to England by way of France, spending some time in Paris to see the sights and the great variety acts of the day, such as Maurice Chevalier, Mistinguett and the Dolly Sisters. If the Londoners liked the Astaires before, this time they adored them; the Empire, Leicester Square was packed nightly with enthusiastic crowds. With the first chorus of 'Oh, sweet and lovely, lady, be good!' the audience was theirs, and it soon became clear that the critics were with them too. This time there was no hesitation about recording songs from the show; just five days after the opening they went into the studio, with George Gershwin as their piano accompanist, to record 'Lady, Be Good!', 'Fascinatin' Rhythm', 'I'd Rather Charleston' (which Gershwin added to the show for London), 'Hang on to Me', and 'The Half of It, Dearie, Blues' with George adding his vocal encouragement in the background – 'We were having a ball,' said Gershwin.

The Astaires returned to their position as the darlings of London society. They didn't really mingle in show business circles, although they were always friendly to fellow performers. As the leaders of fashion, friends of the Prince of Wales and supreme entertainers, they hobnobbed with the crème de la crème: the wealthy Anglo-Americans such as Audrey Coats, Baba Metcalfe, Edwina Mountbatten; the American-loving English, such as the Prince of Wales; and the Americans they had met in New York. This time they had brought plenty of friends with them, including their Pennsylvania vacation playmates Liz and Jimmy Altemus, and Jock Whitney – John Hay Whitney was his full name. A tremendously wealthy New Yorker, with a vast estate on Long Island and an inheritance of over $30,000,000

[65]

with more to come, Whitney had met the Astaires in New York while he was a student at Yale, one of the preppy fans they so enjoyed. It was natural that Jock, large, awkward and stunningly well-connected to the Paynes, the Whitneys, and the Vanderbilts, should be added to their circle when he came to study at Oxford University's New College, bringing with him his American manservant, Edgar. In fact Adèle, then twenty-nine but admitting to some years less, was seen out on the town so much with Whitney, then just twenty-two, that rumours spread of an imminent engagement. She exploded with glee when quizzed on this: 'Me marry Jock Whitney? Why, he's still at school!' Afterwards there was some making up to be done, for Jock, whose inheritance had also brought psychological problems of shyness and a stutter, was a bit hurt at not being taken seriously. He always maintained that Adèle was just the greatest company he ever found.

It was not only society that courted the Astaires. A particularly good offer from the manager of the hotel on the corner of the Haymarket and Pall Mall (and, alas, no more), persuaded them to move out of the Savoy to the Charlton, which was a gentle five-minute walk to the theatre or to Jermyn Street and just along the road from York House, home of the Prince of Wales and his brother Prince George. With some time on their hands for shopping, that Rolls-Royce could now be ordered. They chose a black Twenty, the smallest model of the range, and Rolls-Royce found them a chauffeur who knew London and could drive them in style. It was a very satisfactory arrangement all round, except for one unfortunate night when Astaire announced that he would drive home at two in the morning after a visit to the Kit Kat Club with Liz Altemus, by then a stunning twenty-year-old. He dropped her off at the Mountbattens' in Park Lane and then, in Grosvenor Square, on his way back to the Carlton, he was suddenly confronted by a small sports car that zipped right around the square and seemed to be headed straight towards him. Fred, confused by driving on the left side of the road, veered, and, before anyone knew what had happened, the cars collided. A girl in evening dress, looking panicky, hopped out of the sports car and disappeared around the corner. The driver was abjectly apologetic, for the entire near side of the Rolls was dented and damaged. Fred was apologetic, too – he still wasn't sure how much in the right or wrong he had been – but he found himself mesmerised by the man's dress: white tie and tails, with ruby-and-diamond shirt-studs and waistcoat buttons that twinkled in the gaslit street and the headlights of the cars. 'All the time I was hypnotised by those

[66]

ruby-and-diamond waistcoat buttons,' recalled Fred. 'It may sound strange, but that was all I could think of at that time.' Both men were unharmed, but the situation was awkward and they wanted to be on their way. The sports car limped off and Fred caught a cab back to the Carlton. 'I was up early next morning,' he said. 'I had to break the news to Delly that we had no Rolls for a few days.' After that, he hastened to Cartier, to treat himself to some ruby-and-diamond baubles like the ones he had seen in the early hours of the morning. He got his studs, but he never did find out the young driver's name.

The royal Princes were still their greatest fans. On 9 August, Adèle received a note from the Duchess of York – today Queen Elizabeth, the Queen Mother – apologising for having seen them only twice recently and suggesting that Adèle and her brother might come to lunch to see 'the baby', at the Duke of York's Mayfair home. 'The baby' was just four months old, a cheerful child who would in time grow up to be Queen Elizabeth II. The Astaires were delighted and excited as they directed their cab driver to Bruton Street, but even they were not really aware how extraordinary the invitation was: the King's first grandchild being shown off at a special preview to these American dancers long before the British public had even seen a photograph!

The King himself had heard about the friendship between his sons and this American couple, and decided to discover what attraction they held. He and Queen Mary, a rather forbidding couple and certainly not regular theatregoers, came to the Empire in Leicester Square in August. They were impressed by what they saw, and according to the Prince of Wales, the King pronounced: 'They seem a very decent sort of American'.

Between shopping sprees and social rounds, Fred played golf and went to the racetracks, with the guidance of an ever-widening circle of contacts. Jack Leach introduced him to people like the journalist and crime writer Edgar Wallace. 'Edgar thought he knew everything about racing,' said Leach, 'but in fact no one knew less.' Jack 'explained' to Fred that every owner's horses are the best in the world; it's the draw, the jockey, or something else that is to blame when they don't win, never that the horse is just not good enough. Another jockey, Brownie Carslake, illustrated the point with a story about Edgar Wallace: Brownie realised that unless he came up with a plausible reason for his mount being out of the frame, he would never be booked by Wallace to ride for him again. 'What happened?' growled Wallace, when Carslake had predictably limped in last. 'Well,' said Carslake, well prepared, 'he's green and very backward.' 'Green? What do you mean green?', said Wallace. 'He's nine years old.'

Astaire, in his enthusiasm for jockeys and their life, decided that he would have a go himself, and went up to Newmarket Heath to ride out with the horses in the early dawn. 'I don't think that horses approve of me,' Astaire said, for no matter how docile a hack Leach found for him, the second he got up it would start to buck and play around. But on the track he felt truly at home and, in a country where it was legal, he was a tremendous better. Backstage at Leicester Square, with his Cockney dresser George Griffin, he worked out vastly complicated schemes of doubles, trembles, Yankees, any-to-come roll-ups; they always had a new scheme to beat the bookies. 'We called him Cash Astaire, the Big Punter,' said Leach. 'To distinguish him from Ready Money Riley, a big gambler who always betted in readies. If Fred had £10 on the nod with a bookie, he also had £2 in cash, so that if he won he could collect some money straight away. Fred did have some wins, but more by luck than judgement.' One of his earliest victories came in the Guineas, when Leach was to ride Adam's Apple. He told Fred that he thought his rival Call Boy was a sure thing, so Fred contrarily put £5 on Adam's Apple at 20 to 1, and it won by a short head. 'Who the hell would listen to you?' he afterwards told Leach. On another occasion the trainer Harvey Leader told Fred that he fancied his chances with a two-year-old called Dark Warrior, to be ridden by Jack Leach at Manchester. However, when the horse arrived at the track the course was water-logged and it was only at the insistence of the owner that the by-now hopeless Dark Warrior ran at all. 'He wasn't much of a swimmer,' said Leach. 'We told everyone to save their money and the price drifted right out.' But to the jockey's surprise, and Astaire's delight, with a 'pony', £25 each way, Dark Warrior romped home.

So devoted was Fred to the turf that he decided to become an owner himself, a move that would at least get him into the paddock to see the racing from the owners' stands, without having to peer over heads in the grandstands. So Jack Leach helped him to buy some horses and then managed them for him. (And in his turn Leach called his daughter – Fred's goddaughter – Gillian Adèle, after the sister of 'the best mover I have ever seen'.) Fred registered colours of buff blouse and cap and a blue sash with the Jockey Club and Alfred Butt gave him a present he always treasured, a model of a china racehorse with a jockey wearing the Astaire silks.

For all the fun the Astaires were having, Fred and Adèle did notice a change in London. The nine-day General Strike which started the week after they opened did not affect their box office – Londoners seem to crave pleasure during any adversity and continued to go to the theatre and the West End regardless of current events – but there was a subtle alteration in attitudes when it was settled. The downturn in the economy that the strike presaged brought its own feelings of change and gloom. Traditional musical vaudeville was in trouble, with music halls all over Britain making way for the more extravagant and escapist world of the cinema. The movies were no longer simple shorts like *Fanchon the Cricket*, but complicated, sophisticated, and hugely expensive undertakings: MGM had just spent over $4.5 million making the biblical epic *Ben Hur* and that, judging by the queues outside cinemas, was what the audiences wanted. The Astaires, always aware of new trends, could see the silver screen taking over their whole world; nowhere was this more obvious than at their own theatre which, after 326 performances of *Lady, Be Good!*, closed down so that the site could be redeveloped as a movie-house.

That was a closing night to remember. Even the Prince of Wales couldn't get seats, until Alfred Butt prevailed on some less exalted folk to give up their box. After many cheers and encores, the curtain fell for the final time. The Prince had organised a post-performance party at York House, St James's Palace. It was some party! The band played long into the night and the Prince and Adèle led the dancing. She announced that Jock Whitney was an expert dancer who just might be persuaded to demonstrate his version of the latest craze, the Black Bottom. At the Prince's request Jock, though he claimed that he was barely familiar with the dance, dove in with huge enthusiasm. Adèle said: 'He sure had the bottom to do it, too, I'll tell you that.' But when Fred, who claimed Jock was the slowest Charleston dancer he had ever witnessed – George Raft was the fastest – called out: 'Look out, Jock, the floor is beginning to sag!' Jock's large figure lost its balance, and to great applause he ended flat on the floor.

Adèle suggested that the Prince show his paces too, but he declined – 'I don't think I'm ready to show off my tap dancing yet,' he said. There's always been an element of mystery concerning the Prince's dancing. In Court circles it has been said for many years that Fred Astaire taught the Prince of Wales to tap dance, and certainly the Prince had on one occasion sent Astaire some shoes to have taps affixed. Astaire recalled: 'I did it for him, but I don't know whether he ever tried them.' This may be an instance of modesty on Astaire's part, or

[69]

perhaps he knew the full story and was simply not telling, for the Prince of Wales, once he had his tap shoes, did indeed try them out – not at Buckingham Palace, as the rumour went, but at York House, where Adèle called on several occasions as Tap-Instructor by Appointment. The Prince had sent the shoes to Fred because he could anticipate the public's reaction if Adèle were to render such a service. Tap dancing became quietly popular in the royal household and has remained so to this day.

Tap was not the only fashion note traded with the royal family, for the Duke of York (later King George VI) adopted Astaire's plan of having a pair of braces for each pair of trousers, rather than move one set from pair to pair. There was one question of style that Fred was eager to discuss with the Prince of Wales, but it took him quite a while to summon up the courage to ask the prince the secret of the way he tied his neck-ties to get that large knot. At the time the Wales Knot, later known as the Windsor Knot, the double wraparound system that enlarges the top of the knot, was the most fashionable thing in London; every young blade wanted to emulate the dandyish Prince of Wales, but none quite caught that detail. The Prince laughed aloud, and told Fred: 'Of course, my dear Astaire, I'll explain how it's done. But there's no big secret; I just have my ties cut wider than normal and the extra material creates a bigger knot.' It's no great feat to guess that Fred's first call the next day was in Jermyn Street, to order some extra-wide ties!

When it was time to go home once more, Fred and Adèle parted sadly from their friends and, with the beautifully repaired Rolls carefully stowed in the hold, set sail for the New World. George Gershwin had only been in London for the start of the run. Back in New York, he had been working away on another show especially for the Astaires. This time, however, Alex Aarons and Vinton Freedley planned to introduce a proper story line; they hired the newspaper columnist and ex-Harvard wit Robert Benchley to write the show with Fred Thompson, co-author of *Lady, Be Good!*. But Benchley, who was also the drama editor of *Life* magazine, found the going rough. *Smarty*, in which Fred was cast as Adèle's guardian, was not so smarty and even definitely shakey in Philadelphia, and another writer, Paul Gerard Smith, was called in to doctor the script. One of Astaire's favourite tunes, 'The Man I Love', written for Adèle, was dropped after the first week and the livelier but nonsensical 'The Babbitt and The Bromide' was added. But, as Ira Gershwin later explained, 'The Man I Love' did survive to become a classic: 'It was in a couple of shows that didn't happen. Then Lady Mountbatten, who was a great admirer of my brother, heard it and took a copy of the sheet music back to London with her, where I guess it was played at parties and clubs.' For *Smarty*, business was bad, and it only got worse when the show was renamed *Funny Face* and moved to Wilmington for three days. 'We played to two hundred pregnant housewives,' said Adèle. Fred recalled in *Steps in Time* how he sounded off to his faithful dresser Walter: 'I hate flops – and this is one. We might as well face it: this damn turkey hasn't got a prayer. I'm sick of this racket anyway.' At least his complaints had the effect of cheering Adèle up. 'Let him moan,' she said, 'it's the first chance he's had in years. He loves it.'

Fred's despondency was overdone. While everyone was worrying about learning new lines and new songs, the show had gradually been evolving into a viable entity, and when it finally arrived at the Alvin Theatre (recently rebuilt and now owned by and named after the producers Alex Aarons and Vinton Freedley) on 22 November 1927, the Astaires found themselves with a glittering and happy audience and a show that was an instant hit. In retrospect one wonders how anyone could have been nervous about a production which was liberally filled with songs that have lived on so well. ''S Wonderful, 'S Marvellous,' sang Adèle; Fred sang and danced 'High Hat' with a male chorus and crooned 'My One and Only' to Gertrude MacDonald. Just to ensure success, Fred and Adèle did their 'Oompah Trot' at the end of 'The Babbitt and The Bromide', a patter song made up of the 'conversations' between the eponymous hero of Sinclair Lewis's novel and Bromide, named for the sedative the British army was said to add to its tea to put the men off sex. Fred said that he never did understand it, he knew the Babbitt side but was puzzled by the bromide: while Vinton Freedly understood the bromide part but was puzzled by the Babbitt.

The pre-opening tension had got to the cast. Even the usually unflappable Adèle was so worried before the première and so relieved afterwards that on the second night of *Funny Face*, she arrived at the theatre with one too many martinis inside her. She and Fred managed their first routine, Astaire flashing smiles to cover her mistakes and just rescuing her from falling into the pit. As they danced off, Fred remembered many years later how he patted her hard on both cheeks, saying: 'Come on, Delly, take a bow.' She managed a bow and a smile but as they came off she started to cry. 'You hit me, you hit me,' she sobbed. Fred managed to calm her and steer her to her dressing room.

[71]

She had fifteen minutes before her next entrance, and her maid was quickly instructed to sober her up. When Fred next saw her, she was icily dignified, announcing coldly: 'You hit me.' 'I know,' he replied, 'but you were impossible – something had to be done. Let's forget it. I'll give you twenty bucks tomorrow.' When the performance was finally over, Fred made his apologies to Adèle, who by now was quite calm. She made no answer, but continued to take off her make-up in the mirror. There was only one thing she had to say: 'Where's my twenty bucks?' Next day a small diamond brooch from Cartier arrived for the very sober and reformed young lady, but it was a few days before their relationship returned to normal.

7
Adèle

In the script of *Stop Flirting* there's a moment when Adèle says to the 'older' Freddie, a mite petulantly, that she is now a grown-up – eighteen! – and Fred snorts in disbelief. And well he might, for Adèle was actually twenty-seven years old that year. During the run of *Lady, Be Good!*, on 18 September 1926, she celebrated her thirtieth birthday; or, more accurately, she celebrated *a* birthday, for she had long since decided that she was indeed the ageless sprite that the critics and fans perceived – the very Peter Pan that Barrie had invented. Nonetheless, this milestone made her suddenly more aware of the passage of time. She and Fred had always had a rather vague plan for the future: they would become famous stars, makes lots of money, and then retire to an idyllic rural life. More specifically Adèle, who never relished the hard work that went into performing, would get married and raise children, and Fred would go on to a brilliant solo career. They had indeed become famous and they were making money; although their lifestyle kept pace with their earnings, Fred made sure that something was put by for the bad times he expected around every corner. There was no thought of slowing down: they were having too much fun to give up. Adèle, at five foot three and 106 pounds, with midnight hair, large mouth, and expressive brown eyes, was the ideal foil for her five foot seven, 128 pound, brown-haired, brown-eyed, lantern-jawed brother. He was elfin and pixieish, she was spritely and pretty. Their dancing and performing partnership was flawless, and they were also a marvellous twosome offstage, their very different natures making them the best of friends. As youngsters, Fred had always been catching up, while Adèle had relied on flair and intuition to get by. Fred slept little and was up before dawn working out improvements to their routines; Adèle would sleep blissfully for ten hours lulled by the knowledge that if a problem existed, Fred would be dealing with it. He always suffered from awkwardness and shyness when he didn't have a script; she was

[73]

incurably cheerful and forward. He was always calmly polite; her language would have shocked a sailor. Fred would say, apologetically: 'Adèle is extremely frank. She finds it hard to keep back anything she has to say and out it comes.' Yet she was uncompromising and if she heard his apologies, she would retort: 'Why the fuck shouldn't I say what I feel?'

The rows they had were short-lived, and jokes were long-running. After they did *Funny Face*, Adèle became Funny Face to him, and he became Sap, the fool, to her. Fred was for ever pressing her to come to the theatre earlier, to go through their paces 'just one more time', but she was invariably reluctant; then, when he was at his most exasperated, she would give a performance of such brilliance that he would be lost for words. But if he were late for her, then there would be hell to pay. Fred recalled one occasion when he kept her waiting a couple of minutes: 'And she had sewn up my trouser legs.' And during the *Funny Face* run, when Fred had been 'getting her goat', he decided to get her a real one – a Tibetan mountain goat borrowed on a $50 deposit from Central Park Zoo, and delivered to the stage door on a long silk ribbon 'from a devoted admirer'.

Away from the theatre, they went their own ways, Fred to the racetrack or pool-hall, Adèle with her friends to shop or play – she loved tennis, golf and riding, though she never did learn to swim – and also to cope with her continuous stream of admirers. From the age of thirteen she had been courted assiduously by a variety of desirable and less desirable men, from the classy and wealthy to the theatrical sharks. Her sexual education had begun early, in the fumbled embraces of stagehands and young performers. Despite Ann's protective chaperonage, she fell madly in love at the age of twenty-one with the critic and writer George Jean Nathan, who with H. L. Mencken founded *Smart Set* and *American Mercury* magazines. 'He was greasy looking, fat, and a real smart-ass,' said one of Adèle's closest friends. Nathan at one stage said that he wanted to marry her, and it was to him, she told Cecil Beaton many years later, that she lost her virginity: 'Mother was furious.' Indeed Ann did her best to end the affair, and Fred certainly was no fan of Nathan, although Adèle herself blamed her own friends for trying to ruin it. Liz Altemus said that Adèle claimed that Liz had deliberately shut a taxi door on Nathan's hand because she did not like him – indeed she did not like him one bit, but she denied that the incident was premeditated.

By the time of *Funny Face*, Adèle had acquired another persistent suitor: William Gaunt, an Englishman working in New York for his family's Yorkshire wool business. He wined and dined Adèle assiduously and on 10 February, five months after her thirtieth birthday, he announced that they were engaged. The relationship was stormy, and it was not long before Adèle told her brother that she was afraid of Gaunt and wanted to break off her engagement. Gaunt blithely continued to claim her as his fiancèe, telling a New York newsman: 'Yes, its true, we got engaged recently. I've known Adèle for a long, long time now – perhaps a year. It doesn't take long to get married.'

Next, James T. Walker, the publicity-hungry Mayor of New York got in on the act and announced that he was Adèle's new boyfriend, which she hastily denied: 'We've just danced together a few times, that's all,' she said. And there were others, among them Billy Leeds, an American millionaire whose mother had married Prince Christopher of Greece. Billy, who was five years younger than Adèle, had recently distinguished himself by sailing the Atlantic in a small boat. Despite his marriage to Princess Xenia of Russia, he was regularly seen escorting Adèle to society functions.

Adèle was ready to quit the social rat-race; all she needed was the excuse, or man, to do it. The problem was to find someone she wanted to marry. She was sufficiently wealthy, independent and bright to realise that many of the men who might make her extravagant offers would not suit her at all. Her preference was for a self-confident, rich man like Jock Whitney or Billy Leeds – an Anglophile American or, better still, with her taste for things English, an Englishman. Englishmen were polite and well-mannered, unlike most Americans, of whom she said: 'They talk loud and they tell you where they've been and who they know. Who cares? That's Americans. You never hear an Englishman doing that.'

One Englishman that Adèle took a particular shine to was the effete photographer Cecil Beaton, who had taken some impressive portraits of the Astaires, and who was twenty-five years old when Adèle almost helped him to lose his virginity in New York. In fact (as his 1947 diary reveals) it was on a Wednesday that he first slept with Marjorie Oelricht, who volunteered her services when Beaton told her that he had never been to bed with a woman. The same week – on Friday – Adèle continued his education. This was, Beaton told his diary, a more serious affair. He had always adored Adèle and she was convinced that any man could be swung from homosexuality to heterosexuality – like another, later, lover of Beaton, Doris Castlerosse, she thought there was no such thing as an impotent man, only an incompetent woman. Despite her endeavours, and their occasional forays, Beaton decided that on the whole he was more attracted to men. Adèle later told her friend Lady Anne Tree, 'He was very sweet and very shy. He came out of the bathroom with a little towel around his waist.'

There was one new interest to take her mind off her private life. Walter Wanger, a former army Intelligence officer who had become a senior producer at Paramount Pictures in New York, came to see *Funny Face* and afterwards asked the Astaires to make a screen test, for he thought the show could make a good movie. Unhappily, no record remains of that footage of Fred and Adèle, but Paramount executives had roughly the same opinion of the duo as did those early Broadway scouts: Adèle was praised as 'lively', but Fred's evaluation read: 'Can't act. Can't sing. Balding. Can dance a little.' Hardling encouraging! But despite the reports, Wanger wanted to go ahead with the project. However, the money men decreed that one of the two Broadway acts Wanger wanted to launch on film would have to be held over. They already knew that comedy worked well on the screen, but there was nothing to suggest that dancing would be much of a draw. So Fred and Adèle lost out to Wanger's other Broadway stars, the Marx Brothers, who went on to make their first movie, *The Cocoanuts*, with him.

The Astaires went back to partying with Liz and Jim Altemus, Jock Whitney, and a host of friends: weekending on Long Island; seeing their royal British friends when they were in town; and entertaining the grandest in the land. They both believed that this was the only life for them. Fred, paraphrasing Scott Fitzgerald, observed: 'The rich are different. They do not just have more money. They have more everything.' He was impressed by Jock Whitney's way of ordering his cigars by the dozens of boxes. One day, when they were playing golf together, Jock drove off the first tee into the wood. 'Fucks,' he said, and it struck Fred as significant that his friend even used expletives in the plural.

Jock's valet, Edgar, who had been with him at Oxford, was taking flying lessons, although Jock was so unnerved by his aerial chauffeuring that he went to huge lengths to avoid going up with him. Astaire's man – when he arrived back in New York with the Rolls he decided he really needed a driver – also wanted to learn this useful skill; so Fred advanced him the money for lessons, and either drove the car himself or took cabs when necessary.

During the break after the nine-month Broadway run of *Funny Face*,

Adèle's friendship with Billy Leeds led to an unfortunate incident out at Oyster Bay, Long Island. He was showing her his powerful new speedboat, Fantail, when the boat caught fire from a defective engine. He and Adèle just managed to scramble ashore and push the boat off before it exploded, leaving her with a badly charred shoulder, face, and hands and Billy, nearer the blast, only slightly better off. Happily the damage to both of them was fairly superficial. After a brief stay in Manhattan Hospital, Adèle was well enough to sail to London for the by-now-routine West End transfer of the show, although the opening was postponed for a few weeks to allow her to recuperate fully.

George Gershwin travelled with the Astaires as their resident rehearsal pianist, and the British comic actors Leslie Henson and Sydney Howard were added to the cast of *Funny Face* at the Prince's Theatre (now the Shaftesbury). The London run was memorable on several counts: during the second week, a night watchman blew up the theatre – unintentionally, but he *had* been searching for a gas leak with a lighted match. The results were predictable: the theatre and the surrounding streets exploded as though hit by a bomb. Performances went on at the Winter Garden, while an assault course of planks and walkways was constructed over the holes of the Prince's so that determined patrons could reach the show when it moved back to its proper home. The difficulties had not the slightest adverse effect on the show, although Leslie Henson said: 'Coming to see it now is tougher than riding the Grand National.'

The mood in London was light and happy. There was talk of financial crisis, but then there always is, and it didn't seem to dampen people's spirits. All the Astaires' old friends could be found at The Silver Slipper, the new Regent Street club owned by Kate Meyrick, or at her old club at 43 Gerrard Street, or at the Savoy Grill. Noël Coward had now made his first screen appearance and had seen *Easy Virtue*, *The Vortex* and *The Queen was in the Parlour* filmed. He told them that he couldn't recommend the movie-making life highly enough: 'You don't have to learn your lines at all,' he enthused.

It was a happy year they spent in London; the only shadows were cast by the King's illness (he was at one time thought to be on his deathbed, but revived dramatically when the Prince of Wales hurried back from Africa to attend him) and the news from America that financial disaster really had struck. On 24 October the stock market shuddered, and five days later, on Black Thursday, it finally crashed; millions of dollars were wiped away. Fred heard the news with horror.

[77]

He had always been a cautious investor, but even the most conservative investments were worth little or nothing now. But as the days and weeks passed, and he saw how badly Britain had been affected, he couldn't help noticing how the very rich stayed that way; it was only those lower down the ladder who were really hurt, for the very rich could trim their sails but still maintain a Sybaritic lifestyle.

Show business was affected in two ways by the Crash: the bad news was that some of the high-flying entrepreneurs were caught by the chill draught blowing through town – people like William Fox, founder of Fox studios, who was worth $3 million in September (when he bought New York's Roxy Theatre for a million dollars) and broke in November; but the good news was that people craved escapist entertainment.

Funny Face played well until 22 January 1930. As always, there was a huge demand for closing-night tickets: it was an essential part of smart life to be there. After the performance, Adèle's dressing-room suite was crowded with fans offering congratulations, among them Prince Aly Khan, the handsome eighteen-year-old playboy son of the Aga Khan (the fabulously wealthy spiritual head of 70 million Muslims) with a friend of his, Lord Charles Cavendish, the twenty-three-year-old younger son of the Duke of Devonshire. Adèle was taken by the tall, good-looking Englishman, who joined the group that went out to dinner afterwards. That weekend, while Fred stayed in London, Adèle set off for Paris for a few days at the invitation of Prince Aly Khan, who was taking a break from his legal studies in London. She told Fred on her return that the party had included young Charlie Cavendish. 'He's awfully nice', she said, adding that she had accepted an invitation from him to spend a weekend at The House, his parents' home.

Adèle was not quite prepared for what she found. When she arrived at Charlie's home, 160 miles north of London in the picturesque Peak District hills, she was utterly taken aback by the vast size and fantastic array of neo-classical buildings that is Chatsworth. Adèle was not often known to be lost for words, but this time, she recalled, she was notably quiet. 'Welcome to The House,' said Charlie, for Chatsworth, the stately home of the dukes of Devonshire since the 17th century, is not a castle, not a palace; it is a fabulous amalgam that has always been known simply as The House. There was, as Adèle discovered, a 19th-century theatre in the North wing, 17th-century gold-leafed window frames and finely carved façades, walls hung with paintings by Rubens, Gainsborough, Reynolds, and Rembrandt, and sculptures dating back

[78]

to the 5th century – it was, and is, a building of such over-powering splendour that even the wealthiest American banker could not have conceived it. Adèle, the little girl from Omaha, found it all simply wonderful, a fairytale in real life. Her visit was brief and beautiful, and she was fascinated by everything she saw: she had stayed with aristocrats before, but never in quite such magnificence. She was intrigued by the whole family, including the reclusive Duke Victor who, since his stroke a few years before, simply growled at visitors; in turn, Charlie's brother, sister, and friends were fascinated by Adèle. Charlie was shortly off to New York to work in J. P. Morgan's bank, and Adèle promised to show him around.

When she got back to London, Adèle told her mother, 'You know, I think I could live in a house like that all the time.' And elsewhere Lord Charles Cavendish was singing her praises to his friends: 'She is the most marvellous girl.'

His family was delighted to see Charlie so happy, for he had long been something of a problem. He drank too much, gambled too much, and seemed to have no sense of application, direction, or purpose. Sixth of the seven children of the ninth Duke of Devonshire and younger of the two sons, Charlie was a victim of the British system of primo-geniture, whereby the eldest son inherits the title, the lands, and the money. His relatives attributed his erratic behaviour and eccentricities to an accident that befell him as an undergraduate at Trinity College, Cambridge. He had fallen on his head while riding in a point-to-point steeplechase, had refused to go to bed, and shortly thereafter took a similar spill. As one of the family remembered, although he did recover, he was never known to refuse a drink for the remainder of his life.

Charlie's elder brother, Edward, then thirty-six, was the heir to the dukedom and carried the courtesy title of the Marquess of Hartington, which meant that he would be addressed as Lord Hartington but could not sit in the House of Lords until he inherited his father's title. Charlie himself was known as Lord Charles, as the system decrees that the sons and daughters of dukes and earls are known by the courtesy title Lord or Lady with their first name. The advantage of primogeniture was, and is, that the great estates, houses, and art collections are kept intact; the disadvantage was that younger sons were often not encouraged to consider themselves worthwhile for anything much. There was often some awkwardness about them: for example, Prince Bertie, the Duke of York, later King George VI, was a second son who stuttered quite badly. Quite often, second sons would go off the rails. Charlie's father,

Duke Victor, had been Governor General of Canada, and Charlie had a wretched and lonely youth. The one thing he had acquired from his family was his father's love of horses. Duke Victor had always encouraged bravery, paying all his children five shillings if, after they fell off a horse, they immediately remounted.

The family title, Devonshire, is a strange one for a clan whose fortune lay in Derbyshire and who have never had any property in or connection with the county of Devon, which lies some 250 miles to the southwest. The present Duke, eleventh of the line, says he suspects that when his ancestor Lord Cavendish was offered an earldom in 1618 in exchange for a contribution of £19,000 to the coffers of Queen Elizabeth I – a later contribution secured the dukedom – he had already prepared a noble design with the letter D for Derbyshire, but was thwarted when he discovered that the name had already been taken by the Stanleys, whose forebear had been created Earl of Derby in 1485 after placing Richard III's crown on the head of the victorious Henry VII at Bosworth Field.

Duke Victor had managed to fix Charlie up with a job at J. P. Morgan's bank in the hope that he might at last acquire a career and a purpose. The Duke had little thought for the danger of plunging Charlie into Prohibition New York; his only concern was that, once there, his son should learn a useful trade. For Charles Cavendish it was a faint hope. Parties, night clubs, and a plentiful supply of bootleg liquor enlivened his nights, and his days at Morgan's, where he would sometimes fall asleep at his desk, did not concern him too much, to the exasperation of his employers. Whenever he could think of a reason, he would not show up at all, preferring to play golf with Fred or accompany the Astaires to the racetrack.

For those who still had money, the Depression years were a time of high living and elegance. Charlie, thanks to his allowance from his father, and the Astaires, Broadway stars, had plenty. Charlie became Adèle's most frequent companion and escort: she showed him the town, introduced him to Long Island society, and enjoyed the cachet of having a real live English lord on her arm. She also, rather to her surprise, found herself growing increasingly fond of him – even when he drank too much. He never became aggressive, just friendly and happy, but he did need some looking after. Adèle became his self-appointed guardian, rescuing him from dinners and nightclubs all around town. A typical and oft-repeated entry in his diary of the time read: 'Got frightfully tight.'

[80]

The Astaires had a new rôle to play in the autumn of 1930 when, on Thursday 25 September, at the church of St James the Less, Falls-of-the-Schuylkill, Pennyslvania, two of their closest friends, Jock Whitney and Liz Altemus, were married. Adèle shared the bridesmaid's duties with Jock's sister Joan Whitney Payson; Fred, dashing in top hat and morning suit, was an usher for the groom, who had Bob Benchley as his best man. Jock had courted Liz, who had been the only unmarried American dancing partner of the Prince of Wales (except for Adèle, of course), across Europe and America – he said that she was the only girl he knew who played polo better than a man yet could still look ravishingly beautiful by night-time. She was weighed down like a princess as a bride, with a $225,000 necklace from Jock's mother, a cheque for a million dollars, and the deed to a 2,000-acre estate in Upperville, Virginia and a house in Manhattan from Jock, not to mention the manuscript of Abraham Lincoln's last address and of Walt Whitman's 'O Captain! My Captain!'

The splendour of the wedding contrasted starkly with life in other quarters of the United States now in the grip of the Depression. In that scene, too, the Astaires played their parts, quietly and without fuss. Both Adèle and Fred could be found regularly at the Little Church Around the Corner on 49th Street, where Rev. Randolph Ray, whose services had been regularly attended and collection plate unostentatiously swelled by Fred over the years, had set up his own soup kitchen to help the needy.

But while many went hungry, the career of the Astaires received another boost when they were offered an amazing $5,000 a week by the great showman Florenz Ziegfeld. (There exists some newsreel footage of this show on which Ziegfeld calls for dancers; when the Astaires trot on with Marilyn Miller, he says: 'I mean my other dancers, not my $10,000 a week dancers' – but then Ziegfeld always was prone to hyperbole.) There was no falling out with Aarons and Freedley, but in the world of Broadway musical comedy the name of Ziegfeld still had a special magic. Even though he had lost more than a million dollars in the Crash, he had come bouncing back, with the support of earlier backers, to co-produce with Sam Goldwyn the movie *Whoopee* with choreographer Busby Berkeley and director Thornton Freeland, and then to produce *Tom, Dick and Harry* with his great beauty, Marilyn Miller and the Astaires. Aarons and Freedley just could not match Ziegfeld's offer. They were less than pleased to have their stars pinched from under their noses, but a moderately amicable parting took place, or at least the Astaires felt it was amicable.

Fred later said he had taken on *Tom, Dick and Harry* (later renamed *Smiles*) for 5,000 very good reasons, but he was also attracted by the fact that the show was very loosely based on an idea of Noël Coward's about a couple of society swells (the Astaires) and a Salvation Army girl (Marilyn Miller). The music was by Vincent Youmans and the choreographer was their old teacher Ned Wayburn, author of their 'Baseball Act' – although the Astaires would, as usual, be doing their own choreography. The cast included plenty of bright young talent, including the British-born comic Bob Hope.

Smiles was the name of the show, but there were few smiles backstage after the out-of-town previews, which were an utter shambles. The stage staff used every means possible to keep songwriter Youmans from his endless supply of whisky bottles; eventually Ziegfeld had to get an injunction to prevent Youmans from withdrawing his music, which he tried to do on a number of occasions. The show's director and author, William McGuire, was far keener on chasing chorus girls than delivering rewritten chunks of script on time. Most of the $60,000 underwriting had been provided by New York mobsters who demanded script changes or favours for their special chorines. It was quite apposite that a song entitled 'You're Driving Me Crazy', by the Astaires' vaudeville friends, Walter Donaldson and Eddie Foy, was inserted into the show for Adèle. The situation was epitomized for Astaire by an incident in Boston, when he and Marilyn Miller went out for a drive. Looking down into the Charles River, they were grabbed by a couple of policemen. 'You're not going to do it, buddy,' said the two cops, assuming that suicide must have been their purpose. Astaire said that even for him things were not quite that bad, but to get even for the undignified arrest, he invited the patrolmen to come and see *Smiles*. 'That'll serve 'em right,' he told Adèle.

Ziegfeld did everything in his power to promote the show. On 18 November, several thousand people assembled outside the theatre to see the first-night celebrities crowd in. But the reviews were just as Astaire had predicted: poor to dreadful. Benchley, firm supporter, fan, colleague, and friend though he was, could only bring himself to write in *The New Yorker*: 'Of course no show with Fred and Adèle can be a complete bust.' The one redeeming feature of the show was 'Young Man of Manhattan', set in a Bowery invaded by Fred and a male chorus line in formal clothes. About that number Benchley said: 'There are moments when the back of your neck begins to tingle and you realise that you are in the presence of something pretty darned swell.'

[82]

The 'Young Man of Manhattan' routine had been dreamed up by Fred on one of his 4 a.m. wakings at the Park Avenue apartment. He conjured up a long line of chorus in top hats and tails, and himself in front of them using his cane like a gun, shooting them one at a time, then mowing down any survivors with machine-gun taps. His early-morning improvisation with an umbrella for a cane woke Adèle, who sleepily ambled out of her room to say: 'Hey, Minnie, what the hell are you doing?' 'I just got an idea for the Manhattan number,' he told her. Adèle was unimpressed. 'Well, hang on to it, baby – you're going to need it in this turkey,' she said.

He had indeed hung on to it. The routine began with the seventeen-year-old mouth organist Larry Adler, dressed like a Bowery bum, playing his harmonica, and ended with Astaire, in top hat and tails, knocking off the chorus line and finally shooting Adler. 'It was a very, very good number and the way he staged it was wonderful,' Adler recalled. 'It was an education to work with him.' That education covered many fields. Fred persuaded Larry to participate in the Sunday charity shows, a virtually compulsory part of a Broadway performer's life – sometimes they did as many as five a day. Sponsored by newspapers or other businesses, these shows were an integral part of promoting a show, rather as television chat shows are today. Adler assumed that they would just do a brief version of their *Smiles* duet; not a bit of it. They spent three solid weeks rehearsing a two-minute version of Gershwin's 'I Got Rhythm' – something they were performing for free.

But Adler, young as he was, also felt Fred's sting. The critic Alexander Woolcott, a great fan of Adèle, asked her to appear on his popular radio programme, *The Town Crier*. Adèle asked Adler, rather than her brother, to play the piano for her number, 'If You Would Always Be Good To Me', thinking Fred would not be happy to be merely her accompanist. 'Larry, pick it up half a tone,' she said during a rehearsal, but Adler could not comply. He was self-taught, and only knew how to play in two keys, D or F. Adèle, used to musicians who could busk in any key, couldn't believe there was a problem: 'Don't be silly, Larry,' she said. But unhappily, it stayed in D. After the broadcast, Adèle broke into tears: she felt that she hadn't given her best and had let Fred down. When Adler got back to the theatre, Astaire's black valet Walter pointedly announced: 'Don't mess around with Mr Fred today, he'll kill you.' The next day an envelope was slipped under Adler's dressing-room door: inside, in letters cut from *New York Herald Tribune* headlines, was the message: 'Larry Adler is a cunt'.

[83]

Larry Adler wasn't the only one Astaire jumped on during the sensitive weeks after the opening of *Smiles*: when Adèle sang on the Rudy Vallee show, Fred tracked down one critic and told him: 'If you ever take a rap at us, direct it at me instead of Adèle, will you?'

The cast did what they could to rescue *Smiles*, but it was a lost cause. There were some good moments however, and the Manhattan number was a sure-fire show-stopper. 'Anyone got any chalk?' Fred would call, going back to his dressing room, where he would religiously put a score above the mirror for each show stopped. To make things worse, Marilyn Miller was suffering badly from sinus trouble – some said cocaine was her problem – and would have to leave the production and have an operation, and to top that, police and news reporters swarmed all over the theatre when the gangster Legs Diamond was found shot dead in the bed of another of the show's stars, Virginia Bruce.

Smiles closed after 63 performances, posting a loss of $30,000. At the end, the Astaires claimed that Ziegfeld still owed them $10,000; eventually the case went to arbitration and they were happy to accept an award of $5,000. All in all, *Smiles* was *not* a happy experience.

Fred was left in a state of exhaustion – always so much worse after a failure – and serious questions about the future. Was this the end? Had they used up all their good will with the audiences, and, what would be worse, with the producers? There were few positive aspects to that bitter January of 1931: depression bit deep outside and there was a different depression inside the Astaire household.

While Fred lay low, Adèle worked off her energy and forgot the disappointment of *Smiles* by socialising and having fun, invariably with Charlie Cavendish. On one of those late nights at '21', Adèle – after only one Martini, she swore – turned to him and said: 'You know, Charlie, we get on so well, I think we really ought to get married.' Next morning, the phone rang at the Astaire's Park Avenue apartment. It was Charlie. 'You proposed to me last night,' he said. 'If you don't accept me, I'll sue for breach of promise.' She had, it seemed, become engaged again. She was thirty-three years old; Charlie Cavendish was twenty-four.

It was not totally unexpected, but about the same time Pierpont Morgan became utterly exasperated with Lord Useless, as he was known around the bank. You could take your pick and accept either Charlie's story, that he went to the racetrack one day and never returned to the office, or Morgan's, that he had to ask him to leave.

Fred had come to terms with the ideal of Adèle's eventual retirement

[84]

from the stage and they had quite often talked about it, but now that it was a reality there were adjustments to be made. 'My brother of course will continue his theatrical career,' Adèle reassured well-wishers, but she had as little idea as Fred how the separation would affect the two halves of the Astaire entity. But first, as a cure for *Smiles*, the whole family took off for Europe. Charlie sailed by chance on the same ship as his erstwhile boss, Pierpont Morgan, and being a merry soul acquired his revenge by making ghostly noises outside the banker's cabin. The Astaires travelled with a party of friends that included Jimmy Altemus and Bob Benchley. Adèle and her mother went to Chatsworth, while Fred, Altemus, and Benchley toured the night clubs of Paris and Germany. On their return Jimmy Altemus said it was one of those trips where the revellers themselves knew less about what happened to them than anybody else, especially about the night they found themselves drinking and dancing with some beautiful girls who, they suddenly realised, were not girls at all, but men in drag.

In Britain, reactions to the news of the Cavendish–Astaire engagement were mixed. Charlie himself was not at all sure that it was for real. 'Just think of it happening to me,' he said, 'a thing like that after a night like that.' Adèle was blissfully content with her new situation, and told a New York newspaper reporter: 'Women gain wisdom more quickly than men. Their wisdom enables them to fend off old age with greater ease. To retain their independence and individuality they should never tie themselves to husbands older than themselves. That's an old fashioned custom and should be discarded.' Before she left New York, Adèle had said optimistically that the Duchess had confirmed the family's good wishes, but that was not quite the case. The Duchess, daughter of the Marquess of Landsdowne, was a termagant – 'An unpleasant woman, accustomed to authority' is how her brother-in-law the Duke of St Albans described her to the present Duchess when jokingly warning her against following in the footsteps of 'Granny Duchess' – and she had written a note of chilling formality, suggesting that Miss Astaire call on her. What the grande dame of Chatsworth planned to do to the poor girl is anyone's guess, but in Adèle the Duchess had a formidable opponent. It was nothing new for the British aristocracy to marry Americans: they had been doing it for years, injecting new blood, and, often more importantly, new money into the British system. Consuelo Vanderbilt had been married to the Duke of Marlborough for twenty-five years before they divorced in 1920 and he wed the Bostonian Gladys Deacon. Lord Furness, a shipping magnate, had married the youthful American heiress Thelma Hays Morgan Converse, daughter of Harry Hays Morgan, US Consular General in Buenos Aires, when she was just twenty-one. In more recent times, the Earl of Dudley had married the musical-comedy actress Gertie Millar in 1927. And in other less respectable fields, two daughters of the night club owner and occasional jailbird Kate Meyrick had also married into the peerage: Dorothy to Lord de Clifford in 1926 and, two years later, May to the Earl of Kinnoull. Nevertheless, in certain circles there was obvious disapproval of the match and at Court there was some consternation. The Duchess of Devonshire, Mistress of the Robes and a close friend of Queen Mary, confided to her: 'It's quite dreadful, my son wants to marry an American actress.' 'My dear,' replied Queen Mary, 'I quite understand – my niece has just married a man called Smith.' There was an element of perverse enjoyment for others in her woe, which was itself a source of amusement in the Duchess's circle, for the Smith in question was Captain Henry Abel Smith of the Royal Horse Guards, a cousin of the Duke of Somerset and an eminently suitable and respectable match for his bride, Lady May, daughter of Queen Mary's brother, the Earl of Athlone.

Certainly after the Duchess's initial shock at the thought of having an actress invited to stay in The House, Adèle and her mother made a good impression at Chatsworth. Adèle controlled her outspokenness –quite easily actually, as the splendour and magnificence of Chatsworth, with its Painted Hall, gilt ceilings and vast state rooms, any one of which could have contained several houses the size of Adèle's Omaha birthplace, was enough to overwhelm the stoutest heart. And Ann, always perfectly at ease in any situation, was shown around by the duchess and listened sympathetically to the problems of organising her various houses, for in addition to Chatsworth and 2 Carlton Gardens in London, the Devonshires had mansions at Hardwick Hall and their Bolton Abbey estate as well as the vast Lismore Castle in southern Ireland, which was still being renovated after the depredations during the 'troubles'. Ann and Adèle were ferried around the estates in the Duke's 'Stink Hog', as he called his large brown Rolls-Royce, and enjoyed a life of luxurious ease. They sailed through their visit perfectly, behaving as though it was the most normal thing in the world for them to be waited on by footmen in livery – lemon coats, dark blue breeches and white stockings – and ladies' maids who took care of *everything*: pressed their clothes, squeezed the toothpaste on to the toothbrush, turned their stockings to slip their feet into, and laid out their evening gowns before dinner.

2326 South 10th Street, Omaha, Nebraska – the house where Frederick Austerlitz Jnr was born in 1899.

Fred, aged 5.

Fred and Adèle, brother and sister dance team. Around 1910.

Fred aged 13, and Adèle aged 15½.

With Adèle in *Over the Top*, 1917.

Adèle, aged 16.

The Bunch and Judy, 1922.

Over the Top, 1917.

Stop Flirting, 1923.

With Tilly Losch in *The Band Wagon*, 1931.

Adèle on her wedding day, 1932. (From left) Mrs Astaire, Lord and Lady Charles Cavendish, Marquess of Hartington, Duke of Devonshire and attendants. The Duchess is conspicuously absent.

Lismore Castle, Adèle's new home.

Adèle's premature daughter dies at birth.

Fred married Phyllis Potter on 12 July, 1933.

Together for the first time, Fred and Ginger Rogers in *Flying Down to Rio*, 1933.

Fred Astaire, the image perfected, 1935.

Adèle, however, was troubled about Fred. She felt it was unfair for her to walk out on him after a stinker like *Smiles*; people were bound to think that she was deserting him, and he would have one hell of a job re-establishing himself. So, after they all talked it over, Adèle decided that if they could find a good show to do, she would give Broadway one last shot, and then she and Charlie could get married.

Happily, the Astaires did have several offers, including an attractive one from Max Gordon, a cheerfully enthusiastic entrepreneur, born Michael Salpeter, who decided that he was going to have a Broadway hit. He had bundles of money and some talented people around him, as well as a cheerful apparent innocence. (It was said that Gordon had once been asked what he thought of nepotism in Hollywood. When he was told that nepotism meant hiring one's relatives, he exclaimed: 'You mean they have a word for that?') He also had a package called *The Band Wagon* with a score by Howard Dietz and Arthur Schwartz and book by George S. Kaufman, three men with good track records. Dietz was the ebullient, pushy son of a New York tailor who had come to songwriting via an advertising agency where he had dreamed up the roaring-lion trademark and the Latin motto *Ars Gratia Artis* for Samuel Goldwyn's independent Goldwyn Picture Company, before it was amalgamated with two other companies to become Metro-Goldwyn-Mayer. He was hired by Goldwyn as publicity director, and at the same time began to moonlight as a lyricist. Composer Arthur Schwartz was quite unlike Dietz, a teacher-turned-lawyer-turned-songwriter of perfect serenity. The librettist George S. Kaufman, author of *Once in a Lifetime*, *The Man Who Came to Dinner* and later the mystery lover of Mary Astor's scandalous diaries, developed a committee system with Howard Dietz, whereby Dietz would suggest an idea, Kaufman would do a first draft, then Dietz would rewrite that before Kaufman wrote the final version. Kaufman had already had a major Broadway hit as director of the Ben Hecht–Charles MacArthur play *The Front Page*, and he was not greedy for credit: he insisted that the programme read: 'Entire production supervised by Howard Dietz', despite Dietz's claim that Kaufman had done the major share of the work.

A strong cast was assembled: Frank Morgan, the former Ziegfeld comedienne Helen Broderick, and the beautiful and mysterious Tilly Losch, an Austrian ballerina whose *succès d'estime* in London had been as great as the Astaires'. Tilly, an outspoken and witty character, had recently married Edward James, the rich, good-looking, extravagantly mannered, and effete art collector whose sister Audrey had been pursued by the Prince of Wales.

[87]

If the smell of death sometimes hangs over a show, so also can one occasionally detect the aroma of success. *The Band Wagon* had it. The singing and dancing and comedy were all first rate: with Tilly Losch, Fred danced the 'Beggar Waltz', with Adèle he created the moving 'Dancing in the Dark'. There was a sophisticated stage turntable – the first one used on Broadway – which was the one thing that did worry the cast somewhat. Would it really work to order for numbers like the merry-go-round sequence of 'I Love Louisa'? The try-out in Philadelphia was fantastic, and the revolving stage worked just fine. Producer Gordon positively glowed, but Kaufman took a more guarded view and suggested to Gordon and Dietz, 'It might be a good idea to leave the play in Philadelphia and take the notices to New York.' He need not have worried, for *The Band Wagon* duly worked its magic at Broadway's New Amsterdam Theatre.

Fred, Adèle, and Tilly (who had become a firm friend of Adèle – they could be equally irreverent and outrageous) threw stardust at the first nighters. It wasn't a Ziegfeld audience packed with glamour, but it certainly loved what it saw. *Variety* summed up the opening: 'That laughter made it seem as though ninety-seven per cent of the audience were backers of the show.' And critic Brooks Atkinson in the *New York Times* said on 4 June 1931, 'It will be difficult for the old style revue to hold up its head . . . when revue artists discover light humour of that sort in the phantasmagoria of American life, the stockmarket will start to rise spontaneously, the racketeers will all be retired or dead and the perfect state will be here.' The *Graphic* gave it top marks: 'this revue is without flaw'. Brooks Atkinson's declaration that it was the start of a new era in the artistry of the American revue set the guaranteed seal of success on the show.

Fred and Adèle had both poured everything into this show and they were well rewarded. Reviewers even spoke of Astaire as an actor – his greatest wish. 'The American Theatre could produce a far worse Hamlet,' wrote one. 'He has given us this season's greatest piece of mummery . . . his hoofing, rhythmic and graceful as it is, must be looked on as secondary. He has ripened into a comedian whose spirit is as breezy as his stepping . . . he has become one of the most valuable theatrical properties in the business. . . .' And in the *New York Sun*: 'There is something utterly audacious about the two of them. There is a lightness and a flexibility and dash in whatever they do; whether it is to chase a plump and bearded Frenchman around the revolving stage or to dance in black and white before an immense encircled drum. They may be chatty and intimate, teasing themselves and the audience, they may be bizarre, tantalising figures from a modernist nightmare. They are, in any case, incomparable.' Fred's protective spirit was roused and his feelings mixed when he read another: 'Fred was the backbone of the performance . . . he ran away with the whole affair, leaving even his delightful sister panting for breath.' In the old days he would have been positively furious with that, but now he could not help but laugh when Adèle saw it and said: 'See, I told you I was getting too old for this caper.' The young harmonica player Larry Adler, one of their fellow sufferers in *Smiles*, said he saw the show a dozen times. 'It was, quite simply,' he recalled during my researches, 'the best revue I ever saw.'

The Band Wagon ran from 3 June 1931 into the next year, and then it went on tour. Finally, on Saturday, 5 March 1932, at the Illinois Theatre in Chicago, Fred and Adèle Astaire danced together on stage for the last time. There were tears aplenty that night for the many, many friends and fans who had travelled from New York to be there. The Astaires themselves seemed in rather sombre mood afterwards. They found it difficult to believe it was really happening – a twenty-seven year partnership was at an end. In a corner of Adèle's dressing room their mother quietly tried to dry her tears. Adèle recalled: 'That last show with Fred was a sad occasion. I wasn't sure at the time I was doing the right thing, but it did have to be done. I could see that we would have to go our separate ways even though I would miss his moaning.'

The future beckoned. Adèle's understudy, Vera Marsh, took over adequately enough in *The Band Wagon*, and Adèle herself prepared to set sail for England and matrimony.

8
Finding a partner

While Fred continued to tour *The Band Wagon* with Vera Marsh, Adèle and Ann arrived in England to prepare for the wedding. They had already assimilated a lot of English culture and now did their not inconsiderable best to ensure that everything ran smoothly, aware that they would face antagonism in some quarters. Ann was a slight but almost regal character; her Nebraska accent had long since softened so that it was difficult to place her, although The House with its many servants, poor heating, and negligible plumbing arrangements had caused her to revert to amazed American surprise. Adèle was a natural mimic; after a few days in England she sounded like a native. The success of the mission was jeopardized when Charlie was suddenly rushed to hospital with appendicitis, but he recovered quickly and did his part to ensure that Adèle and her mother were well looked after and comfortable – on his instructions the fires in their grates were tended directly after those of the Duke and Duchess themselves. The warmth was appreciated, as the two women could not help but feel a chill in the air. It seemed that Adèle's nuptials would be in some contrast to the big society wedding of Charlie's brother Edward, Marquess of Hartington, and Lady Mary Cecil, daughter of the Marquess of Salisbury, fifteen years before. In fact the present occasion was to be so subdued an affair that the preparations scarcely affected the routine of The House. Only the immediate family was invited. The ceremony took place on Monday, 9 May 1932, in the elegantly pretty chapel at Chatsworth.

Its one disadvantage is that its location cuts off the morning sun from the living quarters. 'I'm sure God wouldn't mind being worshipped in a slightly different position,' the present Duke says, for the umpteenth time puzzling over the placement.

It was the first time that the 17th-century chapel, with its high ceilings, marble altar, wood carvings by Grinling Gibbons, and paintings from 1691–2 by the Italian Antonio Verrio (his work can also be seen at Windsor Castle, Whitehall and Hampton Court), had ever been used for a marriage ceremony; decorated with myrtle, camellias, and arum lilies, it looked magnificent. The parish organist, T. H. Moseley, played the wedding march and Rev. Foster Pegg, vicar of the Duke's parish of Edensor, proudly officiated.

Adèle looked calm and beautiful in a plain white gown designed for her in New York by Mainbocher. She was attended by three little bridesmaids: Charlie's brother Lord Hartington's daughters Lady Elizabeth, 5 (who many years later was to be the final love and companion of the poet John Betjeman), and Lady Anne Cavendish, 4, and Charlie's sister Lady Maud's daughter Judith Baillie, 6, with Maud's two sons Peter, 4, and Michael, 7 (now Lord Burton), in kilts as page boys. Adèle was given in marriage by Ann, an unusual gesture at a British wedding, where that rôle is traditionally taken by the father of the bride, or a close male relation or friend of the family. Charlie's eldest brother Lord Hartington acted as his best man. It was as well the guests were few, as the magnificent chapel does not hold more than a handful: there were the Duke (who knew a thing or two about ceremonial, having carried King George's crown during the 1910 coronation in Westminster Abbey) and the Duchess; Charlie's brother's wife Lady Hartington; his uncle Lord Richard Cavendish with his wife Lady Moyra; his sisters Lady Maud, with her husband Captain the Hon George Baillie, Lady Blanche Cobbold, and Lady Dorothy Macmillan (married to Harold Macmillan, later Prime Minister); and his brother Lord Hartington's younger son, Lord Andrew Cavendish, then twelve years old and now the present Duke. The local choir sang 'O Perfect Love' and to everyone's surprise and delight, the cantankerous Duke Victor was really quite pleasant to one and all. Charlie even stayed sober for once. For all the splendour, Adèle had little compunction in giving false information for her marriage certificate – while Charlie gave his age correctly as twenty-six, Adèle gave hers as thirty-one, when she was actually thirty-five.

The Duke was quite fond of his rather inept second son and had taken a liking to the sparky bride: as a wedding present he gave them his imposing Lismore Castle, a beautiful fortress built by King John in 1185 on the banks of the Blackwater River in County Wexford. But the Duchess had begun by being suspicious of Adèle – her first reaction to the news of the match had been that obviously Charlie had got the girl pregnant and she should be paid off – and she remained in some doubt as to whether she could trust this American actress to integrate into the family. She made her feelings known by absenting herself from Adèle's introduction into society when the bride, now officially Lady Charles Cavendish, was presented at Court in June. This archaic ceremony no longer exists, but in 1932 it was still a *sine qua non* of life for a young debutante or a newly married lady to make their curtsies to the monarch. The Duchess sent word that she was confined to bed with 'acute rheumatism' although, as Mistress of the Robes she should have been in attendance; moreover, she was a tough old bird who usually let no physical ailment get in the way of her duty. Adèle decided there was nothing to be done except ignore her mother-in-law's action, so, elegantly beautiful in a dusty pink satin robe with a fan-shaped train and with ostrich feathers in her hair, she sailed through the ceremony. She was presented to King George and Queen Mary by the Countess of Airlie, acting Lady of the Bedchamber, accompanied by Lady Balfour, niece of the Duke. It was no secret that the Duchess's absence had been a diplomatic one, but happily her objections did not last long for, against all odds, Adèle made an ideal wife for Charlie. She was loyal, a popular hostess, and a dignified Lady Charles Cavendish – well, as dignified as she could be. Even when she was having fun she managed to do it in a dignified way. The Duchess did, very slowly, warm to her, particularly after Adèle discovered her mother-in-law's penchant for risqué jokes; Adèle's collection was second to none.

It wasn't until the summer of 1932, when the tour of *The Band Wagon* ended, that Fred managed to visit his mother and Adèle in Ireland and to travel with them to London for the Derby and a visit to his tailors Kilgour, French (as they were then known). They searched out all their old haunts and, one night at the Savoy, Fred did something he had never done before. Turning to Adèle he said: 'If you'll be a good girl you can dance with me.' Social dancing always made him nervous; he was convinced that his partner would expect him to do fancy steps and that he would trip on her feet and cause horrible embarrassment when he came tumbling down on top of her. Adèle smiled, then assumed a serious face. 'Well,' she said, 'if you'll be a very good boy, maybe I will dance with you.' And so it was, for the first time in their lives, Adèle and Fred danced together on a ballroom floor for their own amusement. Afterwards Fred recalled to one reporter: 'I was surprised – I found out that she was really rather good. We had lots of fun. It had never occurred to us to dance together in private while we were appearing on stage together.'

Before the wedding, while Adèle had been organising her future life

[92]

with Charlie, Fred had been contemplating his own future, both personal and professional, without her. 'It's about time you thought of settling down, too,' Adèle told him. He was well aware that he ought to be thinking of getting married, but while there had been plenty of girls to escort, there had never been a really mutually special relationship in his life. He had the usual quota of youthful crushes, and some long-time low-key loves, but he had just been too busy for marriage. His heavy work-load also saved him from his own gaucheness, for surprisingly in one blessed with buckets of confidence on stage or at public functions, he remained shy and awkward in private. And his girlfriends had to cope with Adèle's teasing as well as everything else: one night during the brief life of *Smiles*, she went backstage announcing: 'Be extra good tonight, Freddie's got a girl out front!'

For as long as Fred could remember, he had been keen on Liz Altemus, though, as she later recalled during my researches, they were always friends, but never lovers: 'Freddie is my Cyrano, he would fight battles for me. He was not a beau. The other men I knew were all bastards, but those are the ones you fall for. Freddie was far too nice.'

In London he had met Audrey James, elegant and flirtatious, the companion and possible cousin of the Prince of Wales. Fred had always been discreet about his friendship with Audrey for fear of upsetting the Prince. According to Adèle, the Prince of Wales could not have minded anyway, as he had no interest in sex and just wanted to be surrounded by attractive girls. Nonetheless, Astaire remained wary. Soon after Audrey announced that her marriage to Dudley Coats was over, she wed the fabulously wealthy Marshall Field of Chicago. Fred and Audrey, in London and New York, remained frequent companions: whatever there was between them at first evolved into a long and deep friendship that continued through the years. Lillian Bostwick was another favourite, but she was also being courted by the banker Ogden Phipps. Fred was always conscious that in terms of wealth and so-called breeding he could not compete with people like Phipps – had he only realised that he had assets of his own that were envied by others, the story might have been very different.

Fred still felt guilty about deserting Aarons and Freedley. During the run of *Smiles*, George Gershwin tried to make peace between Alex Aarons and Fred by suggesting that Fred help out with the choreography for their new show, *Girl Crazy*. Fred had come to the Alvin Theatre the next day and worked with Allen Kearns, who had been with him in *Funny Face*, and a perky Charleston champion from Kansas,

[93]

Texas, born Virginia McMath but now known as Ginger Rogers. There was a shortage of rehearsal space and so they decamped to the foyer to work on 'Embraceable You', a romantic routine, and on her Charleston number, 'If Not For Me'. He spent a couple of sessions at the Alvin and took a proprietory interest in the show's fortunes, which were in marked contrast to *Smiles*; although the highlight of the show was the young belter Ethel Merman singing 'I Got Rhythm', which Fred quickly co-opted for his extra-show concerts, Ginger was certainly noticed too. Fred took her out dancing at the fashionable Casino in Central Park, where Eddie Duchin's band played, and to the cinema on a few occasions. The relationship had no chance to blossom, for Ginger had a burgeoning movie career, travelling out to the Long Island studios of Paramount each morning with her ambitious mother Lela and returning for the evening performance of *Girl Crazy*. She had already made a handful of features including *Young Man of Manhattan* (no relation to the *Smiles* routine of the same name) and *The Sap from Syracuse*. ('You really are the Sap from Syracuse now, turning down Alex,' Adèle considerately told her brother as *Girl Crazy* prospered.) Ginger enjoyed Fred's company, as she later told Larry Adler: 'How could I not? He was a bit down at the time with *Smiles*, but he danced wonderfully and everyone knew him all around town. For me it was great fun going around with him. He was kinda cute.' But aside from this one dancer, all the girls that Fred found attractive were invariably being wooed by princes or millionaires. In the early days he had felt that he had nothing to offer, but things were different now. He was about to lose his stage partner, and he knew that somebody was needed to replace her. His mother and sister knew, although Fred might not have admitted it, that someone was needed to replace Adèle off-stage too. And happily the right person did come along – in a most unexpected way.

Fred rather imagined that he would eventually fall in love with a young, inexperienced girl with perhaps not too many social ambitions. But such things can't be planned and romance arrived in the shape not of a blushing debutante but of a married woman – and one with a child of her own.

On a Sunday in the summer of 1931, Fred drove out to Long Island, to a 'golf luncheon' organised by Virginia Graham Fair Vanderbilt, the athletically beautiful wife of William Vanderbilt, whose sister Consuelo had married the Duke of Marlborough. Fred found himself and Charlie Payson, husband of Jock Whitney's elder sister 'Mouse' (her given name was Joan) at a table with the heiress Dorothy Fell and a dark, doll-like girl called Phyllis Baker Potter. Virginia Vanderbilt had long since ceased trying to make a match for Fred; anyway, at a lunch party there was no pressure to match couples. Fred already knew the lovely Fifi Fell, wife of Dorothy Fell's brother John, so he felt quite relaxed. Phyllis simply fascinated him, particularly by her way of rolling the letter 'r' like a 'w' when she spoke. Fred was so captivated that he opted out of the golf match on the Vanderbilt's elegant private course which had been his reason for coming out in the first place. Neither of his companions knew anything about the theatre, and they hadn't seen *The Band Wagon* – Phyllis, who came from Boston, had never even heard of the Astaires. But her face was familiar, and Fred finally figured out that he had seen her at the Belmont Park racetrack with her uncle, Henry Bull, president of the Turf and Field Club – a man who figured high on Fred's list of VIPs. Phyllis was dark, dimpled, about five foot three (the same height as Adèle), and that afternoon, thanks to the sunshine and the champagne, quite open with Fred: she had parted from her husband and was planning to bring up her son Peter in a quiet country setting.

There were no sudden flashes of romance, but at the end of the day Fred felt he would like to see more of this bright little girl who seemed so unhappy; he asked if he could call her in New York. She said that she was going away, but would be back in a few days; later on she said that one of the advantages of being married was that you really didn't mind if a man made the call or not. But Fred did telephone. Phyllis invited him round for tea, to meet two-year-old Peter, who was so much a part of her life. Unphased by the domestic complications, Fred became a regular and welcome caller, but he would get slightly edgy if he found her receiving any attention from other men. He said he suffered agonies if there was anyone else around her, but Phyllis, who found herself strangely drawn to this Broadway dancer, remembered differently: 'Nonsense Fweddie. It wasn't you who suffered, it was me,' she would tell him. She learned more about his life by going to see him in *The Band Wagon*, and afterwards she visited him backstage. 'You were vewy, vewy good,' she said. That to him was praise indeed.

Over late dinners, with Peter safely tucked up in bed, Fred learned all about Phyllis Potter. She was the daughter of a Boston gynae-cologist, Harold W. Baker, who had founded the city's Free Hospital for Women. After he died and her mother remarried, Phyllis had been brought up in New York by her mother's sister Maud Livingston and her husband Henry Bull, an affluent couple who had no children of their own. She made her society début in 1926; in December 1927, she married the wealthy young Wall Street broker Eliphalet Nott Potter III; a year later Eliphalet Nott Potter IV, known as Peter, was born. But the couple soon realised that they had rushed without thought into the match and in time Phyllis decided that the marriage had collapsed around her. The separation was not amicable. Eventually a split-custody agreement was made, although Phyllis could not travel without the permission of the court. She managed to have the agreement amended in January 1932, so that she had Peter for nine months of the year – a change that acknowledged her need and the difficulties her husband was causing.

The atmosphere backstage during this period bore witness to Fred's concern over Phyllis and her problems, for he had at last fallen in love. Like any challenge that Fred faced, he tackled his wooing with single-minded dedication. After Fred had gone to Hollywood, Adèle recalled (he was, as always, unforthcoming about his own life so information was always sought from other sources), 'At the time of *The Band Wagon* he was nutty for Phyllis. Moping about and behaving just like he had a flop on his hands when we were out of town. He was very funny about it all. But it was really just a matter of seeing if they could sort out all the dreadful legal complications which were upsetting Phyllis so much.'

Surprisingly enough, Ann Astaire was not quite so enamoured of Phyllis; one might have expected her to be pleased that her thirty-two-year-old son at last had a steady relationship, yet she did little to hide her disapproval. Fred didn't even notice her comments and jibes. He looked at the world through rose-coloured glasses, but what Ann saw was endless complications over Phyllis's divorce plans. What's more, Ann reckoned, if the girl got divorced once, what was to stop her divorcing again and finding yet another new man? Why not pick one of the many beautiful, wealthy, and eminently suitable young society girls who were free? Any one of them would make an ideal wife for Fred, who had long since ceased to be merely a show-business celebrity and was now accepted as part of the American social scene. In Ann's opinion, a divorcée with a young son was the last thing Fred needed now that he was on his own professionally.

Phyllis was also aware of the problems inherent in this relationship. She decided to get away for a while with Henry and Maud Bull, who were heading for England so that Henry could attend the Derby. *The Band Wagon* closed in May and Fred too sailed for Ireland, London, and

Epsom. With the help of Adèle and Charlie, he spent the summer of 1932 showing Phyllis all the sights and places he had come to love. For a man usually obsessed with his career, Fred showed a surprising disinclination to return to the States. Before leaving New York, he had discussed the idea of a show with Cole Porter and heard some of Cole's songs, but he could see nothing to drag him back in a hurry, even when a cablegram arrived asking if he was still going to do *Gay Divorce*. Frankly, he did not much care; he would rather stay with Phyllis in London. But she had a different reaction: she very seriously told him, 'Fweddie, I think you should go back and investigate your career. After all, if we are going to get married you'll have to work – won't you?' It took a while for her question to sink in, but when it did, a delighted Fred headed straight for the shipping office to book his passage back to New York.

Once home, professional problems overshadowed his personal ones, for he now faced the challenge of shedding the vestiges of the old act and scoring by himself. Cole Porter, just back from Hollywood (where he supervised the score for the movie version of his *Fifty Million Frenchmen*), was working with two new producer friends, Dwight Wilman and Tom Weatherly, who had acquired an unproduced J. Hartley Manners play called *Gay Divorce*. It needed a good deal of rewriting, but it seemed like a suitable vehicle for Fred's first solo outing. He was to play a man pretending to be a professional co-respondent for an Englishman seeking a divorce.

It was no trouble to find backers for the show, for Fred's friends were as determined as he that his first solo venture should be a success. The major investor was Jock Whitney, already a keen angel, who refused to be put off by Fred's doubts: he cheerfully opined that it could not possibly be a worse failure than the ill-starred *Here Comes the Bride*, which had cost him $100,000; it ran just seven performances before Claudette Colbert had dropped out with appendicitis. 'This time I know I'm going to make a fortune,' Jock told Fred. Taking the 'Adèle' role was the luscious Claire Luce, a blonde cigarette girl turned Ziegfeld star who was married to the millionaire playboy Clifford Warren Smith. She had some experience of the movie world from her rôle opposite Spencer Tracy in John Ford's 1930 film *Up The River*, and she understood and sympathised with Fred's problems. She worked like fury to get her performance up to the impossible heights Fred expected, and later she recalled: 'I actually felt more sorry for Fred than I did for myself, despite the horrendous schedules of rehearsals that he kept up. He was a very worried man.'

[97]

The try-outs began in Boston. The show was decidedly shaky; the comedians Eric Blore and Erik Rhodes scored, the music was fine, but it was generally agreed that the story did not work. Could Jock be headed for another beating? Fred was determined that it should not be so. The one redeeming feature of the show, which almost alone seemed to rescue it, was Cole Porter's 'Night and Day'. Cole said he had written the song after a luncheon with the mildly eccentric Mrs Vincent Astor, who had insisted that they eat off trays so they would be free from interruption by the servants. They had sat out on the porch despite a downpour of rain, and his hostess complained of the 'drip, drip, drip' that appears in the lyric:

> Like the drip, drip, drip of the raindrops when the summer shower is through,
> So a voice within me keeps repeating you, you, you.
> Night and day you are the one;
> Only you beneath the moon or under the sun.

The song was specifically written for Fred's voice, yet when he heard it he thought it was pitched too high for him. He even approached producer Tom Weatherly, saying his voice would crack if he sang it. In retrospect this was one battle Fred was glad he lost, for 'Night and Day' never failed to stop the show. His dreamy, romantic, flowing choreography was not at all the type of thing he had been doing with Adèle.

He also choreographed a spectacular speciality number of the type that he might well have done with Adèle, in which he and Claire waltzed around, then over, tables and chairs – just as though they were not there. Frequently either Claire or Fred would fail to negotiate one of the obstacles; then, in the way of magicians or jugglers, when they did get it right the applause was all the greater. He missed not being able to talk things over with Adèle: although Ann was at hand to discuss and criticize, and Phyllis did try to understand what was going on, it was not the same as being able to talk to a fellow-professional like Adèle.

However, in Lismore Castle Adèle was following the progress of *Gay Divorce* with interest and concern. She knew Claire Luce and believed she would be a fair foil to Fred. But the letters she had from her mother did not bode well. 'I knew that it would be a tough ride for Fred,' she said. 'But it was just something he had to do. We'd just have to wait and see.' On opening night, 29 November 1932, a cablegram from Ireland arrived at the Ethel Barrymore Theatre. As he read it, Fred's worried face spread into a broad grin, for the message said: NOW MINNIE

DON'T FORGET TO MOAN STOP LOVE ADELE AND CHARLIE.

Could Fred Astaire survive without his live-wire sister? The Broadway audience did not seem too sure. It was one of those late-arriving, noisy, coughing houses. Fred's own feelings were summed up by Phyllis, after he had struggled through the evening. Her comment was: 'What a dweadful audience.' 'So is the show,' he replied. 'I liked some of it,' she said practically. 'I'm glad it's over,' said Astaire, in no mood to be cheered. It was at times like that in particular, when he could see things were wrong, that he was so glad she was not a theatrical type who would have trotted out first-night platitudes.

It was not only Fred who missed Adèle: most of the reviewers mourned the absence of her sprightly personality. One wrote: 'Fred Astaire stops every now and then to look off stage towards the wings as if he were hoping his titled sister, Adèle, would come and rescue him.' And another: 'One thing is certain, after viewing last night's performance we have come to the conclusion that two Astaires are better than one.' The legendary newspaperman Walter Winchell, getting Adèle's new title wrong, came to Fred's rescue – up to a point: 'The personable and talented brother of Lady Cavendish never before seemed so refreshing and entertaining – but *Gay Divorce* has a tendency to go flat for more than two minutes at a time – too often.' Brooks Atkinson wrote: 'In the refulgent Claire Luce, Fred Astaire has found a partner who can match him step for step and who flies over the furniture in his company without missing a beat. As a solo dancer, Mr Astaire stamps out his accents with that lean, nervous agility that distinguishes his craftsmanship and he has invented turns that abound in graphic portraiture. But some of us cannot help feeling that the joyousness of the Astaire team is missing now that the team has parted.' The reviews, fair though they were, reaffirmed Fred's view that in the mind of the theatregoers he was irrevocably tied to Adèle and that without her he needed to move into completely different areas to gain an identity of his own. Straight comedy, maybe? The film business? Many of his own contemporaries had already gone to Hollywood. Maybe the Astaires' disastrous screen test was just a temporary setback; could he perhaps find another chance to test as a solo act? At least there was a current vogue for dancing and singing in the movies: there might just be a place for him on the screen.

Away from Broadway, another drama was being played out, the subject of which was the contested custody of young Peter Potter.

Phyllis, learning that her husband planned to re-marry, had hired the formidable lawyer Fanny Holtzmann (who also represented Fred's friends Gertrude Lawrence and Noël Coward) to help her gain full custody, so that it would be possible for her to travel with her son without permission from the court. It was a tedious, wearing business for Phyllis and just as anxiety-ridden for Fred, desperate for her to be happy and free.

Gay Divorce was running smoothly enough when Fred had a backstage call one night from the one-time juvenile performer Mervyn LeRoy, whom he knew from their vaudeville days. LeRoy had gone into the movies as a straight actor and was now directing Edward G. Robinson in *Little Caesar*, and he was about to start work on the Warner Bros musical *Gold Diggers of 1933*. He really liked *Gay Divorce* and told Fred that it should be turned into a movie; Fred was, needless to say, flattered but self-deprecating. Afterwards he thought that this could be the break he was looking for but – it wasn't. Astaire claimed that when LeRoy mentioned the idea to the studio heard Jack Warner, he barked: 'Who am I going to put in it? Cagney?'

But while Fred worried about his future in New York, his ears should have been burning, for out in Hollywood, David O. Selznick – son of the pioneer film magnate Lewis J. Selznick, brother of the top talent agent Myron, husband of Louis B. Mayer's daughter Irene, vice president in charge of production at the mightily troubled RKO Studios – was desperate to find something to stave off impending bankruptcy for his company. RKO was an amalgam of the Radio Corporation of America and the theatre chains of B. F. Keith and Orpheum. At first a showcase for RCA's sound on film process, it soon gained vast ambitions and an ever-changing management to produce the results. It was David Selznick's turn at the top. And Selznick had his eye on Fred Astaire. On 13 January 1933, he had sent a memorandum, almost his sole means of communication – and fortunately he personally retained his carbons – to director Mark Sandrich and associate producer Louis Brock which read: 'I am tremendously enthused about the suggestion New York has made of using Fred Astaire. If he photographs (I have ordered a test), he may prove to be a really sensational bet . . . Astaire is one of the great artists of the day: a magnificent performer, a man conceded to be perhaps, next to Leslie Howard, the most charming in the American theatre, and unquestionably the outstanding young leader of American musical comedy. He would be, in my opinion, good enough to use in the lead of a million-dollar-picture – provided only that he photographs, which I hope is the case. I trust you and Mr Sandrich will keep confidential the fact that we are considering and negotiating with him, since I am certain that as soon as it becomes generally known that he is at last considering pictures, there will be a wild scramble on the part of all studios to test him.'

Fred would have been amused by the 'at last considering' – it had been on his mind for ages, but there had just been no offers. A test was duly arranged in New York. Fred, feeling none too confident, spoke, walked, and danced to George Gershwin's 'I Got Rhythm'. On 26 January, Selznick sent another memo to Sandrich and Brock: 'I am a little uncertain about the man, but I feel, in spite of his enormous ears and bad chin line, that his charm is so tremendous that it comes through even in this wretched test, and I would be perfectly willing to go ahead with him for the lead in the Brock musical. I should like to have Brock's opinion; but even if he is opposed to Astaire, I would be in favour of signing him for this part if some of the other studio executives have any enthusiasm for the man.'

But once more the fates intervened: just a week after giving the go-ahead to Astaire, David Selznick had a major boardroom row over the division of control between the Los Angeles and New York offices, quit RKO, and joined his father-in-law Louis B. Mayer at MGM. Once installed, Selznick decided to try and get some benefit from his hunch about Fred Astaire. He negotiated with RKO to lend Fred to MGM for a movie that was already scheduled, with Clark Gable, at the peak of his popularity and somewhat reluctant to make the movie, and Joan Crawford, a top star who had recently faded with her last two films, and as an instant response to the success of Warners' *42nd Street*. Selznick believed that with a co-star like Gable and the introduction of the stage performers Nelson Eddy and Fred Astaire, not only could MGM make money but they could also rescue Joan Crawford's career.

The 'loaning' of actors under contract was a common practice at that time in Hollywood, and, for the studios – all eight of whom were ultimately under the sway of Morgan and Rockefeller interests – a highly profitable one. A $1,500 a week man would be loaned for $2,500 and the contract holder would pocket the difference. But Fred knew nothing of these machinations; he had been delighted to be offered $1,500 a week for three weeks by RKO, just about enough time for them to see whether he worked on film. By the end of three weeks RKO would know whether it was worth taking up the first of their four annual contract options – the $1,500 would increase by $500 a week each year.

It all sounded marvellous to Fred, who was blissfully ignorant of the dangers inherent in a contract which gave all the options to the studio. It was with great delight that he told Phyllis of his good news: he was being given a chance in the movies. It would be best, said Fred, for him to go out alone to Los Angeles for the filming when *Gay Divorce* closed: then he could return to New York and, with the launching of his new career under his belt, they could at last get married. It might be risky; unknown dangers lay ahead: but at least he would be able to make some money for his new family. But Phyllis was not totally sold on the details of Fred's latest plan and her answer was firm: 'No, that's no good – if you're going away from me to Hollywood, you'll start running around with some of those girls out there. And whether you do or not I'll always think you did, so we had better get married right now as soon as possible.'

Fred was overjoyed that at last things were happening, and he hastened to make preparation. First he needed his birth certificate to get a licence when Phyllis's divorce came through. Ann searched high and low, but she finally realised the awful truth: Fred did not have a birth certificate – in fact, technically he didn't really exist. So Ann, now resigned to the wedding plans, set off by train for Omaha, to register the birth of her not-so-little son – he weighed in at about 134 pounds now, a big bonny babe if ever there was one. She found that life back in Nebraska wasn't very rosy for her friends and family, for the Depression was biting cruelly. Her elder brother Dan, for so long a real high hat locally – he even took his meals in the dining room while his wife Mamie ate in the kitchen – had lost his job at the Paxton-Gallagher foods company, where he had worked for thirty years. Jack, his crippled son, still lived with his statuesque but unmarried sister Hélène; he worked for Paxton-Gallagher, she for the Mutual Benefit Health and Accident Association. Their brother William at the Armour Packing Company was concerned to keep his job as a clerk; the prospect of finding another was not good. At least Dessa and Adèle, the daughters of Ann's sister Maria (who had died at the age of forty in 1915), were being well looked after by their father William Wilke and his new wife Ora. Ann visited her kin and childhood friends, promising to try and persuade Fred to come back too. At last she managed to register his birth, giving her New York address and Fritz's Detroit home, even though Fritz had of course been dead for some years.

Fred was now a real person, and there was only one more legal hurdle to be cleared. On 24 June 1933, Phyllis' ex-husband had married

Margaret Tiers. Maybe now Phyllis could establish proper custody of young Peter. On 11 July, she appeared before Justice Selah B. Strong in his chambers in Borough Hall, Brooklyn, to testify that she did not intend to marry Fred Astaire until she was satisfied that she could devote all of her attention to her child. She told the same story to waiting reporters from the *New York Times*. The following day, Judge Strong granted her custody of the boy for eleven months of the year with the freedom to take him wherever she liked.

They were at last free to marry. How long would it take to arrange? Where could they be married? They were full of questions. Happily, now the cares were resolved, Judge Strong, who had suspected the situation, stepped in and told them that, if the circumstances were unusual or pressing, he could grant the licence and perform the marriage right there and then. Yes, said Fanny Holtzmann, my client wishes to get married so that she may leave New York for Los Angeles for an urgent business engagement. So it was that at 6 p.m. on the evening of Wednesday 12 July, in the unromantic but imposing grey granite County Court House, Brooklyn, Fred Astaire, thirty-four, and Phyllis Potter, twenty-five, were married. Henry Bull gave the bride away and Supreme Court Justice Thomas Cuff, Fanny Holtzmann, and her attorney brothers, Jacob and David Holtzmann, acted as witnesses. They posed happily for a photographer in the court house corridor and returned to celebrate at 875 Park Avenue.

9
Keeping in the lines

They had a honeymoon of just one day, spent on Captiva, the yacht belonging to Jock Whitney's mother Helen Hay Whitney. Jock had put himself in charge of ship's supplies and the vessel was laden with flowers, champagne and caviar for the twenty-four-hour cruise up the Hudson. On the Friday, leaving young Peter with his nurse in Manhattan, they boarded a Ford triplane, for both of them their first commercial plane trip, and took off on a twenty-six-hour flight, including stop-offs, to California. They were checked into the Spanish Moroccan splendour of the Beverly Wilshire Hotel, on Wilshire Boulevard, where they found their suite awash with white flowers – a present from MGM in the name of Joan Crawford, star of *Dancing Lady*, which, it was explained to Fred, would be his first venture. 'My goodness, this really is a bit extwavagant,' said Phyllis, but Fred said he thought this was just Hollywood-style politeness.

In the summer of '33 Hollywood was still a nascent industry, peopled by young stars and young executives who had grown up in that exclusive world: there had been plenty of stage performers who had been rowed into a cameo movie rôle and then disappeared from sight. Fred, at thirty-four was too old to be groomed for studio stardom. There were some veteran leading men. Al Jolson was twenty years older, Maurice Chevalier was ten years his senior. But they had both started in films many years before: Jolson in 1923 and Chevalier in 1908. Otherwise, senior citizens, such as Ronald Colman and Richard Dix were strong, mature and dramatic players. There *were* film stars in their thirties – both Gary Cooper, huge at the time, and Clark Gable were thirty-two – but they had been around in movies for ten years. Now Astaire found that dancing partners, material and co-stars were foisted on him, and he was treated with scant consideration by people who were younger, less experienced and less talented than himself. That he overcame these tribulations to achieve such artistic triumphs was quite extraordinary. Astaire's early Hollywood years have been chronicled from the point of view of the publicity departments, always eager for an easy headline, but a deeper examination of the time that Fred became an international, rather than an Anglo-American, star reveals a lot more about the man, his family and his motivation.

Hollywood was a massive gamble, but Fred saw no alternative: he didn't want to team up with another dancer, and he had gone about as far as he could on the Broadway stage. He imagined that filming would be like working on stage but without an audience, but when he reported for duty at the studios on 1 August he discovered there were many things he would have to learn about the new medium. The first shock was that the sight lines in cinemas were quite different from those in theatres, where the best seats look up at the performer. The make-up department decreed that for *Dancing Lady* Fred's receding hair – 'My high intellectual forehead' – should be supplemented by a hairpiece; he went along with that stoically. 'I hardly noticed at the time,' he said. 'I guess the camera rather accentuates these lofty characteristics.' Others were not so kind about the toupee and one movie magazine used two pictures of Astaire next to each other: one was a casual photograph of Astaire and Phyllis after their marriage and one was of him on the film set. The captions ran: 'Here is Fred with his wig but without his wife'.

There were, happily, some familiar faces on the movie set, like dance director Sammy Lee, who had worked on *Lady, Be Good!*, and cast member Bob Benchley, who was happily transforming himself from writer to comic actor. Astaire had already arranged for his Broadway dresser, Walter, to come out West as valet and general odd-job man for the brief stay, and from his very first day he took Phyllis to the studio with him: he enjoyed her company on the ride in and then he could also see more of her at lunchtime and the evening – and, as he said, she could keep an eye on all those girls. Once on the sound stage Astaire decided that maybe this game was not so bad after all; an obsessive perfection-ist, he liked the film technique of doing things over until they were right – and he found that he really didn't seem to miss the audience applause. He would far rather know inside that he had done well than receive the cheering of an often undiscerning theatre audience. The unnerving part was watching the rushes of the previous day's work – no matter how well he thought the filming had gone, the rushes were invariably a big disappointment: 'I couldn't bear to see myself. I knew darned well that an inventory of my face would disclose no feature which could be hailed as what a successful movie star should wear. It was awful agony just

[105]

watching.' Fortunately for generations of moviegoers he was not given much time to worry about such things; otherwise he might well have carried out his threat to Phyllis to pull out of the RKO commitment.

Ever since Al Jolson had announced 'You ain't heard nothin' yet' in *The Jazz Singer* in 1927 and had gone on to make *The Singing Fool* the musical had been an obvious subject for the movies; every conceivable stage musical had been quickly adapted and the performance had been shot straight as a two-dimensional play. The craze for all-singing all-dancing movies was so intense it burnt itself out. The Depression years, and audiences hungry for escapist entertainment, had made light-weight optimistic movies the order of the day. Then Warner Bros revived the genre, and Broadway choreographer, Busby Berkeley, with his work on the gritty backstage story, *42nd Street*, directed by Lloyd Bacon, revived the fortunes of the company. The follow-up, *Gold Diggers of 1933*, directed by Mervyn LeRoy, ensured Warner's continued success. The Berkeley technique was to get the camera to do the dancing around endless geometrical patterns of chorus girls, invariably blonde and invariably surrounded by the Big White Set. Recent improvement in film stock meant pure blacks and whites could now be reproduced on screen and thanks to the technicians, like art director Van Nest Polglase (who would design *Flying Down to Rio* as his first Astaire assignment), the Big White Set, both ostentatious and understated, was introduced into films as that quintessential art deco style that has pervaded The American Dream ever since – the large, spacious, clean-lined rooms with white carpets, huge white sofas, and a plentiful supply of white telephones.

Dancing Lady followed the Warner Bros 'backstage' formula and it worked on many levels: it enabled Astaire to feel his way into movies, it gave MGM an added name to the roster of stars who had filmed for them and it made them a deal of money. It was a fairly low key entry into movies. He is introduced to Joan Crawford as the 'famous Fred Astaire' and does just two dances with her – which add up to about six minutes' screen time.

But Fred Astaire was left not knowing what was going to happen next, for, with David Selznick gone, there was no guarantee that RKO would want him any more. When he did arrive at the RKO lot, he was relieved to discover that the new head of the studio was someone he knew: Merian C. Cooper, a film-maker friend of David Selznick who had taken over on Selznick's sudden resignation. Cooper, or Coop as Fred called him, was very involved in setting up a movie about a giant

[106]

ape called King Kong but he did also take a special interest in Fred's *Flying Down to Rio* and its ever-changing cast. The main casting problem that Coop could see was Fred's partner, and after much discussion a suitable candidate was found in Dorothy Jordan, known as Sugar, a bright young actress who had been a chorus girl and Adèle's understudy in *Funny Face*. She had danced with Fred before and worked very well with him.

The best laid plans often go astray and by the filming date other members of the cast (such as Helen Broderick, who had been in *The Band Wagon*, Arline Judge, dancer wife of Mae West's *I'm No Angel* director Wesley Ruggles, and rugged Joel McCrea) had all had to pull out. On top of that Sugar Jordan had upped and offed to marry studio head Merian Cooper and was away on honeymoon. Astaire now had no idea who would be his partner, if indeed he would have one. Many names were discussed; none was confirmed. He didn't know enough to realise just how tenuous his rôle was becoming but silently he put up with the confusing traffic of names. 'All I wanted to do was to stay in pictures,' he said, glossing over the problems. Movies were the one chance he could see of making money, so he kept a tight control of his temper – one flare-up at this stage could have ended his film career. Adèle was really concerned as she read between the lines of his frequent letters.

Shooting of the film with Thornton Freeland, who was only a year older than Astaire, started with the cast still unsettled. Looking back, Fred said: 'It was not until the third day that I was told that there would be a dancing partner for me, and then I must say that I had mixed feelings about who they had in mind. I really didn't think that she'd want to dance with me. She'd been making straight films with some success and I'd heard that she didn't want to make musicals any more. On the other hand I had worked a little bit with her on that show *Girl Crazy*, that Alex Aarons needed some help with, and I did at least know that Ginger Rogers was a pretty good dancer.' That was a very generous view of the situation, as he was actually plunged into gloom. He knew very well that Ginger Rogers was a champion Charleston hoofer and was a hard-working professional but not for a second did he consider her to be anywhere near the kind of partner that he wanted or needed: she simply didn't have the dance technique to match his.

Ginger Rogers was a typical Busby Berkeley girl, and she had been a conspicuous performer in *42nd Street*. At twenty-two already a veteran of East Coast shorts, Ginger and former Lillian Gish stand-in

[107]

Una Merkel were revealed inside a railway carriage full of girls in nightwear singing: 'When she knows as much as we know, she'll be on her way to Reno'. In *Shuffle Off To Buffalo*, Ginger had also been the girl covered from head to toe in silver dollars, singing 'We're in the Money' for the opening sequence of *Gold Diggers of 1933*. Ginger Rogers was no Adèle. What was worse she had hardly any time to rehearse. When she arrived on the set of *Flying Down to Rio*, she had already worked at most studios, had been under contract to both Paramount and Pathé and was getting nowhere fast until RKO liked her work in *Professional Sweetheart* and signed her.

The movie was on the blocks, so Fred continued his non-violent learning process. But the score of the new film sounded promising even though it had been written by Vincent Youmans, composer of the disastrous *Smiles*. Youmans was even more critically drunk than Astaire remembered him, yet *Rio* was one of the finest scores he had ever written. But no sooner had he finished his work on the film than he was committed to a sanatorium where he would die in '46. In the book of the film, the army of RKO contract writers had Astaire playing the best friend of bandleader and pilot Gene Raymond, twenty-five-year-old tall and blond leading man. Dolores del Rio, twenty-eight-year-old cousin of heart-throb Ramon Novarro and cast in her rôle as the exotic Mexican beauty, was to play opposite Raymond. Credited above Astaire were Spanish language player Paul Roulien and Ginger Rogers. Astaire had fifth billing – hardly an auspicious start to his RKO career.

The dance sequences were to be directed by Dave Gould, described by Hermes Pan as 'a promoter and man about the business.' Although he is credited on the titles with the choreography, he planned to get himself an assistant to do the bulk of the work. It transpired that Gould's idea was to provide Fred Astaire with undoubtedly the most important, and unsung, collaborator of his career, a slight Greek-American called Hermes Pan. Pan heard of the dance assistant's job from a dancer he met in the street one day. The arrangement was casual in the extreme. 'What assistant?' asked the commissionaire at the wide green painted gates of the RKO lot when Pan arrived. But he talked his way through, saying he was expected, and he recalled for me how he made his way to Stage 8, where he looked around somewhat puzzled as to what would happen next. He was then approached by a lightly built man, who said: 'What does Dave Gould's assistant look like?' 'That's me,' said Pan. 'Hi,' said the man, 'I'm Fred Astaire.'

[108]

On and off set, Astaire and Pan found many points of contact, and, for the film work that is most remembered, Pan was a major influence. The friendship and working partnership between the two is not surprising, for Hermes Pan, born Panagiotopulos, was a double for Fred. Son of the Greek consul to the Southern States (not quite as grand as it sounds, as he was actually an immigrant Greek who ran a candy store and restaurant in Nashville, Tennessee), Pan was eleven years younger than Astaire, born in Memphis on 10 December 1910. He too had a sister who was a dancer, and like Astaire, Hermes had picked up a few steps while Maria had danced. Also, like the Astaires, brother, sister and mother had arrived in New York with little money and a huge bundle of hope which they checked into the large and none-too-smart Eddison Hotel, just off Broadway. 'I remember we were always pretty cold and pretty hungry,' said Pan. 'When I was twelve years old, I got a job as an errand boy in a chemical laboratory.'

At fifteen he first appeared on the stage of the Astor Hotel doing some solo dances he had worked out in the corridors of the laboratories. 'They'd encourage me to give them a little show,' he said. Then followed a job at the Le Boeuf Sur La Toite speakeasy on 51st Street, wiping tables and so on till the owner, seeing a likely looking attraction, said that if he wanted to do a spot of buck and wing, he could do so – for the tips the punters might give. It was there that Hermes Pan (he had already far too much trouble with his real name to keep it for professional purposes) could be seen doing the Black Bottom and any other fancy steps of the time – a new dance step was front page news in the popular press in those bitter years.

Pan then got a job in the chorus of a show called *Top Speed*, written by songwriters Bert Kalmar and Harry Ruby and librettist Guy Bolton, who wrote the book of the Gershwins' *Lady, Be Good!* for the Astaires, and he worked alongside the *Top Speed* star Ginger Rogers, at the time making her Paramount feature *Young Man of Manhattan*. Pan, having lived on potatoes and Welfare, went on the road with his sister Maria and their mother, who cooked spaghetti along the way, just as Ann Astaire had done for Adèle and Fred. But the Pans found the travel costs were often more than they earned. Pan told Astaire the story of how in Modesto they had run out of money and had to leave their mother as security for their lodgings while they went on to the next date in Antioch, and how they had arrived stony broke in Los Angeles, dreaming of getting work in the movies. In return, Astaire told him the story of the divided hard-boiled egg and the problems he had faced along the way.

[109]

Hermes Pan's great advantage as Astaire's collaborator was that he could be stand-in, double, or anything else that was needed. As Pan had also worked with Ginger Rogers he also knew of her dancing capabilities – or lack of them. So a pattern of working began which was to stay with Astaire for the next important years: as Ginger was always zipping from film to film, Astaire would rehearse with Pan, who would take Ginger's rôle. Then Pan would go off and rehearse with Ginger wherever she was working, leaving Astaire to get on with the next routine. In later years Astaire would always be asked who was his favourite dancing partner. The truth was something he never really could admit in public, for after Adèle, Astaire's most frequent and favoured dancing partner was certainly the light-footed Greek, Hermes Pan, who worked on all the great Astaire-Rogers movies as well as on many of the Astaire films made without Ginger Rogers. Pan, paid $75 a week, more than he had ever earned before, said: 'The great different thing about Fred of course was that he was the first real perfectionist that Hollywood had ever come up against in the dancing world: they couldn't really believe it. Ginger was hardly ever available. That didn't please Fred, who always liked a lot of rehearsal. So the way we did it was this: he'd work out the steps with me – The Continental or whatever – then, having played Ginger to Fred, I would then go off, the dance all ready in my mind and then be Fred to Ginger. We'd work two or three weeks on any one dance, showing her what to do after we'd already spent a couple of weeks, Fred and I, working it out.'

The director assigned to *Flying Down to Rio* was Thornton Freeland, a thirty-five-year-old former juvenile actor who had worked with the great directors D. W. Griffith and Ernest Lubitsch. On day one Thornton Freeland obligingly drew a large chalk line on the floor of the set and told Astaire: 'Keep within these lines. If you get outside you'll be out of frame.' The first run-through was a disaster. 'Cut', called Freeland. Astaire kept dancing, concentrating on his steps, and it took a few moments for him to realize the take was finished. 'That was a hell of a lot of good work for nothing,' said Freeland. 'Didn't you hear me say "Cut"? You kept crossing the line so many times you might have been in a skipping game.' Astaire learned fast.

When he saw the results of the music and dancing Fred was quite disconsolate. He could live with his acting, but the dances – even the Carioca hip to hip, head to head routine – just did not work as he'd hoped. He went to producer Brock and put in a special request: Could he please make sure the dance sequences were cut from the final edited footage? Brock affected not to be surprised at the naïvety and innocence of the request – if the studio paid out money for something, they most definitely wanted to see it up there on the screen – but he managed to placate Astaire by telling him that the request would most certainly be passed on, and persuaded him to continue.

The problems of the new genre did not end with the filming. The sound track had to be dubbed – the mixing of the dialogue, music and sound affects all recorded separately – and then synchronised with the edited film, in the early days of film a time-consuming and difficult task.

Hermes Pan explained how he was not only Astaire's dancing partner, but also the feet of Ginger Rogers: 'Before Fred arrived everything was recorded live and put on film, but that wasn't the way that Fred wanted to work. The routines range over too large an area and there was too much external noise of dancers for us to want to use live sound – particularly with the taps. So what we'd do is go off afterwards – Ginger invariably had another film – and just using regular hard shoes – not with special taps on – we'd dub in the tap dancing sequences. Everyone said we were crazy and maybe we were. But that's the way it worked. Dancing was done on hardboard over concrete and if you get the microphone nice and close it gives a really good sound. Because Ginger was so busy she was never around when we needed to record her taps. So I did them. I'm quite light and just made sure that I danced a little lighter and kept a pretty good eye on the screen. Trying to get things into sync was hell – a beat out and Fred would run the whole thing again. We were running the music and taps on two tracks which did make things easier to work with. But you were talking about a film which would normally have say four weeks of rehearsal for everything – but Fred would spend three or four days filming one number which would make everybody mad.'

If Fred was a hard taskmaster for his partner and other dancers on the film set, then Ginger Rogers was the match for him in other ways. The kind of girl who goes places and does things, she was ambitious, determined, hardworking and just as tough in her own way. Born Virginia Katherine McMath on Sunday, 16 July 1911, in Independence, Missouri, east of Kansas City, she was the daughter of nineteen-year-old Lela Omogene Owens, one of five daughters of a Kansas builder, and her electrical engineer husband, Eddie McMath, whom she had met at a Kansas City dance school and married on her eighteenth birthday, 25 December 1909, in Salt Lake City, Utah. Virginia was their second child; the first had died at birth one year earlier, and another girl born a year later was also to die.

[111]

Lela, a tiny, dark-haired, bright and sparkly girl, had dreams of a world far outside her sleepy existence and had been working in Independence as a stenographer for a local newspaper. When McMath went to work in Ennis, Texas, the marriage broke down and Lela soon returned with the baby to her parents in Kansas. The divorce was unpleasant and on a couple of occasions McMath failed to return the baby after access visits. The courts restricted him to Sunday only visiting and contact between father and daughter became minimal; he died when Ginger, so called from her own first attempts to say Virginia, was eleven years old.

Some years before, when Ginger was five, Lela McMath, leaving the little girl with her parents, had headed for Hollywood, the movies and a new world. She had always been attracted by the glamour of showbusiness, and with her natural good looks, she was sure that she would have no trouble being 'discovered'. With her dreams she took a photograph of herself with Ginger – such a fine portrait that the Kansas photographer who took it managed to have a print, labelled Madonna and Child, hung in the Missouri State Building of Jefferson City.

Not surprisingly, Lela's plans to make some quick money and then have her daughter join her soon foundered. The producers were not all falling over themselves to discover her. She may have been the prettiest girl in Kansas, Missouri, but the competition in Hollywood was something else together. However she was bright enough to think of alternatives and she sat down with some old stories she had written and tried submitting them to various studios, eventually finding a taker for a tale called *The Honor System*. No one actually wanted the story, but Fox did buy the titles, in an age when a living could be made on the fringes of scriptwriting supplying titles at $25 a throw. Lela was delighted to sell and see the film made with her title and starring the dashing actor George Walsh, younger brother of director Raoul Walsh (who lost an eye and wore an eye patch and directed *White Heat*, later maker of *The Roaring Twenties* and other adventure movies). Thanks to contacts made through *The Honor System* she was taken on as an assistant to accompany child star Baby Marie Osborne (who later became a stand-in for Ginger Rogers in the thirties and Betty Hutton in the forties) for filming in New York, where Lela could at least afford to have Ginger join her at the Hotel Bristol on the company expenses. It was at this time that six-year-old Ginger made her screen début at Fox's Fort Lee, New Jersey, studios during the making of one of George Walsh's films, when director Burton George put her into a bit part. Lela, with mixed feelings

[112]

of jealousy and concern for the child, decided she did not want her daughter to be in movies quite that young and Ginger only appeared in a couple of scenes. Ginger's stay in New York was short-lived, as Lela planned to marry again, so the child was sent back to Kansas and, on her own account, Lela Leibrand, as she had become, headed for Washington with her new husband, a shadowy, and short-lived character, about whom little is known. There, as Sergeant Leibrand, Lela got a publicity job on *The Leatherneck*, the Marine Corps magazine, as America entered the European War in 1917.

In Washington Lela managed to exorcise her acting ambitions by appearing in uniform in a training/propaganda film called *All In A Day's Work* – it had been no trouble to pump up her qualifications for the job until it seemed as though she was one of the most experienced film makers in the States. Ginger remembered seeing the film in a Kansas cinema. 'It was so exciting seeing her on the screen in her uniform. I hadn't seen her for a long time and my grandmother said: "You can all go home now," when it was over. "No," I said, "I want to wait here for Mom"'.

For the ambitious Lela, the war and another marriage ended at the same time. Back with Ginger in Kansas it was not long before she found another admirer, insurance man John Logan Rogers, whom she married in 1919. During the seven years the marriage lasted, Rogers legally adopted Ginger and so she became Ginger Rogers. From Dallas, Texas, they moved in '21 to Cooper Street, Fort Worth, and at the age of fifteen Ginger won a local heat in a Charleston competition which led, on Saturday, 4 December 1926, to her beating a hundred finalists to become 'Charleston Champion of Texas' and win a $100 a week four-week booking on the Interstate vaudeville circuit. Lela had the bright idea of immediately signing up the two runners-up, Earl Leach and Josephine Butler, to make up an act which Lela named Ginger Rogers and her Redheads. Ginger herself was a brunette and only became fairer-haired many years later. Three years in vaudeville in the South and Mid-West ended with Ginger getting a a $350-a-week booking on the Paramount-Publix circuit when she sang, danced and gave baby talk 'recaltations about the amunals, including the Mama Nyceroserous and Papa Hippopapimu' – a twee genre popular at the time.

All the while Lela was in the background, pushy, noisy but often right when it came to working out how best to promote her daughter. It was almost inevitable that Ginger, the attractive flapper, dizzy, frisky and modern with her bobbed and curly hair would one day fall in love; it was equally inevitable that Lela would disapprove. Anyway, in 1928 Ginger married vaudeville dancer Jack Culpepper, who worked as Jack Pepper, during a three week lay-off in New Orleans. Lela, presented with the fait accompli, helped them work up an act called Ginger and Pepper which lasted for the ten months of the marriage. As a solo act once more, Ginger met orchestra leader Paul Ash and went with him to New York, where she failed to get a part in the Eddie Cantor musical comedy *Whoopee*, but did land the rôle of Babs Green in the Bert Kalmar-Harry Ruby musical comedy *Top Speed* (with chorus boy Hermes Pan making his professional Broadway début), which opened at the 46th Street Theatre on 25 December 1929. She sang the catchy 'Hot and Bothered' and was noticed by *Times* critic Brooks Atkinson, who wrote of 'an impudent young thing, Ginger Rogers, who carried youth and humour to the point where they are completely charming'. She was also spotted by a Paramount film producer, but her screen test was as unenthusiastically received as Fred Astaire's – the notes in the file on Ginger said: 'Just another Charleston dancer. She can't act, but she's cute and plump and pretty and would do all right for a flapper.' However, she did gain the contract for *Young Man of Manhattan* and the dialogue line: 'Cigarette me, big boy,' a chance she grabbed with both hands.

She already had a little experience having made shorts of her vaudeville act. She had also appeared in the three-reeler *Campus Sweethearts* with Rudy Vallee. She went straight into a starring rôle in another big show called *Girl Crazy*, produced by Alex Aarons and Vinton Freedley, turning down a part in Douglas Fairbanks' *Reaching for the Moon* to stay in New York where she would, at the age of nineteen, be earning $1000 a week from the show and another $500 from her daytime filming in the first full year of the Depression. Lela's theory was that it was wiser to stay on Broadway to build a name, to improve an offer from Hollywood. It was as *Girl Crazy* was preparing for its November 1930 opening that Aarons hit on the idea of persuading Fred Astaire, currently suffering in the abysmal *Smiles*, to give Ginger and her dance partner Allen Kearns some guidance in their dance routines. The show went well but her film career did indeed falter and she left Paramount for Pathé and then, when Pathé did not renew her contract in 1932, to First National where she made the Joe E. Brown comedies, *Hat Check Girl* and *You Said a Mouthful*.

As a newly dyed platinum blonde in Hollywood she dated director

Mervyn LeRoy who got her a small but noticeable part as Anytime Annie in *42nd Street*, 'who only said no when she did not understand the proposition', before covering her in gold coins for his own *Gold Diggers of 1933*. The *42nd Street* film helped her gain an RKO contract. When she was assigned to *Flying Down to Rio* it was purely an experiment by RKO: they had only made a profit with the last of her previous four pictures, *Professional Sweetheart*, although they had no wish to get rid of her as they had earned good money from her frequent loan-outs – after *Professional Sweetheart* she had immediately made three films at other studios.

With Ginger Rogers RKO had also by default acquired her mother. Producer, Pandof Berman, recalled his days working with Lela with some emotion: 'Lela always wanted to be involved with things, particularly Ginger's costumes. We'd plan the costume in advance of filming but Lela would work with the designer and we'd never know what monstrosity Ginger would show up in.' In a fairly futile bid to keep the energies of Lela usefully employed, she was appointed to be 'Head of New Talent' at RKO and did indeed push some new talent, such as Lucille Ball, who appeared briefly as a model in *Roberta, Top Hat*, (one line, back to camera), *Follow the Fleet* (fleetingly) and Rogers' *Stage Door*, and Jack Carson, also in *Stage Door*. But that hardly made an impact on the time she had available to promote, protect and oversee the career of her beloved Ginger. Her only distraction was an obsessive patriotism. Ginger's scripts would be carefully vetted. 'Share and share alike' was excised from Ginger's *Tender Comrade* script in 1943 as being indubitably communistic. Another actress said the line. The casts of the films were also scrutinised carefully. (Lela Rogers' shining hour came later during the heyday of the House UnAmerican Activities Committee, when she did needless harm to the careers of many performers amid the Red Threat hysteria which pervaded Hollywood.) But in 1933, both Ginger and her mother were a bit wary of the *Rio* assignment. 'I would have much preferred to be doing a straight movie,' said Ginger. 'I knew it would be good to work with Fred as he had a great reputation for being a top dancer and a top professional, but I'd heard that he was worried about going into movies. At least I did know him and we could talk about old times in New York.'

That late summer of '33 in Los Angeles seemed to disappear like lightning for Astaire with busy working days, pleasant evenings in the warm California air and early nights. Fred and Phyllis were at that time of newly married life when the warmth of their relationship was enough. Even if the filming was not a success, Fred might be able to try

[115]

again as a straight actor or go into the business side, like Alex Aarons, now a film producer, or his erstwhile partner Vinton Freedley, who was running a highly successful management company. Astaire still had to fulfil the commitment to take *Gay Divorce* to London. There were many reasons why he was excited about the trip, as it would be a proper honeymoon for them and he was looking forward to talking over his new experiences with Adèle; they had not seen each other since they both had married and he had just heard some marvellous news from Ireland: Adèle was expecting a baby in November.

Having flown out to L.A., Phyllis and Fred decided to take the train back to New York, through the mid-Western prairies. It was a trip that reminded Fred of his vaudeville days. In New York they collected Peter, then four years old, and set sail for Southampton. To Phyllis's great relief, Fred and young Peter got along fine; except for one occasion when Peter was made to pick up something he had thrown on the floor and he called Astaire: 'You old damn man'. Phyllis would use that expression herself afterwards when she wanted to tease her husband.

Adèle knew that she would probably not be able to be present for the first night herself, as her baby was due about that time and she was in no condition to make the often rough sea crossing to England. Although Adèle was living a life of leisure, the pregnancy made her irritable. 'Oh, I do wish it would hurry up,' she wrote to Fred. 'I do wish it would arrive. I'm like a pig and slow like a snail and I can't bear it any more. And I do wish Mother would hurry.' For Ann was still steaming across the Atlantic to be with Adèle when the baby was born. Adèle did not have to wait much longer. After feeling worse than usual one day, she went into early labour. In later years, given the techniques and facilities of a modern hospital, all might have been well, but there, in beautiful Lismore Castle, with doctor and midwife in attendance and her husband nearby, on Friday 8 October Adèle Cavendish's little baby daughter lived for no more than one hour. Fred was rehearsing in London when Charles Canvendish telephoned with the sad news. By the time Ann received a wire next day in mid-ocean to tell her of the tragedy, a little oak coffin was being lowered into the ground. Adèle was painfully ill, desolate at the loss and confined to her bed. Everything which had looked so rosy now seemed bleak. When Ann arrived a few days later, she took charge of everything and comforted, bullied and talked Adèle through her lowest moments.

In London, rehearsals for the show continued with Fred in sombre mood. His old friend Lee Ephraim was producing the show with Claire Luce, Eric Blore, and Erik Rhodes from Broadway to supplement an otherwise English cast, and after a successful provincial run it opened at London's Palace Theatre on Thursday 2 November. In Ireland, Adèle and her mother followed all news of Fred's progress and even heard him on the wireless on a BBC broadcast promoting the show. Reception was bad but Adèle recalled: 'I was sitting with Charlie and my mother at Lismore. Fred started to sing. He went on. Why, he was even hitting those high notes that used to scare us. It was grand – Mother and I both cried a little.'

The opening in London found Phyllis hiding in Fred's dressing room, only venturing out to see the 'Night and Day' routine, in which Claire Luce made one hesitant step as she went over a table top, knocking her hip and making Phyllis dive back into the dressing room, where she was comforted by Fred's London dresser George Griffin: 'Don't look so un'appy,' he said. 'Mr Astaire's doin' 'andsome.' When the show was over it was Phyllis's turn to console Fred: 'I'm sure no one noticed.' Although faithful first nighter, Prince George, when he heard of Fred's concern, said that he had noticed Astaire's face. He had reckoned one of the chair legs gave way a bit as they had stepped up. That day's slip had long term repercussions for Claire Luce: the crack to her hip never did fully recover and Claire put down the premature end of her dancing career to the incident. However, the critics found nothing to complain about and the show settled in for a long run.

Astaire's lack of confidence in an Adèle-less show in London had made him book the new family into the Carlton Hotel rather than find somewhere to rent, but it soon became clear that the show would run for a while, and Phyllis found a comfortable small house at 3 John Street in Mayfair which would suit them ideally. When they could put Adèle's bad news from their minds, the Astaires were as happy as sandboys, spending most of their time alone, occasionally making forays out or travelling, with Peter and his nanny in tow, off for country weekends, where there were all kinds of exciting things for a little boy to see and do, although hardly surprising for a child in his circumstances, he was not always entirely obedient. Astaire recalled the occasion they had lunch with Lord Derby's son Lord Stanley – the present Lord Derby – and Peter threw a toy locomotive at him drawing blood from the little boy's head, but doing no serious damage.

Three weeks into the London run of *Gay Divorce*, Adèle and Charles Cavendish, with Ann Astaire, travelled to see Fred. Adèle was

[117]

determined to be cheerful and she announced, not at all seriously, 'We missed Minnie's opening, so we'd better go and see the show quickly before it comes off.' But seeing the show, his first not originated with her, was a tense and nerve-racking experience for both of them. Fred had been looking forward to showing his sister his new tricks and that night everything went just right. Claire Luce and Astaire flowed immaculately over the tables several times, cheered on for encores; the 'Night and Day' routine was romantic, elegant and spellbinding. Fred was not the only one aware of Adèle's presence. When she rose in the intermission there was instantaneous applause around the theatre which she acknowledged cheerfully, for the life and times of Adèle Astaire were a source of constant fascination to the British public.

There is an old saying that Ireland is rather like a mistress, ideal to visit but not live with, and that is how Charlie and Adèle Cavendish now began to feel. There was too much sadness at the castle, so they decided that maybe it would be a good idea to spend the greater part of the year in London.

It was some weeks after Astaire had arrived in town before he even gave much of a thought to Hollywood and the movies, and then when he did think about it, it was only to hope that at least his dancing would have been removed from *Flying Down to Rio* and that his whole performance had been cut from *Dancing Lady*. Phyllis, who was discovering the way to deal with her man, said: 'There's no question about it. You'll have to take up farming.' But the very next morning he had a cablegram from RKO producer Pandro Berman, at twenty-eight the youngest of the bright Hollywood executives, which read: FLYING DOWN TO RIO COLOSSAL SUCCESS STOP OFFERING SEVEN YEAR CONTRACT STOP MAKE SURE FILM RIGHTS GAY DIVORCE STOP REPRESENTATIVE WITH NEGOTIATION RIGHTS ON THE WAY TO YOU STOP.

The only complaint, it transpired, was not that Astaire was in the picture but that he was not in it enough. The Radio City Music Hall launch of *Rio* had been an enormous success, the Carioca routine receiving rave reviews, and *Dancing Lady* was to open shortly in London – at the Leicester Square Empire where Astaire had danced the last night of *Funny Face* with Adèle. As Douglas Fairbanks Jr said to him when he had dropped into the Savoy Grill for a little post- theatre supper: 'What do you mean by revolutionising the movie industry? I've just seen *Flying Down To Rio* and you've got something absolutely new. It's terrific.'

[118]

Astaire was slightly abashed by this and mumbled a reply: 'I'm just trying to do a little dancing.'

The *Dancing Lady* story was far from over, for by the end of '33 not only had Joan Crawford at twenty-nine been restored to the first rank of movie stars but her marriage to Douglas Fairbanks had ended in divorce, and after the first of her intermittent romances with Clark Gable she had married the other *Dancing Lady* leading man, Franchot Tone.

The new year was a time for calm life in the Astaire household, barring incursions from Adèle and Charlie. Fred would meet his friends the jockeys at the Piccadilly Hotel, which was their traditional meeting place, or play some golf. Adèle socialised furiously and agreed, briefly, to be a performer again as a 'chattering lady' in a charity Pageant of Parliament being staged in June. She danced with her fan, Prince George, at the Derby Ball at Grosvenor House and caused a mild scandal at the Royal Courts of Justice when she appeared as a witness in the divorce case being brought against Tilly Losch by Edward James.

Edward James still had a sizeable part of his £1 million inheritance gained when his uncle Frank was killed by an elephant. James, poet godson of Edward VII, whose son he claimed to be, announced an impressive list of Tilly's reputed lovers, including Lord Redesdale's son Tom Mitford, Winston Churchill's son, Randolph, and Prince Serge Obolensky. The names, and the scandal of James's alleged homosexuality, made the eight-day case the *cause célèbre* of the year.

The petulant aesthete, James, who looked younger than his twenty-seven years (his wife made an unlikely claim to be just two years his senior) charged Tilly, the Viennese Jewish bank clerk's daughter earning $1,000 a week when James first saw her in *The Year of Grace*, the review presented by C. B. Cochran and written by Noël Coward, with infidelity in the back of a New York taxi cab on the way to the Empire State Building with the Russian Prince Serge Obolensky, recently divorced from Vincent Astor's daughter Alice. This charge was resolutely refuted by Tilly and many witnesses were called, including James's sister Audrey Field, the former Audrey Coats, who had been pursued by both Fred Astaire and the Prince of Wales. But Tilly's star performers were the couple who were travelling in a separate cab on the same journey: Tory MP Chips Channon, homosexual, American born, wealthy and married to brewery heiress Honor Guinness (and father of present day Tory MP Paul Channon), and Adèle Astaire.

[119]

To confuse things further, James claimed to his counsel that Channon had tried to seduce him and that Adèle could not be trusted. In conversation with the writer and singer George Melly in 1977, James said that Tilly would tell him bitchy stories about Adèle: 'She will tell you all sorts of things about me, but they are not true. She is so hot to get a man and she is unable to, so she has quickies with her stage hands. She calls them into her dressing room and they fuck her on the floor.' James also told Melly that once in New York she had got out of his Rolls-Royce on the driver's side by lifting her legs over the gear lever and deliberately letting him see up her skirt: 'I was shocked. She said to me: "Oh, hello! Did you see the ace of spades?"'.

The high farce in court began when Adèle, in the witness box, said that, as her cab had been running side by side with Tilly's for much of the journey, she thumbed her nose at Tilly – she demonstrated to the court exactly how she made the gesture. The court collapsed with laughter until the judge brought it once more under control. 'Anyway,' Adèle said, 'there's no such thing as a fifty-block kiss.' James's counsel, Norman Birkett, who was to have a glorious career ahead of him, asked Adèle whether a recently acquired sable coat had anything to do with her evidence – he had been told by James that it was a present from Tilly. 'I've always made a lot of money,' Adèle said, 'and nobody has to buy me furs.'

Tilly Losch, even with the legal expertise of the eminent King's Counsel Patrick Hastings, bizarrely paid for by James, lost the case and had to pay around £12,000 in costs. 'I have not a penny in the world,' Tilly said, after the verdict on 26 June. 'I shall keep on dancing. It is my life.'

Newspaper headlines were filled with the extraordinary twists and turns, and society had a field day of gossip even when the case ended. For despite Tilly being convinced that Adèle had lost her the case, the two women remained the best of friends through a perpetual trade in mutual slanders. When there was the upsurge in anti-Semitic feeling and Tilly, with her Austrian accent and dark looks, became an obvious target (although she had become Roman Catholic – she enjoyed the absolution after confession), Adèle, according to Tilly's Irish friend (and later executor) Billy Hamilton, would always spring to Tilly's defence, announcing: 'I hope you realise that I, too, am a Jew.' And Tilly, when anyone made unkind remarks about Adèle, would always chide those who made them.

Against all the odds and most expectations Adèle was a good, considerate and loving wife for Charlie – 'Who said that it would never last?' was the popular joke after they had been married a few months – and she was even capable of sustaining some kind of control on Charlie's drinking by keeping him busy, so that there was a genuine improvement in his habits. The Devonshire family, loyally and enthusiastically, all visited *Gay Divorce*. The imperious Duchess was warming to Adèle and, although she did not like to admit it, quite enjoyed the show. Charlie's elder brother, Edward Hartington, was delighted with his new sister-in-law and insisted that his sons, the sixteen-year-old William Cavendish, Earl of Burlington, and thirteen-year-old Andrew Cavendish, both at Eton, should see their aunt's brother performing on stage. Andrew, the present Duke, was already involved in the family passion for horse racing, which had somehow passed his father by, and was running an illegal bookmaking operation for his fellow students at Eton. He remembered going backstage. 'I was terribly impressed,' he told me, 'because Fred actually produced a racing form book from his pocket.'

10
Top Hat

Fred Astaire had always considered Hollywood essentially second-rate. He had long expressed the view to Adèle that the dancers he saw on film were made to look better than they warranted by the camera. As a professional, he was initially indifferent to seeing himself on screen and had no desire to be 'considered' by some wet-behind-the-ears Hollywood brat.

But when the run of *Gay Divorce* ended he decided he was ready to face working in the movies again, after taking a relaxing break with the Bulls at their holiday home in Aiken, South Carolina. It was at Aiken that Phyllis spotted in an Augusta newspaper that *Flying Down to Rio* was playing locally. Despite Fred's reluctance they drove along, slipped in unnoticed, and even Fred admitted that he enjoyed the film, although he was still embarrassed by the rôle. Afterwards they did not leave the cinema quite so unnoticed, as his distinctive features were spotted by a fan and autographs were eagerly sought.

When they returned to Hollywood to see what RKO had in store for him, Astaire kept a very low profile. From his position as a Broadway star he did get to meet the powerful men in the film world: he told Darryl Zanuck (a fellow Nebraskan born in Wahoo, three years younger than Astaire), who had just left Warner Bros and with Joseph Schenck had formed 20th-Century Pictures, that he didn't like *Rio*. Zanuck had been impressed by the film and would later feel great annoyance that he hadn't snapped up Astaire before RKO. Astaire told his same story of disappointment to the independent producer Samuel Goldwyn. Goldwyn had reacted quite differently to the film and, with the encouragement of his wife and business confidante Frances, immediately contacted Pandro Berman at RKO, who had just used Goldwyn's contract player David Niven for a $5,000 loan out. As a *quid pro quo*, Goldwyn offered to take 'the dancer Astaire' on the same loan-out terms. Astaire was delighted by Goldwyn's plan, grateful that someone wanted him. In his enthusiasm, what Astaire didn't know were the terms of Goldwyn's deal nor Goldwyn's sales spiel of 'I feel sorry for the guy.'

Berman was not taken in by the Goldwyn nonchalance, just further convinced that he had a winner on his hands. Having lost Errol Flynn to Warners, who had snapped him up on a seven-year contract, he had no intention of losing any other stars. Astaire said that he wanted to work with Goldwyn; Berman, in what was one of the very first deals of the kind, offered Astaire five, and, when he wavered, ten per cent of profits to carry on with RKO. For the insecure, newly-wed Astaire and Phyllis, who had quickly realised the rarity of the offer, there was little contest.

Berman also had in *Gay Divorce* something that was a proven success in the eyes of Astaire. So Berman and director Mark Sandrich (who had survived on an almost unremitting diet of short films until one of them, *So This is Harris*, won an Oscar in '33 and he was promoted to make two comedy feature movies), did their best to hurry the progress of the script for *Gay Divorce* with the Hays office. The censorious Motion Picture Producers and Distributors of America Inc, self-appointed guardians of the nation's morals, an organisation run by former Postmaster General Will H. Hays, demanded that the title be changed. The word 'gay' had no homosexual meaning in those days, it simply meant happy and lively, and the Hays objection was that the breakdown of a marriage was a serious and distressing matter that could not be talked about with such levity. Those gentlemen took themselves very seriously, but eventually they did admit a compromise: while a divorce could not be gay, the Hays office did allow that a divorcee might be gay. It seems a piffling distinction, but at the time the industry took such matters ruthlessly and so the change was made – although the title remained *The Gay Divorce* when the movie was released in Britain. Other alterations were also made, so that Fred's stage rôle as a writer became a dancer to explain his habit of breaking into a routine. And, after the success of the Carioca routine in *Rio*, RKO decided that they should create a new dance for this picture too. So The Continental was born.

The Front Office, those grey men examining the heavy ledgers of profit and loss, had decided that they would stick to the proven formula of Astaire, Rogers and a new dance step, and rejected Astaire's suggestion that his stage partner, Claire Luce, would be by far the best leading lady. Ginger Rogers was under contract, available and

[123]

obviously worked well with him, so Ginger Rogers it would be. In his memoirs Fred recounted that he was pleased when Pandro Berman told him RKO wanted Ginger to co-star with him once more, but that was just not so. If he had been at all sure of his own position at the studio he would have done everything possible to find another dancer. As far as Pandro Berman was concerned, Astaire and Rogers, 'The King and Queen of the Carioca' as they were billed in the publicity to popularise the dance, had performed well in *Rio*, making it the fifteenth most successful film in the States that year and about to earn RKO, on the verge of insolvency, $480,000. So Fred went along with what Berman suggested.

Familiar faces, Eric Blore and Erik Rhodes from the stage show, were hired – and a long-legged seventeen-year-old ingénue from St Louis, Missouri, named Betty Grable was also signed. Fred rehearsed his dances with Hermes, Hermes rehearsed them with Ginger, then Fred and Ginger danced for the cameras. The relationship between the stars was professional and businesslike with little warmth – there was neither the room, nor the time for anything else – Ginger was always called formally Miss Rogers and Astaire Mr Astaire, and they called each other that too, until Ginger shortened it to Mr A, and then she became universally called Miss R. Astaire didn't socialise with the cast because he was awkward and because he invariably had other things to do; Ginger never socialised because she usually had a new film script to learn, and anyway her mother thought stars should behave like stars and only talk to their own kind.

New music and new words were added to *Gay Divorcee* and, other than the haunting 'Night and Day', it might not have been recognised as a loose version of the stage play. But the result worked, and when *Gay Divorcee* opened in New York at Radio City Music Hall the lightness of the silly story and the delight of Astaire and Rogers' romantic dancing to Cole Porter's music, made it an immediate success.

Quite by chance RKO had established a new form of intimate, romantic comedy on the screen with the Astaire–Rogers coupling. They were keen to continue the successful formula, so set off in search of another vehicle. Although Sandrich wanted to direct the follow-up, Pandro Berman had other long-term plans for him, so William Seiter, who had already directed Ginger Rogers in three films, was assigned to the next property, *Roberta*. Sandrich, meanwhile, would be preparing a much grander production for Astaire, an original story with a score by Irving Berlin. As it transpired, Sandrich and Astaire were to work together a great deal in the next eight years. George Stevens directed *Damsel in Distress* and *Swingtime*, but all the other movies picked by Berman were directed by Sandrich, and made known a whole series of classic songs. Astaire's own views were simple: 'I was very lucky to be able to introduce such a great bunch of songs. It was nothing to do with me. Just look at those movies: Cole Porter's *Gay Divorcee*, Jerome Kern's *Roberta*, Irving Berlin's *Top Hat*, *Follow the Fleet* and *Carefree*, Jerome Kern and Dorothy Fields' *Swing Time*, George and Ira Gershwin's *Shall We Dance?* and *Damsel in Distress*. I couldn't miss.'

The third RKO production, *Roberta*, was important for many reasons, not least because it was the first movie in which Hermes Pan was properly credited as dance director. Astaire was gaining in confidence each day and the figures from *Gay Divorcee* were looking good – the gross would eventually reach $1,774,000 with profits of $584,000 – and so the front office were happy to allow Astaire to develop his own shooting plan. The Astaire system was established like this: firstly, he would prepare and shoot four or five of the most difficult or complex dance numbers: if the ideas did not work then they would be rethought during the progress of the picture, they could then reshoot at the end. His own solos would be left until last so that there would be plenty of pressure-free time to get them just right. Then would come the overdubbing of the taps with Hermes Pan.

Roberta was based on the eponymous Broadway musical written by Otto Harbach, and Astaire would take the best-friend rôle that had been created by Bob Hope on stage. The film was created for the Broadway musical star, Irene Dunne. The other leading players were Astaire, Rogers and Randolph Scott, a one-time engineering student who had become an actor after meeting RKO owner and tycoon Howard Hughes on a golf course six years previously. The story and music were freely adapted and the resulting mélange included the songs 'I Won't Dance' (from a Kern flop), 'Smoke Gets in your Eyes' and 'I'll be Hard to Handle'. 'Lovely to Look At' was the only new song. The film is not often seen, but in it, for the first time, Astaire arranged that the dance sequences would be shot to his own specifications, with several cameras shooting one dance from different angles and a whole sequence shot in one take, so that after editing there would be a continuity of movement on film. Previously the majority of directors had furiously cut to close-ups of faces, feet or audience to give the feeling of action and frantic business. Astaire wanted the dancers to provide that excitement themselves – and he made another request that

[125]

was considered eccentric in the extreme: he wanted the bodies of himself and his partner to be filmed in long shot, so that both heads and feet would be in the same frame. Unusually, this meant there were only one or two cuts in a long sequence. What was more, Astaire often suggested his own sartorial variations, such as the black and white co-respondent shoes and the ties and scarves he used to hold up his trousers.

In Astaire's vaudeville days he had been keen to acquire Irving Berlin songs, so the prospect of having a whole film written by Berlin especially for him was a delightful one. Berlin was also a particularly fortuitous choice as he not only wrote marvellous music, he understood the film musical genre (his 1926 song 'Blue Skies' had been a great success for Al Jolson in *The Jazz Singer* in 1927) and he knew Astaire's work from the days he had sung Berlin's 'I Love to Quarrel With You' and 'I've Got a Sweet Tooth'. There was a limited vocal ability, but a tremendous strength in actually putting the songs across. So when the assignment had come up, Berlin had been quite happy to leave the New York offices of his Waterson, Berlin and Snyder music publishing company and move out to the West Coast to be composer in residence. He took along with him what he called his 'Buick', an oversized upright piano with a special mechanism for shifting the keyboard and transposing his melodies into any key, for Irving Berlin had taught himself to play the piano in only one key: the key of F-sharp, which includes all the black notes on the keyboard. Ever since his first big hit in 1911 with 'Alexander's Ragtime Band', Berlin had been supreme among American songwriters, so it was a coup to have him along.

The elaborate romantic misunderstandings that were one of the key-notes of the Astaire movies were scripted by Dwight Taylor, who wrote the Broadway play on which *Gay Divorcee* was based, and many of the romantic complications of *Top Hat*. Astaire, at the age of thirty-six, was less than pleased at being cast as a juvenile, 'A rather cocky and arrogant one at that,' he said. As ideas were still being discussed, Astaire had told Sandrich and Berlin about his 'Young Man of Manhattan' shooting and tap routine that he had used in *Smiles*; it was a good idea and he was convinced that so few people had seen the disastrous show that no one would complain about the routine not being original. It was a few days later that Berlin asked Astaire to stop by after filming to listen to a song he had written which might fit the routine. So there, in a side room of Stage 8, Sandrich and Astaire listened for the first time as Berlin, with his slightly throaty, soft voice

[126]

sang the lyric: 'I just got an invitation through the mails, your presence requested, this evening, it's formal, top hat, white tie and tails . . .' and *Top Hat*, the song and the film, was born.

The final item to be settled before filming as far as Astaire was concerned was the matter of his leading lady, although the decision had long since been made by others. Pan Berman realised that the obvious choice was Ginger Rogers. So had Sandrich. One person was not happy with the choice: Fred Astaire himself. Hermes Pan, choreographer on all ten of the RKO series of Astaire-Rogers films, told me: 'It was the Twenty-five Years' War. It wasn't an outright battle, but a clash of personalities and careers. Fred always wanted to rehearse some more, however long he had been going, Ginger wanted to prove herself as a serious actress. And of course Fred didn't want to be totally tied to any one partner.' Pandro Berman was quite unprepared for Astaire's initial reaction to Ginger Rogers's name and said: 'I'll never forget how horrified Fred was when I notified him that Ginger was going to play the part of the titled English lady in the *Gay Divorcee*. But there was resistance of that sort on every picture I proposed. They just didn't want to work together.' And in a masterpiece of understatement Ginger admitted the tensions too: 'Fred was a hard taskmaster, a perfectionist. He always got a little cross with me because my concentration was not as dedicated to the projects as his was. So there were times of stress. Off screen we had little in common. We never travelled in the same clique. I belonged to the tennis group and he belonged to the golf group and never the twain shall meet.'

If Fred gave in fairly gracefully on *The Gay Divorcee*, as the years and films passed he became increasingly concerned and even petulant about the continuation of the partnership. The gist of his complaint he explained: 'Ginger had never danced with a partner before. She faked it an awful lot. She couldn't tap and she couldn't do this and that. Most people didn't put the taps in themselves, but I used to do it because . . . I wanted to kill myself, I guess. But Ginger had style and talent and improved as she went along. She got so that after a while everyone else who danced with me looked wrong.' He hated it when they were referred to as 'a team'. 'Huh, that makes us sound like a couple of horses,' he said at the time, with ill-disguised distaste. 'Miss Rogers and I are not a team. She has her own career as an actress, we just happen to have made some films together.' Angry letters were sent more than once by Astaire to Berman refusing to work with Rogers, as he called her, one more time. Each time a combination of cajoling, flattery, persuasion and money were used to make him change his mind. With *Top Hat*, which made profits of $1,325,000, both Astaire and Rogers were given $150,000 and a ten per cent share of the profits. But each film became an increasingly bitter source of negotiation long before anyone got on to a set.

As a consolation, Fred was promised eight weeks rehearsal, rather than the more usual four weeks. To make sure that *Top Hat* was right, Astaire would work on an empty stage with Pan until all hours. 'Often we wouldn't leave until 2 a.m. or so and then we'd be back again first thing in the morning,' said Pan. It was trial, sweat and sheer hard work that slowly developed into a cohesive entity. Sandrich said that he used Astaire's one-take philosophy as much as possible, but it did have to be modified for practical purposes as one perfect take could take weeks of shooting. 'We went to huge lengths to make the "Top Hat" number look like one take,' Sandrich said, 'but actually it's several.'

The solos were one thing, but dancing with partners in films produced all kinds of problems for Astaire, particularly in the dress that his partners wore. For stagework the element of design insists that the stage wear both looks right and is convenient to work in. For film the comfort of the performer is less important. What is important is that the costumes photograph well and also that the actor or actress will look good in it for the few minutes of film time needed. The feather tornado of *Top Hat* demonstrated the problems that arise: for the song 'Cheek to Cheek', Astaire created a flowing, gentle, romantic dance that was shaping up well in rehearsals with Hermes Pan, and Fred had inspected the fairly full dress Ginger was going to wear. ('They asked me to describe the dress of my dreams,' she said, 'and this was it.') The dress was not ready for rehearsals, and on the day shooting started an hour late while Ginger was fitted into the elaborate creation, trimmed with masses of blue feathers. 'All right, we'll do one run-through first,' said Sandrich. The music started, the song went well –

'Heaven, I'm in heaven, . . .'

– but as soon as the dance started it was far from heaven and, literally, feathers started to fly, firstly gently and then with a vengeance. 'It was like a chicken attacked by a coyote,' said Astaire, 'I never saw so many feathers in my life. I had feathers in my eyes, my ears, my mouth, all over the front of my suit.' The wardrobe lady was quick with her insistence that once the first flush of feathers had flown the dress would stay in one piece, so Sandrich said that they had better go for a take to snatch a print if they could. But as the song went on into the dance routine feathers began to fly once more. The cameramen stopped shooting: 'We just can't see a thing.' There were feathers on the lens, feathers in the air and feathers littering the floor. Phyllis was on the set that day with David Niven and began to giggle: 'She looks just like a wooster, but I think we'd better leave.' Still the feathers kept flying and late in the afternoon Fred threw up his hands. He was white with anger. He yelled at Ginger. She burst into tears, and Lela came charging at him like a mother rhinoceros protecting her young. After a lot of hollering Astaire retired to one side of the sound stage and Ginger and Lela settled down on the other. 'It was my dream dress and they were trying to take it away from me,' said Ginger. 'Mother said: "What's the matter with everybody? That's a beautiful dresss. I'll tell you what, if they don't like it, why don't you tell them to get a new girl?"' A stony silence descended. Finally the designer agreed to spend all night sewing each feather into place and on the third day, though a few feathers still flew, they were able to shoot the dance. Take after take and the major feather fall-out seemed to have subsided. Astaire's anger had subsided. Ginger's frustration had calmed down and a small crowd of spectators had gathered from nearby sets when they heard of the blizzard. At the end of the day Hermes Pan and Astaire sat down, firmly. They would just have to see how it looked in the rushes in the morning. But eventually Pan and Astaire began to laugh. 'What a hell of a day that was,' said Astaire and between them they worked out a little ditty. 'To stop us from going quite crazy,' as Pan explained. They did not realize that they would sing this song many times in the next years: to the tune of 'Cheek to Cheek', it ran:

> Feathers – I hate feathers
> And I hate them so that I can hardly speak
> And I never find the happiness I seek
> With those chicken feathers dancing
> Cheek to cheek.

The fiasco had also revived another unfortunate memory for Astaire of the 'Twit, twit, twit' number he and Adèle had hated so much in *The Passing Show of 1918*. Next morning Astaire sat down for the rushes. They ran the film. The first take was fine. 'Let's see it again,' said Sandrich. They all watched carefully, even Astaire could not see anything too wrong with it. They ran through the other takes, then stopped. The first was universally agreed the best.

Thereafter Astaire often referred to Ginger as 'Feathers'. But the near disaster actually helped to bring Astaire and Rogers closer than they had been previously, as though they had survived a close-run vaudeville routine. To put the seal on the occasion, Astaire ordered from Cartier a small golden feather to give to Ginger as a peace token. (Even on the final print there are feathers on the floor. Producer Berman remembered that scene as not being unique: 'He always fought about Ginger's clothes. Whenever Fred came to me to register a complaint about her appalling taste in gowns her mother would jump into the fray and we'd have a real Donnybrook.')

Astaire often complained about his partners. 'All girls try to add to their costume at the last minute.' His particular hates were bangles and sequins, lead weights in sleeves, or four-inch stiletto heels that not only made his partner tower, but would also leave him with lacerated and bleeding shins.

Astaire hated to be watched by people when he was preparing a dance; but there was one visitor he happily welcomed: Lady Charles Cavendish. She came out with her husband to see what Hollywood was all about. When she landed in America she was eagerly quizzed by reporters about her own plans: when would she make a picture with her brother? Indeed RKO suggested that she and Fred could make *Lady, Be Good!* – this was one partner he could certainly not object to – but Adèle had seen what he had been doing on screen and remembered painfully the *Funny Face* test they had made together. Although she gave placatory answers she realised full well that no way could she, rising thirty-eight, keep up with what her brother was then doing. RKO even started developing a script based on *Lady, Be Good!* but Adèle had one good reason to decline the offer: she was pregnant.

Top Hat was to be the saviour of RKO. With rentals of over $3 million, it would not be overtaken in that decade by any other RKO product and by the end of the year it was the second largest grossing film in the world.

Astaire said: 'We were making movies that we hoped many people would see. Certainly many more than ever saw the stage shows I had done, but it never for one second occurred to me that anyone would be watching the movies after a year.'

Screen writer and director Garson Kanin, who would later direct Ginger in *Bachelor Mother*, remembered that first night of *Top Hat*: 'Never before and never since have I seen an audience stand up and cheer at the end of a picture. A standing ovation for a movie? I sat

[130]

through the picture twice and that evening insisted on going again and taking my brother with me. Twice for him too, which meant four times that day for me. The next evening I was back again.' Garson Kanin was not alone in his reaction and the audiences queued and queued to see *Top Hat*.

Putting aside Astaire's objections – and it is easy to understand his concern about rehearsals when Ginger had sandwiched the making of *Top Hat* between *Star of Midnight* and *In Person* just afterwards – Astaire and Rogers did look marvellous together, and just as fast as fallacious stories suggesting a very close relationship appeared in the fan magazines, so did stories of their disagreements. Astaire remembered: 'I never went to her and said "Grrr", and she never came to me and said "Grrr". I don't remember it as mutual aggression. I spoke to Ginger about that and she didn't understand it at all. Honest to God. Maybe Ginger and I did argue about a step or something, but I don't know anyone who doesn't argue about anything – except for Audrey Hepburn.'

When filming had finished on *Top Hat*, there was time for Phyllis and Fred to have a breather before he started work on the next movie. *Follow the Fleet* was chosen as a follow-up, with an apposite theme around the Navy – the increasing German armaments build up in Europe meant that the military was once more a major source of interest – and another Irving Berlin score. Astaire's rôle, as an ordinary 'gob' seaman, would be a striking contrast to his former screen rôles.

Astaire was by now aware that the profit forecast of *Top Hat* meant that RKO were determined to cast him with Ginger Rogers. Again Ginger's dress caused problems. For the number 'Let's Face the Music and Dance', Ginger wore a gown with heavy beaded sleeves which hung down from the wrist, so that every time she did a quick turn the sleeves would whirl around, requiring Astaire to take evasive action. He reckoned he had the problem beat when the cameras began to roll as planned to shoot the four-minute dance sequence with no cuts. For fifteen seconds everything was fine, then Ginger gave an unexpected twist and a couple of pounds of beaded sleeve whipped across Astaire's face. He kept on dancing, and at the end of what seemed to him like half an hour the take was over. 'How was it for you?' asked Sandrich. 'It was all right for me. Fred, how about you?' asked Ginger. Astaire said he could not remember a thing – he had been knocked out in the first round. Astaire ducked and weaved, but it was twenty takes later and eight o'clock in the evening before they decided to give it a break.

[131]

Almost inevitably the next day they chose the first take, and for Astaire there was a growing, if grudging, respect for Ginger's ability on camera.

Hermes Pan recalled one occasion when Astaire and Rogers had filmed forty-seven takes of a dance routine. Rogers never complained, despite the fact that she had had to endure many hours longer in make-up each day, while Astaire had to change his underwear and shirts two, three or more times a day, sodden after the energetic routine under blazing arc lights. Even Astaire was quite horrified when he realised afterwards what she had been through, but he was just trying for the best results and he expected others to keep up with him. 'She had guts,' he said of Ginger, from him a great compliment indeed. But as Berman said of Ginger's bleeding feet: 'They just worked so hard. But you're right, we would have had trouble if we had worked animals as hard as that.'

But not even Hermes Pan, the trusted and faithful sidekick, could encourage Astaire to take physical risks: 'You couldn't just suggest something to him. You had to win his respect. Work on him. In the number where he dances over chairs, when first I suggested doing that – there happened to be a chair on the stage at the time and I thought it might be a good idea – Fred was quite afraid of it. "Hey, I'll hurt myself or break an ankle or something," he said. By then I knew how to deal with this, so I just said to him: "Okay, okay. We'll do something else". Then when I knew that he was watching a little later I danced onto the chair, put my foot on the back and let it fall over. He was kinda impressed. I'd sneak up on him, then he was quite fine and couldn't do it enough: that tells you quite a lot about Fred, I guess.'

Ginger Rogers was the original trouper, hard-working and tough. If she found she could not keep up with Astaire she was quite capable of faking the action so brilliantly that it was only Astaire himself, Hermes Pan and the director who would really notice. 'We were only together for a part of my career and for every film we did, I did another three on my own. The studio was working me too hard. Fred would rush off for a holiday and call me and say: "Hey, ready to do another?" And I didn't have the sense to say that I was too tired. Those times were murder for me. Oh, I adored Mr A but all the hard work . . . the 5 a.m. calls, the months of non-stop dancing, singing and acting. We just worked it out and had a lot of fun and got very exhausted. And Mr A was quite divine.'

Ginger was, like her mother, a Christian Scientist who believed that illness was in the mind. She was committed to a regimen of clean living:

[132]

no smoking, no drinking, early to bed, lots of tennis and swimming, some fishing and plenty of landscape painting, along with her work for the church – soliciting new members, fund-raising and so on. By her own admission her strongest quality was always her straightforwardness. 'I hate pussyfooting around. I like to be straight from the shoulder with others as I like people to be straight with me. That can make problems, but it is the best in the long run.' Certainly her private life did not involve any pussyfooting, for the one weakness that Ginger did suffer was falling in love. In November 1934 she had married her second husband, actor Lew Ayres, attended by her friend Janet Gaynor, winner of the first ever Oscar for Best Actress, and Ben Alexander, Ayres' co-star in *All Quiet on the Western Front.* Two years later, to the ill-disguised approbation of her mother, they separated and Ginger and Lela – GeeGee and LeeLee to each other – were living together in a mansion on Beverley Crest Drive in Coldwater Canyon, complete with a drug store soda fountain bar and interior arranged by the Astaire-Rogers Big White Set designer Van Nest Polglase. Here Ginger would be visited by her many admirers, including Howard Hughes, Jimmy Stewart and Cary Grant through to Alfred Gwynne Vanderbilt, who even co-hosted a roller skating party with her.

While Ginger socialised away from the cameras, Fred continued to entertain himself at the local racetrack. The Cash Astaire betting systems did not always work, but there was always a new way that would guarantee prosperity and ensure that he wouldn't have to work his way through exhausting dance routines ever again. One system was to back every horse ante-post in the big Santa Anita races – placing the bets some weeks before: if the horse won the odds were good; if it did not run the stake money was lost. He would spend long evenings poring over the form books at his house to get this just right. He was a frequent but not heavy gambler. In 1938 he was $1 up, the next year $400 down.

Many systems were also composed on his film sets with George Griffin. Astaire had brought George out to Hollywood when he was sure that he was going to stay for a few years. Griffin's telegram of acceptance read: YES SIR STOP I WILL LEAVE AT ONCE STOP DIDN'T KNOW YOU WERE IN BEVERLY ILLS THOUGHT YOU WERE IN OLLYWOOD STOP GEORGE. One of the systems that Griffin devised involved counting the number of letters in the name of the last horse in a race card, then counting up that number of horses and choosing that one. 'They even used to win sometimes,' said Astaire. There was a clique of horse race fans at the studios and Astaire, along with Bing Crosby, was one of the original investors in the new Del Mar Turf Club track – 'Where The Surf Meets The Turf' – just outside Los Angeles, and he became a regular attender. The California tracks were also home from home for many of his East Coast friends: Jock Whitney had horses that came out, as did Alfred Gwynne Vanderbilt.

When Astaire had arrived in California he was no wet-behind-the-ears neophyte but already thirty-four years old and a big Broadway star. He was now married and, without Adèle's influence, had settled down. These changes had some immediate effects. 'I suddenly found I didn't want to go out to nightclubs and private parties any more,' he said. 'I'd done all that.' His worst fault, by his own admission, remained that he took his work so seriously. 'I sometimes make myself miserable worrying about it,' he said. 'But I can't help it. I get so wrapped up in it that I probably give the impression of being in a daze, when I don't mean to be.' What that meant in practical terms was that after long days at the studios, where Phyllis would often sit knitting quietly in a corner, they would drive home together to the rented house on North Alpine Drive, have a light supper and be in bed by 10 p.m., ready for another dawn start the next day.

It was not only Astaire's single-mindedness that ensured his success. One of the reasons for the excellence of the scores was the intense rivalry which existed between the composers. Gershwin, often a slow writer (although he always kept an unpublished waltz up his sleeve so that he could instantly 'compose' it for any pretty girl), announced in public that Jerome Kern, writer of *Show Boat* and many light operettas, was a hopeless choice to write *Swing Time* for Astaire. On the grapevine Kern heard this and produced the Oscar winning 'The Way You Look Tonight'. Cole Porter, who wrote *Gay Divorce*, *You'll Never Get Rich* and *Silk Stockings*, would complain that he was having trouble in later life writing lyrics. 'Why don't you use a collaborator?' suggested Astaire. 'I couldn't possibly,' agonised Cole, 'I want to do it all myself.'

[134]

11
Hollywood years

As soon as it looked as though they were going to be staying in Hollywood, Phyllis started to look at real estate, but she was unimpressed by the impractical and garish kaleidoscope of styles she found in the Hollywood and Beverly Hills sprawl of green-verged suburbs. She would, she decided, find a site somewhere so that they could build exactly what they wanted.

Inevitably, Fred was wooed by various studio heads who were eager to sign him from RKO and he and Phyllis were more than aware that mixing with these men could do his career no harm, and so Sam Goldwyn and his former Broadway actress wife Frances Howard became friends.

Through Goldwyn Astaire met the other studio heads, and it was at Sam Goldwyn's beach house in his first Hollywood summer that he heard the newly elected President Franklin D. Roosevelt deliver his Forgotten Man fireside speech on the radio – although the blue ocean at Malibu is far from mid-West hearths. The company there that day was the kind Astaire had become used to: Joe Schenck, United Artists' chairman, actor Charlie Chaplin, CBS founder Bill Paley, and Phyllis. And from New York, Bob Benchley, Jock and Liz Whitney.

Whitney had been persuaded to invest in the new Technicolor process. With his cousin Sonny Whitney and David Selznick, he had formed the Selznick International Pictures company. It was Jock in fact who paid the $50,000 for the pre-publication rights to Margaret Mitchell's *Gone with the Wind* (at the time far more than had ever been paid for the screen rights to any novel) and Jock who battled with the Hays Office to retain Rhett Butler's famous 'Frankly, my dear, I don't give a damn'. Liz Whitney was one of the thirty-one actresses who screen tested for the rôle of Scarlett O'Hara – and it was not solely because she was the backer's wife: she was certainly beautiful and wilful enough for the rôle. But she recalled: 'I guess he only really wanted to bed me.'

Astaire did not simply select his friends from high society. He remained close to his alter ego Hermes Pan, nicknamed The Little Bear by Liz Whitney, and also began a lifelong friendship with the tall, gentlemanly Englishman David Niven, just signed to Sam Goldwyn on a low-money seven-year contract. 'I joined the Hollywood Cricket Club,' said Niven, 'that way I got to meet all the ex-pats. I was playing tennis on a very hot day when my host said that the dancer Fred Astaire had just moved into the house next door, so as I'd met Adèle in London, I thought that I ought to say hello. I wasn't the dancing type, but I felt that if I got to meet anyone connected with the film industry in any way, that sooner or later I must end up by getting a job.' Niven went to knock on the Astaires' door, which was opened by Phyllis, and immediately shut in his face. 'There's a dweadful man at the front door without a shirt on who says he knows your sister,' called out Phyllis.

'It was a very hot day and a hard game I'd been playing,' Niven later apologised.

David Niven was a very social animal and claimed that it was through him that Astaire became friendly with MGM vice president Irving Thalberg and his actress wife Norma Shearer. Thalberg, the same age as Astaire, was a different breed of Hollywood producer to the ones that Fred had known previously; he believed in the bottom line of the balance sheet rather than the extravagant producer's credit, and it was at Thalberg's house on a Sunday night that Astaire could see advance copies of the latest releases along with Gary Cooper, Claudette Colbert, Niven himself, Douglas and Sylvia Fairbanks and Charlie Chaplin and his 'wife' Paulette Goddard (they were never actually married, although they openly lived together as man and wife).

Another man with whom Astaire found an instant affinity was Randolph Scott, his *Roberta* and *Follow the Fleet* co-star, the tall and rugged one-time engineering student from Orange County, Virginia, who had lied about his age at fourteen to serve in the 1914 War. Scott played a good game of golf, and had an easy-going professionalism that Fred admired. Together they fished for marlin off the Mexican coast and played poker in Hollywood.

Henry and Maud Bull soon became far more than guardians to Phyllis, with the shared interest in golf and horseracing, they became like members of the family, and it was not long before they left their East Coast base and moved to California to be near Phyllis and Fred: a cosy foursome who did everything together.

Phyllis, however, was the most important person in Astaire's life, he would hardly take a decision without her acquiescence and he sought her guidance on every sort of subject. His old girl friends from New York – even Liz Whitney – were actively discouraged from visiting and actresses were totally out of bounds. There was probably no need for it, but she protected him, looked after him and made sure he was cosseted from the outside world so that he could concentrate on his work. Despite Astaire's huge earnings for the time – several hundred thousands of dollars a year, a vast amount in the 1930s, although even he never knew exactly how much – he was surprisingly unsophisticated about money matters. 'I will look after your accounts,' Phyllis announced. 'I may not know anything about show business, but I have learned to read a balance sheet.' So in huge ledgers Phyllis would enter earnings, expenditure, tax liabilities and profits. Astaire never looked at them: as long as Phyllis said that things were okay that was fine by him.

The Astaires took a well-earned break in Ireland with Adèle and Charlie before moving on to London. They loved the castle, the people and the luxurious greenery of Lismore and most of all, they were relieved that Adèle's pregnancy had not suffered any complications. She seemed to be taking care of herself and leading a calmer life.

In London, Phyllis had some momentous news for her husband. 'Fweddie,' she said, 'I went to see the doctor this morning and he says I'm going to have a baby.' 'Let's celebrate,' he said, and solemnly pulled the cord to summon room service: 'Could we please have a half bottle of champagne and two glasses?' he asked.

Back in California, Astaire reflected how everything was perfectly organized. He would become an uncle and a father within weeks of each other.

Adèle was happy to see how content Freddie was with his bride and little stepson. She had a close-up view of the work and life of the Hollywood film stars and had satisfied herself that there was nothing there that she craved any more. In fact Charlie had been the one who had entered the Los Angeles cocktail circus with most enthusiasm, but even he had told Adèle that he reckoned the novelty would pall pretty quickly. The doctor reckoned that Adèle was going to have twins, so she was doubly pleased – maybe this would make up for the last disappointment. She was convinced that at least one of them was a boy.

In October she once more gave birth prematurely, to two perfectly formed stillborn twin boys. Prayers for the souls of the infants were said in St Carthage's cathedral in Lismore, at the Roman Catholic church in

[137]

Lismore and at the Cistercian Abbey at Mount Mellerary just a few miles distant. The Cavendishes were at the centre of life in Lismore, so their grief was everyone's. A profound sadness enveloped the small town as the soft muffled clanging of the church bells tolled their lament. At St Carthage's, a few feet from the small grave of the infant girl born just two years beforehand, two more small graves were dug and the caskets with the bodies of the little boys were lowered into the ground.

Adèle wrote a long letter to Fred. 'I told him that he mustn't worry about Phyllis,' Adèle said. 'It was quite different for her anyway. She had already had one healthy child and according to the doctors in those days I was terminally old to be having a baby, so it was not surprising that I had complications.'

Normally it was Fred who was the early riser. But on the morning of Tuesday 21 January 1936 it was Phyllis who hustled Fred up: 'I think we'd better get down to the hospital.' Astaire had wanted her to go earlier, but she had refused, determined not to go one second earlier than necessary.

There was a mad dash down Wilshire Boulevard with Fred at the wheel. Half an hour after their arrival at the Good Samaritan Hospital, Phyllis was delivered of a healthy baby boy, Fred Jr. Astaire was booked into an adjoining room at the hospital, and joked: 'I made a remarkable recovery.' He was kept busy at Phyllis's insistence – she would send him out to the Santa Anita racecourse, and in the evenings Irving Berlin would pop in for a game or two of gin rummy which often lasted long into the night.

Astaire confessed he was surprised at how well he had adapted to marriage. He still had some of his bachelor habits, like keeping his pocket watches and clocks running ten minutes fast to make sure that he was never late, he still went around the house turning off lights that were not needed, and he was obsessively tidy. The only point of contention was when he started to practise putting in the bedroom, but Phyllis quickly persuaded him to abandon that practice.

In Ireland Adèle's friends rallied round, and she dropped the idea, more in jest than earnest, that maybe she ought to go back to work. The word soon got around, and Jack Buchanan who had in recent years also acted as his own film producer, got in touch. Buchanan remembered: 'Of course I had seen Adèle on stage with Fred and I knew she was a very bright actress.'

His next film project as producer and performer was to be *Break the News*, from a French novel about a couple of song and dance men, played by himself and Maurice Chevalier, and he offered Adèle a rôle as the star the two men fight over. It was intended to have one small dancing number – expanded in the finished film. Buchanan's French director, René Clair, was enthused by the idea and so was Adèle. Her letters to the States became more frequent with her increased activity in Britain. The film wasn't the only news from Adèle. She also had all the latest London gossip. When King George V died on Sunday 26 January 1936, he was automatically succeeded by his eldest son, the Astaires' friend, the Prince of Wales. But the Prince was never to be crowned, for in the background lurked Mrs Wallis Simpson, already twice-married and about to be divorced for the second time. The newspapers, under the controlling hand of the Daily Express proprietor Lord Beaverbrook and Daily Mail owner Esmond Harmsworth, Lord Rothermere's son, exercised extraordinary self-censorship, and never once mentioned the affair. The foreign newspapers had no such hesitation, and neither did Adèle who reliably informed her friends that Mrs Simpson was 'the only one who could make the Prince get it up'.

The battle between church, state, King and Mrs Simpson was finally resolved on Friday 11 December 1936 when Edward VIII, as the Prince now was, did the absolutely unthinkable thing and abdicated. The country and the world was divided for many years as to the rights and wrongs of his actions but the person most affected was the Astaire's friend Bertie, Prince Albert, Duke of York, now suddenly and unwillingly created King George VI.

The Duke of Windsor left England on HMS Fury for Austria via France, and a life of exile with Wallis Simpson, to marry in France on Thursday 3 June 1937, with Wallis dressed in a blue crêpe dress by Mainbocher, designer of Adèle's trousseau.

Adèle's filming of *Break the News* started well. Then suddenly, after seeing the second day's rushes, Adèle got cold feet. She said: 'I saw my face on screen in close-up and suddenly thought, "Good heavens, I look as though I'm a hundred years old" . . . I felt it was not the right part for me. It really was a straight part and I didn't like the idea of not having dancing and singing to do. Then I thought of my brother Fred and how disappointed he would be, I reckoned, if he saw it. I thought of the stage audiences who remembered me and the young people who have never seen me – and I imagined them saying: So that was what she was like. I felt I couldn't go on with the part.'

She agonised over the decision but ultimately decided it was best to make the break cleanly and early. Jack Buchanan, as one dancer to

[139]

another, was understanding and refused point blank Adèle's offer of cash to cover the inconvenience she had caused. He later said: 'I wish I could have worked with Adèle but it was not to be, but I did get a chance later to work with Fred.' And Adèle commented afterwards: 'I am not like Freddie, the theatrical tradition and showbusiness wasn't bred in me. For me it was an acquired taste – like olives. And I should have known that I'd had enough.' June Knight stepped into the role.

Back in Lismore, Adèle put show business out of her mind. She had already made some improvements when she first arrived: 'There were two hundred rooms and one bathroom,' she complained. She installed bathrooms in the dressing rooms of the main bedrooms and American equipment into the kitchen to the astonishment and admiration of the Irish. Now she went around the estate seeing where more improvements could be made, to cut costs and make the land more productive.

And from a distance of several thousand miles she acted as a one woman cheerleader for Astaire. BEST EVER she cabled him when *Swing Time* was released. Fred was both pleased and amused to receive the cable. She had sent exactly the same one for *Follow the Fleet, Top Hat, Roberta, Gay Divorcee, Flying down to Rio* and *Dancing Lady*.

She also kept an eye on what other people said about her brother and his dancing. When *Swing Time* opened in Ireland she sent him a cutting from the *Cork Examiner*, writing across the top of the page: 'Must send you this as it is the only unfavourable one by some sour-puss': 'The Singing and Dancing Limit. Ginger and Fred are at it again in *Swing Time*, singing and dancing like anything. One begins to wonder how many more of that type of film the public is prepared to enjoy. I know of at least one member of it who has reached his limit.' When Fred showed Phyllis the cutting her dismissive response was: 'What a dwedful man.' But Fred could not help agreeing that maybe the *Cork Examiner* critic, sitting in his office with clay pipe in his mouth and his Irish blackthorn shillelagh cudgel on his desk, might have a point.

With Charlie, Adèle had other problems. As she bustled around the estate or socialised in England, so her husband was taking increasingly to the bottle. There was a long history of alcoholism in the Cavendish family and Charlie seemed determined to succumb to the demon drink. He went for cures to be dried out, not once, but several times. Each time he would come back fit and vowing to be a new man. But it never lasted long. 'I really don't mind the cures,' he used to say. 'It means that I can drink more afterwards.'

In the evenings, or during the day, Charlie would take himself off to

[140]

Dungarvon, some eight miles away, to the bar run by the Widow Feeney. Adèle would good naturedly go along later to haul him back. 'You see,' Charlie would explain, 'there is really no fun in drinking at home. It's much better to go out to a bar for it.' In the main street of the sleepy, easy-going town of Lismore, where the world seems to have been set to run at half-speed, the population of only a few hundred had – and still have – two churches, the Church of Ireland cathedral and the Roman Catholic church, a couple of grocers and general stores, a shoe shop, a butcher and well over a dozen bars. It would seem that almost anyone with a frontage on the main street would open up as a publican, selling heady black Guinness or Irish whiskey and poteen. The company was good, the talk rich and heady, and the peat fires seductively cosy.

To fill his days Charlie would play golf on the nine-hole Lismore course and follow his small stable of jumpers in the straw Devonshire colours, at Punchestown or Tramore races. It was after the Tramore races that Adèle started a tradition of a huge annual party at Lismore in the evening. It was always a grand affair and the castle staff made sure that it went with a swing, but there was often the volatile behaviour of Adèle to cope with. When Charlie's father, Duke Victor, and the Bishop of Waterford came one particular year, Charlie begged Adèle not to be late and also to behave herself and modify her sometimes frank language in front of the Man of God. This was tempting providence, and Adèle, too far.

At 8.30 the guests began to arrive in the Great Hall, but of the hostess there was no sign. Charlie tried to entertain the Bishop as best he could, mainly by offering him more and more drink. By 9.30 Adèle at last appeared at the top of the stairs in a stunning emerald green dress – unusual for her, as she did not normally wear green – looking ravishing, the dress perfectly setting off her raven hair. An Irish neighbour, William Hamilton, recalled how Charlie went to the foot of the stairs in anguish. 'Darling, how could you?' he said. 'I did beg you to be on time . . .' From halfway down the stairs, where she had paused dramatically, she said, 'Oh Charlie, please don't be like that.' She descended a few more steps and added: 'I've only been thinking of you: I've been clipping my bush into a heart shape.'

The effect was electric. Charlie quickly found the Bishop another drink, the other guests hastily started talking among themselves. But within a matter of minutes, Adèle, with her particular charm, had swept round the hall, pacified everyone and flirted cheerfully with the rather perplexed Bishop, who began to enjoy himself thoroughly.

[141]

There were other long-term results from that night too, as Adèle encountered the young son of one of her neighbours. 'You're terribly good-looking,' she told him, 'but far too pretty for a man. You had better grow a moustache, otherwise everyone will think you're a pansy.' Nearly forty years on the man still wears the moustache he grew as soon as he could afterwards.

Although most men found her stimulating and delightful, Adèle's frankness did not endear her to many women, and she had few female friends. She was close to Clodagh Anson, her unmarried next door neighbour at Lismore (real neighbours were few and far between) who was six years younger than her, the granddaughter of the second Earl of Lichfield on her father's side and the fifth Marquess of Waterford on her mother's side. And then of course there was her perpetual friend and sometime sparring partner, Tilly Losch, who, undeterred by her disastrous marriage to Edward James, was quite ready for another marital adventure.

Although she sometimes complained of being lonely at Lismore, Adèle was warmly welcomed by the more entertaining of the Irish, a decidedly more relaxed race than the British aristocracy. And she did make some good friends like Richard Adare, son of the fifth Earl of Dunraven and Mount-Earl (and much later himself the sixth earl) and his American second wife Nancy Yuille, from Halifax County, Virginia. They would join her on expeditions to Dublin, where they would stay at the American legation and go to plays and parties. The three high living and fun loving Guinness girls, daughters of Ernest Guinness and grandaughters of brewing millionaire Earl Iveagh, all became friends: the eldest, Aileen Plunkett, was married to Lord Plunkett's son Flight Lieutenant Brinsley Plunkett. Maureen was married to Basil, Captain the Marquess of Dufferin and Ava, and Oonagh was married to Dominick, Baron Oranmore and Browne. Between them they knew every racetrack, pack of hounds and social centre and introduced Adèle to all of them.

Whenever possible Fred Astaire would travel, either by himself or with Phyllis, to London and Lismore. Always quietly. Always unannounced. And invariably to the despair of people like David Jones, who was handling his film publicity in Britain.

Astaire, invariably polite when he had to be polite, was always embarrassed to talk about himself, and within the bounds of acceptable behaviour for a star of his importance did his damnedest to avoid journalists. He was aware that his powers of analysis were not strong:

he knew what he did but not how and certainly not why. What did it matter what the steps were called? He had a working knowledge of the game; that was what mattered. But away from the Hollywood fan magazines a new breed of cinema observer was beginning to appear who treated cinema as a serious new art form.

In the forefront of this movement was the *Sunday Observer* critic, Caroline Lejeune, who finally tracked down Astaire in Claridges Hotel. Lejeune reported that she had been keeping a careful eye on sailing lists, printed conveniently in *The Times* and elsewhere, for Astaire's next visit to England. But she was on holiday when she saw a newsreel film of his arrival at Southampton, and the only contact who might be able to assist in an introduction was in the Mediterranean. The film company was kind, but scarcely helpful. They revealed that he had gone to Paris and would be staying at Claridges on his return. They would prefer Caroline to make her own arrangements. She did and a few days later telephoned the hotel; Astaire was out. She found that he was always out. Sometimes she would actually catch him on the telephone: 'He was vague, but quite charming; always on the point of going out, and by the time you got there he was gone.

'Finally I rang him up from a call-box two minutes from Claridge's. He was in, but going out. So was I, and I got there first. I sent up my card, naming the mutual friend in the Mediterranean. So-and-So, I wrote, promised that you would see me any time you came to England. Is that a lie or will you see me now? That brought him. He came down – on the way out with a frown of complete perplexity. "Hullo," I said. "Hullo," he answered absent-mindedly, his forehead puckered over the card. "What is all this? I haven't seen So-and-So for years. How does he know what I'll do?" "He doesn't," I said. "But you've done it. Would you like to ring him up? He's in the Mediterranean." He relaxed with a grin. "I'll take your word for it," he said. "Can I see you for five minutes?" "Seems like it. I'm just on my way – " "Out," I said. We sat on a seat in the lobby for just about the time it takes to sit down and get up again. We tried the porters' seat first. "Can't take this one," said Astaire, springing up suddenly. "That's the boys'."'

They moved up higher. 'Astaire was nervous, restless, on the hop and already out in imagination. Charming, courteous, but simply not there. Mobbed in Paris? He smiled his wry, one-sided smile. "Oh, sort of. I don't know why. That sort of thing's silly and embarrassing. I've been in shows since I was seven. They could always see me. I've not changed." "Haven't you – sort of – limbered up?" "No, only worked.

[143]

It's all practice – and thinking out new ideas." "Where do you get them?" "Oh, anywhere – in the bus, in the street – any place. There is a new step in everything, if you can only find it."'

' "Endlessly?" "Well, there are as many new steps as new tunes in the world." "Can you shape them in your head without moving your feet?" "Not often." "Embarrassing?" "Sometimes – but they know me now, and they don't think I'm quite crazy. When I'm rehearsing a new step they always leave me alone." "Can't you rehearse with anyone watching you?" "Could you write a book with someone reading over your shoulder?" "No," Lejeune said doubtfully. "No," he said positively. "Does the singing bother you?" "Not a bit. I can't sing, so why should I worry? It's all part of the routine, and new routines are the only things that matter. I'm no better than I was at seven, only more people see me. Sorry, but I've got to go." He was up and off like a whirlwind.'

What fascinated Lejeune and other critics was Astaire's panache. Years later another minor matinée idol, the actor George Hamilton, in pursuit of style and flair deduced that no star ever lasted who wore jacket lapels of more than three and a half inches or less than three and a quarter! Just like Astaire. That, as Adèle pointed out (she never did tire of her pleasure and pride in her brother and his achievements) was the least of Astaire's innovative and faddish dress habits. He was obsessive about his appearance and, from the early days of vaudeville, when money was tight, clothes were his one big extravagance. He took as much trouble getting his film clothes right as he did his steps.

Popular fashion has changed much since the turn of the century and Fred Astaire was invariably at the forefront in the world of men's fashion: the trouser braces kept on every pair of trousers were soon replaced by self supporting trousers, and in several films you can see him without a jacket and braces. But he never appeared with bare chest, let alone bare arms or legs, as did Gene Kelly.

His suits were always immaculately tailored with straight trousers, never flared or flapping. In the duet he dances in *The Band Wagon* with Jack Buchanan, the suavest man of the British theatre, Buchanan appears to have surplus trouser material, while Astaire, wearing close but straight cut trousers, presents a far more elegant picture.

Always prepared to buck the accepted trend, his slight, wiry frame sported single breasted suits unbuttoned, when double breasted suits were the norm. After he discarded braces, he developed a habit he had seen rural labourers use in Britain of using a scarf instead of a belt.

George Burns, who became a longtime and close friend, and who, with his wife Gracie Allen, would work with Astaire on *A Damsel in Distress*, was a great admirer of that style: 'But it used to take three neckties for me to keep my pants up,' he said. 'He made me ruin a lot of ties, that guy.'

The famous feet were not large – size eight and a half (and his Los Angeles cobbler gave him every hundredth pair free; during a film he would wear out several dozen). He put on white shoes with a white suit when such a thing on anyone else whould have seemed the height of flashiness; on Astaire it was elegant, if slightly raffish. He affected co-respondent shoes of black or brown leather and white buckskin, or highly shining patent leather, which drew attention to his feet in dance routines. He had his neck ties cut wide, on the same principle adopted by the Prince of Wales, to gain a large knot. He also commited the faux pas of wearing the same coloured tie as shirt. But once Fred Astaire had done it, fashion followed. Like his dancing, his clothes sense seemed effortless. There was to him nothing worse than looking as though he was wearing a new outfit. 'I dislike looking dressed,' he said. 'I distinctly dislike newness in clothing. I never wear a new hat until I have battered it and crushed it so that it looks well worn and comfortable. The same with shoes.' His quick temper – some who admit to temper are being self-deprecatory, but in Astaire's case the mean, ready-to-kill paroxysms were for real – would crack quickly if one of his dancing partners complained about her shoes not being comfortable. 'The sensible ones would run around in them a bit beforehand, just as I do,' he said.

He wore pastels: pinks, yellows and creams, which he would quite often match with brown suede shoes, of the kind favoured in the English countryside. As he grew older, however, he would accept darker colours. For rehearsals, he would wear a union suit, sometimes of flannel, sometimes of towelling. And, like Ginger Rogers, he would chew gum as he worked. He had FA monograms on his two-piece underwear, his shirts, and his two-piece blue silk pyjamas (made in London). He ate sparsely, a large bowl of chicken noodle soup or cup of bouillon at lunchtime, meat and maybe a bowl of ice cream in the evening. He drank lightly, a dry martini, a whisky, some wine, and smoked sparingly (he gave up in the fifties but smoked for his rôle in *On The Beach*, stopping again in 1961).

He adopted many English habits – including the wearing of a silk handkerchief in the breast pocket of his jacket. And if you checked the cuff buttons on his suit jackets you would notice that, as in all the best English tailoring, the last two of the four buttons on the cuff can actually be undone – those buttons were originally put on jackets for holding gloves, but have not been used for that purpose this century.

Off stage he invariably wore a hat covering his 'high intellectual forehead'. The toupee was only worn when he was in performance, whether on stage or at a showbusiness function. It was to him, like the make-up that he wore on camera to hide the small mole under his left eye, just a professional accessory. But he was touchy about it and would follow up any new instant cure for baldness that he discovered. David Niven even remembered him with some alarming rubber suction contraption on his head one day. 'It didn't do him any good at all,' said Niven. 'In fact, I'm almost sure it made things worse.'

Astaire always claimed that he did not read reviews or care what people said, but when the British *Films in Review* commented on the toupee, he was sufficiently roused to send a letter of complaint: 'Your publication has been somewhat familiar to me for a number of years. Now one of your reviewers has overstepped his status with a grossly insulting commentary on me. The man's opinion of me as an artist matters little. It is his deliberate attack and effort to describe me as a decrepit old ham trying to hang by a thread or something that I resent vehemently. I will not tolerate this presumptuous or patronising attitude. The wig described is exactly what I have always worn in all my specials and pictures.'

Astaire's cars, like so much else, were British and the best. For many years he had two black Rolls-Royces, one bequeathed to him by Phyllis's Aunt Maud. In the early Hollywood years he had a housekeeper from Mayfair, a chauffeur from Aberdeen but, when his last chauffeur died, he used to drive himself each day down to his Brighton Way office, just five minutes from his house, and to All Saints' on Sunday.

He said that he was not sentimental, yet he kept a stack of press cuttings and letters from old friends, and was really very pleased when Adèle named a dachshund after him. She explained to neighbours: 'You know those four little worry wrinkles that droop away from a dachshund's eyes and make it look so appealing? Fred's got that look to me sometimes. Maybe that's why I love dachshunds. They remind me of Fred.'

Astaire claimed he didn't like looking back, yet with close friends he would reminisce for hours. To many, Astaire seemed the perfect

[146]

English gentleman, yet he was proud of his Austrian origins, and turned up for an early Hollywood fancy dress party in the uniform of an Austrian hussar, borrowed from one of John Gilbert's films.

With his film career established, Fred continued the battle to break away from the Astaire-Rogers formula. The studio, on the other hand, was equally determined to keep them together.

Ginger, often referred to by Astaire as The Wasp, was due a straight starring rôle, she said, as she had made *Follow the Fleet, Swing Time* and *Shall We Dance?* (Berman persuaded the Gershwins to write this as the first of two films for Astaire) without her usual break for one of her own movies. She had tried unsuccessfully to persuade John Ford to let her play Queen Elizabeth to Katharine Hepburn's Mary Queen of Scots in *Mary of Scotland* – not because of the test (which was fine), but because the studio felt that either people would not recognize her as Ginger Rogers or else they would recognize her and expect her to make a wisecrack. 'Anyway,' said one executive, 'the public won't stand for someone called Ginger Rogers playing a queen.'

Meanwhile Astaire, aided by Phyllis and inspired by the regular, inconsequential but supportive letters from Adèle, sought out new scripts and ideas. Eventually his views won some credence and when Ginger was given *Stage Door*, with Katharine Hepburn, Fred was assigned to make *A Damsel in Distress*, based on a P. G. Wodehouse story, with the comedy duo of George Burns and Gracie Allen as his co-stars. An English leading lady was needed for the tale. Jessie Matthews and Ruby Keeler were suggested and rejected. Eventually a mixed solution was found: one, there would be plenty of solo dances, and two, the leading lady would be Joan Fontaine, sister of Olivia de Havilland and cousin of the British aviation pioneer, Sir Geoffrey de Havilland. Director Mark Sandrich commented: 'You see the snag we are up against is that we have to keep to the same story formulas, not because we want to, but because if there is the slightest deviation the public squawks. I don't think the public wants new things half as much as the people who advise the public.' But the film was really a solo vehicle for Astaire and although he looked suave, debonair and danced superbly, ultimately the audience gave their verdict. They did not want Astaire without Rogers. So reluctantly he agreed to do *Carefree*, with an Irving Berlin score. But for him there would be some bait: he would play an adult rôle, a psychiatrist, and the film would be made in colour. If dance could work on the screen, how much more spectacular would it be in rainbow hues? A marvellous gimmick was planned. The film

[147]

would be shot in black and white to start with, but then he would sing Irving Berlin's lyric 'I Used to be Colour Blind', and slowly the film would dissolve into rainbow hues.

That was the plan. But two things intervened. One, the cost of shooting in colour was going to escalate the costs of the production and an Astaire vehicle was no longer a guaranteed money spinner: since the *Top Hat* profits of $1,325,000, *Follow the Fleet* had made $945,000, *Swing Time* had made $830,000 and *Shall We Dance?* had cleared $413,000. Secondly, the political situation in Europe in 1938 was rapidly deteriorating and there was the terrible danger that RKO might not be able to get a proper European release on the film, thus gutting the potential market by some twenty-five per cent. So Astaire performed 'Colour Blind' in monochrome.

Irving Berlin also wrote a number for the score with especial reference to Astaire and Rogers, 'Won't You Change Partners?'

Always ready to turn everything to good advantage, Astaire justified his many hours swinging a club by choreographing the memorable golf sequence in *Carefree*. The idea first came to him at Bel Air and a practise range was set up at RKO's San Fernando valley ranch while Hal Borne played for him and a team of men retrieved the three hundred or so golf balls which he drove off into the middle distance. Close by was an emergency supply of iced beer to cope with the scorching summer heat. That was one dance sequence which was not all shot in one take; even Astaire reckoned that it was not humanly possible for him to be step perfect and hit every ball spot-on in one go.

That dance also expresses the acting and pantomime element in Astaire's dancing, for although the sequence with the golf clubs and drives is brilliant, the abiding image of the sequence is the expression on Astaire's face as he looks up for Ginger's approval. His face drops as he realises she has gone – he had been performing just for himself.

There was a further gimmick that RKO felt would be a sure-fire winner: for the first time in an Astaire movie he and Ginger Rogers would actually kiss. Much play had been made of the fact that they hadn't touched lips, and the popular theory was that it was Phyllis who was responsible for the no-kissing rule of the early films – a door shuts and reopens to show Astaire with lipstick on his face, or a curtain is discreetly drawn – and it is true that Phyllis was often around the set and kept a weather eye on any girl who might look as though she had set her sights. However, during his stage career, Astaire had played against Adèle as the romantic interest and always retained a chaste

[148]

relationship with her.'It was my idea', he said, 'to refrain from mushy love scenes, partly because I hated doing them on stage and partly because it was different not to have sticky clinches in movies.'

But the kiss became an issue and Mark Sandrich recalled: 'In the film George Stevens made with Fred, *Swing Time*, Dorothy Fields wrote that lyric especially for them: "A fine romance, with no kisses, a fine romance, my friend this is . . ." but the kissless romance worked. Partly as a gimmick, although it was an anti-gimmick to start with.' Ironically, it was Phyllis who suggested, when he got back together with Rogers after the loss-making *Damsel in Distress*, that maybe a kiss would be good box office. Astaire asked Ginger if she would mind them breaking their regular habit to end this international crisis. 'Oh, all right,' she said, very straight faced, 'But you'll have to speak to my agent.'

The scene was filmed with the 'Colour Blind' dance routine shot at twice the normal speed, so that when the kiss sequence was run at the regular speed it would be in slow motion, with the final position held until Sandrich told them to cut. Sandrich let the clinch run on for fifteen seconds to allow for a dissolve of that scene to the next one. 'You'd better come and see what we've done,' Astaire told his wife.

Next morning at the rushes, there was quite a feeling of anticipation in the plush velvet-seated projection room. Astaire was busy trying to explain to Phyllis that although the kiss might seem to go on for ever, it only actually lasted for a few seconds, and that hardly any of it would be used on screen, anyway. Intriguingly, it is Ginger who kisses Fred. But that didn't make the thirty-nine-year-old leading man feel any more comfortable.

There was one more Astaire-Rogers vehicle waiting to go at RKO – *The Story of Vernon and Irene Castle*. With the dismal *Damsel* figures – an estimated loss of $65,000 (fortunately the *Carefree* figures of a $68,000 loss had not yet been accounted) – Astaire gave in once again to the re-pairing of himself and Ginger Rogers. The movie was a straightforward biographical picture of the dancing Castles, whom the Astaires had so admired and who had in turn admired the Astaires when they saw them in vaudeville the year before their *Over the Top* Broadway début. It was in *The Story of Vernon and Irene Castle* that the pressure of working with a perfectionist like Astaire finally told on Ginger – it was the ninth time they had worked that way in just six years.

Hermes Pan recalled: 'I felt the death knell on that film. Their rhythms were just different. I wouldn't decry Ginger as a dancer. She is

[149]

truly wonderful, but a totally different style to Fred.' There were other problems with the Castles film which Astaire had not encountered before. For a start, the real life Irene Castle had right of approval: it was after all her rather romanticised biography of the partnership, for which the studio paid her $40,000, on which the film was based. Irene thought Astaire, despite being several inches shorter than Vernon, was perfect. He had staged some dances for her theatrical comeback after Vernon's death and had been so flattered to be asked by such a great star that he had refused to be paid. On the other hand, she thought Ginger Rogers was terrible. While the studio had cleverly worded the agreement so that Irene could veto any girl other than Ginger Rogers, to Irene McLaughlin, as she then was, there was only one person who could portray the haughty elegance of Irene Castle – and that was herself.

But the only rôle she was offered was that of her own mother. She was apoplectic at that. And when it became clear that the studio was determined to go ahead with Ginger, Irene spent her time on the set being as disagreeable as possible. Ginger hardly helped: she did not want her hair dyed, or even cut into the Castle bob, so a wig was made. She insisted on high necklines on the grounds that she thought her own neck was a little too thick. 'Yes, I know that,' said Mrs McLaughlin, 'but I never had that thick neck.' Ginger gave up with the riding hat she was wearing in one scene: 'I wouldn't have been caught dead without a riding hat,' said Irene. She even attempted early on to get Ginger removed from the film, but there was no way that the RKO brass were going to permit that. Irene did at least have the grace to say: 'I'm sure the studio would rather that I had been dead. They even waited two years for me to kick off after I had sold them the story. But when they found out that I was indestructible they went ahead and made it anyway.'

Although the musical score was appealing, the dances by Pan fluid, with *The Story of Vernon and Irene Castle*, the magic was missing. There were several reasons. The story emerged as a stereotyped success story without extra ingredients – Vernon, having given up vaudeville for dancing, is killed in an accident in the Great War. It was the first time in the Astaire-Rogers pictures that one of them had died during the story. The *New York Times* said: 'Rogers and Astaire have been so closely identified with light comedy in the past that finding them otherwise employed is practically as disconcerting as it would be if

[150]

Walt Disney were to throw Mickey Mouse to the lions and Minnie to be devoured by a non-regurgative giant.' The flirting, mistaken identity and other stratagems of the earlier movies were missing. The final ignominy was that the film lost $50,000 at the box office.

There had been heavy emphasis on turning in good figures since entrepreneur Floyd Odlum had bought a half share of RKO in 1935 with the intention of shaking the place up. Odlum and the other main shareholders, RCA (where David Sarnoff held power) and the Rockefellers family, would no longer tolerate loss-making projects. They brought in George Schaefer from United Artists as Corporate President (production head Sam Briskin, formerly VP in charge of production for eight years at Columbia under Harry Cohn, had already lost his job through his failure to find instant pay dirt, to Pan Berman, who was reluctant to take the top head-above-the-parapet job) who ran the studio so efficiently that by '37 profits were running at $2 million a year. However, in 1938 major shockwaves had blown through the industry with the anti-trust suit filed by the government against Paramount. Although the case, and the eventual settlement ten years later, is referred to as the Paramount Decision, there were eight defendants – Paramount, Loew's, Warner Brothers, 20th-Century Fox, RKO, Columbia, Universal and United Artists – all panic-stricken in their various degrees (in '31 Paramount had 971 theatres, Fox 521, Warner 529, down to Universal with just 66) about how the loss of any of their guaranteed circuits would affect business. There were many contingency plans and discussions as to how to staunch the losses.

That year Ginger Rogers' low budget *Bachelor Mother* with David Niven (which she had furiously resisted as unsuitable for her squeaky clean image – the story had store girl Rogers mistakenly taken as the mother of an abandoned child) made $827,000, so her future was assured. But at the end of 1939 Berman left RKO for MGM and in 1940, RKO had no place for Astaire, and little interest in making musicals. On 27 January, Radio-Keith Orpheum officially emerged from receivership. Their '39 gross income from more popular and prestigious pictures than they had ever before produced had been $52 million and they could start afresh with a working capital that amounted to more than $8 million. The only music films that would benefit in the schedules for the year were co-productions – with Walt Disney and the animated wood doll Pinocchio (which made for splendid prestige, rentals of $3,600,000 and an accounting loss of

[151]

$94,000) and their second Herbert Wilcox-directed Anna Neagle movie, *No, No, Nanette* (which lost just $2,000). But there was another factor that had dogged Astaire's steps for the last three films.

Unwittingly he found himself caught in the crossfire of a monumental battle between Orson Welles and newspaper tycoon, William Randolph Hearst. Welles, the wunderkind who had arrived from New York at the age of twenty-three, had every intention of making his screen début as writer, director and star with his story of Citizen Kane, a megalomaniac newspaper proprietor. Hearst had every intention of stopping him. Kane was not solely based on Hearst, but it certainly drew a deal of real-life inspiration from him. Hearst, lover and promoter of actress Marion Davies through his Cosmopolitan Film Company, was a powerful and vindictive man. As soon as he heard tell of the project at RKO he put his lawyers, print hounds and whatever else came to hand on a massively orchestrated smear campaign against Welles and RKO.

The effect was two-edged. The more Hearst raged the more Welles made his fictional anti-hero behave and live as Hearst did, in his palatial San Simeon castle, where the Astaires had stayed more than once. Hearst's media tentacles extended everywhere and the widely read gossip columnist, Louella Parsons, did her bit in her master's campaign of character assassination.

Hearst's energies gained him the satisfaction of preventing *Citizen Kane*'s release for three years after it was scheduled. When the film finally came out, it lost $160,000, helping RKO into a $185,495 loss for the 1939 financial year. Neither Hepburn nor Astaire had their contracts renewed and, after the Hearst campaign began, the last three films Astaire made at RKO all lost money.

In London, thanks to an introduction by Adèle and Charlie, Tilly Losch became the second wife of the sporting sixth Earl of Carnarvon, whose father had sponsored Howard Carter's discovery of the tomb of Tutankhamun. The Earl, known as Porchy through his subsidiary title of Lord Porchester, was divorced from New York heiress, Catherine Wendell, and had been feeling rather lonely in New York when he had been invited for dinner by Adèle. That night Charlie – *plus ça change* – passed out from an excess of alcohol and was ministered to by the twin angels of Adèle and Tilly. Porchy was smitten, and on Friday morning, 1 September 1939, at London's Caxton Hall register office, Tilly, accompanied by her business manager, became the Countess of

Carnarvon and mistress of Porchy's splendid 17th-century Highclere Castle in Hampshire.

On 3 September Great Britain, with France, Australia and New Zealand, declared war on Germany. However, in Hollywood there were new stars and new films to be made. While *The Castles* was an artistic success but financial flop, RKO experimented with a new genre, the disaster movie, with *Five Came Back* with Lucille Ball, C. Aubrey Smith and John Carradine among the passengers on a clipper plane that crashes into the dense South American jungle: an investment of $225,000 produced profits of $262,000 and plenty of artistic praise for the studio. So there were few tears shed at the departure of their dancing star. Ginger Rogers, on a longer contract, would stay, as her non-dancing movies – *Stage Door*, *Vivacious Lady* and *Bachelor Mother* had all done well.

Astaire had no work, no contract and no future. He was low and, after many hours of hitting a golf ball around the Bel Air course he came to an inescapable decision. There was at least some money that had been saved under Phyllis's stewardship, so he might as well face facts and retire from showbusiness. Maybe he could breed horses, run a little stud farm and shake off the glitter of forty years on stage. It wasn't, he contemplated, much of a job for a grown man anyway.

12
War

Throughout those early Hollywood years, while Fred Astaire had grown from ambitious newcomer to top star, Phyllis was the strength in Fred's shadow. She was solid, dependable, vivacious and, underneath the petite prettiness, formidably tough. If she wasn't at the studio each day, she was nearby; she admitted to knowing nothing about show-business, dancing or movies, yet Fred would ask her advice on everything – and he would take it. Her own opinion of herself was excessively modest: 'I'm not a perfect wife. I can't cook. I can't sew. I hate housework. I can't look after Fred's business affairs. All I can do is sit and look pretty. I help Fred by being around when he needs me.'

As his first Hollywood dance partner, Joan Crawford, said: 'They reinforced each other. Fred was a shy man; Phyllis has always been shy too. On that first picture he made with me, she'd drive him to the studio, wait in the car reading until he finished in make-up and then while he worked she'd sit quietly in a far corner of the set doing needlepoint. He treated her like the great lady she always was. Saturday nights she'd pick him up with a picnic basket and a hot thermos of soup or coffee. They'd have their dinner by the sea, then drive to their ranch, Fred curled up on the seat with his head in her lap. Some men can't allow a woman to drive, but Fred never competed with Phyllis, he enjoyed her abilities . . . he's such a virile man, he's never had to prove it . . . he's kept himself intact and could because he's been so fulfilled in his personal life. I've never seen two people work with such minimum effort at happiness.'

Phyllis was equally self-effacing about her business abilities. When they arrived in Hollywood she had told Fred that he should go ahead and make the money and that she would look after it for him. She made it quite clear that she was so pleased to have found a man with whom she was happy that she had no desire for the extravagant things in life. She read his contracts, kept a wary eye on other stars' careers and looked to the long term. Astaire believed he had started his film career too late and that any dancer had reached his peak by twenty-five. At first Phyllis listened to what he had to say, but she also realised Fred Astaire was no normal person.

Gene Kelly pointed out in the early 1980s: 'I once said that fifty years from now, the only one of today's dancers who will be remembered is Fred Astaire. Now I'm not sure that he won't be playing Hamlet on Broadway when he's 110.'

While Fred had rehearsed and worked and slaved, Phyllis had hunted for real estate, and in the spring of '36 she had found a four-acre plot perched two hundred feet above the smog of Los Angeles on Summit Drive just off Benedict Canyon Drive, where she organised the building of her dream house. 'It will be much better for the boys,' she said, 'and we get the fresh air without having to go miles into the mountains.' The plot was surrounded by orange groves and wild-life, with Pickfair, the huge mansion built by Mary Pickford and Douglas Fairbanks, just above and Charlie Chaplin's house just below.

As the house started to take shape, Fred had spotted the outlines of a swimming pool and tennis court. 'I'm not playing tennis,' he had said; it was the one sport at which he did not reckon to excel, while Phyllis was a good player. 'Don't be silly,' said the ever-practical Phyllis. 'That's not for us. That is for the resale value – or else the children may want to play.' The two acres not covered by the plans, Phyllis announced, would be a run where they would breed pheasants: that was another of Phyllis's long-term ideas, and in time the pheasant run at Summit Drive became another house, which was sold to *Wuthering Heights* director, William Wyler, which paid for the building of both houses.

Then she had found the ranch, just thirty miles outside the Los Angeles city limits. The Blue Valley Ranch, as it was called, was just off Devonshire Street, in the town of Chatsworth, named after the Duke of Devonshire's stately home by a former Devonshire family employee who had moved out there many years before. This would be the place for relaxation and for Fred to carry out his horse breeding plans. Early on he had established a schedule for filming and rehearsing that usually allowed him a break of a month, or two, or three between films. This enabled him and Phyllis to take long trips together, to Mexico, to Europe, just by themselves, skipping crowds and showbusiness. One year, Astaire recalled, they went to Paris for the Longchamps races and thought they had avoided the press photographers and reporters. But at the airport in France they were approached by a cameraman. Astaire reluctantly posed for a picture. 'I spoke too soon,' he said. But as they walked on the man pursued them: 'Attendez, monsieur et madame – that will be cinq francs – five francs, please.' Astaire happily handed him the money and took the claim slip – feeling not at all famous for once.

From *Top Hat* onwards he worked on a percentage of the profits – ten per cent for *Top Hat* – so the money was soon flowing in and growing. Often in the entertainment world a few make huge amounts of money but few manage to keep it. However, the ones who did were the kind of people Astaire identified with. Cary Grant was one. 'I had lawyers, the others had agents,' Grant said. Bob Hope, whose fortune was measured in hundreds of millions of dollars, and Bing Crosby were also careful with money. So was the man behind one of the greatest of all the Hollywood fortunes, Randolph Scott, who put his earnings into real estate, oil, mining and securities.

Astaire, hit once by the Wall Street Crash, had no desire to enter the multimillionaire class – he knew there was no way that he would ever be able to compete with Jock Whitney, for instance, so Phyllis invested cautiously and wisely. When you realise that Astaire was earning over $100,000 a year in the 1930s and living well, but not extravagantly, it is easy to understand how his fortune was estimated at over $20 million. He only had, ate and bought the best, but that in itself can be an economy: he was often thought of as being mean, but Astaire had worked hard to make his money and he had every intention of hanging on to it.

While his own world achieved some stability, in the big wide world everything was changing. And Astaire was one of a group of movie actors who gathered at the Beverly Hills home of the forthright Edward G. Robinson to discuss the increasingly alarming political situation. For many Americans Europe was a long way away, but for Astaire and the Hungarian-born Robinson it was very near. Robinson believed they had a duty to make their feelings known. Fred Astaire was a lifelong Republican voter who preferred to keep his politics to himself as much as possible. However, in his first entry in *Who's Who in America* he added his name to Robinson's 'declaration of independence' which called on President Roosevelt and Congress to sever all diplomatic relations with Germany – 'a boycott that should last until such time as Germany is willing to re-enter the family of nations in accordance with the principle of international law and universal freedom'. They did not

[156]

have to wait too long, as in December 1941 the Japanese air force bombed Pearl Harbor and the United States at last entered the conflict.

In England the old order had already moved on. At Chatsworth in May 1938 Duke Victor, the ninth Duke of Devonshire, had died. Although he had been awkward and irascible he did have his redeeming features – and considered Adèle the best thing to have happened to his family for years. He loved cricket – one of his greatest pleasures was to sit in an armchair with his black spaniel at his feet watching Derbyshire. Once, a Derbyshire batsman hit a six which smashed through a window of the Duke's Rolls-Royce. There was immediate apprehension which was quickly defused when the Duke ordered that the man be sent his congratulations and £10 for hitting such an excellent stroke. But he was not universally mourned. His grandson Andrew Cavendish, the present duke, was not sorry to see the last of the rather frightening old man, whom he remembered at Christmas time presenting his annual Christmas tip, or present, in his study. The young boy and old man both stood there in silence for some time. The Duke then took two pound notes from his desk and handed them silently to Andrew, who just as silently took them and fled.

Charlie's elder brother Edward now became the tenth Duke of Devonshire. Compared with his father he was a model of probity – apart from a particular wariness of clergymen and a positive dislike of nuns. Edward was at heart a politician and had been Under Secretary of State for Dominion Affairs in Stanley Baldwin's short-lived National Government of 1936. He was delighted to resume the post when Winston Churchill succeeded Neville Chamberlain as Prime Minister in 1940. His sons, the Marquess of Hartington and Lord Andrew Cavendish, were in the Coldstream Guards, and in Ireland Charlie felt that he too wanted to do his share for his country. At thirty-three his volunteering was rejected on both health and age grounds, although as the first waves of aeroplanes went up and battled against the Germans, there was a scheme with which Adèle and Charlie could help.

Pilots on active service were in need of recuperation after the months of continual battle flying and the mental fatigue and breakdown that often followed. Adèle offered to take some of these airmen at Lismore, one of the twenty houses in Ireland found by RAF organiser Commander Stephen King-Hall. Charlie was more and more confined to his bed but Adèle did have the help of her mother to look after him and her 'boys'. 'She is brave to stick it out here,' Adèle told her friends, 'when she could be in California with Fred. I appreciate it tremen-

[157]

dously.' Adèle dropped a letter – she was already an accomplished knitter and tapestry maker and had recently taught herself to type rather well on the ten-year-old Royal typewriter used in the Lismore Estates Office – to Cecil Beaton, about the pilots: 'It makes it more personal to have them just two at a time and we can lavish all our time and attention on them. These boys who are with us now are SO good looking (sigh) I only wish I were ten years younger (another sigh) . . . what brave, wonderful youngsters they all are!'

To Adèle, now more British than the British, the war became a Holy one and she entered it with all her spirit. She became quite vicious about Americans like Kitty Miller, wife of theatrical impresario Gilbert Miller, who had fled the country, and especially about Tilly Losch, who had fled both her husband, Porchie Carnarvon, and his country just at their time of need. Tilly, according to Adèle, kept her distant husband happy and supplying her with money by writing him sexy letters, which he would then read out to his friends. 'It is altogether a most unsavoury business,' said Adèle, who decided that she wanted to help nearer the front. Although she said that the real reason that she was leaving Ireland was that she couldn't stand any more salmon! It was the estate's main crop and even after the exports to England there was always masses of fish left. She set off by boat and train for London, where a little thing like a bomb barrage was not going to put her off her stride: it was in April of 1941 that she was caught in a night blitz on London. 'It was my first,' she wrote to her brother, 'and I must say I've never had such an opening night in my life. Really, Fred, it was hell.' She had been at a party at the Dorchester Hotel, a popular venue, particularly with the Americans in London, on the grounds that it was built of reinforced concrete and more resistant to bombs than conventional buildings. The graphic account of the raid which Adèle (who could not stand even prop guns going off on stage) sent to Fred so affected him that he immediately released the text to US newspapers to highlight the British plight.

Even during the worst of the Blitz Adèle led an active social life. On Saturday 19 April, at St Bartholomew the Great in Smithfield, she attended the wedding of Charlie's nephew, Lieutenant Lord Andrew Cavendish, who had just won the Military Cross for gallantry while leading his platoon in battle south of Florence, to Deborah Freeman-Mitford, Debo, daughter of Lord Redesdale. The Mitfords were a truly extraordinary family, talented, attractive and eccentric. Father was the model for the amiable monster Uncle Matt in sister Nancy Mitford's

Pursuit of Love; brother Tom was one of Tilly Losch's admirers; her sister Diana was married to fascist leader Sir Oswald Mosley and sister Unity was a passionate worshipper and groupie of Adolf Hitler – at Munich's English Garden Unity had shot herself in the head, not fatally, when war was declared. Adèle was fascinated to see such a consort of the enemy accepted into a British family but she was beginning to understand that the ways of the English were rather different from the rest of the world's and that, in the right circumstances, your worst foe could sit at the host's right hand. Adèle returned from the wedding quite riveted. 'I was sitting opposite Mrs Hitler in church . . . Unity, I mean,' she told Cecil Beaton.

Their friends too were becoming increasingly involved in the war effort. David Niven, then thirty, who had been commissioned in the Highland Light Infantry as a young man, decided he could not stay in Hollywood while his fellow Englishmen were fighting for King and Country, so ignoring his contractual obligations he headed home. As well as getting a new commission in the Rifle Brigade he also, at a Café de Paris dance, met (and later married) Primula, known as Primmie, daughter of Lord Rollo's son William and the Marquess of Downshire's daughter Lady Kathleen.

Jock Whitney, who had been spending more and more time in Hollywood apart from his wife Liz, and had finally officially separated from her and in 1942 married Betsey Roosevelt, ex-wife of President Roosevelt's son Jimmy, arrived in London as a major in the Eighth Air Command with the Army Air Corps; a year later Jock, by then serving in Intelligence, was shot down and captured in France.

With Charlie in the capable hands of her mother, Adèle joined the American Red Cross, setting off early each morning from her base at the Ritz Hotel on Piccadilly. The obvious use for Adèle, the organisers quickly realised, was as a morale booster, and at the American Red Cross Rainbow Corner snack bar, canteen and meeting rooms on Shaftesbury Avenue she quickly became a star attraction. Night and day she would be there. Singing, dancing with the soldiers and, most importantly of all, acting as elder sister to the GIs on leave. 'With what little time they had in London they really didn't have time to write letters home, so they told me what they wanted to say and then I wrote the letters for them,' she said. She signed the letters: 'Adèle Astaire (Fred's sister)', so there would be no problem exlaining who she was. 'The Americans never did learn to cope with the Lady Charles Cavendish bit,' she said, 'and anyway most of the GIs were far too young to know anything about me, it was Fred they were interested in.'

News reaching America got no better. In August 1942, only three weeks after Fred and Phyllis had sent a message of congratulations and good wishes to their friend Prince George, now Duke of Kent, on the christening of his second son, Prince Michael George Charles Franklin, they received another message from London: on 25 August Prince George had been killed in an air crash while flying in a Sunderland flying boat on a trip to inspect RAF installations in Iceland. He was thirty-nine years old and his son, the new Duke, Prince Edward, was just six weeks short of his seventh birthday.

At Lismore Charlie's health, despite the ministrations of Ann, got no better and in the spring of '44 he suffered a sudden relapse. On Thursday, 23 March 1944, with only enough time to summon the white-robed Cistercian monks with their black hoods from Mount Melleray Abbey (a few miles from the castle in the Knockmealdown Mountains at Cappoquin), with prayers, priests and Ann Astaire by his side, Lord Charles Arthur Francis Cavendish died peacefully in his sleep. The years of alcohol abuse had finally induced a fatal sclerosis of the liver.

When the call came through for Adèle, there was neither time nor facilities in those war-torn years for her to travel to Ireland, so, like a trouper, she continued to turn up at Rainbow Corner, night after night, determinedly cheerful and brave for the soldiers. As soon as possible Adèle made the sad journey over to County Waterford to see the body of her much-loved husband buried by the graves of the three little children that he had never known. In contrast to the small marble plaques, a fine monument was erected to commemorate the man who had brought a new life for Adèle, as Adèle took her mother back to London to continue, even more determinedly, her own personal battle for the freedom of the world.

According to the terms of Charlie's will, £10,000 was left to Adèle, £500 to Ann, who had cared for him as though he were her own, and after some bequests the residue of his £81,815 estate was left to Adèle, with an annuity of £5,000 a year if she should remarry. Before he died he had told Ann: 'Please promise me that if anything happens to me you will try and make sure that Adèle is happy – I know she may want to remarry and I would like her to do so.' Lismore was to be Adèle's: if she should remarry or die it was to pass to Charlie's brother's second son – Lord Andrew, for he, like Charlie, had few expectations under the traditional primogeniture system.

[160]

William Cavendish, the young Marquess of Hartington, elder son and heir of the new duke, was experiencing his own problems. He had fallen in love with Kathleen Kennedy, the bright and beautiful daughter of the former United States Ambassador to London, Joseph Kennedy. Joe Kennedy was a Boston banker, supporter of RKO films when he managed to pick up their stock for next to nothing, long-time lover of actress Gloria Swanson and Roman Catholic head of a large family. His eldest son, Joseph, was a Lieutenant in the US Navy; then there was John, acting as secretary to his father, Rosemary, Kathleen, known as 'Kick' from her initials KK, Eunice, Patricia, Robert and Edward. Kennedy was bitterly opposed to the romance between the twenty-six-year-old Hartington and his twenty-four-year-old daughter for several reasons: the Devonshires were leading Protestants – as a determined Roman Catholic, he considered Hartington not good enough for his daughter – also, he had the lowest opinion of England's chances against Germany and spent much time and a vast amount of energy in trying to get the United States to abandon England to their fate in Europe. The fact that Hartington was heir to a dukedom made little impression on the curmudgeonly Kennedy and he forbade his daughter point blank to marry him.

On the other side, the Duke of Devonshire also strongly disapproved on religious grounds, though he had, thanks to Adèle, become an enthusiast of Americans. It was not a happy situation. Eventually a few weeks after Charlie had died at Lismore, the couple decided they could wait no more and, with Kathleen converting to become a Protestant, they married quietly at London's Chelsea Register Office on Saturday 5 May 1944 – the Duke of Rutland acting as best man.

Their happiness was not to last, as Hartington and the Coldstreams were immediately sent to the Front. A few months later Kick Kennedy's brother Joseph Jr, who had none of the meanness of spirit of his father, was shot down over Suffolk, on Saturday 12 August. One month later Kick was widowed when her husband was killed by a sniper's bullet on the Belgian border. Kick flew to America, where she could be comforted by her family before returning to London. Four years later she too was killed while travelling with a man friend in a private plane which crashed over France. Both Kick and Joseph Kennedy Jr were in time remembered in Robert Kennedy's children, the eldest of whom is Kathleen Hartington Kennedy, now Townsend, and second of whom is Joseph Patrick, the same names as borne by Robert's eldest brother. So it was that Lieutenant Lord Andrew

Cavendish, the second son, Charlie's favourite nephew, whose expectations had been minimal, was suddenly heir to the vast Chatsworth estates.

In the United States, Astaire's retirement after the end of the RKO contract had not lasted long. There were still those who rated his talents, and, to his delight and surprise, there were those who wanted the Astaire name and reckoned they could also capture the magic that created the Astaire profits. MGM, flush with the success of *Gone with the Wind* (David Selznick had made the film as an independent, but Louis Mayer had loaned him Gable, invested $1,250,000, and retained distribution and half the profits – many millions of dollars) and *The Wizard of Oz*, wanted Astaire for *Broadway Melody of 1940* with a score by Cole Porter. Astaire, concerned for his future, was delighted to accept and, in *Broadway Melody*, would at last make his first colour movie. But, as with *Carefree*, colour film stock was sacrificed to bottom line – it had not proved a great profit factor. Hermes Pan had gratefully accepted the security of an RKO contract some years before so he was no longer available. Astaire would have a male dance partner in George Murphy (they would play a club act) and his new leading lady was to be the twenty-seven-year-old tap dancer, Eleanor Powell. George Murphy was debonair with a splendid manner, but no competition for Astaire, and his dramatic energies had been diminished by an involvement in politics, switching from Democrat to Republican (eventually becoming a California senator).

It was only when Astaire began to work with others that he realised just how good Ginger Rogers had been for him. She was not the ideal partner, but at least she had the ability to camouflage her faults on screen. The next ten years would be spent in the frustrating search for the perfect partner, and a suitable vehicle for Astaire that would make the studio money. *The Story of Vernon and Irene Castle* had actually grossed more than *Gay Divorcee*, but as the costs were so much greater the Castle film lost $50,000, while *Gay Divorcee* made $500,000. It was only slowly that Astaire became fully aware of the financial discrepancies, but learn he did.

Paramount wanted him for *Second Chorus* as a college student jazz trumpet player (Bobby Hackett eventually blew the notes, although Astaire became quite proficient on the horn). He was forty-one at the time of release and the script's unlikely explanation was that he had failed his exams a lot. Although Astaire later referred to the film as 'smaller budget' and 'a quickie', everything is relative: it was less

[162]

expensive than any of his four previous films (each cost over $1 million) but Astaire received his $100,000 and the combined salaries of Goddard, Meredith and Shaw pushed the film into a high budget category. At RKO for example, most of the films of the 1940/1 season were budgeted at less than $200,000.

Astaire played opposite Paulette Goddard, Chaplin's mistress, who, in fairness, hadn't claimed to be a dancer since the days when as a Ziegfeld girl, she was billed as Peaches. Astaire was later to claim that *Second Chorus* was the worst film he ever made, although he was again working with Hermes Pan, who had moved to Paramount when Pan's seven-year RKO contract had expired at $300 a week, a sum he occasionally increased for the family by casting himself and sister Marie in the chorus line.

There were two films at Columbia with Rita Hayworth, daughter of dancer Eduardo Cansino (object of Adèle's Astaire's teenage crush) and his Ziegfeld partner Volga Hayworth. Neither *You'll Never Get Rich* nor *You Were Never Lovelier* was a great success, despite having Columbia boss Harry Cohn personally overseeing the latter. But they did establish Hayworth, then in her early twenties, as the top pin-up and sex symbol of the age (in August '45 her likeness was stamped on the first atom bomb dropped on Hiroshima). Hayworth's tempestuous love life ensured she was news. By the release date of *You Were Never Lovelier* she had left her small, tubby manager and husband, former car salesman Edward Judson, and was with her *My Girl Sal* co-star Victor Mature. But another lightning change meant that by the end of the year she was married to Orson Welles. While Astaire (who kept his self-esteem by sticking to his regular $100,000 appearance fee – inflation was not accounted) and Hayworth (on $500 a week for a pretty tight schedule – the film was released within four months of the start of production) worked together, business at Columbia was prospering so much that there was nowhere for them to rehearse on the set, so they were assigned to an address on Santa Monica Boulevard. It was only when they arrived at the place that they discovered they had been sent to the second floor of a funeral parlour of the Hollywood Cemetery. There were problems rehearsing there, Astaire recalled, as whenever a cortège of funeral cars passed by the building they were asked to be quiet.

In a black and white satin and lace nightgown Hayworth was a sensation on the cover of *Life* (11 August 1941) just a month before the release of the movie. Rita Hayworth was everywhere and *You'll Never Get Rich* was her fourth film release in nine months.

[163]

The observant will have noticed a difference between the two Hayworth-Astaire movies in her singing voice: in neither case is it hers. For *You'll Never Get Rich* her words were sung by Martha Tilton and in *You Were Never Lovelier* by Nan Wynn.

Helen Hunt, the make-up lady assigned to Astaire, remembered how she went to help him with his toupee one day and he produced a jewelled pin, in the shape of a Spanish dancer twirling her skirts, that he wanted to give to Rita. 'It was just beautiful,' recalled Helen. But Astaire was concerned about the present. 'I want to give it to her, but I don't want her to feel I'm after her in any way. You know how it is. She's got so many admirers.' Helen Hunt reassured him and the present was given and gratefully received, and Rita took the gesture as one of friendship, although she would have thought none the worse of Astaire if his motives had been base.

Fred felt that top flight success was eluding him, while his co-star, Rita Hayworth was on a tremendous high. However, there were distractions. Phyllis was pregnant again and on 28 March 1942 gave birth to a beautiful little baby girl who was named Phyllis Ava Astaire (the Ava, pronounced Ar-var). Astaire was on the tennis court at the Goldwyns' when a phone call told him of the birth. He was quite besotted by the new baby, more so than he had been with Fred Jr. It was as though he could release his emotions and innermost feeling to this little bundle of blue-eyed babyhood.

To continue his good fortune, Mark Sandrich, who had never lost faith in Astaire's box-office appeal, packaged *Holiday Inn* for Paramount to team Fred Astaire with Bing Crosby. There was a score of old and new Irving Berlin songs, including the début of 'White Christmas'. Crosby was no dancer but had the redeeming feature, as far as Astaire was concerned, of being a good golfer and a keen horse racing man. Astaire's reputation as a hard worker had preceded him and he was surprised to find Crosby was first on the set. Crosby was practical about it: 'Boy, that man can dance. If you're going to be anywhere near him in a picture you'd better get your dancing shoes on early to keep anywhere near him. So I reckoned he would at least be kinder to me if I showed willing.' As it turned out Crosby only does some token dances with Astaire in the movie, leaving the real hoofing to Marjorie Reynolds and Virginia Dale.

Although he settled for less than the usual $100,000 for *Holiday Inn* (he still got his percentage), Astaire's confidence was revived, and RKO started to wonder what they had got rid of so callously. They hastily offered Astaire *The Sky's the Limit* at his original home. His terms and conditions would be met absolutely and, in addition to having a veto over his leading lady – he went along with RKO's suggestion of Joan Leslie – he would also be his own dance director. Co-star Joan Leslie was already a screen veteran at eighteen, having made her screen début under her real name of Joan Brodel as Robert Taylor's younger sister in the 1937 *Camille*. The often rather gauche Astaire of earlier movies gives way to a more abrasive, and ultimately realistic screen persona, with which he was obviously more comfortable. When he plays a drunk scene here and sings Johnny Mercer's evocative 'One More for the Road' (Set 'em up, Joe . . .) there is no hint of the restrained elegance of the drunk scene of *Holiday Inn*. The rewards were reaped both critically and financially and although the film did not reach great heights, it gave RKO a useful profit of over half a million dollars.

Astaire, in uniform for the film, thought that he really should be doing something more positive to help his friends in Europe – it was not much consolation to be told of the morale-boosting value of his movies; he wanted to be at the sharp end.

13
MGM

Colour film stock – the Jock Whitney-sponsored Technicolor and rival systems – had been used effectively for ten years before Astaire got to make his first non black and white movie. But it was an expensive business.

If 'I Used To Be Colour Blind' had actually worked out as planned in *Carefree*, there might have been no anxiety to dabble in colour film, but it was a new – if at the time still pretty crude – idea and so when Arthur Freed talked about a colour movie to him, Astaire agreed, knowing full well that his offer to go to Europe to entertain American servicemen would mean that the likelihood of working on the movie was slim.

Freed was also a songwriter of note ('Singin' in the Rain', 'Temptation', and 'You are my Lucky Star') and had just made *Meet Me in St Louis* with Judy Garland (and even sung on the film soundtrack as the voice of Judy Garland's screen father Leon Ames) and *Du Barry Was a Lady* with Lucille Ball and Gene Kelly, who had also been successfully loaned out to Columbia to make *Cover Girl* with Rita Hayworth and Phil Silvers. Now with the brilliant, volatile and emotional director Vincente Minnelli, Freed planned three Astaire musicals. As the first partner, he had found twenty-one-year-old Lucille Bremer, a Radio City Music Hall Rockette who had been spotted by Minnelli at the Silver Slipper Club in New York and who had appeared in *Meet Me in St Louis* as the elder sister of Judy Garland.

It was on Minnelli's last day of shooting on *Meet Me in St Louis* that he was called aside by producer Arthur Freed and told of the plan to make a film version of the *Ziegfeld Follies* as the most lavish, biggest all-star production ever. A $3 million budget had been put aside for the sixty-five scenes, every writer at MGM was called on to provide additional material, every glittering MGM star was on standby. Along with Lucille Ball, Lucille Bremer, Fanny Brice, Lena Horne, Fred Astaire, Gene Kelly, Red Skelton and Esther Williams already set, Judy

Garland was also pencilled in as a last minute replacement for Greer Garson. That did cause some problem, as by then the romance between Minnelli, thirty-five, and twenty-two-year-old Garland, then married to orchestra leader and composer David Rose, had broken up and she was involved in another romance. He shot her sequence quickly. The real problems with Garland, according to Minnelli, were not the emotional ones but those caused by her compulsive taking of amphetamines and other pills which had started in her teenage years to prevent her putting on weight. They had been dining one night when she had told him: 'I use these pills. They carry me through,' she told him. 'I always have to look my best in front of the camera. You should know that. You expect it of me too. Well, sometimes I don't feel my best. It's a struggle to get through the day.'

Astaire for the first and only time in this decade, was to dance with Gene Kelly, the other leading dancer of his generation. Balletic and sometimes mannered, Kelly, so backstage gossip had it, was a man who thought before he danced, in contrast to Astaire's more natural approach, appearing to dance before he thought. They performed a revised version of 'The Babbitt and the Bromide', the number that Adèle and Fred had danced in *Funny Face*. Gene Kelly felt that 'The Babbitt and the Bromide', with its jokey patter and relaxed duet, should not have been as light and unchallenging as it was, but Minnelli disagreed. 'This was a revue,' he said. 'They should have been kidding their exalted stations. The dancing might have come easily to Fred and Gene, but it was impressive nevertheless. I had seen Fred do the number with Adèle in *Funny Face* in 1927, but their approach was different.'

Kelly and Astaire devised their own choreography, but that caused some problems, for neither wanted to be accused of foisting his quite different dance style on the other. 'We were so polite and generous and nice to each other it was almost boring,' said Kelly. Minnelli recalled: 'One would say: "What if we did so and so?" The other wouldn't react. "Maybe that's not such a good idea" . . .' Astaire's reaction, when told of Kelly's comments, was of mock outrage: 'What does Gene mean by saying the routine was unchallenging? Didn't we beat hell out of the floor together? We were supposed to be a popular team. We weren't trying, after all, to do *L'Après-midi d'un Faune*.'

Astaire's desire to become actively involved with the war effort grew with every report back from Douglas Fairbanks Jr, Jock Whitney, David Niven, Adèle or some other friend. He played military camps, went, accompanied by Phyllis, on a War Bond tour during which a pair of his tap shoes was auctioned for $100,000 worth of Bonds and the shoe laces for $16,000. He also joined the Hollywood Bond Cavalcade Show on a somewhat chaotic two-week coast to coast jaunt along with Lucille Ball, James Cagney, Judy Garland, Betty Hutton, Harpo Marx and Mickey Rooney. At Madison Square the show raised $18 million, helping New York reach a target figure of $5,000 million bonds sold: that kind of news did reach Britain and Adèle wrote to congratulate him. But to him it was not the same as really being involved at the Front. The Draft List reached down to Spencer Tracy, Humphrey Bogart and Fred Astaire, but in their forties they were as low down as it was possible to be – Astaire made Number 156 on the list.

He 'adopted' an RAF squadron and wrote to ask them what they wanted most. The answer was unanimous: autographed photographs of Rita Hayworth. But at last, while Minnelli was preparing a particularly elaborate setting for Ziegfeld, Astaire finally got the call: could he stand by to leave for Europe as soon as possible? For his last day of filming, Astaire, punctured with vaccinations for his trip, hot with fever and dressed in white tie and tails, danced with Lucille Bremer through a sea of bubbles surrounded by rocks on which beautiful mermaids were reclining – that is until the chemical fumes from the bubble-making machines not only caused the maidens' costumes to wilt but also overcame a number of the cast. It was no sadness to Astaire that the scene was destined to end on the cutting room floor.

At last he was off to Europe. In August '44 in New York he was given his briefing and a uniform – he would be given the temporary rank of captain, but without the pips. For all his enthusiasm he was decidedly apprehensive when he said goodbye to Phyllis and the three children – Fred Jr was six, Peter was fifteen and baby Ava was just two. And a complete security blackout meant that, even if he had known where he was going, he could not tell Phyllis.

Astaire, accompanied by accordionist Mike Olivieri, landed at Prestwick airfield in Scotland, where he found that the previous bucket seat C-54 plane from the US had crashed, while his, with thirteen passengers on board had landed perfectly – he had actually told the pilot that he was not superstitious and had rejected the offer of travelling separately from Olivieri on the earlier plane. From Scotland he telephoned Adèle at the Ritz. 'This is Fred,' he said. 'Fred who?' she sleepily demanded. 'Fred Astaire, your brother, you sap.' The squeals of delight put paid to further sensible conversation, but that day he flew down to London and arrived with Olivieri to meet Adèle at Rainbow Corner, where, bursting with pride, she introduced her brother who had flown in to give his support to his British friends. 'If these old bones can stand the racket I'm going to do a bit of hoofing for the boys,' he announced, and the reaction from the enthusiastic audience was deafening.

Bing Crosby arrived by boat to join Fred in entertaining the troops, and London was quiet for them. There were plenty of air raid warnings but no bombs. In France, Astaire and Crosby appeared together at a few venues before Crosby went off with the Third Army and Astaire went with the First. The audiences were vast and appreciative. At the Palace of Versailles, Astaire, in his army boots, danced for 5,000 GIs sitting in the acres of turned off, empty fountains. But away from Paris and the main centres, the going was often rough. On one occasion, Astaire noticed that the last jeep in the convoy of vehicles was not there any more, it was found half a mile back, upside down in a ditch, having skidded off the road, with its cargo of dancing girls in the troupe sitting by the roadside, seemingly quite happy and giggling.

When the convoy stopped in a small deserted Belgian town a little boy approached him: 'I know you,' said the little boy. 'You do? Who am I?' said Astaire. 'Oh,' said the little boy, thinking hard, 'Oh, Ginger Rogers.'

Accommodation was variable. In Holland the company stretched out on coats on the stage of a cinema and slept there at the insistence of the venue's Astaire-enthusiast manager. In Astaire's case the sleep lasted right through an air raid. He was kept awake another night when some bombs dropped a few hundred yards from the troupe's encampment. For twelve hours they were pinned down by the bombardment, although Astaire claimed he spent his time usefully with Chicago comedian Willie Shore, writing a rather good comic song called 'Oh, My Aching Back', about his GI experiences.

But he was relieved to travel back to Paris away from the front line. He and Olivieri were booked into the Ritz, but the conditions there were not quite the same as in peacetime. 'In the previous five weeks I had one bath in a Belgian prison – and that was that – so even the cold water was welcome,' Astaire said. At the Olympia, he gave the first show for the Americans since the liberation of the city and later they were summoned out to General Eisenhower's headquarters, some twenty-five miles outside Paris. They were told the invitation was for a meal and they would not be asked to do a show, but Astaire asked

Olivieri to bring his accordian anyway. They dined, Fred and Mike put on their show and also did a short routine for the appreciative audience of the four black cooks who had been slaving away in the kitchens.

He met up again with Bing Crosby and they spent a couple of days in London before they both caught the Queen Mary, bobbing and weaving her way across the Atlantic to avoid the all-too-frequent U-boat patrols. It had been an exhausting, exciting, shocking and moving experience and Astaire was glad to be away from the battle and surprised to be greeted as a conquering hero in New York. Astaire had hoped that Phyllis would be there to meet him, but he realised that there was no way that she could have known which boat he was on or even which day he would be coming back although through William Hearst Jr, who was working as a war correspondent, he had got a message back saying that he was okay. He took back with him a collection of souvenirs of the trip, from signed photographs of Eisenhower, an Italian automatic revolver, a set of German false teeth, part of a parachute and also a whole load of clothes he had taken and never worn. Throughout the trip he had performed in his army uniform and danced in his regulation boots. 'They worked quite well for taps,' he said, 'and what was more important I think the guys kinda liked it. I was just wearing what they were wearing and not coming in for any special treatment that would keep me apart from them.'

For Astaire there were two important first stops: to call his wife in California and to visit St Bartholomew's on Park Avenue and 50th, just around the corner from the Waldorf Astoria where he usually stayed on his visits to New York. There, amid the hubbub of the city he could thank God for his safe journey in a land where many would not survive.

He always found St Bartholomew's a calming refuge: 'I find great comfort in that magnificent church in the midst of the hurly-burly of city life. I think of everything there – my life, my work, the hidden meaning of the good and the bad things that have happened to me. I come out of there spiritually refreshed. It often helps me to go on. I just love the peace there.' Sometimes he would go down to the Little Church Around The Corner and have tea in the Episcopal Actors' Guild rooms or more often just go and talk to the Rev. Ray about the church's work, just as he would do at All Saints in Beverly Hills, seeing how he could help. Many needy people benefited from his generosity, but he always made it a precondition of any gift that it should be truly anonymous. Over the years the church had received many thousands of dollars from

Astaire, but he always reckoned that whatever he had given could never repay what the church had given him.

Back home again he cheerfully returned to work on his three-film commitment to MGM starting with *Yolanda and the Thief*, a light and nonsensical fantasy.

The only real casualty of *Yolanda* was Astaire's dancing partner Lucille Bremer. According to Minnelli: 'The studio gave her every opportunity to deliver. Nothing was spared to show off her extraordinary dancing ability. However she lacked star quality. But then Lucille never wanted to be a star and it probably showed. She got married as quickly as she could, leaving pictures shortly afterwards. Her defection is sad in a way, for I consider her one of the finest dancers I've ever worked with.'

Astaire was not happy with the lavish Minnelli sets and he wasn't happy with the fantasy treatment of the story of the American con man who swindles an heiress by posing as her guardian angel. Freed, who wrote the lyrics for the rather forgettable music by Harry Warren, wanted Astaire to make his third MGM film about a New York playboy and a Salvation Army girl. But the script was not ready and elsewhere there was suddenly an urgent call for Astaire from Paramount, where dancer Paul Draper, who had worked a double act with mouth organist Larry Adler, had been given his first starring rôle in the Mark Sandrich directed *Blue Skies*, scored by Irving Berlin and starring Bing Crosby, then at the peak of his film career. There was a problem with the film. Crosby, by no means the easiest of men to get along with, was making life impossible for Draper, who under pressure suffered from an almost terminal stammer. After a couple of days on set with Crosby, Draper was virtually speechless and Crosby announced that he was going off to take his sons swimming. Instead he went straight to the front office and demanded that Draper be removed from the film. To find a last-minute replacement while a film is in production is never easy, but Sandrich thought of Astaire and contacted him. Astaire said that he would be interested if they could get Hermes Pan from his current deal with 20th-Century Fox for the film. That was done and within a few days Astaire was back in business.

As 1945 rolled by and the filming of *Blue Skies* continued there was still no sign of *Yolanda* or *Ziegfeld* being released. Could it be they were going to remain for ever on the shelf? Astaire believed that this really was a good time to take stock of his situation and so, after many long and self-searching talks with Phyllis, he decided that he would make the Crosby film his last: he was now forty-six years old and the time had come to hang up his dancing shoes. Phyllis told David Niven that the retirement talk only happened when he had a good round of golf. If he had a bad day there would not be any idea of quitting. But there was also a rude awakening when he went for the usual routine medical check-up before making *Blue Skies*. He was, the doctor told him, getting a bit old to be putting all that strain on his heart by dancing. He was quite shocked by the prognosis, but reckoned that he had come into films with the big stars Joan Crawford and Clark Gable in *Dancing Lady* and now he could go out on a high point with Bing Crosby. So a formal announcement was made: *Blue Skies* would be Fred Astaire's last movie.

Crosby was always happy to be working with Astaire. 'There never was a greater perfectionist,' said Crosby. 'There never was or will be a better dancer and I never knew anybody more kind, more considerate or so completely a gentleman. If my work in the pictures I made with him is any good it was because some of his class rubbed off on me. I am notoriously a sloppy, slovenly workman. I love Fred and I admire and respect him. I guess it's because he's so many things I'd like to be and am not.' There was a little dancing for Crosby, five years younger than Astaire, but not much. 'When you're in a picture with Astaire you've got rocks in your head if you do much dancing,' Crosby said. 'He's so quick footed and so light that it is impossible not to look like a hay digger compared to him.' Astaire, always sensitive to public reaction, was delighted and rather surprised by the public response to the news of his upcoming retirement. Sackfuls of letters poured in saying don't retire, don't stop. 'It was rather as though I was shirking in my duty – very strange,' he said. 'There was one letter I do remember. Someone wrote to say that I wouldn't go through with it and that I would go on dancing until I was seventy-five . . .'

Filming had hardly started when Astaire's friend and most success-ful director Mark Sandrich died suddenly of a heart attack at the age of forty-five – which gave Astaire even more pause for thought about his own health. Sandrich was replaced by Stuart Heisler, who had just directed *Along Came Jones* and worked as second unit director on John Ford's *The Hurricane*. By then Astaire was determined that he and Hermes Pan would shoot his dances his own way, as he would have done with Sandrich. Heisler was happy to let him do that – when it came to setting up, editing, synchronising dance on film there was no one, after all, better than Astaire.

Astaire attacked his part with grim determination. The script was

[172]

hastily rewritten to include the Berlin song 'Puttin' on the Ritz'. With Hermes Pan and his assistant, Dave Robel, Astaire created a sequence in which he dances in morning dress, grey cravat and black tail coat, with a chorus made up of Fred Astaire's own images, not one image repeated but two separate images used alternately, to make a perfectly drilled chorus of eight. The tight, controlled sequence of Astaire's so-called 'last dance' may have looked easy, but it was in fact tremendously complex. There were shades of the *Top Hat* number, but it was a more mature, mean, unsmilingly aggressive Astaire this time. The number was shot last of all in the picture, and when filming was completed the publicity stills were taken of the Last Dance to be spread across the world. Forty years in showbusiness and he was happy to be getting out. As the last photograph was taken, Astaire carefully removed his toupee rug. He stared at it for a moment, like Hamlet contemplating Yorick's skull. Then, in full view of the entire cast and crew he threw the hairpiece to the floor and jumped on it with undisguised glee.

A technical hitch to his planned retirement was that Astaire was still under contract for one more film with MGM. He pleaded with his agent Leland Hayward to negotiate a way out of the deal. It took time, but by threatening that Astaire would do some unspeakable things on set, and would probably, because of his increasing years, hold up filming for inordinate lengths if they held him to the terms, it was agreed to let him go . . . but, if he ever did decide to make a comeback he would be obliged to fulfil the remainder of his contract to MGM. Astaire was satisfied with that.

At the beginning of November 1945 there were three Astaire films on the stocks awaiting release: *Yolanda*, *Ziegfeld* and *Blue Skies*. Hollywood and the American public, reckoned Astaire, had obviously had enough. The message had been clearly spelt out and he was right to be going. He had done his best but his style was no longer wanted. He had made a buck, saved a few, so there was no danger of his family starving.

Once before, he claimed, he had been replaced by a dog act – admittedly a dog act did stay on that Douglas Fairbanks vaudeville bill after young Fred and Adèle Astaire had been dropped after their one matinée performance – maybe that could happen again now. After all, at that time the collie Lassie (in real life a male dog named Pal) was residing in a $380-a-day suite at the New York Plaza and riding high at the box office.

Astaire was happy to spend time at home with baby Ava and out on

[173]

the golf greens. He said that golf brought out the best and, sometimes, the worst in him: 'The only time that I've ever sulked is when I thought that I had won a golf tournament only to find that I had been disqualified because I had unwittingly driven two balls off the first tee. My keenest personal ambition was to actually win a golf tournament. I'm not asking for a silver cup – if I could only win one little penknife or something, with my name engraved on it. I've come close, but I've never won a tournament. Before I took up golf I fancied myself as a great baseball player.'

He might not have won a tournament, but in the middle of the War years he did take time off to send a telegram to Adèle: HAVE DONE IT AT LAST STOP HOLED IN ONE YESTERDAY. He was playing (off a National American handicap of nine, equivalent to a highly respectable seven in Britain) with a number four wood at the thirteenth hole of the Bel Air Country Club, in a game with Randolph Scott and was justifiably proud of the achievement. However, Astaire said that his dancing, far from helping his golf, was actually a hindrance as he was not used to keeping his arms stiff, so his drive, undoubtedly elegant, was inclined to looseness.

It was not only with fellow performers that he played, Phyllis too made a good partner and opponent; although she weighed just a hundred pounds, he reckoned that she could hit a ball as well as anyone at the club. She was also fit through her tennis and once delighted Astaire by winning the mothers' fifty-six yards dash at Fred Jr's school.

'The first great shock of retirement,' he said, 'was finding that there are no days off.' But this gave him plenty of time for the race track. Astaire's caution about becoming an owner was a regular point of discussion with New York trainer Clyde Philips. It would, after all, be difficult to emulate his success in the UK, where his first horse, Dolomite, which cost him $500 in partnership with Sidney Beer, won some races and was sold for $1,000 a couple of years later, as he did not have an American Jack Leach. It took Astaire fifteen years from the time that he had first discussed the matter with Philips to the day he actually sent him a wire, asking him to find a couple of reasonably priced horses. But he struck lucky first time out. Philips bought a three-year-old colt called Triplicate for $6,000, who won on his first outing in Astaire's name at Jamaica, New York, by five lengths. Henry Bull, who had been a keen amateur steeplechase rider, had offered Astaire the use of his colours – dark blue, yellow sash and red cap – which Fred was delighted to accept. Within a short time Triplicate and the other horse, called Fag, bought for $5,000, were showing a return. Fag was third first time out in a claiming race, won his second claiming race and was bought for $4,000, leaving Astaire with a tidy profit from prize money and sale.

For some years in England, and now in the States, Astaire's one complaint was that he had never seen a horse of his win a race, he was always somewhere else. But on Thursday 7 June 1945 at Santa Anita, Triplicate won the seventh race, and that autumn picked up a further $5,000 third prize money in the Santa Anita Handicap. The next year Trip, as he was known, in a field of twenty-three was just beaten into second place in the Santa Anita Handicap – the following week in the mile and a half $50,000 San Juan Capistrano, in front of a 60,000 crowd, Trip romped home by five lengths and through the crowd Astaire struggled to the Winners' Enclosure, followed by a delighted Phyllis. She had been catching on fast in this game, and along with Astaire was becoming aware that owning a successful race horse takes on all the agonies, dramas and problems of big business: it certainly did not seem like a hobby.

Triplicate's finest hour was yet to come, for that year Trip was entered for Hollywood Park's $100,000 Hollywood Gold Cup. There was some high drama, as Astaire's regular jockey, J. D. Jessop, had been suspended and Basil James, the alternate jockey Astaire wanted, was out East and flying conditions were terrible. What could be done now? Fruitless phone calls and enquiries were made all around. Just when there seemed not the slightest hope of getting the jockey to Los Angeles on time, an unexpected saviour appeared. Astaire was not alone in following the fortunes of Triplicate, and RKO studios' owner and airlines millionaire Howard Hughes heard on the grapevine of Astaire's plight. Out of the blue a message was sent to Astaire's home: Hughes would get James to the racetrack – bad weather or not. Astaire accepted the offer with alacrity and one of Hughes' pilots, flying through storms and turbulence for much of the way, delivered a rather shaken jockey to the track.

Astaire recalled: 'I was more nervous than before any opening. We had a good jockey, but he didn't know the horse.' Moaning Minnie need not have worried. Triplicate came from the back to just catch Louis B. Mayer's filly, Honeymoon, by a neck, in a time to equal the track record. Randolph Scott said that it was one of the truly wonderful days of his life, as they cheered Trip into the stands. And when Astaire collected the Gold Cup he felt he really had climbed another peak of his ambitions. The winner's share of the purse was $81,000 and Cash Astaire the Big Punter had $400 across the board – winning $6,000. 'That,' said Astaire, convincingly but quite accurately, 'put me about even for life on betting.'

With his horses doing well, his children growing and *Blue Skies* getting good houses, Phyllis was eager to help Fred find other things to occupy his planned retirement. He still had a flood of fan mail. At one time he was receiving around 2000 letters a day. And most of the letter-writers wanted to know the same thing – how could they learn to dance like Fred Astaire? Astaire could only give one answer: try Arthur Murray, the one time vaudevillian who had made some $20 million from his Arthur Murray Dance Studios across the States and who had the dance market virtually sewn up. Phyllis suggested that now he was retired Fred should start his own dance studio. If only a fraction of the letter-writers turned up, he would still do very well from it. So, with former RKO publicity man Charlie Casanave, Astaire began to get the operation together. Neither he nor Phyllis had any experience of running their own business and so it was not surprising that the first studio, at 487 Park Avenue, in New York, caused some headaches. The building work on the main Adèle Room, as it would be called, was way behind schedule. January became September. *Life* magazine moved in and took hundreds of pictures – not a snap appeared. When they did open eventually there was no business. As Astaire said: 'I don't know what happened to all those people who wrote to me, but they certainly weren't at the studio.'

Phyllis felt very guilty about the operation since she had pushed Fred to go ahead, but he said that was silly: 'I wanted to go ahead with the project – it was my idea.' For two years the business staggered along before he was faced with the choice of injecting more capital or closing down the studios altogether. He was determined that the business should succeed so he decided that he would put more money in, even though this meant that he would have little option but to consider filming again.

14
Laughter and Garland

At The White House, in Washington, DC, Adèle spotted the Conservative politician Harold Macmillan talking with the dour John Foster Dulles at a presidential reception. 'Darling,' said Adèle, warmly embracing stately Old Etonian publisher Macmillan, and showering him with kisses. Dulles looked unamused. 'Oh, do you know my sister-in-law Lady Charles Cavendish?' said Macmillan, whose wife, Lady Dorothy, was Charlie's sister, to the amazed Dulles. Then he turned to Adèle. 'Adèle, tell me, my dear, what are you up to now?' he said. 'Oh, darling, I'm about to get married.' 'That's wonderful,' said Macmillan. 'Who to?' 'Oh, I've forgotten his name,' said Adèle blithely, 'but he's something very big in Dillon, Read.'

Where laughter was, there was Adèle. She had quickly decided that she would nurse her own great sadness about losing Charlie and the babies to herself. But that personal sadness seemed a minuscule thing compared to the tragedies of war suffered by so many in Europe. Within herself she still felt young and lively. On her forty-ninth birthday she told a friend: 'At my age I don't mind admitting how old I am; I'm forty-six.'

As soon as the war was over she and her mother headed for New York on one of the first available boats. She wasted no time in railing at a photographer from *Life* magazine who wanted to take some new pictures as she landed. 'What?' she said, 'After the last ones you took of me? You made me look ghastly. That nearly ruined my glamour life.' But she agreed anyway. What was she planning to do in the States? the man asked. 'Well, I'm planning to stock up on essential things. Particularly little panties. It's been so long since we could get any in England I'd almost forgotten about them.'

There was an emotional reunion with Fred when they arrived in Los Angeles, and Adèle was both surprised and delighted by his decision to retire. 'It was different for me,' she said later, 'but showbusiness and dancing and worrying were in my brother's blood – it was not just his work, it was his life.'

Among the American friends Adèle looked up was a good looking and slightly awkward soldier she had met at Rainbow Corner in London, now returned to civilian life as a banker. It was this man, Kingman Douglass, a widower with three grown-up sons, who lived on an estate at Gordon in Middleburg, Virginia, whom she was talking about to Macmillan. Douglass was quiet, easy-going and wealthy, and Adèle, who was invariably attracted to the very theatrical or the very noisy, rather liked the calmness that surrounded him.

When she returned to Lismore in '47 Adèle asked Andrew Cavendish, the new Duke's son and heir, to visit her at Lismore, for a rather delicate mission. She was, she told him, contemplating getting married again. If she did that, Andrew would inherit the castle and she had actually grown rather fond of the place and the people. As Andrew and his wife had a home in England she wondered if she might spend some time at Lismore each year? There was another matter. Both she and Fred had been hit by the stock market crash in 1929 and she had not been on stage since 1931, so even with the money Charlie had left her she was not well off and she did value her independence. Could Andrew speak to his father about her situation? Andrew already had an inkling of what Adèle had to tell him and he was delighted to help. A settlement was worked out. The old Duchess, despite Adèle's misgivings, was delighted to hear of Adèle's new plans and happiness and the new Duke was to help her with what Andrew Cavendish called 'a most generous sum'.

Andrew was equally happy to come to an arrangement about Lismore. She could stay there as if it were her own for three months of each year and, while being practical about the deal, he suggested that she pay a rental each year, way below the commercial level but enough to cover the wages of the staff and incidental costs of running the establishment. For the benefit of the Devonshire tax affairs, this in effect meant that Andrew was acquiring the beneficial right to the castle in exchange for Adèle's settlement. On Monday 28 April 1947 Lady Charles Cavendish became the second Mrs Kingman Douglass. She had, she said, no regrets about her resignation from the aristocracy. Some of her friends were surprised that she had found such an undemonstrative man as her new husband, but she was well satisfied with her choice. Some also found disconcerting the habit he had of clearing his throat between words. 'The poor man's just got catarrh,' she would explain.

In America when *Blue Skies* was eventually released it was one of the top ten grossing films that year and Astaire felt he had really ended his career on a high note. Admittedly he did get itchy feet occasionally, and to his own amazement even found himself dancing at home for his own pleasure, something he had never done before. But he was then forty-seven. 'My hoofing days are over,' he confirmed.

The MGM films had not fared badly either when they were eventually released – *Yolanda* had lost money but *Ziegfeld* which had cost a staggering $3 million grossed more. $5½ million. Freed remained an enthusiast for Astaire and believed that if he could find the right vehicle and pair Astaire with another big name, as Paramount had done by teaming him with Crosby, he would have the possibility of creating a really worthwhile and moneymaking project. Astaire was flattered to be considered and pleased that the films had done well, but he still gave the same answer: 'Sorry, Arthur, I've retired.' Then one day he had a phone call from Freed, who did not sound his normal, cheery self. 'Frankly, Fred,' he said, 'We're in a fix. Gene Kelly has just busted his ankle playing volley-ball and he was due to start work on *Easter Parade* with Judy Garland which starts shooting Monday. And Irving Berlin is doing the score. Could we talk about it?'

'Okay, okay. I'll call you back,' said Astaire, as Freed became more and more glum. Astaire was convinced that this was set-up to get him to make a comeback, so he called Gene Kelly.

'I really am out,' said Kelly. 'And they are in a hell of a hole. Would you possibly think about it?'

'Why don't you wait for your ankle to mend?' said Astaire. 'I really don't want to take this away from you.' Kelly explained that so much pre-production work had been done that if the film did not go now, it might never happen.

Kelly, thirteen years younger, was a very different performer from Astaire, although his natural successor as a dance star. He shunned white tie and tails. 'I look all wrong in a dress suit. Like a truck driver out on a date,' he said. If the production had been based around him, it seemed unlikely that it would fit Astaire. But on the other hand the picture had many things going for it. He liked Berlin's music, he liked working with Freed, Judy Garland was the young star of the age and the money would at least cover some of the expenses incurred in setting up the dance studios.

Received history has it that Astaire was the natural and only considered co-star, but that was not so. Top of Freed's list was Bing

Crosby, still riding high under contract to Paramount for another Road movie and the Billy Wilder directed *The Emperor Waltz*; not for a second did Paramount consider letting Crosby go – quite rightly, as it turned out, for *Road to Rio* was the biggest box office movie of the year (ironically *Easter Parade* was rated equal with it in the same period). Larry Parks, who had played Al Jolson in Columbia's *The Jolson Story*, was another possibility, as was Frank Sinatra, fresh from his triumph in MGM's *It Happened in Brooklyn*. Donald O'Connor was another unlikely possibility. Freed narrowed the choice to Astaire, then O'Connor, or possibly the suave Peter Lawford, already under contract for the movie in the rôle of Gene Kelly's best friend.

Astaire had little idea of what he was walking into. Screenwriter Sidney Sheldon, in later years famed for his novels such as *Master of the Game*, had already won an Oscar the previous year for his *Bachelor and the Bobby Soxer* with Cary Grant and Myrna Loy, also thought Freed was joking when he was told of Kelly's accident. 'No, it's not a joke,' said Freed. 'And there aren't going to be any postponements. We're starting work on Monday. I've sent a script to Fred Astaire.' Sheldon, who was then thirty, exploded. Astaire was old enough to be Judy's father. He said: 'I never thought it would work.' There were further setbacks; Cyd Charisse, who was preferred as she was small enough for Astaire, had broken a leg and the studio's casting, Ann Miller, refused to do a test with Astaire. She had after all made twenty-four movies already. In fact Astaire was less concerned about talent than her height. Robert Alton, who had worked on *Ziegfeld*, was dance director and was put out that Astaire wanted to use Hermes Pan as well. Judy Garland was fighting her own dark demons. After she had finished making *The Pirate* with Gene Kelly and Minnelli, now her husband, she had given birth to her daughter Liza, and had then quietly been committed to an asylum. Irrational jealousies and mood changes plagued her. Psychiatry had helped somewhat, and on good days she even entertained those on the set with tales of her committal. She said: 'It was very dark that night. Well, maybe it wasn't, but I was so out of it, that I couldn't make out anything. These two burly attendants met us at the car. They walked with me across the grounds. Suddenly I tripped. They picked me up. I couldn't seem to control my feet . . . I tried to walk, but I kept stumbling. They held me up the rest of the way. "This has to be the end of me", I thought. They got me inside and somehow I fell asleep. I woke up next day and didn't feel too bad . . . and I looked out of the window. I noticed this nice green lawn. Then I suddenly saw why I kept stumbling. I'd been tripping over the croquet wickets.'

On the set of *Easter Parade*, she found she had some new emotional croquet hoops, mainly in the person of her director husband. They were a few days into filming when Freed took Minnelli aside and told him that he had something difficult to say. Minnelli's first reaction was that the front office had decided to scrap the picture. 'No, it's not that, but Judy's psychiatrist thinks it would be better all round if you didn't direct this picture,' said Freed. So out went Minnelli and in came Charles Walters, the choreographer of *Ziegfeld Follies*, who had just completed his first director's assignment with the Betty Comden and Adolph Green musical *Good News*. Astaire, originally depressed with the change, found that Chuck Walters gave him a completely free hand. As a former dancer Walters appreciated Astaire's supremacy and as a film man acknowledged his great experience.

The result of the chaos and trauma was box-office and screen magic. Judy Garland picked up her steps quickly and made no effort to compete with Astaire. Her energetic and powerful performance contrasted well with Astaire's low-key approach. It was the first time in his career that Astaire made a film which was the top grossing movie in the world. All those hours and years of work had at last been rewarded; not only was he delighted but it did seem, maybe, that his retirement from the screen had been somewhat premature. So the Astaire-Garland years were set. A smidgin off his half-century with a girl half his age, Astaire had found a new partner and a new purpose.

He gained something else that was important to him too: an Oscar. Surprisingly, while many of his contemporaries had gained a statuette over the years, Astaire had not. Hermes Pan had won an Oscar for his 1937 Dance Direction of *A Damsel in Distress*, and in fact although that category was only awarded over three years – 1935, 1936, and 1937 – Pan had been nominated on each occasion. Ginger Rogers had won Best Actress in 1940 for her role in *Kitty Foyle*, Joan Fontaine had won in 1941 for *Suspicion* and yet another Astaire dancing partner Joan Crawford had won in 1945 for *Mildred Pierce*. *Easter Parade* won an Oscar for scoring but there was nothing for Astaire and he did not think much of the situation. There was a growing feeling in Hollywood that Astaire deserved some official recognition. Fired by Arthur Freed, at the next Academy Awards ceremony on Thursday 23 March 1950 at the RKO Pantages Theatre in Los Angeles there was a Special Award Oscar for Fred Astaire 'for his unique artistry and his contributions to the

[181]

technique of musical pictures'. Honour was satisfied and Astaire even showed his new-found belief in the system by the very next year acting as Master of Ceremonies at the Awards.

Although Judy Garland only ever made *Easter Parade* with Astaire, that was not the way it was planned. When a studio has made the most successful movie of the year, even when that studio boasts More Stars Than There Are in Heaven, it is desperate to find another crock of gold at the end of the same rainbow. So Freed was determined, and Astaire was not unwilling, to line up two more Astaire-Garland projects. Freed had the ideal script in *The Barkleys of Broadway*, written by Adolph Green and Betty Comden, about a musical comedy couple who break up when the girl wants to be a straight actress – not a million miles from the Astaire/Rogers tale.

So while Garland and Astaire were announced as being together again for the new movie, there was one mighty big catch. Garland's drug and alcohol dependency problems could not take the strain of another film straight after *Easter Parade*. On the set of *The Barkleys*, Judy cracked early. In the old days the studio would have waited for her to recover, but this was now happening too often. As the cast waited – Astaire used the time for extra rehearsals with Pan – Louis Mayer decided he had had enough and $100,000 of Judy's annual $300,000 salary was stopped on the grounds of the wasted pre-production costs of *Barkleys*. Astaire was left in the lurch, just as he had almost been for *Easter Parade*, but who could be found as a replacement? Who was capable of dancing to Astaire's standards and, more importantly, doing it instantly? The studio reckoned there was one person. It was ten years since Rogers and Astaire had danced together. But unknown to the studio Fred and Ginger had kept in touch on and off during those ten years, and their attitude towards each other was like that of an amicably divorced couple. There had been plenty of hollering at the time but it did not seem so painful in retrospect. And while Ginger may have been the one to win an Oscar – she had been particularly pleased with the telegram from Astaire after he had seen her in the rôle, so far removed from their light comedy, it read: 'OUCH' – Astaire was now right at the top again and had no worry about holding his head high. 'The old team hooked up again,' explained Astaire. He also did not know that Ginger and Lela had taken the precaution of sending a note of congratulations to Freed after *Easter Parade*, so that her name was not far from his mind when searching for a replacement. Rogers would be rewarded with $12,500 a week (Garland had been on $5,769).

[182]

So the old team went back to work. After the first take on the first day of filming Astaire called Hermes Pan over to ask if Ginger had grown. She hadn't, but Lela Rogers had persuaded Ginger that she looked better in higher heels. Tall partners drove Astaire wild: she did not wear the high heels for long.

But the problems with Judy were still not over. She started to believe that Ginger, among whose former lovers was director George Stevens who made *Swing Time* and *Damsel* with Astaire, had been planning a coup all along. In a bitchy gesture she sent Ginger a congratulatory floral bouquet – in the shape of a shaving mug, a none too subtle reference to the peach fluff on Ginger's cheeks which always caused such problems to make-up and cameramen. 'What lovely flowers,' said Ginger, showing no signs of recognising the intended insult.

Another day Judy burst on to the set, somehow charming her way past the heavy studio security. Walters said it would be best if she left. But Judy, full of imprecations against Ginger, refused to go. Finally Walters himself led her away in no tame frame of mind and ordered that she be taken home and security be tightened. The time wasted was annoying, but the incident was unnerving for the whole production.

The Barkleys was not as great a hit as *Easter Parade* and Freed spent the next three years unsuccessfully trying to pair Garland and Astaire – Garland at twenty-seven represented contemporary success, while Rogers, more than ten years her senior at thirty-eight, was no longer a glamour star and certainly Astaire didn't relish another resurrection.

However, even if Astaire and Rogers no longer quite had the youthful magic of the RKO days, the memory of that time, combined with a new spurt of cinema-going did turn in a $5.5 million gross on a $2.3 million budget. But, for all the profit there was a new spectre hanging over Hollywood: it had started with a trickle but by the time *The Barkleys* was released, sales of television sets were running at the one million mark. The thinking in Hollywood boardrooms was that people would never stay home to look at a wooden box, but then there was always the fear of the unknown, even among the visionary pioneers of California. When some suggested that television would become hugely important, the backlash of interest in cinema made profits soar – but for how long? As many had failed to make the transmogrification from stage to film, from silent movies to talkies, so many believed that the stars of the big screen could never be squeezed into a nine-inch cathode ray tube. Fred Astaire himself, always being one for innovation and trends, was one of the first in Hollywood to acquire a television; his friends thought of it as an

[183]

intriguing gimmick, but it could have been him confronting his own demons. If this new idea were to catch on, then it could spell the end for the movie industry. No one could foresee how it would instead eventually create such a dramatic metamorphosis and growth. In 1949 there were 940,000 television sets in the United States. Within two years that would have reached 10,320,000 in a pattern that thereafter would double the number of viewers every few years.

Meanwhile, a new era had begun for Adèle. Once more she was Fred's American cheerleader, critic and greatest fan, while Douglass became assistant director of the CIA. Although the ideas of the nation's security being anywhere near the hands of Adèle was an odd one, she declared she had been positively vetted without a stain on her character.

With Douglass, or sometimes alone, she travelled America, from East Coast to West. She travelled the Caribbean, acquiring a little house there which she painted a smoky pink. She travelled to London and Europe. Each June, July and August she went with her mother to Lismore, where the staff looked forward eagerly to her visits. Sometimes she would take Fred and Phyllis, or other friends, and laughter would echo round the courtyard.

'It was marvellous having Lady Charles Cavendish here,' said one retainer, who thirty years after still called her by that name. 'There was always plenty going on when she was here.' For the castle and neighbourhood it was like a three-month annual party having Adèle back and the local Irish would change their plans to make sure they were around for their refresher course of Adèle.

She never neglected to visit the graveyard of St Carthage's, putting flowers on the graves of Charlie and her three little children. And sometimes Ann, remembering her own child, would go and stand in silent prayer. The Dean of the Cathedral told me he found Ann Astaire gazing at the small solitary marble grave plaque of the little girl one day. The hollows of the small cross carved into the stone had filled with water and Ann carefully picked some yellow primroses and placed them in the water. 'It was a sad but marvellous moment,' said the Dean.

One of the greatest fascinations over the years for Fred Astaire had been to try and write his own material for stage and films: he was once asked what he would like to have been in another life and replied: 'A horse'.

From the earliest days when he trudged round the New York music publishers trying to find new songs for Adèle and himself, he had developed a tremendous respect and liking for the people who created the words and music he sang. He knew how hard it was. As a teenager he had tried his hand at it and during the Broadway years spent every spare moment scribbling words and music down on envelopes, on the backs of menus, and magazines. Songwriters, a jealous and introspective breed, invariably racked with self-doubt, appreciated Astaire's treatment of their songs. He did not mess around with them, changing words, rhythm or style. In his view, given the limitations of his voice, he just sang the song as well as he was able. As far as they were concerned, he turned melodies into magic.

If Astaire himself was self-deprecatory, Irving Berlin rated his ability as a singer very highly: 'It's nothing new to say that Fred Astaire is a great dancer. We all know that. But what was even more important to those of us who ever wrote songs for him was that he was also a great singer. I'm talking about writers of the calibre of Jerome Kern, Cole Porter, George and Ira Gershwin, Vincent Youmans, Harold Arlen, Johnny Mercer, Dorothy Fields, Howard Dietz, Arthur Schwartz, Harry Warren, Alan Jay Lerner, Burton Lane and many others. Fred introduced and was responsible for more hit songs than many of the top singers. He knew the value of a song and his heart was in it before his feet took over.'

In fact, outside his small circle of personal friends and racing folk, songwriters were his second choice of ideal companion, and some of them became close friends, including George Gershwin, who died of a brain tumour just after the filming of his *Damsel In Distress*. Gershwin was an old fan of Astaire and had played piano on *Lady, Be Good!* tracks recorded in London in 1926. Gershwin's incredible talent and appetite for sexual conquests fascinated Astaire.

Another close friend was Cole Porter, whose wife was a cousin of Phyllis'. He always gave Astaire encouragement in his own efforts, which had started back in the vaudeville – the first stage performance of a Fred Astaire written song was in 1927 when actress Joyce Barbour sang his 'Tappin' the Time', which had lyrics by the unlikely pair of Jimmy Altemus and Jock Whitney, in the London show, *Shake Your Feet*. He used to jokingly claim that the Whitney-Altemus collaboration was his most successful tune. 'Why,' he said, 'it sold four copies. I bought three myself.'

Sometimes he had succeeded in producing good material, even

[185]

though his 'If Swing Goes I Go Too' (for which he wrote words and music) was cut from the final version of *Ziegfeld Follies*. Sometimes he worked with other writers, such as Johnny Mercer, or with his long-term collaborator Tommy Wolf. From a financial point of view songwriting appealed to him particularly: for once you had written your song the money would, hopefully, just come rolling on in, not only in your lifetime, but for the fifty-year lifespan of the copyright period. His cheques from the collection agency ASCAP, the American Society of Composers and Publishers, were always most welcome – not for the cash alone, but for what the cash represented in terms of songs bought and performed. Like all songwriters, who always believed that the big one is just around the corner, Astaire would never give up. Even the hugely wealthy Irving Berlin would sit in his New York apartment every day to write a new song, and Astaire never lost faith in his own talent, for as long before as February 1936 his self-penned *I'm Building Up to an Awful Let-Down* reached Number Four in the US Hit Parade.

The third film of his MGM contract was *Three Little Words*, a biopic about songwriters Bert Kalmar and Harry Ruby. Garland was in such a state she could not even be relied on to turn up at the studio, spending much of the time in the sanatorium and finally Louis Mayer, offered to pay her $50,000 of the $100,000 he had stopped for the *Barkleys* if she would make *Summer Stock* for him with Gene Kelly. It was carefully planned so that if she loused up she could be excised from the final print without too great a loss. As a new partner for Fred, Freed chose the petite twenty-four-year-old Cincinnati blonde Vera-Ellen, born Vera-Ellen Rohe, a former Radio City Music Hall Rockette. Kalmar and his writing partner Harry Ruby spent most of their time at loggerheads and it is amazing they even spoke for long enough to produce the songs, 'Nevertheless', 'Who's Sorry Now?' and 'I Wanna Be Loved By You', (sung for the film by the boop-boop-a-doop girl Helen Kane, but mimed by eighteen-year-old Miss Burbank beauty contest winner Debbie Reynolds). Neither Kalmar nor Ruby (who, for a time as Edwards and Ruby, had worked the circuit with Harry Cohn, later boss of Columbia) wanted to be a songwriter. Kalmar, the elder by ten years, longed to be a magician; Ruby's sole ambition was to be a baseball player.

After that Astaire went to Paramount for *Let's Dance*, with Betty Hutton, who had replaced the ailing Judy Garland as Annie Oakley in *Annie Get Your Gun*. *Let's Dance* had Hermes Pan working once again with Astaire. The film was nothing special, although Astaire was left with the memory of Paramount's 'Blonde Bombshell' Betty Hutton, who would in time work her way through five marriages and much psychiatric help, running off weeping to her dressing room each time she missed a step. Astaire, grim-faced and silent, would pace the set while someone was sent to appease her.

Writer Allan Scott, who worked on the early Astaire-Rogers canon, did not really make a great deal out of the threadbare story of two showbusiness partners who reunite after five years of private life, just as Astaire and Rogers had done after ten years with the *Barkleys*. But Astaire did gain another trophy for his mantel shelf: in March 1951 he was awarded a Golden Globe as Best Actor in a Musical by the Hollywood Foreign Press Association – it was a second-rate award, but welcome.

Arthur Freed had another project at MGM, with June Allyson, wife of film star Dick Powell, for a movie called *Royal Wedding*. The screen play was by lyricist Alan Jay Lerner (who later wrote *My Fair Lady*) and it centred around a brother and sister vaudeville dance team, not unlike Fred and Adèle Astaire, who travel to Britain at the time of the wedding of Princess Elizabeth to Lieutenant Philip Mountbatten of Greece. Winston Churchill's twenty-six-year-old actress daughter Sarah, far too tall as a dancing partner for Fred, was announced as Astaire's love interest and any similarity to the Astaires' own story was purely intentional. But the project seemed to be dogged by gremlins. The first ten days of rehearsal were fine, then June arrived one morning and said that she did not think she could go on with the picture as she was pregnant.

Ginger Rogers was approached but she was working on another film. How about July Garland? She appeared to be better recently. The script went to Judy Garland. She was delighted with it. So the rehearsals were only held up for a week. But then director Chuck Walters, who had already had two traumatic experiences with Judy, asked to be taken off the film. Now without a director they went ahead on the dances. Disaster again. Judy Garland, brilliant and disaster prone, went through one of her bad patches. After the first two weeks she did not show for rehearsals. The air was purple with Astaire's swearing and cussing.

On 20 June 1950, with a broken water glass, Judy Garland, twenty-nine years old, slashed her neck in a futile and pathetic suicide bid. Costs were rising all the time and they were five weeks into the schedule with not a foot of film in the can.

Arthur Freed scouted furiously around: Jane Powell, a blue-eyed twenty-six-year-old blonde from Portland, Oregon, and a former teen

[187]

singing star of the radio, was available and at five foot one an ideal height, although she was not primarily a dancer. But Astaire had worked with non-dancer material before – so MGM issued a formal statement: 'With the responsibility and in justice to other artists the studio had only one recourse, which was to take Judy out of the picture, assume whatever losses were involved, recast it and go ahead. The substitution of any artist in any picture is never made on an arbitrary basis, and certainly a person of Miss Garland's talent is not easily replaced. The replacement is not a hasty move, prompted by pique or irritation. It is the last resort, arrived at with great regret after all other means have failed.'

Astaire was entirely practical and told Pan: 'It's better for that woman to drop out now than when we are actually shooting. I should never have agreed to work with her again.' A director was found in Stanley Donen, former child dancer-turned choreographer who had co-directed *On the Town* with Gene Kelly, with whom he had made his Broadway debut at sixteen. The dance high spot, as in the recent Astaire vehicles, was his solo. He danced around a room. Upside down, around the side, and so on. Set in the studio was a huge box in the shape of a room with all the furniture, lights, camera and fittings heavily attached to the sides and rigged so that the whole room could slowly rotate while Astaire continued to dance.

It was after *Royal Wedding* (*Wedding Bells* in the UK – so as not to be seen to be blatantly cashing in on events) that Astaire's contractual commitments caught up with him. He had retired once to get out of filming *The Belle of New York*. This time is seemed unavoidable. The story of a playboy and a Salvation Army girl was reminiscent of several other stories of its time. But as a musical stage show *The Belle of New York* had been successful in Europe (it ran just 56 performances in New York) so the front office thought it should make it on film. But not for Astaire. The shots of Astaire, so carried away by romance that he simply floats to the top of the arch at Washington Square looked, despite the best efforts of the photographic department, plain daft. There was eight months' shooting for little result, but as Astaire pointed out: 'I was in *Belle of New York* for eight months beating my brains out and all I got out of it was . . . a fortune. There's one thing about having a flop at a major studio that has it all over a stage flop. You do get paid.'

Undismayed, Arthur Freed decided that he would try an update of another tried success: the Astaires' most successful stage show from

[188]

1931, *The Band Wagon*. The revue would be updated and turned around and played for laughs with Astaire as a has-been trying to make his return with youngster Cyd Charisse, who had been seen as a chorus girl just whizzing past him in the *Ziegfeld Follies* and had danced memorably with Gene Kelly in *Singin' in the Rain*. The plan was to keep the numbers from the original but for time reasons four routines were scrapped. Freed decided that having the Howard Dietz-Arthur Schwarz songs from the revue, the picture needed a proper story. Why not base the part on the Astaire of a few years previously when he was in voluntary retirement? The writers of the story would be based on Betty Comden and Adolph Green. In which case, the best people to write the script would be Comden and Green themselves. 'We wanted to put in all the clichés,' said Green, 'How the troubles out of town can happen. How it happens that friends can turn to you and say: "How can you smart people get together and turn out such a mess?"'

The director would be Vincente Minelli who, although Astaire had found him a bit ethereal, had proved himself capable of a great dance movie with *An American in Paris*. Astaire's co-star Jack Buchanan was suffering from intensive orthodontistry combined with fears of being shown up by Astaire, and Astaire's on- and off-screen preoccupation was worrying about the height of Cyd Charisse.

The battle between ballet and modern dance was for real with former Broadway choreographer Michael Kidd. Minnelli thought he was inspired, marvellous. Astaire thought he was pretentious. He also annoyed Astaire by turning up earlier and staying later than even Astaire, the great workhorse. 'Their attitude,' said scriptwriter Betty Comden, 'reminded me of the lack of common ground between the movie hoofer and the ballerina which we had in our script.'

Astaire never knew quite why it happened, but during the movie he suffered an extraordinary crack-up. He was concerned that it might be a genuine mental breakdown. Minnelli was forever altering things during filming. The first scene was in a hotel room where the cast of the flop in the film are gathered after the opening night débâcle. Astaire was trying to follow Minnelli's increasingly confusing direction. Lines, places changed as the people jostled in the small space. For an hour Astaire pressed on. Then suddenly, late in the afternoon, something snapped. He heard himself say as if in a dream: 'That's it. I can't think. I've got to get out here.'

These was a sudden hush of horror around him. Fred Astaire, the most single-minded professional, was walking off the set. Minutes passed as Astaire sat at the side, his head in his hands. It was about five

[189]

minutes, but after what seemed to those present like a lifetime, he got up and walked back on the sound stage. 'All right,' he said. 'I'm ready now.' Later that evening he went to the director. 'He told me that he was very sorry, that he didn't know what happened,' said Minnelli. 'What could I do? I told him that I drove everybody crazy – it was about true, too. But frankly I hadn't realized that Fred had stormed off. I was too busy concentrating on the scene and my reaction to his apology was automatic.'

Astaire had an altercation with musical star Nanette Fabray, whom he thought, quite rightly, was scene-stealing. Fabray asked Minnelli what was the matter with Astaire. But he did not know. It was something to do with the 'I Love Louisa' number. 'Whatever it was you were doing, don't do it,' he said. Even more puzzled she asked Astaire: 'Please tell me what I did. I'll do anything you say, but I don't know what I did.' 'You know quite well,' he snapped. 'I went through that with Betty Hutton and I'm not going through it with you.' She never did find out her mistake, but Astaire, in time, did pronounce himself satisfied.

The film was also a time for reunions. The stage show lyricist, Howard Dietz, long-time MGM vice president in charge of publicity, came to the Culver City set for the shooting of *The Band Wagon*. The energetic Dietz was a popular figure who survived the ups and downs of MGM with a brazen cheek. One day he ran into Louis B. Mayer outside the studio. 'Howard', said L.B., looking at his watch, 'you're supposed to work until six. You're leaving so early.' Dietz, unflappable, answered: 'Yes, Mr Mayer, but you have to realize that I also get to work very late.' Mayer nodded: 'Yes, that's true,' and he continued on his way.

One regular visitor to the set, who would watch fascinated, was Minnelli's seven-year-old daughter Liza, who would stand alongside Cyd at the ballet bar as she limbered up. Minnelli would get the costume department to run up miniature copies of Charisse's dresses, which Liza would proudly wear around the house. Judy Garland, by then married to Sidney Luft, was back in California filming *A Star is Born* with George Cukor, and had little time for her daughter, so she was always delighted to go off and see her father. Liza remembers those days still: 'After school, which was dreary, I would go to see my father. "Oh please, Daddy, be making a musical," I would say. Then at three o'clock, I would go to the studio. I remember so well watching Fred dance – it was wonderful and so exciting. I remember Daddy calling Fred "Baby". He called everybody "Baby". It was just magic.'

15
Phyllis

Phyllis Astaire was companion, helpmate, adviser and mother of Astaire's children – and bride, as he often called her. They lived totally for each other and although it was a contented family unit, the two boys, Peter and Fred Jr, were merely accessories to their contentment rather than an integral part of it, with their routine carefully organised so that they were out of Fred's way and would not disturb him.

Ava was different. From the second she was born she became an Astaire lady – wilful, influential and loyal. No matter how tired or irritable Fred was he would always find time for Ava; and she too, quite naturally, played up to him in later years. The boys were particularly independent characters: Peter attended Brearley School and then Fermata School in Akin, and Fred Jr went to Webb College. When Fred Jr was younger, Astaire was often asked if his son would follow in his father's eminent footsteps, but he really did not mind: 'I have no hopes as to what he does. If he shows extraordinary dancing abilities and wants to become a dancer, I'll help him all I can, but first I would warn him of the dangers of a theatrical career. I have always enjoyed my work, but believe me, it isn't always fun.' But none of the children did show any tendency toward a showbusiness life and Astaire firmly blocked any suggestion that he should appear in public with the children. Peter however did show particular interest in one subject as a kid. As David Niven remembered: 'We did think that Peter was going to be a scientist.' Niven had visited the Astaires one night just before he was about to leave for the War, and was roped in to help when one of Peter's experimental rockets was lying ominously fizzing on the lawn. 'Peter's rocket refuses to take off,' said Phyllis. 'Can you do something?' 'It took off just as I was getting close,' said Niven. 'Happily it just missed me.'

To the outside world Phyllis was at her best when helping others, quietly and considerately. After the war, when David Niven arrived with his new bride Primmie, it was Phyllis who took her under her wing, and guided her around Los Angeles and Hollywood. Tragedy struck the Niven family when Primmie, at the age of twenty-five, was killed in an accident during a Sunday night game of Sardines being played by the English colony at Tyrone Power's house – she opened what seemed to be a closet door and in the darkness fell and tripped down the cellar steps inside and suffered a blood clot on the brain – and it was Phyllis who took charge of arrangements for four-year-old David Niven and his young brother Jamie, while Fred played golf with their father. Phyllis joined Lilli Palmer while she painted large cartoon figures of Mickey Mouse and Dumbo the Elephant on the walls of their nursery, and when Niven met and married his second wife Hjordis in London, the Astaires made her, too, feel a total member of their family.

When *The Band Wagon* opened there were excellent reviews and healthy-looking takings – it eventually made around $4 million profit – so there were no longer any pressing demands for Astaire to carry on hoofing. It was an ideal time to fade away, with no press conferences, no announcements and no front page headlines, and especially no 'last dance' picture spreads in the magazines.

With Phyllis he went down to Guyama, Mexico, on a fishing expedition and decided from there on in to take things a bit easier. Phyllis had plans to rebuild the ranch house so that they could live there for more of the time. But that summer of '53 at Belmont Park, Phyllis, for the first time that Astaire could remember, said she felt ill. It was a dizzyness, with a headache, and she asked to be taken home early. Next day she seemed fine, and turned down his suggestion that he call a doctor.

They had been planning to spend some time over Easter in San Antonio, Texas, with Fred Jr, who was posted there at Lackland Air Base for his Air Force basic training. It was a good time. The children were becoming adults and Astaire was looking forward to a new period of relaxation. Then at Santa Anita racetrack, Phyllis again complained of dizziness, insisting that she would soon feel fine.

Next day, she wouldn't see a doctor, but when she skipped a dance class function of Ava's and asked to be excused their dinner with Cole Porter, Fred knew something was wrong. Not waiting for her agreement he drove her straight to the family physician. The first checks were okay; they would wait for the return of the X-rays for the final clearance. The X-rays returned and this time the prognosis was not so good, for the doctor had found what looked like cancerous growths on the lung. Immediate surgery was essential.

The Easter trip to see Fred Jr was cancelled and instead he was granted special emergency leave to return home. Next day Phyllis insisted on travelling to the ranch to see the new filly foal from one of their brood mares and she did the full rounds of the stables and animals, looking and touching everything she could. Phyllis returned to the house, breathing hard. When they were in the car, ready for the ride home, she held out her hand to Fred: 'I wonder if I'm going to die?' she said, very softly. 'Don't be silly,' said Fred. 'You just need the operation and some rest and then you'll be fine. I know everything is going to be fine.'

The operation was performed at St John's Hospital on Good Friday. Astaire's faith at least brought comfort and strength to him. However, the operation was not satisfactory and to Astaire's horror Phyllis would have another one immediately. The second operation took place in the early morning of Easter Saturday and Astaire, with his closest friends, David Niven and Hermes Pan, waited, not knowing how to help, not knowing what to say. They stayed there for two hours. Then the surgeons, tired, came out of the theatre and a doctor told Astaire: 'She's doing fine, and she should be getting better straight away.' But he was cautioned that Phyllis would need extensive further treatment and rest.

Fred Jr, who had just arrived on compassionate leave from Texas, returned to his base after a couple of days. Phyllis was put on an intensive course of X-ray treatment in downtown Los Angeles, but her recovery was so swift that she did not even complete the course and came home with just one nurse. Three months after the first surgery, Phyllis decided that the nurse was not needed any more.

Life seemed to return to normal when Phyllis suggested that maybe Fred should do some work, rather than moping around the house. It was just an idea, but then 20th-Century Fox's production chief, Darryl Zanuck, saw them dining at Romanov's one evening and contacted Fred's agent with the idea of doing a modern musical version of *Daddy Long Legs*, Jean Webster's American classic of a wealthy businessman who anonymously sponsors an orphan girl's education. The girl Zanuck wanted to play the orphan was the gamine French ex-ballet dancer Leslie Caron, who had scored so heavily with Gene Kelly in *An American in Paris*. Astaire was tempted by the plan, but first he took Phyllis to Akin with the Bulls for a gentle vacation. When they returned to Los Angeles Phyllis had another setback and returned to St John's for more surgery. Fred Jr was called from Texas; again the operation was judged to be successful. Phyllis returned home and there was some

[193]

slight improvement, but she could not seem to regain her old strength and vitality. 'Fred, I'm all right,' she said to him. 'I really think that you must go on with your plans for *Daddy Long Legs*. It will be a marvellous film for you. Please do not worry about me.' Only at her insistence did he go ahead with the plan, leaving Ann at home all day to nurse Phyllis and look after Ava.

The rehearsals for *Daddy Long Legs* started in July. The minister from All Saints called regularly at the house and each day prayers were said for Phyllis in the church. But one day she lapsed into a coma. Astaire knew she would snap out of it. 'She looked like a beautiful child,' he said. 'She never lost her sweet facial expression.' But on the morning of 13 September 1954 at 10 a.m. her heart ceased to beat. She was only forty-six years old.

'My wife was a wise, remarkable woman,' the distraught Astaire said. 'She looked the same at forty-six as she did the day I met her. To me she stayed twenty-two always. I'd look at myself growing older but she was always the same. We had a wonderfully happy marriage.'

Shooting, due to start in September, was hastily rearranged so that Leslie Caron could be doing some of her solo numbers, while Astaire's rôle was held in abeyance. 20th-Century Fox producer Sam Engel recalled: 'The day after Phyllis's funeral Fred sent for me. He was in a bad way – sort of in a daze. The week before we had a talk in which he said he couldn't go on with the picture. He then had made me an offer that was unheard of in Hollywood. He wanted to pay all the expenses of the production out of his own pocket. I told him to forget it – that maybe God would intervene and Phyllis would pull through. Well, I showed up at Fred's house the day after the funeral and Astaire said: "Sam, what I told you last week still goes. The kids are shattered and I'm shattered. The worst thing is that Phyllis wanted me to do this picture. But I can't. The prospect of going to the studio and smiling is just impossible." I told him: "Don't worry about it Fred. If you feel the way you do, that's it. However I think you'll be making the greatest mistake of your life if you don't go to work right now." Fred shook his head and said: "Sam, I just can't."' Studio head Darryl Zanuck decided that they must carry on somehow. There was too much work and cash already committed to the project to cancel and various alternatives were considered. Maybe David Niven and Hermes Pan, who were trying to persaude Astaire that the best thing he could do was to get back to work, might prevail. But just in case, Maurice Chevalier was put on stand-by to take over.

[194]

The next morning, to Engel's surprise, Fred Astaire arrived at his Culver City offices. 'I don't know if I can make it, Sam,' said Astaire, 'but I'll try. I'm reporting for work.' He returned gradually to walk in the background of some shots, then to dance a bit and finally to act. Pan wasn't available so the dance director was Dave Robel, who had worked many times with Hermes, and Robel had an additional task on set: to look after Astaire during lunch-breaks. Astaire never had been a great one for having too long a break and now that he had nothing to do or think about he was plain dreadful to be around. Engel said: 'It was a frightful ordeal for the poor man. He'd be dancing as if nothing had happened and then he'd come over in a corner and talk to me. He'd say: "I don't know if old Dad can make it", and tears would come to his eyes. I'd say: "It's okay, it's all right to cry." He'd say: "It's rough, Sam, real rough, going home and she's not there." Then he'd talk about how Phyllis had wanted him to do the picture and then he'd go back to work. When the film was released his performance was such that no one would have suspected the private agonies he had gone through.' Leslie Caron also remembered it as a tense time: 'I rehearsed, tried to work, but filming was not held up for long – maybe two or three weeks, that was all.' Astaire had some trouble with the script too. At one point he complained to screenwriter Harry Ephron, father of novelist Nora Ephron: 'That love scene. I can't play it. Cary Grant can play it. I can't.' But he was slowly talked into a very chaste screen kiss.

With the death of Phyllis, Ava became a most important part of Astaire's life. He was sure that the twelve-year-old child would not get over the death of her mother for a long time, but hadn't realised how adaptable children are. Ava recovered far faster than her father did, rising to the occasion with amazing depths of understanding of his loss. She looked after him, he realised later, far more than he ever looked after her. In practical terms, Ann took charge of the house, so Astaire had no worries about his domestic life. Ava had in her the essence of his three favourite people: the mannerisms of Phyllis, the firm-jawed determination to get what she wanted of his mother and the freedom of spirit of his sister Adèle. All the family adored her, and it was not surprising that she was cheerfully spoiled as a kid. If Fred had called Phyllis from the studios in the middle of the day, he would ask Ava's advice. Even when she was just a tot of four years old he called one day to ask: 'Should I put $4,000 on Triplicate this afternoon?' After consideration, back came the precocious reply: 'Well, yes. But how much will I get out of that?'

To begin with, his mother – he always called her Mother, and she always called him Sonny, whatever his age – just tried to encourage him to live life as normal, but she was all too aware that Summit Drive was a home packed with memories and ghosts for him. And so, with the passing of time, she asked if he would be wanting a smaller house. No such idea had even crossed his mind, but Mother knew best and he realised that he needed new work, new pressures, and new pleasures if he was to recover at all from the blow he had suffered. Several times he told his mother that it was no use, he couldn't go on. But always, with her common sense, the wisdom of the church and the incentive of working for Ava, he managed to come round. Leslie Caron said that she was invited back to his house: ' "Come and meet my mother", he said. She was seventy-seven at the time, with a fine, pink complexion and as sprightly as anything. "Oh, you're the girl that's dancing with Fred," she said. She talked about him as though he was only a teenager or something like that. But of course they are from that incredible Nebraska stock where people can go on for ever.'

Ann found Astaire a site for a new home on San Ysidro Drive, just around the corner from Summit Drive, so that Ava could still see all her friends. Ann also organised the architects and everything else that needed doing, although Astaire was aware that just as she was looking after him, she too needed some care. 'She liked to wander out alone. I would get very worried and have to send my chauffeur after her to check she was all right,' he said. Between them, Fred, Ava and Ann made San Ysidro Drive a new home. Round a blind corner and hidden back from the road, it was the essence of his previous Los Angeles homes. With Phyllis he had always slept in twin beds, lest his 4 a.m. rising should disturb her, now there was just one single bed. Instead of the other bed he had a drum set, a piano and a record player. The house was long, low, cool, white and unfussy with two wings, one for Ava and one for him, with room for Ann or Adèle in the middle. The library, with a backgammon table – a favourite game he had learnt when it was fashionable in London in the twenties and thirties – opened into a billiard room, where Fred could indulge his passion for three cushion billiards or, less frequently, pool. The bookshelves were jammed with horse-racing form books dating to 1923. The Oscar and the Golden Globes from the Hollywood Foreign Press Association were clustered together in a corner with pride of place given to the Hollywood Gold Cup won by Triplicate: a portrait of the proud bay hung over the fireplace with a small Irving Berlin naïve painting of a bird with a top

[196]

hat nearby. In the dining room the chairs were reproduction Sheraton, the silver was English Georgian style and on the wall was a painting of a classically pillared dreamscape by Ava Astaire. In the living room – to be totally British, he would have called it the drawing room but that does not sound quite right for a California room that opens on to a palm-fringed swimming pool – he kept a few, very few, pieces of nostalgia. A photograph of George and Ira Gershwin, one of Cole Porter. The chairs and stuffed sofas had recently been re-covered quite sombrely, but for some years they had retained alarmingly vulgar cheetah-patterned material. There were also silver-framed photographs of Fred and Phyllis, of Fred and Adèle, of Fred and Ava, of Adèle and Charles Cavendish, and on one of the sofas there was a delicate needlepoint cushion lovingly stitched by Adèle. On one side was an elegant floral design; when it was turned over there was the delicately stitched message FUCK OFF.

Aside from his golf, the horses and his music he also now had more time to indulge another, more unusual interest which had started when he was touring as a youngster. After the bell-hops and train guards the other source of knowledge, wisdom and authority in uniform were the police. And as Astaire developed and grew, so his fascination for the world of crime grew too. He became one of the first regular citizens in Los Angeles to have a short wave radio licence, so he could listen to police broadcasts. He would ignore the small-time calls on the crackling radio, but when he heard a call on the emergency frequencies – codes three and four – he would race over. Hermes Pan would shake his head in puzzlement at Astaire's latest exploits: 'He does the damnedest, most unexpected things – and can't explain them. One night, for example, I saw a crowd in the street in Los Angeles about four o'clock in the morning. A man had been stabbed and was lying in the sidewalk. A police car drove up and who should pop out of it but Fred. He had been riding in the prowl car with the cops. When he got lonely or bored at night he often used to do this – in Los Angeles, in New York, even in Melbourne, Australia. He really wasn't sure why he did it himself. I asked him once and he said: "It's like going on a good hunting trip, and you suddenly run into some excitement." ' Astaire played down his commitment to the police force: 'I don't want it to sound as though I do it all the time. You'd think I sat around every night waiting to go round. I've done it very seldom in fact but it is fun. It interests the hell out of me. I went one night with Douglas Fairbanks Sr and all we saw was a fire and a fight. And when we were filming *On the*

Beach in Australia Greg Peck and I went out one night. Nothing was happening, but we did go to the morgue. We saw a lot of unpleasant things, but it was rather enlightening to know you can look at all that. But the smell is awful.' This pursuit was not without its own surprises, as when he covered a bank robbery and the thief was caught hiding in bushes at the back of the building. Astaire was walking back to the police car with the handcuffed thief when the criminal turned to him and said: 'Mr Astaire, can I have your autograph?', so Astaire obligingly scribbled it for him on the same piece of paper he had used to draw the plans for robbing the bank.

On more than one occasion he had to get out of the way of gunfire in a hurry. Once the toppling wall of a burning building missed him by inches and on another occasion he spent a few tense moments with his hands in the air when a policeman thought that he might be a suspect in a stake-out.

The fifties were a time of change. In 1949 Astaire had been in the front row of the MGM family photograph taken to celebrate the company's silver jubilee and in the early fifties, right up to *The Band Wagon*, he was still making the string of mainstream Freed-MGM musicals. But the pattern of life had changed. Although the movie companies steadfastly refused to sell their catalogue to television, Columbia, Universal and Paramount had set up divisions to cater specifically for the new medium. As cinema audiences started to slump, the search was on for gee-gaws and gimmicks: 3-D, Cinema Scope, and even experiments with the appalling process of aromatic cinema (Mike Todd's Smell-O-Vision and the competing AromaRama thankfully were not foisted on the public until the end of the decade).

What place was there for a fifty-year-old song and dance man in the modern world? Frankly, not much. But there again, in the desperate battle to combat falling profits, any idea would do. And there was no reason why the new idea should not consist of an ageing hoofer appearing opposite a girl young enough to be his daughter. In production discussions there were a number of factors taken into consideration in planning schedules: a box-office name came high on that list, and Astaire's name still had pulling power. So there were some film projects mooted – a film with Crosby, a film with Cagney, a film about a drunkard entitled *Papa's Delicate Condition*. There was even an intriguing idea for him to play Nijinsky. He was, after all, the greatest dancer since the great Russian, although Astaire was none too keen on comparison with the flamboyant Bolshoi star who had become insane at twenty-seven and spent the last thirty-three years of his life in sanatoriums. Even, Astaire was told, if he felt his ballet technique was not adequate, could he not give an impression of Nijinsky? Astaire had more objections than usual: 'One, I am not a ballet dancer and two, I would need at least three years' rehearsal to be able to work up a technique that was even passably good enough.' He didn't mention the fact that it was no rôle for a man in his fifties. Arthur Freed, who tried to interest Astaire and Gene Kelly in a joint project, remembered: 'It was a shame that after the *Ziegfeld Follies* they didn't work together, but there was always something – I'm not even sure they relished the idea.'

Freed eventually found two projects which did interest Astaire: a musical version of Greta Garbo's film *Ninotchka* and a remake of the Astaires' 1927 stage hit *Funny Face*. *Funny Face*, as a show, had always been beset by problems. So it proved with the film. MGM owned the rights to the show; Paramount owned the rights to Audrey Hepburn, the ideal lead as far as Freed and director Roger Edens were concerned. MGM also owned the rights to Edens, the musical supervisor who had worked on *Easter Parade* and *The Band Wagon* and had won praises for bravery and brilliance under fire with his work on *A Star is Born* with Judy Garland. Complicated deals were done whereby *Funny Face* and Edens would be loaned by MGM to Paramount in exchange for a share of profits. Some of the original Gershwin score was used but a new script was written, loosely based on the life of the film's 'visual consultant', the great fashion photographer Richard Avedon. Hermes Pan was not available; he had been doing an increasing amount of work in Italy – so much so that in time he would be given an Italian state pension. So the cast set off for Paris, where half of the picture was to be shot. In Paris it rained, and rained, and rained. Shots were snatched when and where they could be. Dry scenes were reorganised to take place in showers. 'All of my life I dreamed of dancing with Fred Astaire,' said Audrey Hepburn, 'and what do I get? Mud.' On the Left Bank, in the Latin Quarter, Hermes Pan taking time out from his Italian commitments, was visiting Paris. Late one night he had lost his way to his hotel and was wandering the streets when he heard the sounds of great activitiy. Following the noise he found a film crew – and, to their mutual amazement, Fred Astaire. Astaire was delighted by the coincidence and a nearby café was taken over by Pan and Astaire as a temporary headquarters for gossip, discussion of plans for the movie and so on.

As Astaire no longer had Phyllis to travel with, Ava came instead.

[199]

After the postcards of Paris, with tales of *Funny Face* and Audrey Hepburn, Ava, home on school vacation by the time that Astaire returned, asked: 'Couldn't we go to Paris?' Of course we can,' he said, and they set off for Europe a couple of weeks later.

Where Astaire had been worried and working not so long before, he now strolled along with the crowds of tourists through the Louvre, the Tuileries, visiting Nôtre Dame, the Ritz, the Champs-Elysées, walking arm-in-arm with his daughter – as proud as could be. The journey also meant that Astaire had a chance to show Ava something of the places he knew and later to take her to Goodwood races in England, where his two-year-old filly Rainbow Tie was due to run. Glorious Goodwood it is called, and that summer it was indeed glorious. When the Queen, in the Royal Box with Goodwood's owner, the Duke of Richmond, heard that Astaire was there with his daughter, she asked her equerry Lord Plunkett to invite them to her box between races. So for the first time since he had seen her as a white-gowned babe at that luncheon with her parents so many years before, Astaire once more met the child who had become Queen of England. Astaire said he had danced with her mother some years before. The Queen smiled and replied: 'You mean she danced with you.' Ava bobbed a curtsy, but really was not sure what to do next. Other girls certainly did not have a father who was on such terms with the Queen of England, as if all his other achievements weren't enough. Rainbow Tie was sleek, shiny and elegant in the Astaire colours, as she crossed the line. But, alas, not in first place.

Adèle was back at Lismore with her husband and Ann, so Astaire and Ava went over to join them. For Ava it was a magical trip, she was a pretty dark-haired fourteen-year-old and her head was already full of castles and romance so Lismore was perfect, and the sun shone down non-stop, a rare occurrence for Ireland, even in the summertime. Ava's namesake Basil Ava had been killed in Burma when she was three years old, but Ava did get to meet many of Astaire's Irish friends. Then, while Fred stayed with Adèle and his thoughts in Lismore, Ava, looking so like a younger version of her mother, went to London to see the sights.

In the autumn of 1956, Astaire returned to the rehearsals for *Silk Stockings*, with his *Band Wagon* partner Cyd Charisse, now married to singer Tony Martin. Director Rouben Mamoulian, the Armenian who made Greta Garbo's *Queen Christina*, soon found that Astaire was no easy person to work with. 'He is a truly complex fellow, not unlike the Michaelangelos and Da Vincis of the Renaissance period. He's a supreme artist but he is constantly filled with doubts and self-anger

[200]

about his work – and that is what makes him so good. He is a perfectionist who is never sure he is attaining perfection.'

Astaire himself was unimpressed by the allegations: 'I don't dig this brooding analytical stuff. I just dance – and I just act.'

No satisfactory explanation of Astaire's style could even be offered by Gene Kelly, a great and intelligent analyst of dance and, as the only other oustanding screen dancer, so often compared to Astaire – 'It's the bane of both our lives,' Kelly said.

But as one of the MGM crew pointed out: 'The difference is that there have been a lot of imitators of Gene Kelly, but no one has been able to imitate Fred Astaire.'

'I wish I did know what it was with Astaire,' said Kelly. 'If I knew I'd add it to my own bag of tricks.'

At San Ysidro, life was not always calm between Ann Astaire and her Sonny, as they both had quick tempers and it did not take much, usually some silly trivial domestic matter, to set them off. Then Ann Astaire would pack her bags and announce that she was going to Middleburg to see Adèle, or going to Ireland with Adèle, or sometimes just to New York where she still knew many people, who were always keen to see her. She could count many of the more entertaining ladies of Hollywood among her friends and admirers. Chat show host and businesswoman Pamela Mason, ex-wife of James Mason, thought she was marvellous; Shelley Winters thought her divine.

Astaire would sometimes 'Harumph' when he heard unbridled praise of his mother, but he was tremendously proud of her. 'Mother still tells me what to do,' he said, shortly after Phyllis died. 'She has a bad temper which I guess I inherited from her and when she blows her top I get out of the way.' And Astaire looking back to his Broadway days, said: 'The three people who meant so much to me then were my sister Adèle, my mother and my father. My mother was, and still is, one of the most attractive ladies of her generation. Her advice and guidance through the early years have most certainly been greatly responsible for whatever success Adèle and I were able to attain.'

When Ann Astaire announced that she was arriving in Ireland or Middleberg, Adèle always knew that there had been yet another row, but good naturedly took her mother in, invariably lecturing her on not being beastly to Freddie. Adèle, who reckoned she could fix almost anything, found Freddie's loneliness beyond her, even though she did occasionally introduce him to ladies she considered might make him a good match – although she would have been quite horrified and not a

[201]

little upset if her beloved Freddie had actually wanted to marry any of them. Adèle herself was quite happy, and she enjoyed her rôle of hostess whether in Lismore, New York or Washington.

She could still make her mark and delighted in being involved with ventures that amused her. In the days of currency restrictions she busily removed money from Ireland to America, and she used her impressive contacts to fix all kind of things. When millionaire Paul Mellon and his wife Bunny wanted tickets to take President John F. Kennedy and his wife Jackie to see Noël Coward's *Sail Away* in New York there was only one person to ask to make the arrangements. After the Kennedys had seen the show Mellon sent his jet to bring Adèle, Noël Coward and Coward's companion/secretary Cole Lesley up to Cape Cod for lunch with the Kennedys at Hyannis Port. 'Delly,' warned Coward, wagging his finger at Adèle, 'You are not to tell that story with which you had such success in Jamaica in the spring about the honeymoon couple and the bride who had such trouble with her gums . . .' Dentistry, Coward said, came up in the lunch-time conversation with agonising frequency, but Adèle just managed, with plenty of glances at Noël, to behave herself. Coward, as well as being the Astaires' guiding light, also vied to be their greatest fan and said: 'Delly was a true original. She had a tremendous talent, knew everyone and was my favourite person in the whole world.'

That was not Adèle's only brush with the US Presidency, for, although it may have surprised the presidential entourage, it did not surprise her when, during his visit to Ireland in June 1963, just five months before he was cruelly assassinated, Jack Kennedy ordered the presidential helicopter to fly a hundred miles off the planned course so that he could wave to Adèle at Lismore. 'That's the wonderful thing about the President,' said Adèle of the man whose sister had been married to her brother-in-law, a kind of brother-in-law by marriage. 'He never forgets the little things that are so important to any friendship.'

16
Another last dance

Five times in his career Fred Astaire retired. Each time his belief in the retirement was complete, but each time his feet – and usually some extraneous factors – drove him back to dance.

His first 'last dance' had been at RKO when they didn't renew his contract, the second after *The Sky's the Limit*, the third 'last dance' had been in *Blue Skies*, and *The Band Wagon* had been a definite end . . . that is until *Daddy Long Legs* and Phyllis's illness and death had driven him back into professional circulation. Now, after *Silk Stockings*, he could see retirement as a practical reality. His dancing partners were getting young enough to be his grandchildren and he felt now he really had done all he could in movie dancing.

He spent his days as always on the golf course or at the racetrack. Rising early, doing his morning crossword, having one egg for breakfast, in bed by 10.30 p.m., travelling to see Adèle occasionally and generally taking life easily. But there was enough energy left for another project. Various friends and several publishers had been on at him for some time to write his autobiography. At last, with public relations man Cameron Shipp taking down his thoughts and knocking them into shape, *Steps In Time* – a title suggested by Noël Coward on a visit through Hollywood – was published in 1959. He had taken quite a lot of persuasion to agree to the project, even though it was a flattering idea. 'I don't like looking back,' he said, 'and anyway I haven't got up to all kinds of things like those other people who write books have. I've never been a drunkard. I've been happily married just once and I've got a family. What interest could that be? Anyway, I can't remember a whole bookful.' But with Phyllis no longer there, things were different. David Niven, Noël Coward and Randolph Scott all said he needed to keep busy, so he started to write short passages in long hand. The book, like the public man, was polite and factual. It was also intriguingly inaccurate about many details of his life and the general feeling was that there were more unanswered questions at the end of the book than beforehand. He had painted a picture of a bright, simple world where everyone is as pleasant as possible to everyone else. Hermes Pan made his own point: 'That's the trouble with Fred. Everyone thinks of him as Mr Nice Guy and he tried to live up to his reputation by not saying anything bad about anybody. Some of the people in his book gave him some pretty rough times and vice versa.' But Astaire countered: 'That's the way it is. That's all they're getting.'

Steps In Time was dedicated, to Hélène Geilus's amazement, to 'My cousin Hélène and Omaha, Nebraska'. Although he had only ever been back there once in recent times – with Ava, as a teenager, making his fourth visit since he had left at six – he retained a romantic fondness for the idea of the easy-going mid-west town. But he also retained an irrational guilt about his relations there who had not fared as well as Adèle and he had done: there had even been another cousin who killed himself, whom he had heard about from Hélène when she had visited Beverly Hills. Having written his life-story he broke more of his old rules to keep himself occupied, appearing in newspaper advertisements for American Airlines in the *New York Times*: a photograph of Fred on the steps of an aircraft, with the caption: 'Fred Astaire's favourite step – aboard America's famous DC-7 Mercury for luxury'. This was something he had not done since the days of *Stop Flirting* in London, when he and Adèle had endorsed the energy tonic Phosferine: 'Phosferine never lets us down' went the ads. He even made his television début on CBS's *The Toast of the Town* variety show hosted by Ed Sullivan, which in turn led, eighteen months later, to him testing the strength of his long-held view that he was an actor first and a dancer second, when he appeared in *Imp on a Cobweb Leash*, a television play in CBS's General Electric Theatre series, 'Ronnie Reagan's show', as Astaire called it, for Reagan introduced the weekly performance. He justified his previous reluctance for appearing in straight rôles by saying that he didn't think that the public would accept him in a non-singing, non-dancing rôle. But, as he said: 'I did it and seemed to get away with it. No one seemed to mind too much, or maybe no one noticed it.' That gave him the confidence to try more things in the field. One attraction in those early days of live television, before the days of home video recorders, was that the performance was over and forgotten afterwards and there was no danger that the shows would be replayed in fifty years' time, as has happened to his films. Astaire was wary, rather than frightened, of the medium which had started its broadcasting career just two years after he had arrived in Hollywood, but he liked the idea of new things and new challenges. For some time the networks had been after him to do a TV Special of Fred Astaire singing and dancing. But his conversations with other performers told him that television performers invariably complained of insufficient rehearsal time and, as he said, 'I'm not interested in doing anything crummy.'

A solution was found when he decided that he could best control events by making an independent production through his Ava Productions company. A sponsor was found in Chrysler and he started to put together a one-hour show at his own pace. This would then be transmitted live for NBC from the Burbank Studios. But the first thing he needed was a dancing partner. Fred Astaire's favourite dancing partner, other than his sister Adèle, was usually the one that he was about to work with, rather than the one of the moment. Having been teamed for years with Adèle and then with Ginger Rogers, he was always keen to ring the changes and only in exceptional cases – for instance with Cyd Charisse – did he work with the same partner more than once or twice. Now there would be another exception in Barrie Chase. But then Barrie, his twenty-first screen partner, was a special case on several counts.

When asked the inevitable question as to which was his favourite dance partner, Astaire usually used the flip answer: Bing Crosby. But he hardly danced with Crosby. Sometimes he would say Gene Kelly. A more practical and honest answer would have been Hermes Pan, Astaire's rehearsals partner for over 30 years. Astaire never attempted to outdance his partners, but tried to present on screen the best possible dance with the partner in hand. Sometimes one of them, for example Ann Miller or Betty Hutton, did try to outdance him, but that was a futile exercise and only caused him to lose his temper. To reach perfection the dancers had to look good together. Sometimes a long gown, or flowing hem, could cover up the girl's steps, and often, if they were not primarily dancers, he would suggest details to help make the final product looked polished, flowing and a genuine partnership.

It was while working on *Daddy Long Legs* that Astaire, throwing himself into his work with a vengeance born of desperation, had worked with a dancer with whom he felt an immediate affinity. He needed some dancers for a fantasy sequence where Leslie Caron imagines her unknown benefactor in various guises, including that of an international playboy surrounded by beautiful girls: he had scouted around and had found a languid seventeen-year-old called Barrie Chase, who

[205]

was working with his choreographer friend Jack Cole on the Gregory Peck-Lauren Bacall movie *Designing Woman*.

Barrie Chase, after some years of doing line work for TV and movies, had actually been on the point of giving up her dancing when Jack Cole, dance director of *Cover Girl* and *Gentlemen Prefer Blondes* and the 1945 *Kismet*, hired her for the chorus of the 1955 *Kismet* remake. She soon emerged as a featured dancer and stand-in for Dolores Gray and Kay Kendall, and it was while she was there that she first saw Fred some time before he noticed her: 'During the time I was with Jack at MGM I saw Fred quite often. At first he'd just stick his head round the door of our rehearsal hall to see what was going on with those trap drums that Jack uses. What was going on with me was that I was simply trying very hard. But the best I could do was to struggle away, always two counts behind on everything. Fred continued to look in on us, even though after a quick glance around in that timid way of his, he would dart away. One day he asked Jack who I was. More time passed and eventually Fred and Jack and Kay Kendall and I would get together after rehearsal for a cup of coffee or a cocktail.' She was still not sure that she was getting anywhere in her career, but, as she said: 'After I had started dancing with Jack I couldn't bear the thought of going back to the chorus. I began studying drama and doing some acting because there didn't seem any place to go with my dancing.' Astaire asked if she would do the spot in *Daddy Long Legs*, where she can be just seen with her brunette hair hidden under a blonde wig.

Again in *Silk Stockings* Astaire danced with Barrie. This time Astaire is showing Cyd Charisse and her Soviet diplomats the pleasures of Paris: one of the pleasures, with whom he dances, is Barrie Chase, then nineteen. Barrie, born on Thursday 20 October 1938, the year *Gay Divorcee* was released, was the daughter of cab-driver turned writer Borden Chase, who during the twenties had been a chauffeur for dubious gangland figures and had turned to writing after having worked on the construction of New York's Holland Tunnel – it was an incident there, the death of a co-worker, which provided him with the material for *Under Pressure*, the film that was completed when Barrie was just one year old. Her mother, Lee Keith, a talented pianist, encouraged the youngster's interest in dance and enrolled her as a child at New York's Metropolitan Opera Ballet School. When Barrie was six years old the family moved from Kings Point, Long Island, to Encino in the San Fernando Valley, where she studied dance with Adolph Bolm and Maria Bekefi and went to the smart Westlake School for girls, where Astaire's own daughter Ava also went for four years. Aged fourteen she had appeared in *Scaramouche* and in *Hans Christian Andersen*. At the age of fifteen she turned down a job with Sonia Henje's ice-skating troupe – she thought she was too young for touring – at a time when her world was falling apart. Her parents separated, her much-loved horse Rigged Annie was sold and her parents divorced. Although her father had built a comfortable lifestyle with his screenwriting of films, including James Stewart's *The Far Country* and *Winchester '73*, it was a traumatic time for young Barrie, and as soon as possible she moved into her own apartment. Her ambition for classical dance gave way to film and with Jack Cole she learnt about jazz and modern dance. The brief dances and increasingly longer chats with the recently-widowed Astaire added the touch of finesse she needed. 'He didn't only influence my work, he made my career,' she said. By the spring of 1958 she was firmly labelled as the girl with whom Fred Astaire like dancing. She had learnt more than just style from him, but also humility: during the filming of *Daddy Long Legs* she was amazed to realise that in their brief sequence dancing Astaire was also nervous. So when she worked on *Silk Stockings* she was much more relaxed herself – although she had additional problems with a loose shoe that sometimes flew off. But by the spring of 1958 her own career was beginning to thrive and her agent got her the lead rôle in a television episode of *Have Gun Will Travel* with Richard Boone. 'Then, one night,' Barrie said, 'Fred called and told me: "I'm going to do a television special and I want you to be in it." I said, "Marvellous" in a matter-of-fact way because of course I didn't know that I was going to be the partner.' They went to the Villa Nova for dinner and he talked of the plans for a television special that really was special and how he believed that this nineteen-year-old was the one who could help him. He was one year off his sixtieth birthday at the time, but the years meant nothing to him. The only time he even thought about it was when he read how old he was in a newspaper or magazine. He just needed a dancer to work with who could really inspire him to good things. The more he found out about Barrie Chase the more he was convinced she was the one. She was the right height, a shade under five foot five tall, 118 pounds, was hard-working and independent. Like his first partner Adèle, Barrie did not like the colour green and favoured red or black and white. Musically, she enjoyed Rachmaninov and Count Bassie and shared Fred's liking for steak, salad and ice cream. She lived in a new studio apartment in the university-populated Westwood and confessed to a Bohemian streak in herself and her clothes, which was so extreme at one time that she became known, to Astaire, as 'Baggy Pants'.

Barrie, who thought she knew all about working hard, started rehearsing with Hermes Pan and soon found there was a whole new world of endurance with Astaire. There were several weeks for her to get rid of her nerves and build up confidence before the sweat began in earnest: 'After three hours of rehearsing with him I was ready to drop. A couple of times I was so exhausted that they thought they'd have to give me oxygen. Fred just looked at me and told me to rest and he kept on dancing for six hours more.' Astaire often complained that when people reviewed his work they didn't say whether he was good or bad, just how old he was. But it was an extraordinary factor that could not be ignored, for when he prepared for *An Evening with Fred Astaire* he was fifty-nine years old, gambolling like a lamb, and dancing in an ageless way. He explained his regimen: 'I harden my legs, get my breathing going, gradually build up stamina and learn to conserve my energy. I might get winded early in the routine. So I pantomime a little to avoid unnecessary exertion and pace myself to the end. I train just like a race horse. I own an animal that ran very well at Hollywood Park. It liked the track. It ran well at Golden Gate. It liked the track. But at Del Mar it didn't run at all well. Something wrong with that track. I feel the same way with certain floors. If the floor is good I can use ordinary leather shoes. If it is slippery I wear shoes with rubber on the bottom. Or maybe some resin sprinkled on the floor will do the trick. But whatever I do I must get a good grip, without slipping or sticking.'

A three-month rehearsal was unknown in television, but Astaire did it and Astaire got it right. David Rose, composer of 'The Stripper' and first husband of Judy Garland, was musical arranger and he backed up Barrie's comments on the extraordinary concentration involved to make everything right: 'I walked into a rehearsal and there was dead silence for five minutes with Fred and Hermes Pan just staring at each other. Then Hermes said to Fred that he had the answer to their problem. He should step off on the left foot rather than the right.' Producer Bud Yorkin, NBC comedy and variety producer who had worked with Abbot and Costello as well as Cyd Charisse's singer husband Tony Martin, admitted that the show was not without its own traumas. For a start, said Yorkin, there was the tardiness of Barrie Chase, who managed to work herself into such a state before rehearsals that on several occasions she arrived late, sometimes – shades of July Garland – as much as two or three hours. One-time actor Yorkin, who had a bit part in *Follow the Fleet*, had the problem of coping with the Astaire temperament: 'When such things happened, Fred would react in one of two ways. Sometimes he'd just blow his fuse – but never in front of the cast and crew. He'd go into a room and have it out there, in a violent argument. Other times he'd just sulk. He wouldn't say anything, but we could tell that he was eating his heart out.' Despite the problems, *An Evening With Fred Astaire*, networked live on Friday 17 October 1958, went marvellously. If Astaire admired Barrie beforehand, he did so much more afterwards. She knew there was a party afterwards in the Persian Room of the Beverly Hills Hotel but hadn't realised that it was going to be a huge party, so she arrived wearing a blue cotton summer frock. Covered in confusion, she wanted to go home and change but Astaire would not let her: 'You are the star and you look wonderful', he said. He was full of her praises: 'I liken her to a champion stakes filly, the ultimate in the thoroughbred. She has such individuality, training, grace, a winning kind of movement and personality and she takes her work seriously.'

For once Astaire's work was well-rewarded, for at the 7 May Emmy Awards ceremony *An Evening with Fred Astaire* scooped nine awards, the greatest number given to any show in the eleven-year history of the National Academy of Television Arts and Sciences. Best of all, Astaire won the best actor award for himself. It was not, however, a universally popular decision. For some, including TV pundit Ed Sullivan, asked whether Astaire should have been awarded the Best Actor Emmy. Astaire immediately offered to hand the award back – he reckoned he had been an actor since he was six years old and could not see why he should pretend to have stopped now. 'What the devil is all this about anyway?' he said. 'I'm an actor, and this Emmy is for a performance by an actor, isn't it? When I do a difficult pantomime in a dance that tells a story, what do they think it is? Tiddlywinks?' He kept his Emmy. No one would take it back from him. But the sniping was not over and *Variety* reported that MCA, who had fronted the package, had dropped $75,000 on selling the show by the time that all the rehearsals and so on were considered. Astaire blew his top and wrote angrily to the editor: 'Kindly retract erroneous article in last week's *Variety*. Here are the facts: The entire package is mine, via Ava Productions Corp. MCA merely acted as my agent with the sponsor. Nobody had any cut. All the expenses were paid for by me and the show definitely turned in a sizeable profit. Though I was not interested in that phase, I would like to make it clear that I am not completely nuts. I particularly directed that no expense be spared in carrying out my plans, ideas and designs for the show which I had been working on for some time. Thanks, love and kisses and I will do another one when I get the time, Fred Astaire.' He did not say, but the facts were these: the show cost $195,000 to mount, Chrysler and NBC paid $250,000 to Ava Productions, leaving a passable profit and enough to make another two specials the next two years. Through his new popularity, partly through his Emmys and partly through a resurgence of his movies on television (the television rights to 740 RKO films, including the Astaire-Rogers classics, had been sold for a mere $15 million by the General Tire And Rubber Company subsidiary who bought the company from Howard Hughes), to his genuine and ill-disguised delight, Astaire was asked to take on a totally straight film rôle. No dancing, no singing, just acting. The offer for a movie version of On the Beach came at just the right time. 'I had decided not to do any more dancing pictures,' he said. 'I'd done them all you see. Over thirty pictures – and that just about exhausts the possibilities. I was determined not to become a dancing freak at sixty. And I knew the time to quit had come when one critic said of Funny Face – the film I did with Audrey Hepburn – that it had "something old, something new". I was the "something old".' Stanley Kramer, producer of Death of a Salesman and High Noon and director of The Defiant Ones, had originally hoped to get British actor Alec Guinness or Ralph Richardson for the rôle of the scientist Osborn for his planned film of Neville Shute's post-nuclear holocaust story, but neither was available and it was Kramer's wife Ann who saw one of the Astaire movies on TV one night and told him: 'There's your scientist.' 'I thought she was crazy,' said Kramer, 'but then I realized, by God, she was right.' This time he could play his age, although he was not too pleased flying out to Australia for filming – despite the promise of seeing some Australian horseracing – when he sat next to nineteen-year-old ingénue Donna Anderson, making her first trip abroad. She was somewhat nervous about the experience, but told Astaire: 'My great grandmother told me not to worry; she said that Mr Astaire would take care of me.' He was taken aback by that: 'Your great grandmother? Couldn't it at least have been your grandmother?'

Kramer was concerned to get rid of any signs that this was the Fred Astaire that everyone knew, and even at one stage contemplated putting weights in his shoes to eliminate his distinctive jaunty walk. But he need not have worried, for Astaire had taken the preparations not to dance just as seriously as he took the rehearsals to dance. He worked it

[210]

all out for himself and Kramer's delighted comment after the first run-through was: 'You'd think Fred had been playing serious drama all his life.' It was the least glamorous rôle of his career and far from the romantic floating dance exit, Astaire's character of the car-racing enthusiast scientist commits suicide by gassing himself in a locked and grubby garage.

Astaire already had a feeling that his life was going full circle. Films had been made about his contemporaries, like Cole Porter and George Gershwin, and now his old film stories were coming back. MGM had even made a film called *Lovely to Look At*, with Howard Keel, Kathryn Grayson, Ann Miller and Red Skelton, as a remake of *Roberta*. To add the Astaire touch the final scenes had been shot, not by director Mervyn LeRoy, but by Vincente Minnelli – who in his inimitable style was called in for the last three days to shoot the finale, and was still there three weeks later.

Astaire made two more TV specials with Barrie Chase, both praised and admired – a TV Emmy Award for the first and two Emmys for the second. As Barrie and Astaire worked together they grew closer and Astaire found, first to his surprise, then to his delight, that somehow Barrie was beginning to fill the gap in his life left by Phyllis. It took him a long time to come to terms with it, but eventually there seemed to be no way out but to admit to himself that he loved this off-beat, talented dancer. Outsiders and those working around them realised what was happening long before Astaire himself did. He was too busy and concerned about his work to notice how Barrie looked at him, and too involved with his own thoughts to see how he looked at her, but undoubtedly he was falling in love. His immediate reaction was to deny any emotional involvement with Barrie: 'Widowers like myself are in a tough position. If I go out with a young woman and she's very attractive, very lively, very capable of making me forget sadness then people say I'm robbing the cradle. If I go out with some woman of my own age, they say I'm concentrating on grandmothers. Very difficult.' Barrie joined in the denials: 'Nothing could be sillier. Mr Astaire is old enough to be my father. In fact, older than my father.' But she was also effusive in her praise of him: 'Every time I think about his greatness and what he has done for me I want to kneel down and kiss his wonderful dancing feet. He is like a God to me. There's no one else like him in the world.'

There was no doubting the new spring in his step and the new light in his life. Barrie had a strong personality, but then he had always been influenced by strong women – his mother, Adèle, Ginger, Phyllis, even his daughter Ava, at the age of seventeen, was already telling him what to do. Now with Barrie he had found another talented, strong, yet vulnerable woman. He took her to San Ysidro Drive to meet his mother, his daughter, even Adèle and although they were all impressed by her, pleased with the new happiness she was bringing him, still there were the inevitable questions as to quite what she was doing with this older man. To Ann no girl was good enough for her son, not even, initially, Phyllis. To Ava, Barrie was a challenge for her father's affections for her, even though the two girls got on well and remained friends many years afterwards. Adèle, who thought Barrie very sweet and pretty, assumed that Fred was just going through a quite understandable phase. But even if the Astaire clan could cope with Barrie, could she cope with that tightly knit family? It was a daunting prospect.

Astaire began to ask questions among his friends about the success of other marriages between those of different ages and he looked and realised that there were indeed many successful matches. His great friend Randolph Scott said: 'Fred's always saying "I'll never marry again. No one could replace Phyllis." We try and tell him: "No one has to replace Phyllis, and no one ever will. But you can find a new dimension with someone else and at least fill part of the gap in your life."' But the barrier to a permanent relationship came not only from Astaire's fear of committing himself, but also from Barrie. Although Astaire was totally unaware of the age difference, Barrie could not help but realise that at the time of their first TV show he was fifty-nine, three times as old as she was, at nineteen. By the time that they made a fourth TV special together in '68, he was sixty-eight and she was twenty-nine and far too independent a spirit to be tied to a man almost old enough to be her grandfather, with a son two years older than her and a daughter four years younger. She liked him as a friend, loved him as a teacher, companion and father-figure. She was touched, flattered and pleased that she had somehow been able to bring some happiness to an unhappy man, but what she needed was someone young to live her life with, although she admitted that she could not help but be moved by his thoughts.

One Christmas, kidding his own suave image and lack of hair, he sent her a present of a huge white cat wearing a bow-tie and a yellow toupee of hair on its head. But his lifelong awkwardness, combined with a fear of rejection, meant that although he dropped hints aplenty, he

[212]

never did get around to proposing . . . well, anything. He missed the moment when he could have had her for the asking and she would have been happy to become the new Mrs Fred Astaire, and in time they made it increasingly difficult for themselves, and any off-stage romantic partnership would not work. 'Let us just stay friends,' she said. They did.

Barrie Chase was never as sure of her own ability and dedication to her art as was Astaire, and to some of his friends it came as no surprise when she gave up her career to marry Beverly Hills business man Dr Jim Kaufman, and in December 1973 gave birth to a son. Astaire continued to see her and her husband from time to time and was always convinced of her great talent: 'She was good in those shows. She's a sophisticated mover and I was always disappointed that she couldn't go anywhere after that. Of course she's happily married now, but she should be a performer, because she's a very dedicated performer. God, she's tough to get along with. She doesn't think anything is good. When I'm doing things I think they are good, otherwise I wouldn't be doing them. But she never thinks anything is good. She was always saying: "How do you like that?" We did a Limehouse scene in the last thing I did and she hated it, but she was great in it.'

Barrie Chase was not Astaire's only female friend in those lonely years. He was a man of morals and propriety, but he was also a man who enjoyed and needed female companionship and particularly admired and enjoyed the lively and young. Tina Sinatra, at twenty-three the attractive brunette daughter of Frank Sinatra, was among the guests at a small party on his seventy-third birthday, and acted as an escort on his occasional forays into the outside world. But she was at pains to explain their relationship: 'I love him just like I love my father. People find it difficult to understand this kind of relationship, how two people can be close and yet not be romantically involved and planning marriage.' Astaire himself was flattered by the attention: 'I think it is quite romantic that we are being linked together – but romance is beyond my age.' Breezy and bright blonde acress Carol Lynley was another Astaire favourite. Carol Ann Jones, as she was born in April 1942, just one month before Ava Astaire, had been a teenage model under the name Lee; when she made her first movie at the age of fourteen she wanted to expand it to Carol Ann Lee, but as there was already an actress of that name, settled on Carol Lynley. She had been married at eighteen, divorced at nineteen and was bringing up her daughter by herself. There were some who thought that Carol, who had

[213]

been linked with British television performer David Frost, might even become the new Mrs Fred Astaire – he would certainly have been able to provide a comfortable home for Carol and her daughter. But Carol too was an independent, doing just fine on her own and she too had no desire to give up her freedom for anyone.

Top hat, white tie and tails, 1935.

With Ginger in *Carefree*, 1938.

With Hermes Pan and deceptive dance diagrams, 1936.

With Ginger in
Swing Time, 1936.

With Ginger, forty
years on at RKO
lunch for donation
of archives to
University of
California.

With Fred Jr, and a 222lb
marlin, 1953.

With Anthony Quinn and
his daughter, Christine,
Fred escorts daughter, Ava,
to Beverly Hills debutante
Ball, 1959.

Top left: Off set, and 'unshaven' in *Let's Dance*, 1950.

Top right: With Cyd Charisse, 1957.

Below: With his horse, Triplicate, Astaire won the San Juan Capistrano Handicap, 1946.

With Rita Hayworth in *You Were Never Lovelier*, 1942.

With Gene Kelly in *Ziegfield Follies*, 19

With Judy Garland, a couple of swells, in *Easter Parade*, 1948.

Up the wall in *Royal Wedding* (*Weddin Bells* in UK), 1951.

With Barrie Chase on TV
dance spectacular,
Hollywood Palace, 1960.

On 27 June 1980, Fred
Astaire and Robyn Smith
were married. He was 81;
she claimed to be 35. The
two are shown here in
January 1979.

Exit, 'Puttin' on the Ritz', 1946.

17
Going straight

When it was realised that Fred Astaire was back in action the requests started to flood in and, as long as the script was not about a retired hoofer come back for a spot of tap dancing, he read them all carefully.

Opposite Lilli Palmer, Rex Harrison's German-born former wife who had remarried and been absent in Switzerland for some years, he played a disreputable playboy husband who returns for the wedding of his daughter, played by Debbie Reynolds (previously seen with Astaire in *Three Little Words*), in *The Pleasure of his Company*.

Lilli Palmer had taken one look at the script and gone to writer/director George Seaton to ask for changes in one scene where, naturally enough, the Astaire character dances with his former wife. Lilli Palmer's memories of dancing were of the time when as a nineteen-year-old refugee in Paris she had managed to get a job at the Moulin Rouge. She had passed the audition with her singing and a series of acrobatic cartwheels and splits, but at dress rehearsal in unaccustomed high heels she had been woefully unable to keep up with the chorines and had tripped, breaking her ankle on the way down. She had no desire to repeat that performance with Astaire. 'Mr Seaton, I'm sorry, I can't dance,' she said. 'Could this scene take place somewhere else? On a sofa? Under a Christmas tree? Must it be played dancing on the parquet floor of the living room?' 'Yes, it must,' said Seaton. 'We need the music for one thing. For another we're grateful for every chance to show Fred dancing. Surely you can do a little something. Anybody can dance with Fred Astaire.' But Lilli Palmer, he soon discovered, was not anybody. The moment came when, according to the script, Astaire had to grab her and sweep her off her feet. She demures, 'Oh no, I couldn't,' to which he says: 'I promise not to step on your feet.' Lilli Palmer recalled: 'He certainly swept me off in a wonderfully elegant gesture, but I landed squarely with both feet on his, stopping him dead in his tracks. "Good Lord", said he amazed. "I warned you", I said, feeling a certain satisfaction that I had been able to pin down the great Astaire, if only for a moment. The second time he swept me off he never allowed me to land at all and I just hung suspended in his arms, trying to remember my lines while bereft of the support of terra firma.' At one point it looked as though *The Pleasure of his Company* would never be finished, for the Screen Actors' Guild carried out their threat to call the first ever Hollywood strike for more money. The lights went out at the studios at 6 o'clock on Friday night and did not go back on again. The end of Hollywood was widely forecast, prematurely as it turned out, but the knell was definitely sounded. For six months nothing happened, but eventually, to all round relief, the strike was called off and the film completed.

During the lay-off Astaire did the unthinkable, to his mind anyway, and had an unscripted reunion dance with Ginger Rogers. Astaire, as a widower, was considered a splendid catch in Hollywood circles and at a party given by David Selznick – one of the powerful people for whom Astaire would turn out – he was being actively pursued by one eager lady. Eventually cornered, he spotted Ginger Rogers. 'Oh,' he said, 'I've just seen Ginger. I must go and have a word with her.' Off he darted. Ginger was certainly surprised to be asked for a dance, she knew he disliked social dancing, but as Astaire revealed the reason for his behaviour she promised to protect him, carefully steering him away from danger.

There were other straight films for him to make, but none of that period was outstanding, as he realised himself: 'Films are a bit like race horses, the ones you expect to do well sometimes are no use at all.' Certainly he always put the maximum effort into each one and if he was disappointed by something he was always professional enough to keep his views to himself. However he openly abhorred the trends of the cinema for sexual exploitation and violence and when Anne Heywood appeared bare-breasted in *Midas Run*, he complained: 'It was not in the script; I'm not a prude and I don't mind bad language or anything else, but this gratuitous nudity is stupid.'

He went to London to film *The Notorious Landlady*, with Jack Lemmon and Kim Novak and directed by Richard Quine, a fellow child vaudevillian who had recently made *The World of Susie Wong*. Filming was held up one day outside Buckingham Palace when it transpired that shooting permission had not been cleared. A young newspaper reporter asked Astaire how he felt about standing outside Buckingham Palace. Astaire was polite: 'I have been inside a few times before, you know, I do know the inhabitants somewhat.'

[216]

Without Phyllis, he had lost interest in the Dance Studios and decided that he wasn't cut out to be a businessman, although they had done quite well with a nationwide chain of 135 schools and even, briefly, with a British-franchised operation. This was fronted by actress Anna Neagle, and it opened in '61 in Old Bond Street with a fifty-guinea membership fee and finance from hotelier Charles Forte and British Ford Chairman, Sir Patrick Hennessy, among others. But the British venture did not last long, as rock 'n' roll had taken over from formal dancing and people did not flock to the studio, which lost money and was soon closed down. In the States some studios thrived: for instance in Omaha, where the classes are packed to this day. Others, particularly on the West Coast, did less well, and some of his business managers had been getting into trouble for their high-powered sales techniques, so when an offer came, he happily sold out of the company, with the West Coast Studios being closed: 'It's safer if they are a long way from me.' Despite his legal lack of involvement, as his name stayed, so did he, agreeing to talk, on occasions, publicly and unpaid, to promote the studios.

When he didn't mope and pace his house, he continued his interest in the new and the up-coming and accepted the chance to work with bright new boy Francis Ford Coppola in *Finian's Rainbow*. For Coppola he even agreed to dance a few steps. The film was, unhappily, a dud, even with Hermes Pan working on it and a cast that included the former child star Petula Clark and one time rock 'n' roller Tommy Steele. 'It was a big disappointment,' he said, putting his feelings mildly. Astaire, always prepared, had learnt all his lines before arriving for filming: 'It was just as well, Coppola had me hanging out of trees and all kind of crazy things. If I hadn't known those lines backwards I would have forgotten everything.' Tommy Steele recalled that he was totally in awe of Astaire and he had likewise learnt all his dances in advance. One day, while Steele was doing a little warm-up, he was stopped by Astaire. 'Where did you get that step?' asked Astaire. 'Gene Kelly taught me,' said Steele, rather proud of himself. 'Mmm,' said Astaire, 'he never could do that one.' Astaire's own dancing in the movie was more of a frolic, as he said: 'I've had romantic dancing. I've done it all and I don't want to do it any more. In *Finian's Rainbow* things are different. This time, thank goodness, I didn't get the girl. Matter of fact, all I ended up with in this film was a rainbow.'

Back in Los Angeles his straight television work included an appearance over four episodes of the *Dr Kildare* TV hospital soap opera

[217]

– it was his mother who suggested that he should be on *Dr Kildare*, and thanks to her viewing habits he became an expert on several of the long-running soaps, including *As the World Turns* and *The Guiding Light*, and always knew who was doing what and with whom. Astaire said: 'My mother still watched my stuff on television, but got a little confused when the commercials came on. "Fred, what is that fellow with the beer can doing in your play?" she'd say. Things like that.' He was Robert Wagner's safe-cracker father in the *To Catch a Thief* series, where Wagner was a debonair master thief. 'I didn't want to play goody-goody parts all my life,' said Astaire. The Wagner and Astaire relationship went back some way, as Wagner explained: 'When I was a kid, I used to hang around the Bel Air golf course and say, "Good morning, Mr Astaire," to him. And Fred would say back to me: "Good morning, Mr Wagner."' Wagner was the kind of young friend Astaire enjoyed: stylish, conservative and successful.

For two full programmes he was the sole guest on Dick Cavett's ninety-minute networked TV show. If Astaire could be enticed on to a programme and given a good reason for being there – Cavett was a fellow Nebraskan – he would always give top value. He sang, he talked, and even danced a little. 'That,' he said afterwards, 'is most definitely that. I am not interested in being the oldest living dancer in captivity. My last television special people were looking at me with that look of awe as though they expected me to drop dead at any moment and didn't want to miss the great moment. Well, I'm not going to do that.' As if to prove that he was still interested in tomorrow rather than today he and Ava went off to dine with the British model-turned dancer Twiggy and her manager boyfriend Justin de Villeneuve. He leapt on to a lamppost and twirled Twiggy around. 'You,' he told the chirpy aspirate-dropping Londoner, 'are absolutely beautiful.'

His name went around the world once more when MGM made *That's Entertainment*, a compilation of movie clips from MGM musicals, and producer Saul Chaplin felt that Astaire and Kelly, along with Crosby, Liza Minnelli and Taylor, were the natural hosts for the journey down memory lane. To introduce a *Band Wagon* clip, he walked through the Grand Central stage set where he had walked twenty years before: now it was a dilapidated mess and spoke volumes about what had happened to movies since then. It might have been cheap programming but it was also highly successful, although there must have been mixed memories for Fred with numbers like 'Triplets' with

[218]

Nanette Fabray and 'A Couple of Swells' with Judy Garland, but he did admit that some of the things had worn well. The line-up of Elizabeth Taylor, Frank Sinatra, Bing Crosby, Liza Minnelli, James Stewart, Donald O'Connor, Clark Gable and swimming star Esther Williams was positively glittering and so successful that *That's Entertainment II* was immediately put into production. This time Astaire and Kelly, the two men who had made dancing respectable, by themselves were asked to do the introductory and linking honours. Kelly was sixty-three and Astaire seventy-seven when they agreed to do *That's Entertainment II*. But Astaire, who had made such a point throughout his film career of not repeating himself, was concerned lest the public should think he was past it. They had better find something new for him to do this time, he was very tentative in his approach to Gene Kelly: 'Do you think maybe we ought to do a few steps? If we don't then everyone will think we've got fallen arches.' Kelly said: 'Why not? If we keep control on everything, and if we don't like what we do we can just junk it.' New lyrics were written for the song 'That's Entertainment' and when the music started, according to Kelly: 'We just started to move about, it was inevitable. But we agreed not to jump over six tables. We didn't have the time or the anatomical condition.'

There was a price to pay for his re-emergence as a performer: Betty Ford, wife of Omaha-born President Gerald Ford took Astaire under her ample wing and insisted that he should be invited to White House functions – after all she was the First Lady and had (hadn't every girl?) always dreamed of dancing with Fred Astaire. So as soon as Vice President Ford took the top office after the resignation of Richard Nixon, Fred Astaire and singer Pearl Bailey, the favourite of Gerald Ford himself (in '75 she became a UN delegate), were invited to 1600 Pennsylvania Avenue. Astaire, who in fact never really liked wearing white tie and tails, went, as a White House invitation is the nearest an American gets to a command performance; it was a pity that Betty Ford was unaware of Astaire's views on social dancing: 'I like a crowded ballroom best because then I don't have to move around so much. It worries me to death when some girl wants me to do fancy steps with her, because I know she won't be able to do the ones that I can do. I was never a good ballroom dancer. I've even had complaints about it.' Astaire was placed on Mrs Ford's right hand – and whether the sight of Betty Ford nursing one of her salmon pink satin shoes in the ladies' rest room later was the result of a deliberate act of vandalism on Astaire's

[219]

part, is a moot point. 'It was purgatory,' he admitted to friends – and put Mrs Ford high on his list of least favourite partners. And he also escorted her – by command again – to a testimonial Life Achievement dinner at the American Film Institute for his former neighbour William Wyler; he'd been planning to go to Palm Springs to play golf, so was less than happy at the arrangement.

Helen Hayes had tried some years previously to get Astaire to play Puck in *A Midsummer Night's Dream* – he had other commitments at the time – but he did work with her in Ross Hunter's TV movie *A Family Upside Down*, in which he played a house painter with a coronary who refuses to be mollycoddled and sent to art therapy classes – 'I'm a painter, not an artist,' he snaps to his screen son Efrem Zimbalist Jr, who had to pick him up from the stairs. It was a true movement of generations, as Zimbalist said: 'That was exactly what he had done to me when I was a kid – carried me upstairs to bed.' Astaire won an Emmy for the part (no complaints this time!) and he felt it did open new rôles for him: 'Most of the things I'm sent are the theatrical father. You know, the old hoofer who has hung up his dancing shoes and now talks about the good old days. I won't play 'em, because I don't believe 'em. The shows I've done are a lot of fun. They aren't pretentious or trying to prove anything, they are for entertainment – period. If people don't like it that's their problem: it is definitely not mine. That's been my showbusiness attitude for many years. It's the only way. Nowadays people have forgotten a seven-letter word – decency.'

He wouldn't countenance anything political or with a heavy message theme, and he even sometimes let drop his careful guard on his true feelings: 'I will not be part of anything crummy or distasteful. There's so much wonderful stuff, but some of it – well, I just don't know how they do it. Take a picture like the Poseidon thing, *The Poseidon Adventure*, and it's a hit picture because it's unusual, the effects and all that kind of thing. But the script and the language is just so asinine and atrocious. It's so dumb. Just to think: well, now we're allowed to do this, let's do it. It's unbelievable the dumbness of the dialogue and the characters and so stupid the way it's handled. I always like Gene Hackman as an actor, but he has these unbelievable things to say – he's screaming at the other fellow all the time. It's just about the worst movie in many ways. And still it has its drawing power because it's a very extraordinary thing when this ship goes upside down, so you wait and wait for this thing to happen. It leaves you with a spectacle, and that's all there is to it, but it's so offensive. You just have to say: Oh, come on!' But it wasn't the disaster movie genre itself he minded, as he made a guest-starring appearance as a confidence trickster who gets trapped in *The Towering Inferno*, with an all-star line-up of Steve McQueen, Paul Newman, William Holden, Faye Dunaway, Robert Vaughan, Robert Wagner, among others, in one of the better disaster movies, which topped box-office receipts for the year, to Astaire's delight – it was always good to be associated with a success.

Forgetting the adage about not working with animals, he made *The Amazing Dobermans* surrounded by dogs. He had talked to the woman who knew most about the animals: Liz Whitney Tippett, still living at Llangollen, now with her aviator husband Col Tippett. Liz, as stylish as ever, with one of her Rolls-Royces in her racing livery and another that had belonged to Elizabeth Taylor, said: 'Fred, don't you be crazy. Those animals will have you for breakfast.' A few weeks later he sent her a photograph of himself covered in Dobermans. 'They didn't eat all of me,' he told her. And that nudity rule of his was broken in *Un Taxi Mauve*, an Irish, Italian, French co-production made in Ireland, with Peter Ustinov as a slightly sinister figure and Astaire as a sprightly Irish taxi driver, when Charlotte Rampling went elegantly topless, but as Astaire said: 'That wasn't in the script.' Sometimes his enthusiasms got the better of him. Just after he had finished *The Dobermans* he was trying out the skateboard belonging to his grandson Frederick, son of Fred Jr. He fell off and broke his left wrist and had to spend six weeks with his arm in a cast – at seventy-eight he was lucky the damage was not worse: 'Gene Kelly warned me not to be a damned fool, but I'd seen the things those kids got up to on television doing all sorts of tricks. What a routine I could have worked up for a film sequence if they had existed a few years ago. Anyway I was practising in my drive-way. I wouldn't have minded if I was doing something smart-ass. I don't even know why I did it. My grandson kept on telling me: "keep your weight forward". Then down I went with my wrist under my hip. In all my years of dancing I never went down like that, I've always known how to break a fall. My doctor called me a dummy. A friend who is a Catholic priest rang me laughing his head off: "I'm glad you didn't do it falling out of bed. At least you did it like you were going someplace."' But he was made a life member of the National Skateboard Society. His young grandchildren were puzzled by what it was that their grandfather did: they had been told by their friends that he was famous, but could not see any sign of this. 'I'm an actor,' he said. 'You can't be,' came the reply, 'We've never seen you on television.' Having established what were their most popular shows he asked his agent to get in touch with the producers of *Battlestar Galactica*, where a part was quickly written for him in August 1979 as Chameleon, an inter-gallactic villain who was claiming to be the father of Starbuck, played by Dirk Benedict. After that there was no problem with the kids, who treated him with a new awe. He was then left with a new problem: to convince them that he was not someone from outer space.

He was not taken with the new generation of dance movie with John Travolta in *Saturday Night Fever*, and pronounced himself not over-impressed: 'He's not a dancer. What he did in those dance scenes was very attractive but he is basically not a dancer. I was dancing like that years ago, you know. Disco is just jitterbug. It's not new to me.' But he was intrigued enough to be interested when a project with Travolta was discussed, to be called *Terribly Terrific Teddy*, with Astaire as a dance instructor and Travolta as a taxi driver who becomes his pupil – shades of *Swing Time* from forty years before; but a combination of Astaire's real doubts as to what he could do dancewise and Travolta's other arrangements meant that nothing happened.

18
Ann

In 1971, Kingman Douglass, now retired from his partnership with Dillon, Read, died at his home in Arizona. But of course Ann, with seemingly inexhaustible energy, was at hand to help Adèle in any way she could, and thankfully Ann was still there when Adèle had a fall and had to have four steel pins put into her hip.

'My dancing days are over,' Adèle moaned. But of course they were not, and it was not too long before Adèle was back in her traditional high spirits. She flitted between Virginia, Arizona, New York, California and Jamaica, where she could catch up with Noël Coward, Cecil Beaton and the international gossip.

Sometimes it was Noël rather than Fred who tried to persuade her to return to the stage. 'What? At my age?' she said. 'You must be joking.' She was amazed, and pleased, by the interest that the Astaires still seemed to elicit. In London, dancer Lionel Blair planned a new production of *Lady, Be Good!* and invited Adèle to come and see it. She was shocked by the prospect: 'Good God! I don't believe they want to put that old dog on again. I wouldn't dream of going to see them, although they were good enough to invite me. It's old hat. There is no point in trying to go back to the past. Fred feels exactly the same way I do. We hate the past, but we both look forward to the future with great pleasure. I feel extremely with-it. And I think if I went anywhere I would rather go and see The Beatles' film *Yellow Submarine.*'

While Fred agreed with Adèle that he had no desire to live in the past, in Hollywood there were repeated attempts to get the Astaire-Rogers duo back together. Ginger was keen on the idea, as she was none too happy to slide into character parts when in her own mind she was still the glamorous star of former times. She spent her time at her 4R Ranch at Medford, Oregon, painting, fishing and appearing on television programmes reminiscing about the old days. She had, she said, no secrets and no diets to offer to the world, except an old-fashioned belief in apple-pie American values. Not far off seventy, she explained: 'I use lanolin on my elbows and knees and wash with soap, take off my make-up with cold cream you buy for three ninety five a jar and drink ice cream sodas. It's all the power of positive thinking.' And when it came to positive thought, Ginger and her mother Lela, who still oversaw her career, always had a bundle. Not that everyone could cope with the combined forces of the Rogers ladies: Paul Gregory, producer of her '59 stage play *The Pink Jungle*, recalled, not without retrospective amusement, that Ginger Rogers was a nightmare to deal with and he put down his exodus from showbusiness to her: 'She's a totally manufactured commodity. We'd give her a new scene, and she couldn't remember the lines. She couldn't sing and, surprisingly, she couldn't do the dances. And all through the horror of it she was smiling and grinning and was unreal. There's no denying her appeal to the public. That's what makes her so dangerous. She almost smiled me into bankruptcy. God knows I don't mind her being a Christian Scientist. I just wish she'd put a little more emphasis on the Christian.'

Then, just as she had with the Castles movie, Judy Garland, battered by drugs and alcohol, once more unwittingly came to the rescue of Ginger, just when she was beginning to despair of ever finding a meaty rôle in front of the camera – like Astaire Ginger Rogers could not stand the trend of horror movies and steadfastedly refused all offers to appear in them. Garland dropped out of playing the mother to Carol Lynley in the movie *Harlow* and Ginger stepped into the rôle, giving an impressive, powerful performance – *Harlow* was made in '65, and had far better reviews than the Carroll Baker version made the same year. That led to Ginger taking over the lead rôle from Carol Channing in *Hello Dolly!* on Broadway and then travelling to England to be paid $12,000 a week to play *Mame* at London's Theatre Royal, Drury Lane, as always travelling and behaving like a Star with a capital S in an age when people no longer behaved like that. She still wanted to play the glamorous rôles and would complain: 'They just don't write parts for people like me.'

Ever since the heady days of Triplicate, Fred still maintained a passing interest in the racetrack, winning a few useful races, and, occasionally, becoming quite overcome by the brilliance of his own horse's performance. One weekend he was so enthused that when he woke very early on Sunday morning he got some thick yellow Scotch tape and set off by car to put a yellow sash on some of the nearby squat blue city mail boxes – giving a passable likeness to his blue and

[224]

yellow sash colours. Trainer Philips had died shortly after Trip's big win, although the head groom Laurence Campion took over the training duties and Triplicate had gone on to win the $75,000 Golden Gate Handicap that year, pushing his winnings to nearly $250,000. Astaire, who always enjoyed his moans, made Adèle roar with laughter at his latest complaint: because of his winnings he had gone into a higher tax bracket. Triplicate won several more races, but had recurrences of his early ankle trouble and so at the age of seven he was retired to stud in Kentucky and was eventually sold to Japan where his progeny still race. In England he had a useful filly called Mavis, who won four races in a row, Nick the Greek, High Hat and the filly Rainbow Tie, trained by former jockey Harry Wragg, who won five races as a two-year-old and was eventually shipped to California to Astaire's Blue Valley Ranch. At one stage Astaire was trying to buy a steeplechaser with Gregory Peck so that they could have a runner in Aintree's Grand National, but they failed to find a suitable animal and the plan fizzled out. In Australia he also had a couple of Stan Murphy trained youngsters which he had bought while filming *On the Beach*, but they failed to live up to expectations. But his favourite place of all, possible even more so than California, was the English racetrack.

When he was in London for *The Midas Run* Astaire took time out to see his racing chums and in particular his racing manager and friend Jack Leach. They went out on the town together to talk of horses and old times. At that time in the States Astaire had a couple of fillies, Sharp Curve, a miler who could not get an inch over, and To Glory, and a colt, His Money. Both men were widowers and Leach said: 'We were two young old bald-headed bachelors, going on the town as though they still had all the dash and flair they had when they first met forty years beforehand.' Astaire said to Leach: 'You rotten bastard, you've still got some of your own hair.'

Astaire also took advantage of the film company's travelling expenses to visit Adèle in Lismore when he had finished shooting *The Midas Run* in London, and found Adèle in her self-styled 'saucy seventies' had decided that she would become part of history, thanks to Fred's *Midas Run* co-star, Roddy McDowall.

Adèle had first met McDowall, British-born and the former child star of *Lassie Come Home*, when he was working on his photographic book *Double Exposure*. He was a stills photographer of note and he also owned one of the world's best collections of early motion pictures, and now McDowall suggested that she should meet Dr Howard Gotlieb at

Boston University, the man who set up and ran the first 20th-century archive in America: Adèle should donate some of her extraordinary collection of photographs and memorabilia to Gotlieb's collection. Adèle liked the bright and gossipy McDowall and was intrigued by the idea. When next in Boston she went to see Gotlieb, a bespectacled, cheerful man who in his white work coat looked more like a doctor than a librarian. He explained his operation to Adèle: 'Everyone has a doctor and a lawyer to look after their needs. So they should also have a curator to look after their papers.' So Adèle joined the people, famous and not so famous, at the Mugar Memorial Library on Commonwealth Avenue, where the vast archive is housed. Gotlieb asks his subjects for all kinds of personal matter so that in future years the details can be studied; the plan also was to include the detritus of life as much as the useful things; Adèle would be placed alongside distinguished contributors, including McDowall, but also Mary Astor, Bette Davis, and Douglas Fairbanks Jr from the entertainment world, and D. H. Lawrence and H. G. Wells from the world of literature. Adèle entered into her task with gusto, and trunkfuls of her memorabilia started to pour into Boston: there were letters, notes, telegrams, programmes and plenty of fascinating photographs – including one of Adèle in the nude sunning herself on a beach. 'I think,' said Gotlieb, 'that says quite a lot about Adèle. We had, after all, asked her for all her material and so it would never have entered her mind not to have sent us everything. I liked her very much. She was wicked, witty and charming.' And, inevitably, she persuaded her brother that he, too, should join the list of contributors to the archive.

But it was almost impossible for Adèle to have a totally calm relationship with anyone and her enthusiasm for being part of the Special Collections was such that she wanted to give them a beautiful and spectacular emerald necklace which had come from the Devonshire family and was worth many thousands of pounds. As much as the piece was admired, Gotlieb turned down the gift as there were no facilities at the university for the safe-keeping of jewellery. He explained to the rather miffed Adèle: 'We have to limit ourselves to papers, unless there are truly exceptional circumstances.' Adèle was as forthright as ever: 'If they don't want it, well, fuck 'em.' Happily peace was restored again shortly afterwards.

The introduction into the field of academe brought about another change in Adèle. She had always been a great reader, but hardly scholastically inclined. Now, suddenly, she started to read text books on all sorts of arcane subjects to add to her regular diet of novels and biographies. And if anyone would ask her, she was delighted to act as reviewer. For the *Boston Herald* she reviewed Judith Krantz's sensational novel *Scruples*, and gave it a favourable forecast, with reservations only based on her own practical experience of international high life. She even nursed ambitions to write herself: 'I'm going to write a book one day and call it: *Can a Pretty Little Girl from Omaha, Nebraska, Who Became a Broadway Star and Married into the British Aristocracy, Be Happy? – You Bet Your Sweet Life She Can.*'

The one thing that Adèle really disliked about growing old, other than not being able to keep up the pace of her youth, was that she was denied the company of many young people. Few of her own generation still had much appetite for life and the younger ones who did amuse or entertain her were inclined to be too effete for the red-blooded Adèle. She still saw all her old friends who had survived, even Tilly Losch, whom she met one day at an exhibition of photographs by Cecil Beaton. Afterwards Tilly asked Beaton how he thought Adèle looked. 'The same as you would look if you'd had your face lifted as often as Adèle,' the waspish Beaton replied. Tilly, always a gossip and often a trouble maker, thought, quite rightly, that Adèle would appreciate the crack: she did, and as she had never had cosmetic surgery she treated Beaton's remark as a great compliment to a woman of her age. However, he was livid when he heard that he had been repeated. In the letter he had from Adèle where she mentions it he ringed Tilly's name in green ink, adding BITCH by it. After that, the thirty-year friendship between Tilly and Beaton was at an end, although Tilly and Adèle remained as fond as ever.

The next generation of Astaires showed little inclination for the world of showbusiness, and certainly their father made no effort to make out that it was too much fun. Ava, who had shown a marked artistic streak when she was studying at Westlake, toyed with the idea of entering the world of drama, but ultimately preferred her art and painting. When the time came for her to make her début, there was no prouder father as Astaire danced with her, and, by his own admission, was so nervous that he trod on her feet.

Ava wandered through the Los Angeles arty set, seeing the Bohemian side of life, when she wasn't helping her father as companion, escort and inspiration. When he needed a name for for his music company, Ava Productions had been the obvious title. When he needed another company for the TV special, Vasta Productions, a combination of Ava and Astaire was created. She is even credited with co-writing the Astaire song *I Love Everybody But You*, although she said her contribution was limited to the title. They travelled together to Hong Kong and the Far East and pretty soon it was Ava who was deciding where they should go and what they should see. She didn't like the Hollywood set very much: 'I really don't like going out too much where everyone knows who you are. I guess I get that from my father.' But she enjoyed so much that she was quite happy with the situation. That is, until she met Carl Bostleman, a Boston socialite and would-be entrepreneur, who had been working as an interior decorator and salesman. They fell in love and when Ava was twenty-six, in 1968, they were married by the minister of Astaire's All Saints Episcopalian Church on the lawn of San Ysidro Drive.

Unhappily the marriage, which seemed such a good idea at the time, soon broke down and within two years they were divorced, as Ava had met and fallen for a talented artist called Richard Clayton McKenzie, a widower fourteen years her senior. Her attraction was immediate to this rather Hemingway-like figure with his fierce beard and kindly eyes. His wife had died a year beforehand and he was trying to readjust, living in a midtown Los Angeles apartment block, scruffy but with some class – and there was a laid-up, dilapidating Rolls-Royce marking the back of the place. His Richard McKenzie Gallery on La Cienega sold his paintings and those of his friends, and took commissions.

The first Fred Astaire knew of his existence was when Ava presented him with a McKenzie oil-painting. He was by no means a wealthy man, but Ava suggested that with the money her father had given her they could move to London, and he could paint full-time. On 17 May, for the second time at San Ysidro Drive, Ava Astaire was married – this time by Judge George Zucker, a friend of Astaire and a judge of the California Municipal Court. Ava was twenty-eight, McKenzie was forty-one. 'Look after her,' Astaire told his new son-in-law, as they shook hands afterwards. McKenzie said that he would. And so he did. Or maybe it is she who looked after him. They lived in London for a while, then moved to Ireland where they found Castlepoint, a dramatic and remote house at Schull, County Cork, on the most south-easterly extremity of Ireland, washed by the wild Atlantic winds and nursed by the warm Gulf Stream. This didn't mean losing touch with her father, as Ava explained: 'Daddy loves Ireland and would like to be there as often as he can.' And when he wasn't there, the transatlantic lines were certainly kept busy. Even in Ireland Ava and Dick could keep an eye on her father's achievements, and said that they couldn't help laughing when they saw him in *Towering Inferno*, dishevelled and grimy, surrounded by thousands of gallons of water. It rather put paid to the Astaire sophisticated image, but it didn't stop him from being nominated for an Oscar as Best Supporting Actor. Although he didn't win that, he did win a Golden Globe and a British Academy of Film and Television Arts award for the same performance. The first person he called with the news was Ava. Once or twice a year the McKenzies would travel to California or Fred would stay with Adèle at Lismore, about three hours' drive away – nothing in local terms. And for any Hollywood function where he needed an escort, Ava would be there, with her husband a few paces behind.

The Astaire children played an essentially peripheral role in his life. Although he would assert that the children came foremost, they did not. First, second and third came work. Filming, rehearsing or worrying about it. Or worrying about not doing it. Then came the family. With Ava first.

Peter, sharing Astaire's great fascination, had joined the police force. He had always read the detective books Astaire kept around the house and decided that this was the life for him, becoming Sheriff in the Los Angeles County Sheriff's Department and serving in Santa Barbara. When he retired from the force he became a dealer in lumber and real estate and ran his own private detective agency. His wife Janet presented Astaire with his first grandchild, named Phyllis Maud, the first of three children.

Fred Jr, having worked as a charter pilot, briefly worked in theatrical production, before settling down to run his father's ranch and look after real estate. In the summer of 1961 his wife Gale presented Fred with yet another generation when Fred Henry Astaire was born, again the first of three children on Fred Jr's side – making six grandchildren in all. The one cause of a mild regret for Astaire was that Ava, with that superb breeding of his mother and sister, had no children of her own: they might have been quite something.

In New York the reclusive, private, rich and famous Adèle, as she was invariably described, was not so unapproachable and she became firm friends with one youngster, Maureen Solomon, a graduate from the New York University Film School, who had delivered some flowers to the address listed in the phone book for Kingman Douglass. She had

[229]

called and was amazed when Adèle happily chatted for an hour about everything under the sun. Solomon, later a television script writer, said: 'She was warm and bright and loved to hear the latest gossip. At the time she was fuming about a congressman who had his mistress on salary. She said to me: "Politicians are all tricky. Why should we as taxpayers have to pay salaries to their secretaries, those broads with boobs they hire to have sex with?"' Adèle was also concerned about the sexual state of the world outside of Congress too. 'Do you think there are any real men left? They're all gay now, it's terribly depressing and I really don't know how anyone makes babies now if they're not fucking.' When she was being more serious she had decided that she had little time anyway for the American man. 'They talk loud and tell where they've been and who they know. Who cares? That's Americans. You never hear an Englishman doing that.'

Even in her later years Adèle's hair was a rich chestnut and she always looked elegant and well turned out, keeping herself trim by following the Gayelord Hauser regime, eating sparsely and regularly doing her cardiovascular exercises. 'You must look after yourself,' she said. 'After all, ageing does start when you're sixteen years old and that was a few years ago for me.' She did not claim any particular reason for the Astaire longevity and neither could she see any end to it whenever she was asked – and she was always being asked – when Fred really would be retiring. She would seem to ponder the question: 'We are both extremely energetic. It is the good and clean lives we lead. As far as my brother is concerned, he will stay in showbusiness as long as he is in demand. All the girls, young and old, seem to love him.'

And her age almost, but not quite, caught up with her. In 1977, Aileen Stux-Ryber, one of the Guinness girls, formerly Aileen Plunkett, and the elder sister of Maureen, Marchioness of Dufferin and Ava, gave a magnificent eightieth birthday party for Adèle at her Luttrellstown Castle in Clonshill, County Dublin. Adèle was actually eighty-one then. But that did not stop her showing that she still had plenty of life in her. It only needed someone to say that the assembled company were too old for dancing on tables, when Adèle rose, got up on the table – and a very fine table it was too – and danced, to the delight of the assembled company. The hostess, a mere seventy-three, was none too amused: 'It's terribly vulgar,' she said. 'That's the trouble with Aileen now,' said Adèle, when she heard that she had been chided for her high spirits, 'she's so bloody boring.'

In 1975 in Beverley Hills one night she sat next to Helen Rayburn, wife of television's *Match Show* game host Gene Rayburn, who was immediately invited skiing with her in Jackson Hole, Wyoming. After that, slowly the idea emerged that maybe she really would do something about that book on her life she had talked of writing many years before, although Adèle's view was: 'No one's interested in an old bird like me.' Helen Rayburn suggested that Adèle could talk about her showbusiness life into a tape recorder and use the material as captions to some of her photographs. The project was started, Adèle going up to stay at Osterville Country Club on Cape Cod, a few hundred yards from where the Rayburns had a house, but it was never completed. For things started to go wrong for Adèle. From Lismore she was told that it might be better if she did not spend the summer there in 1979 because of extensive building work going on. Poor Adèle quite erroneously took that as a slight, as she loved the castle and the area and the churchyard where her babies lay, and she thought that maybe she was not wanted there anymore. The following year she was not well enough to go back to Lismore. Instead she had to have a cataract operation on one eye and spent a miserable summer in Phoenix, Arizona, although the imagined rift with Lismore was healed – had she only realized just how much she was loved there, she would never have imagined there was any problem.

In 1973, Ann Astaire, aged ninety-five, was examining some curtains she thought needed replacing at San Ysidro Drive when she fell off a chair. She broke a hip and, because of her age, it did not seem to heal properly and she had to use a steel zimmer frame to help her get around the house. If Astaire was upset, Adèle was even more so. 'I really would not want to spend my life in one of those things,' she said. But Ann struggled on and seemed to manage quite well.

In July of 1975 Astaire, cheered by the interest of a BBC radio version of his life story, came to London to make some new recordings, both by himself and with his old pal Bing Crosby. He was taking time off on the morning of Saturday 26 July for breakfast at Claridges with BBC television producer Richard Drewett, who was discussing with him an appearance on the British TV chat show hosted by Michael Parkinson. Negotiations had not been going well and Astaire was planning to pull out of the arrangement. But the coffee had only just been poured when a page came looking for Astaire. He was gone for some time. Producer Drewett wondered whether Astaire had just walked away. Minutes ticked by. Eventually he did return to the table and sat down. 'I'm sorry. You'll have to excuse me if I'm not very together. I just heard from America, my mother has died.'

Drewett was shocked and suggested that they postpone the meeting. 'No, no,' said Astaire, 'We're here now, there's nothing we can do, so let's talk about the show.'

Ann Geilus Astaire, five months short of her ninety-seventh birthday, had died peacefully in her sleep at San Ysidro Drive.

Astaire had learnt the value of work to paper over gaps in his life: he appeared on the *Michael Parkinson Show* a few months later. Backstage Parkinson told Astaire how, as a kid, he used to copy the way that Astaire and Duke Wayne used to walk. Then Parkinson walked out on to the studio set and fell straight down the set stairs. He went back to re-do the sequence for the recording to find Astaire helpless with laughter. 'Guess you got mixed up between me and Duke,' Astaire said.

The death of Ann had a tremendous effect on both Fred and Adèle. She had been the one unifying factor in their lives and the absence left a deep gap for both of them. Adèle unhappily started to suffer, for the first time in her life from various bugs, viruses and illnesses caused by increasing age, although her stepson Kingman Douglass Jr said: 'She had enormous recuperative powers and soon would be up and telling you in Marine-type language what she thought of the world.' Fred tried to keep himself busy, driving to his office most days and seeing to his mail or playing a gentle game of golf, his life only enlivened when the grandchildren or Ava called, or Hermes Pan would visit from his nearby Cherokee Lane home for some supper cooked by Fred – Fettuccine al Fredo, or something like that. Fred and Pan still went to previews to keep up with what was happening, but at the end of the day there was still an empty house to go home to. But there was one project that increasingly occupied his thoughts. Astaire, eighty years old and just singled out in a best dressed man award as 'the best dressed man of our time – the strongest influence of freestyle elegance in the twentieth century', went to spend the Christmas holidays of 1979 with Adèle in Arizona, to laugh with her, to talk about old friends. And Astaire had something to say that he never imagined he would be saying; he had decided that he wanted to get married to a girl, called Robyn Smith. Adèle had always known that men could behave in a very silly way when it came to dealing with women, but it never occurred to her that her brother would contemplate getting married again at eighty. That was too ridiculous for words.

19
Melody and Robyn

Fred Astaire first met Robyn Smith on 1 January 1973.

No one ever did discover what got into the small $25,000 bay filly in the fifth race at Santa Anita on that New Year's Day. At the 2.40 off in the warm California afternoon Exciting Divorcee, slowly out of the shoot, trailed eighth of twelve at the quarter mark. But on the turn she caught her stride and rallied wide of the dozen runners into the straight. Willie Shoemaker on Lady Broadcast had saved ground as they went round, and at the half Exciting Divorcee, with Al Vanderbilt's distinctive red silks, with checkered black sleeves and a large black circle on the blouse, was trailing just behind Lost Moment and Lady Broadcast in a close field. The rolling thunder of the hooves on green turf pounded past the stands and the cheering crowds.

As they pounded into the last of the six furlongs, there was Exciting Divorcee, pushed from on top with the jockey's determined fierceness, the jaw gripped tight. Other riders, knowing that Shoemaker, with whip flying, was half a length ahead in the final stretch, would have despaired, but Robyn Smith was not the despairing kind, and like greased magic she edged past Lady Broadcast and Lost Moment, into the lead, and by a short neck crossed the line first, with Shoemaker on Lady Broadcast just behind. For a second the grim face relaxed into a half smile of contentment. Robyn Smith smiled when she won.

Watching the race in the box of Alfred Gwynne Vanderbilt II, were the horse's trainer Bobby Lake, and Fred Astaire. Astaire and Vanderbilt had known each other – literally man and boy – for just under forty years, since the day when Vanderbilt's mother, the Bromo Seltzer heiress Margaret McKim, had taken the teenaged Vanderbilt to see the Broadway hit musical show *Funny Face* and afterwards backstage to meet Fred and his sister Adèle. Now that slight youth had grown into a big, sturdy man and Fred Astaire was just a few months shy of his seventy-fourth birthday, sometimes wondering what had

[233]

happened to that passage of years. Astaire had been studying the form book and although the Kentucky-bred filly, by Candy Spots out of French Girl, was a no-hoper – seventh of eight and last in the two previous December outings at New York's Aquaduct racetrack – the horse had reminded him of his *Gay Divorcee* movie, and out of friendship for Vanderbilt he had punted $200 on it, and was quite delighted when the announcement came over the racetrack speakers: First, Exciting Divorcee, owned by Mr A. G. Vanderbilt, trained by R. P. Lake, ridden by R. C. Smith. Exciting Divorcee paid $16.60 to a $2 stake.

When Cash Astaire had collected his frankly unexpected sixteen-hundred-dollar pay out, he couldn't help but remark: 'Twenty to one she paid. If they all came in like that I wouldn't have to worry about working, we could just spend our lives betting on her.'

Later, in interviews he gave just before they married, he would always claim that she had won at twenties. So what if it was some ten to one at the track? That's as near twenty as anything else. And anyway, racing folk are prone to a bit of exaggeration. How else could they consistently beat the odds?

Astaire's racing luck had deserted him after Phyllis died, and on the occasions he did go to the track he complained that on the California circuit, with its stalls starts, there were just not enough places in the races to even enter your horses, let alone win any good races. But he started to take an interest in the racing career of Robyn Smith, and he was delighted to see the gutsy girl prosper. By March of '73 she had won some decent races on North Sea and Crowd Pleaser. As the standard of her horses rose so did her winnings and she settled herself comfortably in the top bracket of jockeys with '73 earnings of an extraordinary $634,055, from 501 rides with 51 winners, 51 seconds and 58 thirds. There was no stopping the rumours that she was just a fortune hunter tagging along with Al Vanderbilt, but she continued to shrug off the gossip disdainfully. 'I'm a good rider and win races,' she said, 'that is what is important. I'm legitimate.'

She hit her peak earnings that season; but she kept up the pace, with $434,329 from 37 winners and 410 rides in '74, $316,009 from 25 winners and 256 rides in '75, and $312,761 from 24 winners and 261 rides in '76. But although this was impressive, Robyn was aware that she could not continue the pace for ever and she was increasingly having disagreements with Al Vanderbilt, her most important owner, and in '77 from just 169 rides and 13 winners her total was $180,822. Many a jockey would have been quite content with those earnings and put it down to 'just a bad season', for Robyn Smith there was something more. Her plan had been that once she had found a patron of Al Vanderbilt's stature and proved herself in the saddle, then other big-time owners would be begging her to ride for them. That did not happen; in the final analysis most owners still preferred to put up a man for the big races. Vanderbilt was not improving his stock sufficiently for her ambitions. She was still nowhere near the annual winner's record of 515 winners in one season by Sandy Hawley, or the cash earnings of Willie Shoemaker, forty-six that year, with a career total of some $75 million.

On the positive side she did have two important pluses in her career. In March she became the first girl to ride in the Santa Anita Handicap, when she rode Austin Miller to a fair fifth place – Astaire, whose Triplicate had previously won the race, lost his money on Robyn that time. Secondly, she was the first girl jockey to be one of the riders nominated for Santa Anita's George Woolf Memorial Jockey Award, named after the legendary jockey who won the inaugural Santa Anita Handicap in 1935. So good was Woolf that Santa Anita legend still remembers the walkover 1942 Pimlico Handicap with winner-take-all conditions, when no owner considered it worth while to challenge Woolf on a famous horse called Whirlaway. Despite it being a no-contest the horse still had to run the course to collect the purse. Woolf, in common with other great jockeys, was not much given to words, but on this occasion, as he was riding the horse from the paddock, he leaned over and volunteered to the trainer Ben Jones: 'Any special instructions, boss?' the reply was quick: 'Yes, Georgie, don't fall off.'

Robyn Smith lost out on the award to Texan Frank Olivares, but she did reckon that something had been won by being on that short list. The other turning point that year was that Robyn Smith and Al Vanderbilt, who had been continuing their public rows and makings-up to an increasingly fierce extent, finally parted. He had been divorced in '75 and many expected Robyn and Vanderbilt to marry, but that did not happen; it seemed to be on then off. Now it was off. This time it was not to be a break for just a day or two or three; it seemed permanent.

'Her life is very full,' he told *Sports Illustrated* for a profile article on Robyn. 'She knows just what she wants to do and she's going to do it. I asked her once what she wanted most and she said she wanted to be the best rider in the world. In the world, just like that. I suppose she could have said the best rider in the world ever, but she just didn't think of that at that moment.' To make the best rider in the world she needed to

[235]

be accepted by other owners and she felt that her association with Vanderbilt, although a good and useful one, had run its course. With the continual control of her weight and the tantrum-inducing depression caused by it, she had already become the cause of her own destruction. She wouldn't be the only one to lose out. Trainer Bobby Lake, who had trained the Vanderbilt horses from '72 to '77, was informed that they would be leaving his stables.

'I suppose Robyn had ridden about half of Mr Vanderbilt's rides with me. I guess they fell out over something,' Lake said with much loyalty. 'She still had rides here, but of course Mr Vanderbilt did have a lot of horses.'

Robyn's version of events has her going from New York to Los Angeles, where she had an apartment in the comfortable $750 a month Villa Barita building at 456 Fairview, Arcadia, just a few hundred yards from the Santa Anita track, to make a television commercial, although there is no record that has been found of any television commercial plans for Robyn Smith that year.

Fred Astaire was surprised to get the phone-call. Quite out of the blue, Robyn Smith called him. 'She just rang me up and asked me out to dinner,' he said. 'I was a little shocked. I was used to doing the asking myself. But I went.'

Robyn claimed Astaire fell in love with her the day that Exciting Divorcee paid $1,660, and says that she fell in love with him that day they went out to dine. When they first met she had heard of him, but had never seen any of his films; in the years between times she had made a point of catching up with those, but in little more of a way than one takes an interest in the careers of those you have met socially. 'He was so cute, humble and charming,' she said. 'After that, it was not a case of an older man pursuing a younger girl. I pursued him.'

Astaire was frankly intrigued by this girl who had single-mindedly driven her way to the top of her world: it was the kind of professional commitment that he understood and one that he admired. Her youth didn't worry him: as his old colleague George Burns said: 'At our age there aren't many women our age around to go out with.' Robyn also played a fair game of golf. And, as someone with early baseball enthusiasms could appreciate, she could throw a ball like a boy, with the wrist rather than with the elbow movement used by most women. Robyn herself told him of the gossip about her past which he might hear: 'There are some things that happened in my childhood that I really can't remember, and others that I don't want to remember because I just can't handle them.'

Fred did hear the gossip, for there was much of it about. Her looks, her friendship with Vanderbilt, her large winnings all conspired to foster the stories. But the truth itself was far stranger than anything that the gossipmongers could invent, for she was not in fact Robyn Smith at all.

Robyn Caroline Smith, as she now called herself, was actually born Melody Dawn Constance Palm in San Francisco on Friday 14 August 1942 at 12.18 a.m. to Constance Palm and her husband Bill, a worker on the President Line shipping fleet. She was the fourth child born to Constance, a blonde from Portland, Oregon, who had already had an eventful and even complicated life: she was on her fourth marriage and already had three children, Madeleine and Burton from her first marriage to Marc Land, and Fred Miller Jr from her third husband Fred Miller. In between times the eldest two children had been boarded out through Roman Catholic adoption agencies and Constance, a self-confessedly devout Catholic whose mother came from County Galway in Ireland, had travelled in search of the bright lights and good things of life in Hollywood and had even worked as an extra on Cecil B. de Mille's 1934 *Cleopatra* which starred Claudette Colbert. In Hollywood Constance met and married a playboy called Fred Grant as her second, and his third, partner – Grant had an income of $800 a month from his father's mail order business that advertised Grant's patent medicine for 'temporary relief for epileptics, and sometimes a cure'. After a few months the marriage ended and he gave her a Nash Brougham car and a police dog called Marje as a separation settlement. Constance had returned to her native Portland, Oregon, where she met and married Bill Palm. They moved to San Francisco and, shortly after Melody was born, Constance was hospitalised with a feverous erysipelas virus: her husband was at sea so Fred and Melody were put into a nursery, with the plan that, through a Catholic agency, they would be temporarily put into foster homes. Melody, aged four, was placed with Jane and Orville Smith, owner of the Heppner Lumber company in Heppner, Oregon.

In time Constance recovered and met, as she described it to me, 'an elderly gentleman', called Hartley Gordon. It was, according to her, only a platonic friendship, but Hartley Gordon did have a large house and plenty of room for the children who she wanted to get back, yet when she tried to retrieve her daughter it transpired that there were adoption papers out in the name of the Smith family for Melody. 'I never signed them,' claimed Constance. Then there began a massive

[237]

legal battle between Constance Palm, the Smiths and Catholic Charities Incorporated to decide what should happen to the child. In May 1948 the case reached the Supreme Court of Oregon in the Pendleton Term and, in a furiously argued suit with claim, counter claim and the allegations of legalistic chicanery, and all the mud that is slung from side to side in such cases, the judgement was made for Constance Palm, and Melody arrived back with her little suitcase, nightdress and toothbrush. Constance made Hartley Gordon her fifth husband and briefly the family was united again.

But not much in Constance's life stayed without problems for long: shortly afterwards Hartley Gordon died and the children were once more sent to a variety of foster homes. Melody grew tall and good-looking and excelled at sport, especially swimming, and in time graduated through Madeleine Grade School and in '61 from Mary-crest High in North East Portland, having spent her last few years fostered with Frank Kucera and his wife in Gresham, Portland.

'She rang me and asked if I could give her some money for her graduation photographs, which I did,' said Constance. 'She gave me the small one and gave the big one to the Kuceras. She was a gorgeous, lovely girl. Then the last time that I spoke to her was on Mothers' Day, 14 May that year. She rang me and I told her that I'd heard that she was planning to go back and live with the Smiths.' The Smiths by this time had prospered further and Orville Smith, as an expansion of the lumber business, had also bought the million-dollar Stetson-Ross industrial machine company in nearby Seattle. 'Melody said to me: "Go to Hell, Mom" I can tell you I was hurt, I really was. And that was the last time I spoke to her.'

Her mother had already given her blessing to a trip to Hollywood that Melody was planning to make with a schoolfriend who was the daughter of a former stand-in for the sultry actress Yvonne De Carlo. After all, it was no more than Constance had done when she was younger. That was that, as far as Melody Dawn Palm was concerned. Hello, Hollywood. Hello, new life. Goodbye, Portland, Oregon. In the next half-dozen years Melody Dawn disappeared completely to be replaced by Robyn Caroline Smith. No one in Portland, Oregon heard from her. Her mother had married yet again, a Mr Dittot, had a daughter Sharon and been widowed. The Kuceras heard not a peep. Her friend returned from Los Angeles, but Melody was determined to stay on. The newborn Robyn tried to get work in movies and television commercials without success. She went to the parties around town where there was always a demand for pretty girls and there she met film producer Martin Ransohoff, who made *The Cincinnati Kid* with Steve McQueen and whose Filmways company was involved at the time with a whole stream of low-budget pictures with director Sam Arkoff. Arkoff referred to that time as the Golden Era. It was pretty thinly plated gold with productions such as *Muscle Beach Party*, *Beach Blanket Bingo* and so on. Arkoff did not remember Robyn among the hordes of bikini-clad extras. 'Robyn Smith? Melody Palm? No, I don't remember the names,' said Arkoff with a laugh, 'but then we only went by distinguishing marks on the body anyway.'

Robyn went along to Columbia Studios, where she tried to enrol in their acting workshop, but her screen career only ever existed in her wishful thinking. And to go with that she reinvented her own past. She said her parents were now both dead, and that she had been brought up in Hawaii. She had been an English major at Stanford in the class of '66. Later she said, when that was shown to be a fabrication, that it was unfair to blame Stanford for that because she was under contract to MGM, where the publicity people had dreamed up her past. But MGM had no aspiring actresses under contract at the time and had never heard of Robyn Smith. By all accounts what is true is that in the spring of 1968 she was taken on a date to the palm-fringed Santa Anita racetrack, an auto-clogged trip down the full length of Sunset Boulevard and then off to Arcadia, and suddenly, at the age of twenty-five, she fell in love with the power and the thunder of the horses, the colour and swirl of the crowds. She could have just crawled into a hole in Hollywood, found a job and waited to find herself a husband, or else she could go out and make a name for herself: it was the latter that Robyn Smith was determined to do.

She had not found the medium in the acting world, where the body and the casting couch seemed to come a long way ahead of doing anything for real, and she was not one inclined to hang around all day making idle chatter with other would-be actresses, so the very next day she was out at the track. She had never ridden as a kid – childhood asthma had put her off too much contact with the animals she could have had, and at five foot seven she was a bit on the tall side but she had met Californian trainer Bruce Headley socially and so begged him to allow her to ride for him in the early mornings. There is a touching honesty in her description of those first days. She said, 'The horses weren't scared, but, boy, I was. Invariably the horses would run away with me, but it was dark in the morning at that time and Headley couldn't see.'

[239]

But she was determined and stories of the beautiful new exercise girl at Santa Anita spread north, where the tales reached Kjell Qvale, owner of the British Motor Company in San Francisco, selling Rolls-Royces from a chandeliered and palatial marble showroom a couple of blocks from the Opera House on Van Neff. By then girl jockeys were just allowed to ride professionally and, in the words of one racing commentator, everyone wanted to see a girl jockey ride, rather like dirty movies or girls wrestling in jelly, everyone wants to see it once – and Qvale, on the board of directors of San Francisco's Golden Gate Park gave Robyn her very first mount on Saturday 5 April 1969. She rather shrugged off the experience, but Golden Gate got the publicity and Robyn Smith, by declaring her birth date as 14 August 1944, rather than the true date of 14 August 1942, was under twenty-five years old and therefore eligible for her trainee jockey's licence. She duly became indentured as an apprentice to California trainer Gerry Dutton.

Qvale was not the only one interested in the idea of a glamorous lady jock. As her fame and name spread to the East Coast, in New York there was a more sinister, but, on the surface, interesting proposition for Robyn Smith from New York trainer Buddy Jacobson.

Jacobson, although successful, was another can of worms altogether. In more recent times he could be found in Clinton, the Siberia of the New York penal system, serving twenty-five years for the murder of Jack Tupper, drug-dealer boyfriend of Jacobson's ex-girlfriend Melanie Cain, a model who had inspired Jacobson to lop several years off his age, set up a New York apartment block as a dormitory establishment for aspiring cover girls and start his own model agency as a further source of glamour. His thriving racetrack career had been much neglected with the new interest in sex but his interest did continue, and he was particularly interested in the stories of the beautiful chestnut jockette, as they were rather sneeringly called by many racing types – the sign on the women's changing rooms at Aquaduct even read 'Jockettes' at one time. So on the strength of his extravagant offers of wonderful rides that she would have, Robyn went East, along with her two pet rats, Salt and Pepper. When Jacobson met her, he spotted the determination and guts in the girl, but he did not see any sexual pushover, although he did recognise the track potential in her attitude. She rode a few times for him, rejected his leering attention and that was that. She was in New York, staying at a small hotel near Aquaduct racetrack and down on her money and down on her luck. Her aim was always that she wanted to reach the top; there seemed a likelihood that she was about to reach the bottom instead.

Girl jockeys are a subject of some contention in the racing world. In *The Thoroughbred of California* magazine of May 1969, Frank Tours said about nineteen-year-old Barbara Jo Rubin, who had ridden quite successfully for Jacobson, and about the newcomer Robyn Smith: 'A lot of noise for little reason'. Even the most liberated and free-thinking of the racing fraternity – not noted for its liberality or its freedom of thought – hold that women, in general, do not have the strength in the straight to make a horse win, when it is edging the frame. The majority agreed – and still do agree – with Frank Tours, that girls look after horses well, they ride exercise well, they groom horses well, but: 'they don't ride them well in the afternoon.'

People reckoned without the Smith determination: her natural body weight was around 125 pounds, but she knocked that down to 105 pounds for the optimum riding weight. She was always small on top, but with the weight loss became positively flat-chested. Her face became drawn and gaunt and her breeches hung off her hips – the only colour came from the sun and the freckles on her nose. So she wandered the barns at Aquaduct, pleading for a chance to ride. Melodrama always high in her heart, she would come out with the 'Sometime you're going to beg me to ride for you, mister,' line, out of some old, corny movie, to the less enthusiastic people she tried. Even she admitted that times were tough. 'Time was running out,' she said. 'People were getting set to move south. I get very defensive when I'm down and out, so I acted like a rich girl. You know, I lied about things to build myself up. Of course, even then I thought I was a great rider. That was no front.'

As her luck would have it, one November morning the rain was extra tough at dawn when she went to see trainer Frank Wright from Tennessee. 'I had chased her away from the barn once before,' said Wright, 'but I guess someone had sent her back as I had been one of the first to use exercise girls and my wife is a show-ring rider. Robyn just stood there outside with the rain running out of her boots. I said "Well, please come inside." ' She started by riding gallops for him and on 5 December rode her first runner for Wright, a horse called Exotic owned by a Detroit dentist. The animal had a penchant for finishing last, so there was little to lose, and when Robyn's driving shank and hunger pushed the animal to within a nose of fourth place, everyone was highly pleased and she picked up more rides. Robyn did find that if there was one thing worse than being a girl jockey, it was being a good-looking girl jockey.

[241]

Early on she got used to the 'I'd like to use you Robyn, but my wife won't let me,' from the trainers. 'That's just lame,' she would say. But she worked out something important pretty quickly: although in theory the trainers picked the jockeys, they only did so with the say-so of the owner. If the trainer liked her and the owner was one of those who claimed that a good girl could not ride half as well as a bad man then she was stumped. So if the owners called the shots, they would be the ones she would get to know, and her looks could act for her – as well as against her on that front. It was not too difficult. Early on when a newspaper reporter asked her about ghosting her autobiography as first of the new breed of girl riders she said, to put him off: 'Why don't you do one of the other women jockeys – Arline Ditmore or Donna Hillman?' 'Donna Hillman? You mean the pretty one?' the man said. 'No,' she replied, quite practically, 'I'm the pretty one.' But she had found a fountainhead in her life: 'All I want to do is to be happy and racing makes me happy. It's the only thing that does.' Not only did it make her happy, but girl or no girl, she started to earn some money. In the 1969 season she had thirty-three mounts, two winners and modest prize money of $5,117. Was she satisfied with that? No, sir. The following year she had only thirty-four rides, to her frustration, but another two winners and $10,947 in winnings. Things were, as far as she was concerned, even worse. 'I know I'm good. I just need the rides,' she said. It was her determination that would give her the leg up to the big time, then, by making sure that she hung round the right places, she had the break she had been looking for. She met trainers like Californian Bobby Lake, who believed that in the right circumstances girls could be good in the saddle and win races; she met Alfred Gwynne Vanderbilt, who had some six dozen horses in training. Now that was the kind of trainer she wanted to work for and there was the kind of patron she needed. She got both.

By the end of the '71 season she had hoicked her earnings up to $278,246 from the meagre $10,000 of the previous years and she persuaded Vanderbilt to switch his horses to Bobby Lake, who prepared to move from his California base for the '72 season. In 1972 she both finished her Apprenticeship with 20 rides that netted her $12,263 and sailed through her Journeyman period with 42 winners from the 36 rides and $393,369. Of course there are other jockeys that earn that kind of money, but they are few and far between. To keep up that rate of earning she had to be sure to ride races in which she could show well, so she took to advising Vanderbilt where the horses should

[242]

be placed. 'Sure, she liked to win,' said Bobby Lake. 'Who doesn't? And that is the game. She's a good judge of a race. She knew where to place them.' Vanderbilt and Robyn Smith became inseparable. But there were two sides to the togetherness: sometimes they would be seen walking hand in hand (she was claiming to be twenty-seven at the time, although she was actually twenty-nine; when they first went together he was fifty-nine years old) and sometimes she would row with him when his friends were around, put him down, even ignore him if she did not get her own way. But Vanderbilt was besotted by the headstrong girl, so before long they would be back to the hand-holding.

When her apprenticeship ended she hoped the world would be begging for her services. It was not quite like that, even though she had at last made a name for herself. She loved the track and she loved the horses. 'I'll sometimes go to the stables and just work the horses late at night. I like to graze them. I like to be around them. Particularly the ones that win for me, it's sort of their reward. And not all of it is the animal. I just like to be alone. I don't think I'll ever get married. I'm just a loner.' And it was with horses that Robyn at last relaxed, no longer wearing that look of suspicion that she had with people. Racing folk said she would smile on a horse but rarely off one, and it was almost affectionately that she became known as 'The Bitch'.

She had no real social life: in bed by nine, up exercising with the dawn. 'She never went out much,' said Lake. 'She was a heaver – always worrying about her weight.' 'Heaving', as it is known, is not a practice altogether frowned on in racing. Many race riders have trouble keeping to their riding weight and with Robyn's height it was particularly difficult and as less weight means more winners, so she would take appetite suppressants and every now and then eat a large meal. The heaver, the chucker, just goes to the bathroom, makes themselves vomit and then continues on as before. The experienced heaver can perform the trick purely by thinking about it. No salt, no fingers down the throst, just a mental picture and out it comes, and the most determined types – such as Robyn – go straight back to the table and tuck in to another steak or two.

Her reputation as a rider, not just a girl, did spread. Alan Jerkens of Hobeau Farm, a man much respected on the track, admired her spirit and gave her some rides: he reckoned she started well, was always out of the gate fast, but that she too suffered the criticism of the girl jockeys that they do finish slowly. Until you have sat on a horse at speed and seen a good jockey in action, there can be little conception of how a rider

[243]

can almost pick up the horse and drag it over the finishing line in a hard decision. 'Jerkens put her on live horses,' said another trainer. 'That was like the Good Housekeeping seal.' The extra pressure made things difficult for her and the pills she popped to keep down her weight made her depressed. She was liable to weep tears of frustration if she could not ride a horse she wanted, or if some other things should get in her way.

She was stood down for ten days for boring out of a turn, which caused another jockey to be unseated. She became impossible for many. She got rid of her agent, George DeJesus and cut Vanderbilt. She said: 'He was too demanding.' He said: 'I was losing patience with her.' One day she lashed a stable man across the face with a shank over some trivial incident – but she was undeterred. 'I'm going to be highly successful, so there'll be a much more interesting life for people to write about in ten years' time,' she said.

With success came recognition and other problems. There were Robyn Smith stories all around. There were even Robyn Smith jokes: 'Did you hear Robyn took off her bikini top at the pool and was arrested for indecent exposure? No. What happened? They dismissed the case because of insufficient evidence.' But the Vanderbilt rumours didn't phase her too much. 'I know what they're all saying,' she said. 'I'm used to it. It's just a, well, more of a daughter thing. I mean, there's no romance. I'm a whole lot closer to Mrs Vanderbilt than I am to Mr Vanderbilt. Nobody wants to hear that. But I think Mr Vanderbilt is a wonderful man. There's no one nicer.'

Happily for her riding, by the beginning of '73 there had been a rapprochement with Vanderbilt and her earnings for '72, with 44 winners in 381 rides, were $405,632. For all her suspicions of the outside world, for all the problems she was facing inside herself, Robyn Smith was riding high, and through Vanderbilt, she had met the people who could help her further. She was also doing what she had never done as a Beach Party Bingo starlet, meeting the big name stars, just at a time when it did not really matter to her, but she had to admit that she had been rather taken by Vanderbilt's slightly built friend Fred Astaire whom she had met at Santa Anita.

With the affair with Vanderbilt over, it was quite logical for her to follow up the influential contacts she had made through him: hence her phone-call to Astaire, a man who was bound to have other contacts in the horseracing world. But over dinner she found that he was surprisingly shy and awkward – and rather likeable. Their friendship

[244]

grew, and on the days that she wasn't riding – which became increasingly frequent – she would call by his house to talk. She talked to him of her plans of becoming a trainer, in the way that many jockeys do, knowing their riding days are numbered.

That season Robyn continued her riding at the lower key caused by her loss of Vanderbilt. The figures speak for themselves: in 1978 she won $104,450 from 87 rides, in '79 she rode just five times and won only $2,400, but she spent much of her time with Fred Astaire. It was not long before the story of Astaire's glamorous new escort hit the newspapers. The paragraphs started in January 1979 and gathered momentum when he gave her the money for a car to replace her crushed Volkswagen, which had been a gift from Vanderbilt. 'What I liked about Fred,' she said, 'was that I preferred his company and companionship and friendship to anyone else. Fred's honest and down to earth, and such a gentleman. But I don't want to fall in love and get married. I want to concentrate on my career.' 'Why,' said Fred, somewhat plaintively,' Couldn't people say June and October, rather than June and December?'

When Astaire told Adèle of his plans that Christmas in Tucson, Arizona, she could hardly believe he was being serious, and she told him: 'Don't be ridiculous, Freddie.' But serious he was. He returned to Los Angeles and proposed to Robyn. 'Look, shouldn't I just move in with you?' she said. 'No, we're marrying and that's that,' he said. And that was about that.

Firstly Ava had to be told. Her reaction was to come hurrying out from Ireland to see what on earth was happening. Then Adèle had to be pacified. 'He's just being fucking stupid,' she told friends in her matter-of-fact, down-to-earth way. At New York's River Club, her traditional New York base, Adèle made her displeasure known. Anything she found out about Robyn Smith was not complimentary. She rang her Irish friend Billy Hamilton. 'Have you seen the story in Suzy's column about us all being against Freddie's marriage? Do you think anyone will recognize where the information came from?' She didn't seem at all upset when Hamilton told her that of course everyone would know the information had come from her – it was verbatim what she had told him and others in the last few days.

Opposition from the family had no effect. His friends were also just as concerned. The prime assumption was that she was after his money, but then only a couple of his friends had bothered to work out how much money she had been making as a jockey. The far-reaching

[245]

Astaire friends had phone-lines buzzing across the globe; some of them decided that something should be done. But who could tell Fred that he was in danger of making a dreadful fool of himself? One name did emerge: Liz Whitney Tippett, Mary Elizabeth of Astaire's youth. She listened to the proposition and said a flat 'No': 'Listen, if you know Freddie you'll know that if I were to try and persuade him not to go ahead, that will make him more determined than ever to do so.' Of course she was right. She did drop Freddie a line asking him to stay, but that offer was politely declined.

It was in March, 1980 that the world found out that Astaire, just short of his eighty-first birthday, was to marry again, with the first congratulations coming from Alfred Vanderbilt. Fred, inundated by media from around the world, arranged that ABC Television's $1 million-a-year Barbara Walters should interview him at his home for the networked 20-20 news programme. He dismissed their age difference: 'It never occurs to me. I don't even think about it that way. It has nothing whatsoever to do with it. I've always admired pretty girls – and I still do. She's a beautiful female. I know that when you are eighty years of age you're not meant to do that sort of thing. But who the hell is going to tell me what to do? The generation gap? Heck, I never think about it. I'm not a professional octogenarian. I don't like playing the rôle of an old guy who is a creep. Anyway I just don't feel anywhere near eighty. I just can't believe that I'm not fifty any more. We haven't thought about whether it's love – I'm too sophisticated for that, but I don't know. I lost my wife in 1954 and it never occurred to me to marry again. But these things can happen. My married life was perfect. There were no rules. And we certainly didn't discuss everything. I didn't want to know everything about her and she didn't want to know everything about me. Anyone who gets into that kind of relationship is asking for trouble. When my wife died it was just terrible. And she was so young . . . she was only forty-six. It took me a long time to pull myself out of it after I lost her.' But at last he had found someone who had succeeded in giving him everything he reckoned he needed. So, on Tuesday 24 June 1980, at 1155 San Ysidro Drive, with the smog clearing slightly to let in the California sun, Robyn Smith and Fred Astaire were married. Robyn, as could be expected, gave her name as Robyn Caroline Smith, her parents as Orville and June Smith and her birthdate as the 14 August 1944, living out her reinvented past. But Certificate 02147 in the Los Angeles County Records shows that Astaire too was not beyond altering the facts: he gave his highest school grade completed as the same as Robyn – twelve. While she did indeed graduate from high school, Astaire, often to his embarrassment when he considered it, never did get past grade eight. His absent family could not pretend they were pleased. Ava had little good to say of Robyn and Adèle behaved to most people as though the marriage had just not happened.

In December, six months later, Adèle, who had increasingly been feeling her age, had a heart attack and was taken to Scottsdale Hospital, Arizona. Fred immediately flew out to see her. Her strength was not up to much, but enough for Sap and Funny Face to be reconciled at her bedside. On Tuesday 6 January she suffered a stroke and, nearly three weeks later and with her brother nearby, Adèle died, aged eighty-four, on Sunday 25 January, without ever regaining consciousness.

20
Finale

Robyn moved into Ava's room in the single storey house and Astaire continued to share his room with two pianos and a drum kit for his nocturnal meanderings. But certainly there was to be no question that this was just a token marriage. Astaire wanted and desired the physical closeness of Robyn and with her having at last found the father figure she craved and Astaire in turn having found that mixture of feminity, strength and sexuality he so missed, the marriage was launched.

It wasn't to mean, they both agreed, the end of their work. 'He still liked to make a buck,' said Robyn, in a shrewd comment on the piles of scripts which he would read. From the previous year her riding commitments actually increased. From thirty mounts she made a credible $38,115, but she had come to terms herself with the fact that she was not going to be the most successful jockey in the world and she had lost her desire for starving and abusing her body with her new-found stability. Astaire, as much as anything to show he had not gone gaga, accepted a rôle in a film being made by British director John Irvin from Peter Straub's novel *Ghost Story*, and set off for Vermont. He still saw his close friends, like Randolph Scott, Gregory and Veronique Peck, and Hermes Pan still stopped by for an occasional meal. He still went to parties when he wanted to. At the Pecks' New Year's Eve bash he told Robyn that he would leave at midnight – she had to drag him away at 3.30 a.m. At Frank Sinatra's sixty-fifth birthday party in Palm Springs he stayed until last. 'He's okay when you've actually got him out,' said Robyn. But newspapers began to buzz with rumours that the marriage was in trouble. On the set of *Ghost Story* Astaire was seen in the constant company of twenty-one-year-old production assistant Suzy Peterson. Could she be the new fancy in Astaire's life? In fact, nothing could be more wrong. For the four stars of *Ghost Story*, Astaire, Garbo's leading man in *Ninotchka* Melvyn Douglas, 80, Douglas Fairbanks Jr, 72, and Orson Welles' Mercury Theatre and *Citizen Kane* partner John

Houseman, 78, had all been given minders for the duration of the film and Suzy was the girl assigned to Astaire.

Houseman explained:'All of us old men were given a keeper and a house – I had a beautiful blonde from Hawaii – that way they reckoned that they might actually get us to the set each morning.' But pretty girls or not, Astaire found the cold of Saratoga Springs in New York and Woodstock in Vermont began to get to his bones. He complained to Houseman about two things, the cold and the fact that Houseman always looked so cheerful: 'You're always smiling, I wish you wouldn't because you make me look like an old complainer.' Houseman, although born Jacques Hausman in Bucharest, had been through the tough training grounds of an English public school education at Clifton College and his time working with Welles, and he hardly noticed the sub-zero temperatures. Astaire, suffering quite badly, also complained that Robyn would not come out East to join him; instead there was talk from the racetrack of her going to Argentina with a string of horses and race them there for a millionaire Argentinian friend. So persistent were the stories that several newspapers picked up a report that the marriage was at an end and that Robyn was asking for a $5 million separation settlement. The rumours were such that Astaire decided to break his lifetime habit of not commenting on press stories and volunteered to speak to *People* magazine about the happiness that Robyn and he had found together. He firmly explained that no, as far as he was concerned, he was not an old man and yes, they were married and they were going to stay that way. But between the lines could be read the story of two very strong-willed people adjusting to a new life together. Robyn was a delight, he said, adding diplomatically: 'She can be quick-tempered.' Robyn added to that: 'Fred knows how to handle me. There have been lots of men who have been interested in me and I've had lots of attention but there's a big difference between that and being truly cared for. I'm just glad that it was Fred and not me who's been said to have been running around. This is the first time in my life that I've felt really loved – really happy – and I don't intend to let go of that. Fred cares more for me than he cares for himself and that's saying an awful lot.'

For all the complications it had caused, *Ghost Story*, the story of four old men haunted by the murder they committed as youngsters – Tim Choate played the young Fred Astaire – did not work well, much to Astaire's disappointment. What was more Melvyn Douglas died before it was released. Director Irvin, experienced in television (he directed Sir Alec Guinness in John Le Carré's *Smiley's People* was unversed in

Hollywood ways and overshot the film, so that the final edit of the film owed more to front office demands than the performance of the stars.

There had been plans for Robyn to travel to Britain to race in the autumn, but they were called off as finally Robyn had decided to concentrate on one aspect of her life: the marriage, and she knew that Astaire did not, in his heart of hearts, really want her gallivanting around all over the place. From the Autumn of 1981 Robyn Smith raced no more. There was no announcement, she just told the enquirers that she was not available. Astaire was pleased but sorry at the same time. As he told friends: 'She has retired but not at my request or because I thought it was dangerous. I told her she was a champion in her own time – the first woman to win races at big-time racetracks.'

Astaire had lived through a long period when his work had been of purely nostalgic interest, but at last he did start to be acknowledged for his contribution to American movies and music. The songwriters' collection agency ASCAP awarded him a Pied Piper Award for 'being one of the best friends that words and music ever had', and he was honoured by the American Film Institute as the ninth recipient of their Life Achievement Award. When Astaire turned up at the Beverly Hilton ceremony wearing a tuxedo with a bright pink sash around his waist, it did seem as though there was some unity in the Astaire family. Robyn sat on his right hand, Ava and Richard MacKenzie, without beard, and Fred Jr and his wife sat on his left. As master of ceremonies David Niven said to the packed $300-a-ticket testimonial: 'I can assure you the poor man is going through hell.' But the clips and the tributes from his partners Cyd Charisse, Eleanor Powell, Audrey Hepburn, Barry Chase, made it, as Niven said, 'Heaven for us.' One noticeable absentee on that evening was Ginger Rogers, who, it was said, had an engagement in New Orleans. 'I had a letter from Ginger,' Astaire said, 'I couldn't read half of it, her handwriting . . . I'll have to go home and study it.' In fact Ginger was very sore about not being there and she had kept the day free until the last moment, but Astaire had let it be known that he would rather that she was not present – otherwise the great scene-stealer would undoubtedly have done something dramatic. Astaire said: 'If I had a little thing I could squirt in my eye, I could cry, I really mean it. And he did pay tribute to Adèle. 'Adèle was the one who had talent in the family,' he said. 'I just went along for the ride.'

With Robyn at last retired, Astaire spent his time in gentle pursuits. Some golf, some pool and some music. He regularly spoke to his old friends like Irving Berlin and commiserated with him about the songs

[250]

which now came so slowly – it rankled with Berlin that Jerome Kern had continued writing until the day he died at sixty-one. Berlin had written little that was truly memorable since the 1954 movie *There's No Business Like Showbusiness* when he was sixty-six. Astaire, acknowledging he was a mere amateur compared to the great Berlin, had written little at all since the death of his main songwriting partner Tommy Wolf (together they had written 'City of the Angels' about Los Angeles and 'Life is Beautiful', the title track of a Tony Bennett LP and a sometime theme of Johnny Carson). He still took a keen interest in the movies, sometimes arranging to attend private preview screenings. There was even a film being made at MGM that was going to use some old Astaire footage, a multi-million-dollar extravaganza called *Pennies From Heaven*, written by British playwright Dennis Potter and based on a critically acclaimed BBC television series about a 1930s song-sheet salesman who mixes his sales with fantasies about Hollywood movies and his sex life. Astaire and Robyn walked silently from the viewing theatre, but when he got out of earshot of the Paramount people he let rip. It even, to Astaire, with its mixture of coarse language from the salesman (played by Steve Martin) and some of Astaire's own early screen footage, which Astaire was powerless to stop them using, managed to hit pits way below 'the Poseidon thing'. 'I have never spent two more miserable hours in my life. Every scene was cheap and vulgar. They don't realise that the thirties were a very innocent age, and that should have been set in the eighties – it was just froth; it makes you cry it's so distasteful.' He had no desire to return to those former times himself: 'Reminiscing is for the birds. Only the future counts. What I accomplished in the past, if anything, means little to me. I never understand people when they talk about the good old days of showbusiness. Sure there are good things and bad things but the truth is that showbusiness is better now than it ever was when I started. Anyone who doubts that should look at some of my old films on television. I mean people can turn it on and look at it for nothing, and sort of look at it and hate it and say: "Gee. Ho-ho: Isn't that funny?"'

But that was far from the reaction of those who enjoyed the movies or studied them at film school and university to try to gauge the secret of Astaire's flawless techniques. What was it about Astaire that made him so good at what he did? What was it that inspired such devotion, loyalty and inspiration in others? As much as anything it was his own selfless – or maybe selfish – devotion to his craft. While Astaire was earning several thousand dollars a week, his faithful pianist Hal Borne, (heard on some of the soundtracks as duettist with Astaire, noticeably in *Let's Dance*), and dancing partner Hermes Pan would have been working the same long hours for one tenth or less than Astaire was getting – on the early films Pan had $75 a week compared to the $1,500 earned by Astaire. Did Pan have any regrets? Did he not ever feel a twinge of jealousy of Astaire's success? 'Yes,' he said. 'I suppose I may have had a twinge of jealousy. Certainly it would have been nice to have had a bit more recognition and earned more. But when I started, $75 was more than I'd ever seen before and I did boost it by doing a bit of dancing myself,' said Pan, whose own appearances included being in the *Top Hat* chorus. 'But I never had any regrets. It was a pleasure and a privilege to work with Fred.'

Astaire, not being entirely honest with himself on detail, put his success down to a dedication of enthusiasm. 'I was wildly enthusiastic about everything I did. I've never been impressed with what I've done professionally as much as people think I should be. I never took my dancing as seriously as everyone else did. I never felt "Oh, gee, look what I did". I never even wanted to see it on film after I had done it. I never ever felt that "Gee hooray" thing about filming. The fun comes when it's over if it's a success. And if it isn't a success at least it's over. The advantage of films over the stage is you have your evening free. The holidays are longer. And the salaries, unquestionably, are much higher than anything that the stage could afford.'

But there is more to it than that. Somehow, throughout his career, striving for acceptance from Ak-Sar-Ben to Broadway, always in the shadow of Adèle (for many years he even carried around in his wallet a newspaper clipping of the review which read: 'The girl is better than the boy'), he had managed to scale every possible height. From his early days of vaudeville, through radio – 'There is so much progress it is hard to take it all in,' he said. 'Why I can remember hearing about the first crystal receiver and I couldn't believe a voice could be coming out of that thing.' – to gramophone records ('Lovely to Look at', 'Cheek to Cheek', 'The Way You Look Tonight', 'Nevertheless' and 'Something's Gotta Give' all reached Number One in the Hit Parade), to motion pictures and television, where he proved himself a consummate straight actor in the 1960s' Fred Astaire Theatre series, he had always aimed for the highest and invariably got there too.

He was a complex man. A distillation of excellence. A sometimes schoolboy sense of humour – a long-time running joke on the sets between him and Pan was for one to ask: 'Would you like some water?'

at a moment of exhaustion, before throwing a glassful of water at the other when they said 'Yes'. And his feet became so much part of the man that he would sometimes confuse directors, usually on purpose, by conducting conversations with the aid of his tapping feet. He chased Ginger Rogers, like a character on Keats' Grecian urn, always pursuing, with his feet. He made love with his feet. So to him it made perfect sense to speak with his feet, too. But for Astaire there was always that little bit further to reach, maybe to get as good as his mother wanted or to equal the feats of Adèle. 'Don't be silly,' she chided him whenever he made one of his attempts to get her back on stage, 'You're the dancer in the family.' Astaire himself was not so sure: 'I don't actually say: I can hardly wait to dance. People don't do that. Nureyev might do it. I don't think he loves it that much either. I just think he happens to be supreme and he knows it and that's it.' He admitted that when he first arrived in motion pictures he did not see much chance of success as a dancer: 'Most of the dancing I had seen in motion pictures didn't seem to have any great authority as art or entertainment. Maybe it was the screen that took away the three-dimensional quality, maybe it was that there was no audience. The first time that I thought it might project was when I saw the Carioca on screen. I didn't like it as a dance, but it went over with the audience. So I thought: "If they think that's good, surely I can do something better than that." '

He had ambivalent feelings about his own work. Sometimes he would say it made him weep to watch his old movies, other times he would sit up and watch one of them on late-night television and pronounce himself quite satisfied with what he saw. But the nostalgia lived on around him. In England, at Wilton House, the stately home of the Earl of Pembroke, otherwise film maker Henry Herbert who launched Prince Andrew's one-time girlfriend Koo Stark to fame in *Emily*, there is a pair of Astaire's shoes in a glass display with a letter from Astaire in the grand entrance hall. 'It's the one thing everyone enjoys,' said the Earl. Richard Quine, director of Astaire's *Notorious Landlady*, had Astaire's top hat in the entrance hall of his Beverly Hills home. Quine, like Astaire, had been a child vaudevillian, and when he started his collection of hats he asked Astaire if he still had his famous top hat. The not-so-hard-bitten and unsentimental Astaire did have it and gave it to Quine on one condition: that it was not displayed as though Astaire was dead, for as he said when he was approached to sell the movie rights to his book *Steps In Time*: 'I'm alive, not dead. Why go into the past? However much they offer me – and the offers come in all

[253]

the time – I shall not sell.' He meant that to last after his death too, as he specified in a clause of his will that, despite his own avid reading of biographies of others, he did not want any film about himself. 'It is there because I have no particular desire to have my life misinterpreted, which it would be.' And he added, as if by way of the best explanation he could offer: 'I have had various sadnesses in my life.'

In an age when everyone was keen to maximise the potential of their properties, MGM decided to stage a revival of the stage show of *Funny Face*, to which they owned the rights. Six foot six dancer and choreographer Tommy Tune and Astaire's friend Twiggy, the waif-like London model girl who had been conspicuously good with Tune in the Ken Russell-directed movie of Sandy Wilson's flapper musical *The Boyfriend*, were signed for the lead parts. But with shades of former troubles the try-outs were disastrous. The Gershwin score, an assortment of numbers from previous shows, was still marvellous but the book, completely re-written from both the original stage show and the film, caused myriad problems. But, just as happened fifty years previously, the show reached town to rave reviews, audiences and bookings were splendid and the St James Theatre on Broadway was booked for many months ahead. Written into the plot were such details as someone talking of Perth Amboy, New Jersey – venue of the first gig of Fred and Adèle Astaire. Pride of place in Twiggy's dressing room on the opening night went to a hand-written note wishing her well from Fred Astaire.

For all the huffing and puffing, the old team did get back together again in July of '82. Fred Astaire and Ginger Rogers made a personal appearance when the last vestiges of thirty years' worth of scripts, musical scores and papers from RKO were donated to the film archives at the University of California at Los Angeles. Astaire and Rogers joined Jane Russell, 61, Joel McCrea, 77, Rudy Valee, 80, and a host of other stars including the former Pat Ryan, later Mrs Richard Nixon, who as a twenty-three year-old had an extra's rôle in *Becky Sharp*, the first ever feature produced in Jock Whitney's Technicolor. Ronald Reagan, star of RKO's *Cattle Queen of Montana*, was too busy playing president at the White House to attend. 'I could dance right here and now,' said Ginger. But Astaire demurred: 'I guess it's a bit too crowded to do any steps here.' Ginger Rogers, now five times divorced, fervently still expounded the Christian Scientist philosophies, believed in her God and in what her late mother helped create for her. 'I'm Mrs America,' she said. Last year, between spending time at her Palm

FINALE

Springs house and painting, Ginger had once more been at the 4R Ranch. 'I am writing my life story,' she said. If it were to tell just half her story it would certainly be interesting, even as seen through the eyes of Lela and Ginger.

Astaire had been honoured and compared to the greatest classical dancers of his century. He appeared with Rudolf Nureyev on television, was honoured alongside the great choreographer George Balanchine at the first Kennedy Center awards in 1978, and heard Mikhail Baryshnikov pose the rhetorical question: 'What do dancers think of Fred Astaire? It's no secret. We hate him. He gives us a complex because he's too perfect. His perfection is an absurdity. It's too hard to face.' To the last he kept up with each new trend. His status meant that all doors were open. He discussed the success of the *Thriller* video with Michael Jackson; he discussed affairs of the world with Ronald Reagan.

What can you say about this God-fearing, church-going, police-car-chasing friend of bookmakers, the powerful, princes and kings?

That he loved and admired women? That he was a supreme interpreter of music and dance? That his name was synonymous with class and fine things, understated elegance, exquisite clothes and taste? That he was, and will remain, a prince among men? The supreme dancing man? The way that he would sum up his incredible three quarters of a century of showbusiness is, as he said: 'I made a buck.' But to the last he was not bereft of ambition. He still had not won the Derby. He still had not had a Number One song. And he still did not have that golf trophy – no, not even the penknife.

In London the tailors at Kilgour, French and Stanbury still stitch away cross-legged in the basement of their Savile Row premises – the lease expired at Dover Street – and they still have Astaire's measurements. At Kensington Palace Princess Diana, the Princess of Wales, presented Prince Charles with a pair of tap shoes, so that he could join her in her practical enthusiasm for Astaire's dancing. The young princes William and Harry have started attending their own junior dance class and their mother told friends that she would be pleased if they could learn a spot of tap.

Robyn's mother left the small Portland, Oregon, $17-a-night apartment hotel in the winter of 1983 to move nearer her eldest daughter Madeleine in Los Altos, California. 'All I would like,' she said, 'is to see Melody again. It doesn't matter what she calls herself, she is still my daughter.'

In California Astaire had been taking life easily and felt that he had

[255]

not energy or enthusiasm to travel to New York for the Gershwin Festival. So he stayed at home with Robyn and he read scripts. She still sometimes talked of training horses.

At Lismore, at St Carthage's Cathedral, some mindless souvenir-hunting vandal had taken the small marble plaque which marked the resting place of Adèle's twin baby sons. Still the hollowed-out cross on the grave of her firstborn girl sometimes fills with rain and sometimes someone will place wild flowers in the trough.

At the small Mulberry Street coffee and jazz venue off Laurel Canyon Boulevard in Studio City a rather good little rock band called Astaire had been playing. The leader was Fred Astaire III.

When Astaire was given a Capezio dance award, he was not well enough to travel to collect it alongside Rudolf Nureyev.

'He wouldn't be beaten,' said Robyn. Yet an inner ear problem made him unsteady on his once-so-nimble feet. Arthritis could make even dressing himself difficult that winter of 1986.

He still liked to see scripts, but Robyn would be sure to check them to ensure that they did not tell the story of a former dancing star now in his dotage.

On 12 June 1987 his doctor suggested he be admitted to Century City Hospital with a respiratory complaint. Pneumonia developed, he was put on a respirator and a week later he died – just passed gracefully away – on 22 June, cradled in Robyn's arms.

'He was ready to go,' Robyn, her voice breaking and her face unable to hide the tears that had been shed, told a press conference convened just six hours after his death. 'That's the way he wanted. He died holding on to me.'

Ava was in Ireland, Fred Jr at home. They had both said what were intended as final farewells on previous occasions.

At eighty-eight his death was not unexpected, but none the less shocking for that. A genuine sense of loss. Of a man, of a star, of a symbol of perfection and of youth for millions. Many obituaries had already been written, within hours many more were spoken, by everyone from President Reagan to the barman of the Ritz. 'He's not gone,' the barman said, 'He's going to be around for a while yet. Style lives on – it always will.'

And Robyn drove home to San Ysidro Drive.

APPENDIX

Acknowledgements

Thanks must first go to Fred Astaire for being such a great performer, a unique man, and for making this story possible. He was never crazy about intimations of immortality. His views on biographies were ambivalent. He loved reading them and had assisted a number of colleagues writing about other people; but he hated the thought of being the subject of one himself.

He liked to think of his movie dancing career as having been a job well done. He sometimes admitted that those early movies were, of their day, 'okay'. Other times, he would call them 'rubbish'. That came about through a practical overview and the realization that those early film performances were, and would be, considered more than just the few years of his life and career that they actually constituted.

Four years ago he told me that he was being pressed to update his own 1957 autobiography but that he had no desire to do so. He had no interest in another book about himself, he said. He looked, as always, to the future, not the past. So it was for me to take a longer-term view. Hopefully, some will at least learn that there was a fuller life.

My journey – travelled while Astaire was in his final years – would not have been possible without the information and assistance so generously given by so many. Some wished to talk without acknowledgement: that wish is respected. But all I must thank for their openness, wit, and the pleasure of their company. Among the many whose assistance I can acknowledge were: Her Majesty Queen Elizabeth the Queen Mother, His Grace the Duke of Devonshire, the Rt Hon the Earl of Pembroke, the late and present Rt Hon Earls of Stockton, Larry Adler, W. Harold Becker, Leslie Caron, Charles Castle, Dorothy Dixon, Richard Drewett, Gerry Dutton, Dr Howard Gottlieb, Bob Gotlieb, Cary Grant, Dr Charlotte Fienmann, Marion and Patrick Filley, Anthony Haden-Guest, Billy Hamilton, Anthony Holden, John Houseman, Tab Hunter, Gene Kelly, Ivor Key, Frances and Fred Labib, Robert Lacey, Bobby Lake, Sheridan Morley, Mrs Constance Miller, Hugh Montgomery-Massingberd, David Niven, Lilli Palmer, Hermes Pan, Michael Parkinson, Ginger Rogers, Irene Selznick, Helen Rayburn, Neville Shulman, Maureen

Solomon, Tommy Steele, Mrs M. E. Whitney Tippett, Twiggy, Hugo Vickers, Brian Vine.

Also, in Boston: Boston University (Special Collection)

Lincoln, Nebraska: Nebraska State Archives

Lismore, Co Waterford:Lismore Estates Office

London: British Film Institute; British Library; Westminster City Library

Los Angeles: Academy of Motion Picture Arts and Sciences; American Film Institute; California Racehorse Breeders' Association, Santa Anita; Los Angeles City Hall; Los Angeles Herald Examiner; Los Angeles Times

New York: Borough Hall, Brooklyn; Lincoln Centre for the Performing Arts; New York City Hall; New York Public Library; Sports Illustrated

Omaha: Douglas Historical Society; Omaha Historical Society; Omaha Public Library; Omaha World-Record

Portland, Oregon: The Oregonian

San Francisco: Herald Examiner

Washington, DC: Library of Congress.

Additional archives, in the USA: *After Dark*; *Interview*; *Life*; *New York Times*; *Time*; *US*; *Variety*; *Vogue*

In UK: *Daily Express*; *Daily Mail*; *Daily Telegraph*; *Observer*; *Ritz*; *Sporting Life*; *Stage*; *Sunday Express*; *Sunday Times*; *The Times*

My particular appreciation and gratitude also goes to Paul Sidey, my editor, Richard Cohen, Michael Sissons, Bridget Tomlinson, Rowena Webb, Pat McCreeth.

Invaluable help came from Ian Black, Rupert Collins, Quentin Falk, James Ferguson, Vanessa Ford, Jenny Jeger, Andrew Gifford, Natasha Gilmore, Ann Haller, Christina Matthews, Pat Miller, Bob Payton, Amanda Satchell, Joe Steeples, Caroline Warne, Wilf Weeks, Helen Wright, and most especially from my assistants and amanuenses Jenny Lord and Lisa McCaffery. My special thanks to Harvey Mann, the picture editor, for his great work and the many thousand miles travelled.

Grateful acknowledgement is made to Chappell Music Company for permission to reprint previously published material. Excerpts from 'I've a Shooting Box in Scotland' by Cole Porter and excerpts from 'Night and Day' by Cole Porter. Used by permission.

London, SW1
June 1987

Chronology

1869	Frederic Austerlitz born
22 December 1878	Johanna Geilus born
17 November 1894	Johanna weds Frederic Austerlitz
18 September 1896	Adèle born
10 May 1899	Frederic Austerlitz Jr born
1905	Johanna, Adèle and Fred leave Omaha
1906	Liz Altemus born
1906	'Juvenile Artists presenting an Electrical Musical Toe Dancing Novelty'
1908	Phyllis Baker born
10 December 1910	Hermes Panagiotopulos born
1917	*Over The Top*, 44th St Roof Theater
1921	Astaires meet Noël Coward, NY
1923	*Stop Flirting*, London
1923	meets Prince of Wales
1924	Fritz dies
April 1926	meets newborn Princess Elizabeth
1926	Phyllis makes her début
December 1927	Phyllis marries Eliphalet Potter III
1929	Peter Potter born
25 September 1930	Liz weds Jock Whitney
1931	Astaire meets Phyllis
June 1931	*The Band Wagon* opens, NY
5 March 1932	Adèle's last performance
May 1932	Adèle weds Lord Charles Cavendish
24 June 1933	Eliphalet Potter remarries
12 July 1933	Fred marries Phyllis
27 May 1933	Fred signs RKO contract, LA
2 November 1933	*Gay Divorce*, London
8 October 1933	Adèle has stillborn daughter
December 1933	*Dancing Lady*, *Rio* open, NY
12 August 1935	*Your Hit Parade* radio series début

August 1935	*Top Hat* opens
27 October 1935	Adèle has stillborn twin boys
21 January 1936	Fred Astaire Jr born
11 July 1937	George Gershwin dies
20 October 1938	Barrie Chase born
1939	RKO contract ends; Fred retires
1940	Liz and Jock divorce
28 March 1942	Ava born
14 August 1942	Robyn Smith born, San Francisco
1944	Lord Charles Cavendish dies
1946	*Blue Skies* – 'last dance'
1946	Triplicate wins Hollywood Gold Cup
7 March 1947	first dance school at 487 Park Ave
28 April 1947	Adèle weds Kingman Douglass
1949	*The Barkleys of Broadway* with Ginger
14 February 1950	Fred wins Oscar (Special Award)
13 September 1954	Phyllis dies
April 1955	first TV appearance
1955	Peter Potter weds
October 1956	*An Evening with Fred Astaire* on TV
1957	*Silk Stockings*; retires
1959	*On The Beach*, first straight rôle
1968	Ava weds Carl Bostleman, LA
17 May 1970	Ava weds Richard McKenzie, LA
1973	Kingman Douglass dies
26 July 1975	Ann Astaire dies
1976	Barrie Chase marries Dr Jim Kaufman
24 June 1980	Fred marries Robyn Smith
24 September 1980	ASCAP Pied Piper Award
27 January 1981	Adèle dies
11 April 1981	AFI Lifetime Achievement Award
1984	talks to Michael Jackson about *Thriller* video success
12 June 1987	Fred admitted to Century City Hospital, Los Angeles, with suspected pneumonia
22 June 1987	Fred Astaire dies

Key

Shows:

1. Over the Top
2. The Passing Show of 1918
3. Apple Blossom
4. The Love Letter
5. For Goodness Sake (also in London, as Stop Flirting)
6. The Bunch and Judy
7. Lady, Be Good! (also in London)
8. Funny Face (also in London)
9. Smiles
10. The Band Wagon
11. The Gay Divorcée (also in London)

Films:

1. Dancing Lady
2. Flying Down to Rio
3. Gay Divorcee
4. Roberta
5. Top Hat
6. Follow the Fleet
7. Swing Time
8. Shall We Dance?
9. A Damsel in Distress
10. Carefree
11. The Story of Vernon and Irene Castle
12. Broadway Melody of 1940
13. Second Chorus
14. You'll Never Get Rich
15. Holiday Inn
16. You Were Never Lovelier
17. The Sky's the Limit
18. Ziegfeld Follies
19. Yolanda and the Thief
20. Blue Skies
21. Easter Parade
22. The Barkleys of Broadway
23. Three Little Words
24. Let's Dance
25. Royal Wedding (UK as Wedding Bells)
26. The Belle of New York
27. The Band Wagon
28. Daddy Long Legs
29. Funny Face
30. Silk Stockings
31. On the Beach
32. The Pleasure of his Company
33. The Notorious Landlady
34. Finian's Rainbow
135. Midas Run (UK as A Run on Gold)
36. That's Entertainment
37. The Towering Inferno
38. That's Entertainment II
39. The Amazing Dobermans
40. Un Taxi Mauve
41. Ghost Story
42. That's Dancing

Partners

ADÈLE ASTAIRE:
'Make Adèle rehearse? No. She was so talented she didn't need to. I always felt that Adèle was the key member of the team and that without her I'd be nothing.'
(Stage shows 1, 2, 3, 4, 5, 6, 7, 8, 9, 10)

TILLY LOSCH:
'Marvellous, a real talent.'
(Stage show 10)

CLAIRE LUCE:
'She was good in that show – I suggested that they get her for the film, too.'
(Stage show 11)

JOAN CRAWFORD:
'I didn't do much with her. I just did what I was told in that one. She wasn't a dancer. I sometimes think that film put my career back two years.'
(Film 1)

GINGER ROGERS:
'She is a great showman and a very effective performer. In the beginning she faked it an awful lot, but she had talent. She improved as she went along – she got so that after a while everyone else who danced with me looked wrong.'
(Films 2, 3, 4, 5, 6, 7, 8, 10, 11, 22)

DOLORES DEL RIO:
'An exotic dancer.'
(Film 2)

HARRIET HOCTOR:
'A lovely little ballet dancer.'
(Film 8)

JOAN FONTAINE:
'I always considered *A Damsel in Distress* a very mediocre film, although the music was outstanding: 'Foggy Day', 'Nice Work If You Can Get It' and a few others like 'Things Are Looking Up', which didn't become a hit but was good for the show.'
(Film 9)

[263]

ELEANOR POWELL:
'Eleanor was an out and out tap dancer. She danced like a man. She slammed the floor and did it great and that's fine and suddenly she's on her toes in the ballet sequence – it did look kinda funny.'
(Film 12)

PAULETTE GODDARD:
'The worst film I ever made was *Second Chorus*. It was the first film released on television and they are always showing it. She wasn't a dancer.'
(Film 13)

RITA HAYWORTH:
'A great dancer but a different style to me.'
(Films 14, 16)

MARJORIE REYNOLDS:
'I did that drunk dance with her. It was difficult to get it just right.'
(Film 15)

VIRGINIA DALE:
'I did little with her.'
(Film 15)

JOAN LESLIE:
'She was seventeen at the time. I didn't pick 'em younger, they just seemed to come that way.'
(Film 17)

LUCILLE BREMER:
'Capable – she was one of Arthur Freed's finds.'
(Films 18, 19)

JUDY GARLAND:
'She could learn a routine in a flash, but she was not primarily a dancer.'
(Films 18, 21 also signed for 14, 23, 25)

ANN MILLER:
'She's pretty vigorous.'
(Film 21)

VERA-ELLEN:
'Technically just about perfect. A beautiful dancer.'
(Films 23, 26)

BETTY HUTTON:
'She worried about everything so I didn't have to worry so much. She was a loud dancer.'
(Film 24)

JANE POWELL:
'She surprised everybody by her handling of the dances.'
(Film 25)

CYD CHARISSE:
'Proficient and warm.'
(Films 18, 27, 30)

LESLIE CARON:
'A ballet dancer really, but technically good. I called her the sergeant major.'
(Film 28)

AUDREY HEPBURN:
'She never complained, never argued about anything.'
(Film 29)

BARRIE CHASE:
'She has such individuality, training, grace, a winning kind of movement and personality and she takes her work seriously.'
(All TV Specials)

Shows

OVER THE TOP
28 November 1917, 44th Street Roof Theater NY (78 performances) / *Cast:* Fred and Adèle Astaire, Justin Johnstone, Mary Eaton, T. Roy Barnes (replaced by Ed Wynn), Craig Campbell, Ted Lorraine, Joe Laurie, Vivian and Dagmar Oakland, Betty Pierce / *Producer:* L and J Shubert / *Director:* Joseph Herbert / *Dance director:* Allan K Foster / *Set designer:* P Dodd Ackerman / *Music director:* Frank Tours / *Sketches:* Philip Bartholomae, Harold Atteridge / *Music:* Sigmund Romberg, Herman Timberg / *Lyrics:* Charles J. Manning, Matthew Woodward / *including* 'Frocks and frills', 'Where is the language to tell?', 'Justin Johnstone Rag'

THE PASSING SHOW OF 1918
25 July 1918, Winter Garden NY (125 performances) / *Cast:* Fred and Adèle Astaire, Frank Fay, Willie and Eugene Howard, Charles Ruggles, George Hassell, Sam White, Lou Clayton, Nita Haldi, Dave Dreyer, Jessi Reed, Nell Carrington, Isabel Lowe, Virginia Fox Brooks, Arthur Albro, Dorsha, Edith Pierce, Aileen Rooney, Emily Miles, Olga Roller / *Producer:* J. and L. Shubert / *Director:* J. C. Huffman / *Dance director:* Jack Mason / *Set designer:* Watson Barratt / *Music director:* Charles Previn / *Sketches:* Harold Atteridge / *Music:* Sigmund Romberg, Jean Schwartz / *Lyrics:* Harold Atteridge / *including* 'I can't make my feet behave', 'Squab farm', 'Bring on the girls', 'Twit twit twit', 'Quick service'

APPLE BLOSSOMS
7 October 1919, Globe Theater NY (256 performances) / *Cast:* Fred and Adèle Astaire, John Charles Thomas, Wilda Bennett, Roy Atwell, Rena Parker, Percival Knight, Juanita Fletcher, Alan Fagan, Harrison Brockbank, Florence Shirley / *Producer:* Charles Dillingham / *Director:* Fred C Latham / *Dance director:* Edward Royce / *Set designer:* Joseph Urban / *Music director:* William Daly / *Book:* William LeBarron from the story by Alexandre Dumas / *Music:* Fritz Kreisler, Victor Jacobi / *Lyrics:* William LeBarron / *including* 'On the banks of the Bronx', 'A girl, a man, a night, a dance'

THE LOVE LETTER
4 October 1921, Globe Theater NY (31 performances) / *Cast:* Fred and Adèle Astaire, John Charles Thomas, Carolyn Thomson, Alice Brady, Marjorie Gateson, Will West, Bessie Franklin, Jane Carroll / *Producer:* Charles Dillingham / *Director and dance director:* Edward Royce / *Set designer:* Joseph Urban / *Music director:* William Daly / *Sketches:* William LeBarron / *Music:* Victor Jacobi / *Lyrics:* William LeBarron / *including* 'I'll say I love you', 'Upside down', 'Dreaming'

FOR GOODNESS SAKE*
20 February 1922 Lyric Theater NY (103 performances) / *Cast:* Fred and Adèle Astaire, John C Hazzard, Marjorie Gateson, Charles Judels, Vinton Freedley, Helen Ford / *Producer:* Alex A Aarons / *Director:* Priestley Morrison / *Dance director:* Allan K Foster / *Set designer:* P Dodd Ackerman / *Music director:* William Daly / *Book:* Fred Jackson / *Music:* William Daly, Paul Lannin / *Lyrics:* Arthur Jackson / *including* 'All to myself', 'When you're in Rome', 'Oh Gee, oh, gosh', 'French pastry Walk', 'The whichness of the whatness'
* also in London as STOP FLIRTING, 30 May 1923, Shaftesbury Theatre [later at Queen's and Strand] (418 performances) / *Cast:* Fred and Adèle Astaire, Jack Melford, Mimi Crawford, Marjorie Gordon, Henry Kendall, George de Warfaz / *Producer:* Alfred Butt / *Director:* Felix Edwardes / *Dance director:* Gus

[266]

Solhke / *Set designer:* Phil Harker / *Music director:* Jacques Heuvel / *including* 'All to myself', 'I'll build a stairway to Paradise', 'Oh gee, oh gosh', 'It's great to be in love', 'The whichness of the whatness'

THE BUNCH AND JUDY

28 November 1922, Globe Theater NY (65 performances) / *Cast:* Fred and Adèle Astaire, Johnny and Ray Dooley, Grace Hayes, Roberta Beatty, Philip Tonge, Six Brown Brothers, Carl McBride, Augustus Minton, Patricia Clark / *Producer:* Charles Dillingham / *Director:* Fred G Latham / *Set designer:* Gates and Morange / *Music director:* Victor Baravalle / *Book:* Anne Caldwell, Hugh Ford / *Music:* Jerome Kern / *Lyrics:* Anne Caldwell / *including* 'Pale Venetian moon', 'Peach girl', 'Morning glory', 'Every day in every way', 'Times Square', 'How do you do, Katinka?'

LADY, BE GOOD!*

1 December 1924, Liberty Theater (330 performances) / *Cast:* Fred and Adèle Astaire, Walter Catlett, Alan Edwards, Cliff Edwards, Gerald Oliver Smith, Kathlene Martin, Patricia Clark, Phil Ohman and Vic Arden / *Producer:* Alex A Aarons, Vinton Freedley / *Director:* Felix Edwardes / *Dance director:* Sammy Lee / *Set designer:* Norman Bel Geddes / *Music director:* Paul Lannin / *Book:* Guy Bolton, Fred Thompson / *Music:* George Gershwin / *Lyrics:* Ira Gershwin / *including* 'Hang on to me', 'So am I', 'Fascinatin' rhythm', 'The half of it', 'Dearie', 'Blues', 'Juanita', 'Swiss miss', 'Oh lady, be good'
* also in London LADY, BE GOOD! 14 April 1926, Empire Theatre (326 performances) / *Cast:* Fred and Adèle Astaire, William Kent, Buddy Lee, George Vollaire, Ewart Scott, Sylvia Leslie, Gloria Beaumont, Irene Russell / *Producer:* Alfred Butt with Alex A Aarons and Vinton Freedley / *Director:* Felix Edwardes / *Dance director:* Max Scheck / *Set designers:* Joseph and Phil Harker / *Music director:* Jacques Heuvel / *including* songs as NY, with 'I'd rather Charleston'

FUNNY FACE

22 November 1927, Alvin Theater NY (250 performances) / *Cast:* Fred and Adèle Astaire, William Kent, Victor Moore, Allen Kearns, Betty Compton, Ritz Quartette, Gertrude McDonald, Phil Ohman and Vic Arden / *Producer:* Alex A Aarons, Vinton Freedley / *Director:* Edgar McGregor / *Dance director:* Bobby Connolly / *Set designer:* John Wenger / *Music director:* Alfred Newman / *Book:* Fred Thompson, Paul Gerald Smith / *Music:* George Gershwin / *Lyrics:* Ira Gershwin / *including* 'Funny face', 'High hat', 'He loves and she loves', 'Let's kiss and make up', ' 'S wonderful', 'My one and only', 'The Babbitt and the Bromide'
* also in London FUNNY FACE 8 November 1928, Prince's Theatre, London (263 performances) / *Cast:* Fred and Adèle Astaire, Leslie Henson, Bernard Clifton,

Rita Page, Sydney Howard, Eileen Hatton, Jacques Frey, Mario Braggiotti / *Producer:* Alfred Butt, Lee Ephraim with Alex A Aarons, Vinton Freedley / *Director:* Felix Edwardes / *Dance director:* Bobby Connolly / *Set designer:* Joseph and Phil Harker / *Music director:* Julian Jones / *including* songs as NY with 'Imagination'

SMILES

18 November 1930, Ziegfeld Theater NY (63 performances) / *Cast:* Fred and Adèle Astaire, Marilyn Miller, Tom Howard, Eddie Foy Jr, Paul Gregory, Larry Adler, Claire Dod, Georgia Caine, Edward Raquello, Kathryn Hereford, Adrian Rosley, Aber Twins, Bob Hope, Virginia Bruce / *Producer:* Florenz Ziegfeld / *Director:* William Anthony McGuire / *Dance director:* Ned Wayburn / *Set designer:* Joseph Urban / *Music director:* Frank Tours / *Book:* William Anthony McGuire / *Music:* Vincent Youmans / *Lyrics:* Clifford Grey, Harold Adamson, Ring Lardner / *including* 'Say, young man of Manhattan', 'Hotcha ma chotch', 'Be good to me', 'Anyway, we had fun', 'If I were you', 'Love, I'm glad I waited'

THE BAND WAGON

3 June 1931, New Amsterdam Theater NY (260 performances) / *Cast:* Fred and Adèle Astaire, Frank Morgan, Helen Broderick, Tilly Losch, Philip Loeb, John Barker, Roberta Robinson, Francis Pierlot, Jay Wilson, Peter Chambers / *Producer:* Max Gordon / *Director:* Hassard Short / *Dance director:* Albertina Rasch / *Set designer:* Albert Johnston / *Music director:* Al Goodman / *Sketches:* George S Kaufman, Howard Dietz / *Music:* Arthur Schwartz / *Lyrics:* Howard Dietz / *including* 'Sweet music', 'Hoops', 'New sun in the sky', 'Miserable without you', 'I love Louisa', 'The Beggar Waltz', 'White Heat'

THE GAY DIVORCE

29 November 1932, Ethel Barrymore Theater NY (248 performances) / *Cast:* Fred Astaire, Claire Luce, Luella Gear, G P Huntley Jr, Betty Starbuck, Erik Rhodes, Eric Blore, Roland Bottomley / *Producer:* Dwight Deere Wiman, Tom Weatherby / *Director:* Howard Lindsay / *Dance director:* Carl Randall, Barbara Newberry / *Set designer:* Jo Mielziner / *Music director:* Gene Salzer / *Book:* Dwight Taylor / *Music and lyrics:* Cole Porter / *including* 'After you, who?', 'Night and day', 'I've got you on my mind', 'You're in love'
* also in London THE GAY DIVORCE 2 November 1933, Palace Theatre (118 performances) / *Cast:* Fred Astaire, Claire Luce, Olive Blakeney, Claud Allister, Eric Blore, Joan Gardner, Erik Rhodes, Fred Hearne / *Producer:* Lee Ephraim / *Director:* Felix Edwardes / *Dance director:* Carl Randall, Barbara Newberry / *Set designer:* Joseph and Phil Harker / *Music director:* Percival Mackay

Films

FANCHON THE CRICKET
1915, Famous Players (20 mins, b & w)
Cast: Mary Pickford, Jack Standing, Lottie Pickford, Jack Pickford / *Director:* James Kirkwood / *Story:* Fanchon, the little wild girl of the woods, falls for a wealthy youth, who is then disinherited. On his sickbed Fanchon extracts a reconciliation with his father. Fred and Adèle Astaire, as uncredited extras, join a group of local dancing youths.

DANCING LADY
December 1933, MGM (90 mins, b & w)
Cast: Joan Crawford, Clark Gable, Fred Astaire, Franchot Tone, Robert Benchley, Nelson Eddy, May Robson, Willie Lightner, Art Jarrett, Ted Healy / *Executive producer:* David O Selznick / *Associate producer:* John W Considine / *Director:* Robert Z Leonard / *Dance director:* Sammy Lee, Eddie Prinz / *Set designer:* Merrill Pye / *Musical director:* Louis Silvers / *Screenplay:* Allen Rivkin, P J Wolfson, from novel by James Warner Bellah / *Music:* Burton Lane, Jimmy McHugh, Richard Rodgers, Nacio Herb Brown / *Lyrics:* Harold Adamson, Dorothy Fields, Lorenz Hart, Arthur Freed / *including* 'Hey, young fella' (song chorus), 'Hold your man' (Lightner), 'Everything I have is yours' (Jarrett), 'My dancing lady' (song Jarrett, dance Crawford, chorus), 'Heigh-ho, the gang's all here' (song and dance Astaire, Crawford, chorus), 'Let's go Bavarian' (song Astaire, Crawford, chorus), 'That's the rhythm of the day' (song Eddy, dance Crawford, chorus) / *Story:* Fred Astaire in guest appearance as himself in backstage story of a Broadway musical with Clark Gable as producer Patch Gallagher who chooses chorus girl Joan Crawford for leading role.

FLYING DOWN TO RIO
December 1933, RKO (89 mins, b & w)
Cast: Fred Astaire, Ginger Rogers, Dolores Del Rio, Gene Raymond, Paul Roulien, Eric Blore, Etta Moyen / *Producer:* Louis Brock / *Director:* Thornton Freeland / *Dance director:* Dave Gould / *Dance assistant:* Hermes Pan / *Set designer:* Van Nest Polglase, Carroll Clark / *Music director:* Max Steiner / *Screenplay:* Cyril Hume, H W Hannemann, Erwin Gelsey, from play by Anne Caldwell based on story by Louis Brock / *Music:* Vincent Youman / *Lyrics:* Edward Eliscu, Gus Kahn / *including* 'Music makes me' (song Rogers), 'The Carioca' (song Moten and two uncredited singers, dance Astaire, Rogers, chorus), 'Orchards in the moonlight' (song Roulien, dance Astaire, Del Rio), 'Flying down to Rio' (song Astaire, dance chorus) / *Story:* Dancer Fred Ayres (Astaire) and band vocalist Honey Hale (Rogers) help aviator / bandleader Roger Bond (Raymond) to win Belinha de Rezende (Del Rio) by staging aerial display at opening of her father's hotel.

[269]

THE GAY DIVORCEE

October 1934, RKO (107 mins, b & w)

Cast: Fred Astaire, Ginger Rogers, Alice Brady, Edward Everett Horton, Erik Rhodes, Eric Blore, Lilian Miles, Betty Grable / *Producer:* Pandro S Berman / *Director:* Mark Sandrich / *Dance director:* Dave Gould / *Dance assistant:* Hermes Pan / *Set designer:* Van Nest Polglase, Carroll Clark / *Music director:* Max Steiner / *Screenplay:* George Marion Jr, Dorothy Yost, Edward Kaufman, from stage musical THE GAY DIVORCE by Dwight Taylor / *Music:* Cole Porter, Con Conrad, Harry Revel / *Lyrics:* Cole Porter, Herb Magidson, Mack Gordon *including* 'Don't let it bother you' (song chorus, dance Astaire), 'A needle in a haystack' (song and dance Astaire), 'Let's k-knock k-knees' (song Grable, Horton, dance Grable, Horton, chorus), 'Night and day' (song Astaire, dance Astaire, Rogers), 'The Continental'* (song Astaire, Rhodes, Miles, dance Astaire, Rogers, chorus) / *Story:* At English coastal resort Brightbourne Mimi Glossop (Rogers) mistakes dancer Guy Holden (Astaire) for the professional co-respondent hired to establish grounds for her divorce.

* 'The Continental' *was the first movie song to win an Academy Award*

ROBERTA

February 1935, RKO (105 mins, b & w)

Cast: Fred Astaire, Ginger Rogers, Irene Dunne, Randolph Scott, Helen Westley, Lucille Ball, Candy Candino and Gene Sheldon / *Producer:* Pandro S Berman / *Director:* William A Seiter / *Dance director:* Hermes Pan / *Set designer:* Van Nest Polglase, Carroll Clark / *Music director:* Max Steiner / *Screenplay:* Jane Murfin, Sam Mintz, Glenn Tryon, Allan Scott, from stage musical *Roberta* by Otto Harbach, adapted from novel *Gowns By Roberta* by Alice Duer Miller / *Music:* Jerome Kern, James F Hanley, Oscar Hammerstein / *Lyrics:* Otto Harbach, Dorothy Fields, Ballard Macdonald, Bernard Dougall / *including* 'Indiana' (song chorus), 'Let's begin' (song Astaire, Candido, dance Astaire, Candido, Sheldon), 'Russian song' (song Dunne), 'I'll be hard to handle' (song Rogers, dance Astaire, Rogers), 'Yesterdays' (song Dunne), 'I won't dance' (song Astaire, Rogers, dance Astaire, piano/piano accordion Astaire), 'Smoke gets in your eyes' (song Dunne, dance Astaire, Rogers), 'Don't ask me not to sing' (song Astaire, chorus), 'Lovely to look at' (song Dunne, chorus, Astaire, Rogers, dance Astaire, Rogers), 'The touch of your hand', 'You're devastating' / *Story:* In Paris danceband leader Huckleberry 'Huck' Haines (Astaire) falls for cabaret singer Countess Tanka Schwarenka (Rogers) from his hometown; John Kent (Scott) inherits the salon where his love Stephanie (Dunne) is chief designer.

TOP HAT

August 1935, RKO (101 mins, b & w)

Cast: Fred Astaire, Ginger Rogers, Edward Everett Horton, Helen Broderick,

Erik Rhodes, Eric Blore, also featuring Lucille Ball / *Producer:* Pandro S Berman / *Director:* Mark Sandrich / *Dance director:* Hermes Pan / *Set designer:* Van Nest Polglase / *Musical director:* Max Steiner / *Screenplay:* Dwight Taylor, Allan Scott, adapted by Karl Noti from play *The Girl Who Dared* by Alesander Farago, Aladar Laszlo / *Music, lyrics:* Irving Berlin *including* 'No strings' (song Astaire, dance Astaire), 'Isn't this a lovely day?' (song Astaire, dance Astaire, Rogers), 'Top hat, white tie and tails' (song Astaire, dance Astaire, chorus), 'Cheek to cheek' (song Astaire, dance Astaire, Rogers), 'The Piccolino' (song Rogers, dance Astaire, Rogers, chorus) / *Story:* Jerry Travers (Astaire) falls for Dale Tremont (Rogers) who runs away to Venice, believing that he is the husband of her best friend. He follows to rescue her from her rebound marriage to dress designer Beddini (Erik Rhodes).

FOLLOW THE FLEET
February 1936, RKO (110 mins, b & w)
Cast: Fred Astaire, Ginger Rogers, Randolph Scott, Harriet Hilliard, Lucille Ball, Betty Grable, Joy Hodges, Jenny Gray, Dorothy Fleisman, Bob Cromer, Tony Martin / *Producer:* Pandro S Berman / *Director:* Mark Sandrich / *Dance director:* Hermes Pan / *Set Designer:* Van Nest Polglase / *Musical director:* Max Steiner / *Screenplay:* Dwight Taylor, Allan Scott, from play *Shore Leave* by Hubert Osborne / *Music, lyrics:* Irving Berlin *including* 'We saw the sea' (Astaire, chorus), 'Let yourself go' (song Rogers, Grable, Hodges, Gray, dance Astaire, Rogers, Fleisman, Cromer), 'Get thee behind me, Satan' (song Hilliard), 'I'm putting all my eggs in one basket' (song Astaire, Rogers, piano playing by Astaire, dance Astaire, Rogers), 'Let's face the music and dance' (song Astaire, dance Astaire, Rogers) / *Story:* Sailor and former dancer Bake Baker (Astaire) and ex-partner Sherry Martin (Rogers) team up to raise money to salvage a ship.

SWING TIME
August 1936, RKO (103 mins, b & w)
Cast: Fred Astaire, Ginger Rogers, Victor Moore, Helen Broderick, Eric Blore, Betty Furness, Georges Metaxa / *Producer:* Pandro S Berman / *Director:* George Stevens / *Dance director:* Hermes Pan / *Set designer:* Van Nest Polglase / *Settings for Bojangles:* John Harkwider / *Music director:* Nathaniel Shilkret / *Screenplay:* Howard Lindsay, Allan Scott, from story *Portrait of John Garnett* by Edwin Gelsey / *Music:* Jerome Kern / *Lyrics:* Dorothy Fields *including* 'It's not on the cards' (dance Astaire, chorus), 'The way you look tonight' (song Astaire), 'Waltz in Spring time' (dance Astaire, Rogers), 'A fine romance' (song Astaire, Rogers), 'Bojangles of Harlem' (song chorus, dance Astaire, chorus), 'Never gonna dance' (song Astaire, dance Astaire, Rogers) / *Story:* So that he can marry his hometown love, dancer and gambler John 'Lucky' Garnett (Astaire) plans to make his fortune in New York where he falls for dance instructor Penelope 'Penny' Carrol (Rogers).

SHALL WE DANCE?
April 1937, RKO (116 mins, b & w)
Cast: Fred Astaire, Ginger Rogers, Edward Everett Horton, Eric Blore, Harriet Hoctor, Jerome Cowan, Ben Alexander / *Producer:* Pandro S Berman / *Director:* Mark Sandrich / *Dance director:* Hermes Pan, Harry Losee / *Set designer:* Van Nest Polglase / *Music director:* Nathaniel Shilkret / *Screenplay:* Allan Scott, Ernest Pagano, adapted by P J Wolfson from story *Watch Your Step* by Lee Loeb, Harold Buchman / *Music:* George Gershwin / *Lyrics:* Ira Gershwin *including* 'Beginnner's luck' (dance Astaire), 'Slap that bass' (song Astaire, uncredited singer, dance Astaire), 'Walking the dog', 'They all laughed' (song Rogers, dance Astaire, Rogers), 'Let's call the whole thing off' (song, dance Astaire, Rogers), 'They can't take that away from me' (song Astaire, dance Astaire, Rogers), 'Shall we dance?' (song Astaire, dance Astaire, Rogers, chorus) / *Story:* To staunch rumours that he is married to musical comedy star Linda Keene, née Thompson (Rogers), the dancer Peter 'Pete' Peters, alias Petrov (Astaire), decides to marry and then divorce her.

A DAMSEL IN DISTRESS
November 1937, RKO (100 mins, b & w)
Cast: Fred Astaire, George Burns, Gracie Allen, Joan Fontaine, Reginald Gardiner, Constance Collier, Ray Noble, Jan Duggan, Mary Dean, Pearl Amatore, Betty Rone / *Producer:* Pandro S Berman / *Director:* George Stevens / *Dance director:* Hermes Pan / *Set designer:* Van Nest Polglase / *Music director:* Victor Baravalle / *Screenplay:* P G Wodehouse, Ernesto Pagano, S K Lauren, from novel by Wodehouse and play by Wodehouse and Ian Hay / *Music:* George Gershwin / *Lyrics:* Ira Gershwin / *including* 'I can't be bothered now' (song, dance Astaire), 'The jolly tar and the milkmaid' (song, Astaire, Duggan, Dean, Amatore, Rone), 'Put me to the test' (dance Astaire, Burns, Allen), 'Stiff upper lip' (song Allen, dance Astaire, Burns, Allen, chorus), 'Sing of spring' (song chorus), 'Things are looking up' (song Astaire, dance Astaire, Fontaine), 'A foggy day' (song Astaire), 'Nice work if you can get it' (song Duggan, Dean, Amatore, Astaire, dance, drum solo, Astaire), 'Ah, che a voi perdoni, Iddio' (Flotow from *Marta*, song Gardiner, sung by Mario Berini) *Story:* American dancing star Jerry Halliday (Astaire) falls for Lady Alyce Marshmorton (Fontaine); Burns and Allen play his press agent and secretary.

CAREFREE
August 1938, RKO (83 mins, b & w)
Cast: Fred Astaire, Ginger Rogers, Ralph Bellamy, Luella Gear, Hattie McDaniel, Clarence Kolb / *Producer:* Pandro S Berman / *Director:* Mark Sandrich / *Dance director:* Hermes Pan / *Set designer:* Van Nest Polglase / *Music director:* Victor Baravalle / *Screenplay:* Ernesto Pagano, Allan Scott, adapted by Dudley Nichols, Hagar Wilde from story by Marian Ainslee, Guy Endore /

KEY

Music, lyrics: Irving Berlin / *including* 'Since they turned Loch Lomond into swing' (song, harmonica, golf clubs, dance Astaire), 'The night is filled with music' (instrumental), 'I used to be colour blind' (song Astaire, Rogers), 'The Yam' (song Rogers, dance Astaire, Rogers) 'Change partners' (song Astaire, dance Astaire, Rogers) / *Story:* Psychiatrist Tony Flagg (Astaire) uses his hypnotic powers to persuade singer Amanda Cooper (Rogers), that she loves him rather than her fiancé.

THE STORY OF VERNON AND IRENE CASTLE
March 1939, RKO (90 mins, b & w)
Cast: Fred Astaire, Ginger Rogers, Edna May Oliver, Walter Brennan, Lew Fields, Marge Champion / *Producer:* George Haight / *Director:* H C Potter / *Dance director:* Hermes Pan / *Set designer:* Van Nest Polglase / *Music director:* Victor Baravalle / *Screenplay:* Richard Sherman, Oscar Hammerstein II, Dorothy Yost, adapted from book *My Husband* by Irene Castle / *including* 'Oh, you beautiful doll' (song chorus), 'Glow-worm' (song chorus), 'By the beautiful sea' (song chorus), 'Yama Yama Man' (song Rogers), 'Come, Josephine in my flying machine' (song chorus), 'By the light of the silvery moon' (dance Astaire), 'Cuddle up a little closer, lovey mine' (song chorus), 'Only when you're in my arms' (song Astaire), 'Waiting for the Robert E Lee' (dance Astaire, Rogers), 'The Darktown Strutters' Ball' (song uncredited French singer), 'Too much mustard' (Castle Walk) (dance Astaire, Rogers), 'Rose Room' (Castle Tango) (dance Astaire, Rogers), 'Pretty baby (Très jolie)' (dance, Astaire, Rogers), 'When they were dancing around' (dance Astaire, Rogers), 'Little brown jug' (Castle Polka) (dance Astaire, Rogers), 'Dengozo' (Maxixe) (dance Astaire, Rogers), medley: 'You're here and I'm here', 'Chicago,' 'Hello, 'Frisco, Hello', 'Way down yonder in New Orleans', 'Take me back to New York town' (dance Astaire, Rogers), 'It's a long way to Tipperary' (song chorus), 'Who's your lady friend?' (song, dance Astaire, chorus), 'Keep the home fires burning', 'Smiles', medley: 'Millicent Waltz', 'Night of gladness', 'Missouri Waltz' (dance Astaire, Rogers), 'Over there' / *Story:* Screen biography of the Castles husband-and-wife dancing team (Astaire, Rogers), from their first meeting to Vernon's death in World War II air-crash.

BROADWAY MELODY OF 1940
February 1940, MGM (102 mins, b & w)
Cast: Fred Astaire, Eleanor Powell, George Murphy, Frank Morgan, Ian Hunter, Douglas McPhail / *Producer:* Jack Cummings / *Director:* Norman Tauros / *Dance director:* Bobby Connolly / *Set designer:* Cedric Gibbons / *Music director:* Alfred Newman / *Screenplay:* Leon Gordon, George Oppenheimer, from story by Jack McGowan and Dore Schary / *Music, lyrics:* Cole Porter / *including* 'Please don't monkey with Broadway' (song, dance Astaire, Murphy), 'I am the Captain' (song, dance Powell, chorus), 'Between you and

[273]

me' (song Murphy, dance Powell, Murphy), 'I've got my eyes on you' (song, piano, dance Astaire), 'Jukebox Dance' (dance Astaire, Powell), 'I concentrate on you' (song Douglas McPhail, dance Astaire & Powell), 'Begin the Beguine' (song chorus, dance Astaire, Powell, Chorus) / *Story:* Down on their luck dancing team Johnny Brett (Astaire) and King Shaw (Murphy) are spotted by Broadway producer Bob Casey (Morgan) who wants Brett to partner Claire Bennett (Powell) in his new production, but after a mix up Shaw gets the part.

SECOND CHORUS
December 1940, Paramount (84 mins, b & w)
Cast: Fred Astaire (trumpet by Bobby Hackett), Paulette Goddard, Artie Shaw, Burgess Meredith (trumpet by Billy Butterfield), Charles Butterworth / *Producer:* Boris Morros / *Director:* H C Potter / *Dance director:* Hermes Pan / *Set designer:* Boris Leven / *Music director:* Ed Paul / *Screenplay:* Elaine Ryan, Ian McLellan Hunter, from story by Fred Cavett / *Music:* Artie Shaw, Bernard Hanighen, Hal Borne, Victor Young, Johnny Green / *Lyrics:* Johnny Mercer, Will Harris, E Y Harbourg *including* 'I'll dig it' (song Astaire, dance Astaire, Goddard), 'Sweet Sue' (trumpet Hackett, Butterfield), 'Love of my life' (song Astaire), 'I'm yours' (song Astaire, trumpet by Hackett, Butterfield), 'Concerto for Clarinet', 'Poor Mr Chisholm' (song, dance Astaire) / *Story:* Jazz trumpeter Danny O'Neill (Astaire), competes with Hank Taylor (Meredith), for a place in Artie Shaw's band and the love of Ellen Miller (Goddard).

'YOU'LL NEVER GET RICH'
September 1941, Columbia (88 mins, b & w)
Cast: Fred Astaire, Rita Hayworth (sung by Martha Tilton), Robert Benchley, Martha Tilton / *Producer:* Samuel Bischoff / *Director:* Sidney Lansfield / *Dance director:* Robert Alton / *Set designer:* Lionel Banks / *Music director:* Morris Stoloff / *Screenplay:* Michael Fessier, Ernest Pagano / *Music, lyrics* Cole Porter / *including* 'The Boogie Barcarolle' (dance Astaire, Hayworth, chorus), 'Dream dancing', 'Shootin' the works for Uncle Sam' (song, dance Astaire, chorus), 'Since I kissed my baby goodbye' (song chorus, dance Astaire), 'A-stairable Rag' (dance Astaire), 'So near and yet so far' (song Astaire, dance Astaire, Hayworth), 'Wedding Cake Walk' (song Tilton, dance Astaire, Hayworth, chorus) / *Story:* Drafted dance director Robert Curtis (Astaire), falls for chorus girl Sheila Winthrop (Hayworth)

HOLIDAY INN
June 1942, Paramount (100 mins, b & w)
Cast: Bing Crosby, Fred Astaire, Marjorie Reynolds (sung by Martha Mears), Virginia Dale, Louise Beavers / *Producer:* Mark Sandrich / *Director:* Mark Sandrich / *Dance director:* Danny Dare / *Assistant:* Babe Pierce / *Set Designers:*

[274]

Hans Dreier, Roland Anderson / *Music Director:* Robert Emmett Dolan /
Screenplay: Claude Binyon, Elmer Rice, idea by Irving Berlin / *Music, lyrics:*
Irving Berlin / *including* 'I'll capture your heart singing' (song Astaire, Crosby,
Dale), 'Lazy' (song Crosby), 'You're easy to dance with' (song Astaire,
chorus, dance Astaire, Dale, Reynolds), 'White Christmas' (Crosby,
Reynolds), 'Happy holiday' (song Crosby, Reynolds, chorus), 'Holiday Inn'
(song Crosby, Reynolds), 'Let's start the New Year right' (song Crosby),
'Abraham' (song Crosby, Beavers, Reynolds, chorus), 'Be careful it's my
heart' (song Crosby, dance Astaire, Reynolds), 'I can't tell a lie' (song Astaire,
dance Astaire, Reynolds, chorus), 'Easter Parade' (song Crosby), 'Let's say it
with firecrackers' (song chorus, dance Astaire), 'Song of Freedom' (song
Crosby, chorus), 'Plenty to be thankful for' (song Crosby), 'Oh, how I hate to
get up in the morning' / *Story:* Jim Hardy (Crosby) leaves his dancing partners
Ted Hanover (Astaire) and Lila Dixon (Dale) to open up the Holiday Inn with
Linda Mason (Reynolds) as the chief attraction. Hanover, deserted by Dixon,
tries to steal Mason away.

YOU WERE NEVER LOVELIER
October 1942, Columbia (98 mins, b & w)
Cast: Fred Astaire, Rita Hayworth (sung by Nan Wynn), Adolphe Menjou,
Xavier Cugat, Gus Schilling, Lina Romay / *Producer:* Louis F Edelman /
Director: William A Seiter / *Dance director:* Val Raset / *Set designer:* Lionel Banks /
Musical director: Leigh Harline / *Screenplay:* Michael Fessier, Ernest Pagano,
Delmar Daves, story by Carlos Oliveri and Sixton Pondal Rios / *Music:*
Jerome Kern / *Lyrics:* Johnny Mercer *including* 'Chiu Chiu' (song Romay,
chorus), 'Dearly beloved' (song Astaire, Wynn, dance Hayworth), 'Audition
dance' (dance Astaire), 'I'm old fashioned' (song Wynn, dance Astaire,
Hayworth), 'Shorty George' (song Astaire, dance Astaire, Hayworth),
'Wedding in the Spring' (song Romay), 'You were never lovelier' (song
Astaire, dance Astaire, Hayworth), 'These orchids' (song chorus) / *Story:*
Dancer and gambler Robert Davis (Astaire) is mistaken by Buenos Aires
hotelier's daughter Maria Acuna (Hayworth) for a mystery admirer.

THE SKY'S THE LIMIT
July 1943, RKO (89 mins, b & w)
Cast: Fred Astaire, Joan Leslie (sung by Sally Sweetland), Robert Benchley,
Robert Ryan, Eric Blore / *Producer:* David Hempstead / *Director:* Edward H
Griffith / *Dance director:* Fred Astaire / *Set designers:* Albert S D'Agostino,
Carroll Clark / *Music director:* Leigh Harline / *Screenplay:* Frank Fenton, Lynn
Root, from the story *A Handful Of Heaven* / *Music:* Harold Arlen / *Lyrics:*
Johnny Mercer, Bert Kalmar, Frank Loesser / *including* 'My shining hour'
(song Sweetland, chorus, dance Astaire, Leslie), 'A lot in common with you'
(song, dance Astaire, Leslie), 'One for my baby (and one more for the road)'

(song, dance Astaire), background: 'Three little words', 'Can't get out of this mood', 'I get the neck of the chicken' / *Story:* Flying Tigers pilot Fred Atwell (Astaire) calls himself civilian Fred Burton to spend a few days in New York, where he meets magazine photographer Joan Manion (Leslie).

ZIEGFELD FOLLIES
January 1946, MGM (110 mins, Technicolor)
Cast: Fred Astaire, Lucille Bremer, Judy Garland, Lena Horne, James Melton, Red Skelton, William Powell, Marion Bell, Cyd Charisse, William Frawley, Virginia O'Brien, Grady Sutton, Charles Coleman, Harry Hayden, William B Davidson, Harriet Lee, Lucille Ball, Fanny Brice, Kathryn Grayson, Gene Kelly, Victor Moore, Esther Williams, Edward Arnold, Bunin's puppets, Hume Cronyn, Robert Lewis, Keenan Wynn, Rex Evans, Joseph Crehan, Eddie Dunn, Gary Owen, Rod Alexander / *Producer:* Arthur Freed / *Director:* Vincente Minnelli, George Sidney, Robert Lewis, Lemuel Ayres, Roy Del Ruth / *Dance director:* Robert Alton, Eugene Loring, Charles Walters / *Set designers:* Cedric Gibbons, Merrill Pye, Jack Martin Smith / *Music director:* Lennie Hayton / *Sketches:* Pete Barry, Harry Turgend, George White, David Freedman / *Music:* Roger Edens, Giuseppe Verdi, Harry Warren, Hugh Martin, Philip Braham, Charles Ingle, George Gershwin / *Lyrics:* Ralph Freed, Earl Brent, Piave, Arthur Freed, Ralph Blane, Douglas Furber, Charles Ingle, Kay Thompson, Ira Gershwin / *including* Ziegfeld Days medley: 'It's delightful to be married', 'Sunny, I'm an Indian', 'If you knew Suzie', 'Here's to the girls' (song Astaire, chorus, whip Ball, dance Charisse, chorus), 'Bring on the wonderful men' (song O'Brien), 'Libiamo ne'lieti calici' (song Melton, Bell, chorus), 'This Heart of Mine' (song Astaire, chorus, dance Astaire, Bremer), 'Love' (song Horne), 'Limehouse Blues' (song Lee, dance Astaire, Bremer), 'Wot cher' (song chorus), Madame Crematon (song, dance Garland, chorus), 'The Babbitt and the Bromide' (song, dance Astaire, Kelly), 'There's beauty everywhere' (song Grayson) / *Story:* Tribute to impresario Florenz Ziegfeld introduced by Astaire.

YOLANDA AND THE THIEF
October 1945, MGM (108 mins, Technicolor)
Cast: Fred Astaire, Lucille Bremer (sung by Trudy Erwin), Frank Morgan, Mildred Natwick, Leon Ames / *Producer:* Arthur Freed / *Associate Producer:* Roger Edens / *Director:* Vincente Minnelli / *Dance director:* Eugene Loring / *Set designers:* Cedric Gibbons, Jack Martin Smith / *Music director:* Lennie Hayton / *Screenplay:* Irving Brecher, story by Jaques Thery and Ludwig Bemelmans / *Music:* Harry Warren / *Lyrics:* Arthur Freed / *including* 'This is a day for love' (song chorus), 'Angel' (song Erwin), *Dream Ballet* including 'Will you marry me?' (song Erwin, chorus, dance Astaire, Bremer, chorus), 'Yolanda' (song, dance Astaire), 'Coffee time' (song chorus, dance Astaire, Bremer, chorus) /

Story: Conmen Johnny Riggs (Astaire) and Victor 'Junior' Trout (Morgan) persuade wealthy Patria heiress Yolanda Aquaviva (Bremer) to believe Riggs is her guardian angel and to entrust him with her fortune, then fall into the hands of Mr Candle (Ames), her real guardian angel.

BLUE SKIES

September 1946, Paramount (104 mins, Technicolor)
Cast: Bing Crosby, Fred Astaire, Joan Caulfield, Billy de Wolfe, Olga San Juan, Cliff Nazarro / *Producer:* Sol C Siegel / *Director:* Stuart Heisler / *Dance director:* Hermes Pan / *Assistant:* David Robel / *Set designer:* Hans Dreier, Hal Pereira / *Music director:* Robert Emmett Dolan / *Screenplay:* Arthur Sheerman, adapted by Allan Scott from idea by Irving Berlin / *Music, lyrics:* Irving Berlin / *including* 'A pretty girl is like a melody' (song chorus, dance Astaire), 'I've got my captain working for me now' (song Crosby, de Wolfe), 'You'd be surprised' (song San Juan), 'All by myself' (song Crosby), 'Serenade to an old-fashioned girl' (song Caulfield, chorus), 'Puttin' on the Ritz' (song, dance Astaire), '(I'll see you in) C.U.B.A.' (song Crosby, San Juan), 'A couple of song and dance men' (song, dance Crosby, Astaire, piano Nazarro), 'You keep coming back like a song' (song Crosby, chorus), 'Always' (song chorus), 'Blue Skies' (song Crosby), 'The little things in life' (song Crosby), 'Not for all the rice in China' (song Crosby), 'Russian Lullaby' (song Crosby), 'Everybody Step' (song Crosby, dance chorus), 'How deep is the ocean?' (song Crosby, chorus), '(Running around in circles) Getting Nowhere', 'Heat wave' (song San Juan, chorus, dance Astaire, San Juan, chorus), 'Any Bonds today?' (song Crosby), 'This is the army, Mr Jones' (song Crosby), 'White Christmas' (song Crosby), background: 'Tell me, little gypsy', 'Nobody knows', 'Mandy', 'Some sunny day', 'When you walked out', 'Because I love you', 'How many times?', 'Lazy', 'The song is ended' / *Story:* Mary O'Dare Adams (Caulfield) leaves husband Johnny Adams (Crosby) because of his love of running night clubs; his friend Jed Potter (Astaire) reconciles them.

EASTER PARADE

June 1948, MGM (103 mins, Technicolor)
Cast: Fred Astaire, Judy Garland, Peter Lawford, Ann Miller, Jules Munshin, Richard Beavers, Pat Jackson, Dee Turnell, Bobbie Priest / *Producer:* Arthur Freed / *Associate producer:* Roger Edens / *Director:* Charles Walters / *Dance director:* Robert Alton / *Set designer:* Cedric Gibbons, Jack Martin Smith / *Music director:* Johnny Green / *Screenplay:* Sidney Sheldon, Frances Goodrich, Albert Hackett / *Music, lyrics:* Irving Berlin *including* 'Happy Easter' (song Astaire, chorus), 'Drum crazy' (song, dance, drums Astaire), 'It only happens when I dance with you' (song Astaire, dance Astaire, Miller, Garland), 'Everybody's doin' it' (dance Garland, chorus), 'I want to go back to Michigan' (song Garland), 'Beautiful faces need beautiful clothes' (dance Astaire, Garland), 'A fella with an umbrella' (song Lawford, Garland), 'I love a piano' (song

Garland, dance Astaire, Garland), 'Snooky ookums' (song Astaire, Garland), 'Ragtime violin' (song Astaire, dance Astaire, Garland), 'When the midnight choo-choo leaves for Alabama' (song, dance Astaire, Garland), 'Shakin' the Blues away' (song Miller, chorus, dance Miller), 'Steppin' out with my baby' (song, dance Astaire, chorus), 'A couple of swells' (song, dance Astaire, Garland), 'The girl on the magazine cover' (song Beavers, Miller, chorus), 'Better luck next time' (song Garland), 'Easter Parade' (song Garland, Astaire, chorus), background: 'At the devils's ball', 'This is the life', 'Along came Ruth', 'Call me up some rainy afternoon' / *Story:* Dancer Don Hewes (Astaire) piqued when his partner Nadine Hale (Miller) deserts him for Broadway stardom boasts he can teach chorus girl Hannah Brown (Garland) to be just as good.

THE BARKLEYS OF BROADWAY
April 1949, MGM (109 mins, Technicolor)
Cast: Fred Astaire, Ginger Rogers, Oscar Levant, Billie Burke, Jacques Francois, Gale Robbins, George Fucco, Clinton Sundberg, Inez Cooper / *Producer:* Arthur Freed / *Associate producer:* Roger Edens / *Director:* Charles Walter / *Dance directors:* Robert Alton, Hermes Pan / *Set designers:* Cedric Gibbons, Edward Carfagno / *Music director:* Lennie Hayton / *Screenplay:* Betty Comden, Adolph Green / *Music:* Harry Warren / *Lyrics:* Ira Gershwin / *including* 'Swing Trot' (dance Astaire, Rogers), 'Sabre Dance' (by Aram Khatchatchurian, piano Levant), 'You'd be hard to replace' (song Astaire), 'Bouncin' the Blues' (dance Astaire, Rogers), 'A weekend in the country' (song Astaire, Rogers, Levant), 'Shoes with wings on' (song, dance Astaire), excerpt Piano Concerto in B-Flat Minor (by P I Tchaikovsky, piano Levant), 'They can't take that away from me' (song Astaire, dance Astaire, Rogers), 'Manhattan Downbeat' (song Astaire, chorus, dance Astaire, Rogers, chorus), background: 'Angel', 'This heart of mine' / *Story:* Successful dance team Josh and Dinah Barkley (Astaire, Rogers) quarrel when she decides she wants to give up musicals for straight drama.

THREE LITTLE WORDS
July 1950, MGM (103 mins, Technicolor)
Cast: Fred Astaire, Red Skelton, Vera Ellen (sung by Anita Ellis), Arlene Dahl, Keenan Wynn, Gloria DeHaven, Gale Robbins, Debbie Reynolds (sung by Helen Kane), Phil Regan / *Producer:* Jack Cummings / *Director:* Richard Thorpe / *Dance director:* Hermes Pan / *Set designers:* Cedric Gibbons, Urie McLeary / *Music director:* Andre Previn / *Screenplay:* George Wells, based on lives of Kalmar and Ruby / *Music:* Harry Ruby / *Lyrics:* Bert Kalmar *including* 'Where did you get that girl' (song, Astaire, Ellis, dance Astaire, Ellen), 'She's mine all mine' (song chorus), 'Mr and Mrs Hoofer at home' (dance Astaire, Ellen), 'My sunny Tennessee' (song Astaire, Skelton), 'So long oo long' (song

Astaire, Skelton), 'Who's sorry now?' (song DeHaven), 'Come on, Papa' (song Ellis, dance Ellen, chorus), 'Nevertheless' (song Astaire, Ellis), 'All alone Monday' (song Robbins), 'You smiled at me' (song Dahl), 'I wanna be loved by you' (song Astaire, Kane), 'Up in the clouds' (song chorus), 'Thinking of you' (song Ellis, dance Astaire, Ellen, Dahl), 'Hooray for Captain Spaulding' (song Skelton, Astaire), 'I love you so much' (song Dahl, chorus), 'You are my lucky stars' (song Regan), 'Three little words' (song Astaire, Regan) / *Story:* Would-be magician Bert Kalmar (Astaire) and would-be baseball player Harry Ruby (Skelton) team up to write songs.

LET'S DANCE
August 1950, Paramount (111 mins, Technicolor)
Cast: Fred Astaire, Betty Hutton, Roland Young, Ruth Warwick, Lucille Watson / *Producer:* Robert Fellows / *Director:* Norman Z McLeod / *Dance director:* Hermes Pan / *Set designers:* Hans Dreier, Roland Anderson / *Music director:* Robert Emmett Dolan / *Screenplay:* Allan Scott, Dane Lussier, from story *Little Boy Blue* by Maurice Zolotow / *Music, lyrics:* Frank Loesser *including* 'Can't stop talking' (song, dance Hutton, Astaire), 'Tiger Rag' (dance, piano Astaire), 'Jack and the beanstalk' (song Astaire), 'Oh, them dudes' (song, dance Astaire, Hutton), 'Why fight the feeling?' (song, dance Hutton), 'The Hyacinth' (music box, dance Astaire, Watson), 'Tunnel of Love' (song, dance Astaire, Hutton, chorus) / *Story:* Don Elwood (Astaire) helps his former dance colleague Kitty McNeil Everett (Hutton) fight the attempts of her mother-in-law to take away her son.

ROYAL WEDDING (UK: WEDDING BELLS)
February 1951, MGM (93 mins, Technicolor)
Cast: Fred Astaire, Jane Powell, Peter Lawford, Sarah Churchill, Keenan Wynn / *Producer:* Arthur Freed / *Associate producer:* Roger Edens / *Director:* Stanley Donen / *Dance director:* Nick Castle / *Set designers:* Cedric Gibbons, Jack Martin Smith / *Music director:* Johnny Green / *Screenplay:* Alan Jay Lerner / *Music:* Burton Lane / *Lyrics:* Alan Jay Lerner *including* 'Ev'ry night at seven' (song Astaire, dance Astaire, Powell, chorus), 'Sunday jumps' (dance Astaire), 'Open your eyes' (song Powell, dance Astaire, Powell), 'The happiest days of my life' (song Powell, Astaire), 'How could you believe me when you know I've been a liar all my life?' (song, dance Astaire, Powell), 'Too late now' (song Powell), 'You're all the world to me' (song, dance Astaire), 'I left my hat in Haiti' (song Astaire, chorus, dance Astaire, Powell, chorus), 'What a lovely day for a wedding' (song chorus) / *Story:* Brother and sister dancing team Tom and Ellen Bowen (Astaire, Powell) visit London where they both fall in love and both get married on the same day as Princess Elizabeth.

THE BELLE OF NEW YORK

February 1952, MGM (82 mins, Technicolor)

Cast: Fred Astaire, Vera-Ellen, sung by Anita Ellis, Marjorie Main, Keenan Wynn, Alice Pearce / *Producer:* Arthur Freed / *Associate producer:* Roger Edens / *Director:* Charles Walters / *Dance director:* Robert Alton / *Set designers:* Cedric Gibbons, Jack Martin Smith / *Music director:* Adolph Deutsch / *Screenplay:* Robert O'Brien, Irving Elinson, adapted by Chester Erskine from stage musical by Hugh Morton (C M S McLennan) and Gustave Kerker / *Music:* Harry Warren / *Lyrics:* Johnny Mercer / *including* 'When I'm out with the Belle of New York' (song chorus, dance Astaire, Ellen), 'Bachelor dinner song' (song Astaire, dance Astaire, chorus), 'Let a little love come in' (song chorus), 'Seeing's believing' (song, dance Astaire), 'Baby doll' (song Astaire, dance Astaire, Ellen), 'Oops' (song Astaire, dance Astaire, Ellen), 'A bride's wedding day song' (Thank you Mr Currier and thank you, Mr Ives)' (song Ellis, dance Astaire, Ellen, chorus), 'Naughty but nice' (song Ellis, dance Ellen, Pearce), 'I wanna be a dancin' man' (song, dance Astaire) / *Story:* Playboy Charles Hill (Astaire) falls for salvationist Angela Bonfils (Vera-Ellen) and renounces his former life but misses the wedding because of a hangover.

THE BAND WAGON

July 1953, MGM (111 mins, Technicolor)

Cast: Fred Astaire, Cyd Charisse, sung by India Adams, Oscar Levant, Nanette Fabray, Jack Buchanan, Leroy Daniels, Ava Gardner / *Producer:* Arthur Freed / *Associate Producer:* Roger Edens / *Director:* Vincente Minelli / *Dance Director:* Michael Kidd / *Set Designers:* Cedric Gibbons, Preston Ames / *Music Director:* Adolph Deutsch / *Screenplay:* Betty Comden, Adolph Green / *Music:* Arthur Schwartz / *Lyrics:* Howard Dietz *including* 'By myself' (song Astaire), 'A shine on your shoes' (song Astaire, dance Astaire, Daniels), 'That's entertainment' (song Buchanan, Fabray, Levant, Astaire, Adams), 'Beggar Waltz' (from Giselle) (dance Charisse, chorus), 'Dancing in the dark' (dance Astaire, Charisse), 'You and the night and the music' (song chorus, dance Astaire, Charisse), 'Something to remember you by' (song chorus), 'High and low' (song chorus), 'I love Luisa' (song Astaire, Levant, Fabray, chorus), 'New sun in the sky' (song Adams), 'I guess I'll have to change my plan' (song, dance Astaire, Buchanan), 'Louisiana hayride' (song Fabray, chorus), 'Triplets' (song Astaire, Fabray, Buchanan), *The Girl Hunt* – Ballet (narration written by Alan Jay Lerner, spoken by Astaire, dance Astaire, Charisse, chorus) / *Story:* Aging dancer Tony Hunter (Astaire) makes his Broadway comeback with young ballet star Gabrielle Gerard (Charisse) and straight drama director Jeffrey Cordova (Buchanan), which threatens to be a disaster.

DADDY LONG LEGS
May 1955, 20th-Century Fox (colour by Deluxe/Cinemascope)
Cast: Fred Astaire, Leslie Caron, Terry Moore, Thelma Ritter, Fred Clark / *Producer:* Samuel G Engel / *Director:* Jean Negulesco / *Dance Director:* David Robel, Roland Petit / *Set Designers:* Lyle Wheeler, John Decuir / *Music Director:* Alfred Newman / *Screenplay:* Phoebe and Henry Ephron, novel and play by Jean Webster / *Music, Lyrics:* Johnny Mercer, ballet music Alex North *including* 'History of the Beat' (song, dance, drumming, Astaire), 'C-a-t spells cat' (song Caron), 'Daddy Long Legs' (song chorus), 'Welcome Egghead' (song chorus), Daydream sequence: 'Texas Millionaire', 'International playboy', 'Guardian angel' (dance Astaire, Caron, chorus), 'Dream' (song chorus, orchestra, Astaire, Caron), 'Sluefoot' (song chorus, orchestra, dance Astaire, Caron), 'Something's Gotta Give' (song Astaire, dance Astaire, Caron), 'Dancing Through Life' – Ballet: 'Paris', 'Hong Kong', 'Rio de Janeiro' (North) (dance Caron, Astaire, chorus) / *Story:* Jervis Pendleton (Astaire) is the secret benefactor of a French orphan, Julie Andre (Caron); they meet and fall in love.

FUNNY FACE
March 1957, Paramount (103 mins, Technicolour/Vistavision)
Cast: Audrey Hepburn, Fred Astaire, Kay Thompson, Michael Auclair / *Producer:* Roger Edens / *Director:* Stanley Donens / *Dance Director:* Eugene Loring / *Set designers:* Hal Pereira, George W Davis / *Visual Consultant:* Richard Avedon / *Music director:* Adolph Deutsch / *Screenplay:* Leonard Gershe, from his unproduced stage musical *Wedding Day* / *Music:* George Gershwin, Roger Edens / *Lyrics:* Ira Gershwin, Leonard Gershe / *including* 'Think pink' (song Thompson, chorus), 'How long has this been going on?' (song Hepburn), 'Funny Face' (song Astaire, dance Astaire, Hepburn), 'Bonjour, Paris!' (Astaire, Thompson, Hepburn, chorus), 'Basal metabolism' (dance Hepburn), 'Let's kiss and make up' (song, dance Astaire), 'He loves and she loves' (song Astaire, dance Astaire, Hepburn), 'On how to be lovely' (song Thompson, Hepburn), 'Marche Funèbre' (song uncredited French singers), 'Clap yo' hands' (song Astaire, Thompson), ''S wonderful' (song, dance Astaire, Hepburn) / *Story*: photographer Dick Avery (Astaire), transforms dowdy bookseller Jo Stockton (Hepburn) into a glamorous fashion model and takes her to Paris.

SILK STOCKINGS
May 1957, MGM (117 mins, Metrocolor)
Cast: Fred Astaire, Cyd Charisse (sing by Carol Richards), Janis Paige, Peter Lorre, Jules Munshin, George Tobias, Joseph Buloff, Wim Sonneveld, Betty Uitti, Barrie Chase, Tybee Alfra, Belita / *Producer:* Arthur Freed / *Director:* Rouben Mamoulian / *Dance directors:* Eugene Loring, Hermes Pan / *Set designers:* William A Horning, Randall Duell / *Music director:* Andre Previn /

Screeplay: Leonard Gershe, Leonard Spigelgass from stage musical by George S Kaufman, Leueen McGrath and Abe Burrows, based on story *Ninotchka* by Melchior Lengya and screen version by Charles Brackett, Billy Wilder, Walter Reisch and Ernst Lubitsch / *Music, lyrics:* Cole Porter *including* 'Too bad' (song Lorre, Munshin, Buloff, Astaire, Uitti, Chase, Alfra), 'Paris loves lovers' (song Astaire, Richards), 'Stereophonic sound' (song, dance Astaire, Paige), 'It's a chemical reaction, that's all' (song Richards), 'All of you' (song Astaire, dance, Astaire, Charisse), 'Satin and Silk' (song Paige), 'Silk stockings' (dance Charisse), 'Without love' (song Richards), 'Fated to be mated' (song Astaire, dance Astaire, Charisse), 'Josephine' (song Paige), 'Siberia' (song Lorre, Munshin, Buloff), 'The Red Blues' (song Sonnevald, chorus, dance Charisse, chorus), 'The Ritz Roll and Rock' (song, dance Astaire, chorus), background: 'I've got you under my skin', 'Close', 'You'd Be So Nice To Come Home To', 'You Can Do No Wrong' / *Story:* Four Russian commissars, including Nina 'Ninotchka' Yoshenko (Charisse), are sent to Paris to bring home the Russian composer who has agreed to write the score for a film of *War and Peace*, produced by Steven 'Steve' Carfield (Astaire).

ON THE BEACH
December 1959, United Artists (133 mins, b & w)
Cast: Gregory Peck, Ava Gardner, Fred Astaire, Anthony Perkins, Donna Anderson / *Producer, director:* Stanley Kramer / *Set designer:* Fernando Carrere / *Music director:* Ernest Gold / *Screenplay:* John Paxton, novel by Nevil Shute / *Music:* Ernest Gold (background score includes *Waltzing Matilda*) / *Story:* in the aftermath of an atomic holocaust British nuclear scientist Julian Osborn (Astaire) seeks solace in drink and racing cars.

THE PLEASURE OF HIS COMPANY
May 1961, Paramount (114 mins Technicolor)
Cast: Fred Astaire, Debbie Reynolds, Lilli Palmer, Tab Hunter, Gary Merrill, Charles Ruggles / *Producer:* William Perlberg / *Director:* George Seaton / *Dance Director:* Hermes Pan / *Set designers:* Hal Pereira, Tambi Larsen / *Music director:* Alfred Newman / *Screenplay:* Samuel Taylor, play by Cornelia Otis Skinner and Samuel Taylor / *Background score:* Alfred Newman *including* 'Lover' by Richard Rogers and Lorenz Hart (song Astaire) / *Story:* Globe-trotting playboy Astaire turns up on the eve of his daughter's wedding and tries to persuade her to travel with him instead of getting married.

THE NOTORIOUS LANDLADY
June 1962, Columbia (123 mins, b & w)
Cast: Fred Astaire, Jack Lemmon, Kim Novak, Lionel Jeffries, Estelle Winwood / *Producer:* Fred Kohlmar / *Director:* Richard Quine / *Set Designer:* Cary Odell / *Music director, background score:* George Duning / *Screenplay:* Larry

Gelbart, Blake Edwards, from novel by Margery Sharp / *including* background 'A Foggy Day' by G & I Gershwin, medley *The Pirates of Penzance* by W S Gilbert & A Sullivan / *Story:* American diplomats Franklin Armbruster (Astaire) and Bill Gridley (Lemmon) become involved in a mystery when Carlye Hardwick (Kim Novak) is suspected of having killed her husband.

FINIAN'S RAINBOW
August 1968, Warner Brothers – 7 Arts (145 mins, Technicolor)
Cast: Fred Astaire, Petula Clark, Tommy Steele, Don Francks, Keenan Wynn, Barbara Hancock, Al Freeman Jr / *Producer:* Joseph Landon / *Director:* Francis Ford Coppola / *Dance Director:* Hermes Pan / *Set Designer:* Hilyard M Brown / *Music Director:* Ray Heindorf / *Screenplay:* E Y Harburg, Fred Saidy, from their stage musical / *Music:* Burton Lane / *Lyrics:* E Y Harburg / *including* 'This time of year' (song chorus), 'How are things in Glocca Morra?' (song Clark), 'Look to the rainbow' (song Clark, Astaire, dance Astaire), 'If this isn't love' (song, Francks, Clark, Astaire, chorus, dance Astaire), 'Something sort of grandish' (song Steele, Clark), 'That great Come-and-get-it day' (song Francks, Clark, chorus), 'Old devil moon' (song Francks, Clark), 'When the idle poor become the idle rich', 'When I'm not near the girl I love' (song Steele), 'Rain dance' (Hancock, chorus), 'The Begat' (Wynn, chorus) / *Story:* Irish emigrant Finian McLonergan (Astaire) is pursued to Fort Knox by a leprechaun from whom he has stolen a crock of gold.

MIDAS RUN (UK: A RUN ON GOLD)
May 1969, Selmur Pictures (104 mins, Technicolor)
Cast: Fred Astaire, Anne Heywood, Richard Crenna, Roddy McDowell, Ralph Richardson, Cesar Romero, Maurice Denham, John le Mesurier, Fred Astaire Jr / *Producer:* Raymond Stross / *Director:* Alf Kjellin / *Set designer:* Arthur Lawson, Ezio Cescotti / *Screenplay:* James Buchanan, Ronald Austin, from story by Berne Giler / *Background score:* Elmer Bernstein / *Title song (Heywood) lyric:* Don Black / *Story:* Senior British secret service man John Pedley (Astaire) masterminds the hijacking of a government shipment of gold he has been assigned to guard and then recover; co-pilot of getaway plane is played by Fred Astaire Jr.

IMAGINE
1973 (81 mins, Eastmancolor)
Cast: John Lennon, Yoko Ono / *Producer, director:* John Lennon, Yoko Ono / *Story:* Promotional film for *Imagine* LP; Fred Astaire and Dick Cavett appear as fellow Nebraskans in a party sequence directed by Jonas Mekas.

THAT'S ENTERTAINMENT
1974 MGM, (137 mins, Metrocolor)
Cast and co-presenters: Fred Astaire, Bing Crosby, Gene Kelly, Peter Lawford,

Liza Minnelli, Donald O'Connor, Debbie Reynolds, Micky Rooney, Frank Sinatra, James Stewart, Elizabeth Taylor / *Producer, director, writer:* Jack Haley Jr / *including Astaire numbers:* 'Begin the Beguine' (from *Broadway Melody of 1940*), 'The Babbitt and the Bromide' (from *Ziegfeld Follies*), 'Sunday jumps' (hat rack dance from *Royal Wedding*), 'Shoes with wings on' (from *The Barkleys of Broadway*), 'You're all the world to me' (wall and ceiling dance from *Royal Wedding*), 'Dancing in the Dark' (from *The Band Wagon*), 'By myself' (from *The Band Wagon*) / *Story:* Compilation extracts from MGM movies.

THE TOWERING INFERNO

January 1975, 20th-Century Fox/Warner (165 mins, Deluxe Color)

Cast: Steve McQueen, Paul Newman, William Holden, Faye Dunaway, Fred Astaire, Susan Blakely, Richard Chamberlain, Jennifer Jones, O J Simpson, Robert Vaughan, Robert Wagner / *Producer:* Irwin Allen / *Director:* John Guillerman / *Set Designer:* Ward Preston / *Screenplay:* Stirling Silliphant from novels *The Tower* by Richard Martin Stern and *The Glass Inferno* by Thomas M Scortia and Frank M Robinson / *Music:* John Williams / *Song:* 'We may never love like this again' by Al Kasha and Joel Hirshhorn, sung by Maureen McGovern / *Story:* Confidence trickster Harlee Claiborne (Astaire) is trapped by fire in the world's tallest skyscraper.

THAT'S ENTERTAINMENT II

1976, MGM (133 mins, Metrocolor)

Co-presenters: Fred Astaire, Gene Kelly / *Narrator:* Leonard Gershe / *Producer:* Saul Chaplin, Daniel Melnick / *Dance director:* Gene Kelly / *Music director, arranger:* Nelson Riddle / *Special Lyrics:* Howard Dietz, Saul Chaplin / *including Astaire numbers:* 'That's Entertainment' (from *The Band Wagon*), 'That's Entertainment' (new version, with Kelly), 'I wanna be a dancin' man' (from *The Belle of New York*), 'Be a clown', 'Easter Parade' (from *Easter Parade*), 'Bouncin' the blues' (from *The Barkleys of Broadway*), 'Finale' (with Kelly) / *Story:* Second compilation from MGM movies with some original material.

THE AMAZING DOBERMANS

November 1976, Golden Films (96 mins, col)

Cast: Fred Astaire, James Franciscus, Barbara Eden, Jack Carter, Billy Barty / *Executive producer:* Don L Reynolds / *Producer:* David Chudnow / *Director:* Byron Chudnow / *Screenplay:* Richard Chapman from story by Michael Kariake, William Goldstein / *Music:* Alan Silvestri / *Story:* Doberman owner and reformed conman Daniel Hughes (Astaire) befriends undercover agent Lucky Vincent (Franciscus) and helps him catch an extortion racketeer.

UN TAXI MAUVE
(Paris) May 1977, Rizzoli Films (120 mins, Eastmancolor)
Cast: Fred Astaire, Charlotte Rampling, Peter Ustinov, Philippe Noiret, Agostina Belli, Edward Albert Jr / *Producer:* Catherine Winter, Giselle Rebillion / *Director:* Yves Boisset / *Set Designer:* Arrigo Equini / *Music Director:* Carlo Savina / *Screenplay:* Yves Boisset, from novel by Michel Deon / *including* music from Philippe Sarde, The Chieftans, Schubert Sonata interpreted by Roger Woodward / *Story:* Dr Scully (Astaire) drives his patients in a purple taxi and becomes involved with expatriates who are seeking escape in Ireland in Italian/Irish co-production.

GHOST STORY
December 1981, (111 mins, Technicolor)
Cast: Fred Astaire, Melvyn Douglas, Douglas Fairbanks Jr, John Houseman, Craig Wasson, Patricia Neal, Alice Krige, Jacqueline Brookes, Miguel Fernandes, Lance Holcomb, Mark Chamberlain, Tim Choate, Kurt Johnson, Ken Olin, Raymond J Quinn, Barbara Van Zastrow / *Producer:* Burt Weissbourd / *Co-producer:* Douglas Green / *Director:* John Irvin / *Screenplay:* Lawrence D Cohen / *Music:* Phillipe Sarde / *Story:* As an old man Ricky Hawthorne (Astaire) and three friends (Douglas, Fairbanks, Houseman) are revisited by the ghost of Alma Eva (Krige) whom they murdered in their youth; young Hawthorne is played by Tim Choate.

THAT'S DANCING
January 1985 (105 mins, MGM)
Directed, written: Jack Haley Jr / *Cast:* Fred Astaire, Gene Kelly, Ginger Rogers, Cyd Charisse, Nicholas Brothers / *Story:* Compilation of dancing scenes from 1890s to 1984 breakdancing.

Television appearances

THE TOAST OF THE TOWN
13 April 1955, CBS
Variety programme with: Ed Sullivan, Fred Astaire, Will Mastin Trio featuring Sammy Davis Jr, Dorothy Dandridge

IMP ON A COBWEB LEASH
1 December 1957, CBS, General Electric Theatre
Play with: Fred Astaire, Joan Tetzel, Rhys Williams, Joyce Meadows, Howard Smith, Margaret Irving, Walter Woolf King / *Producer:* William Frye, MCA-Revue Productions / *Director:* Robert B Sinclair / *Writer:* Jameson Brewer, John Keasler

AN EVENING WITH FRED ASTAIRE*
17 October 1958, NBC
repeated 28 January 1959
With: Fred Astaire, Barrie Chase, Jonah Jones / *Executive producer:* Fred Astaire, Ava Productions Inc. / *Producer, director:* Bud Yorkin / *Dance director:* Hermes Pan / *Assistants:* Gino Malbera, David Robel, Pat Denise / *Set designer:* Edward Stephenson / *Music director:* David Rose / *Writer of special material:* Herbert Baker / *including:* 'Svengali', 'Change partners', 'Prop dance', 'Baubles, bangles and beads', 'Mack the Knife' (Jones), 'Man with the blues', 'Old Macdonald', 'St James Infirmary', medley: 'Oh lady, be good', 'Cheek to cheek', 'A fine romance', 'They can't take that away from me', 'Nice work if you can get it', 'A foggy day', 'I won't dance', 'Something's gotta give', 'Night and day', 'Top hat, white tie and tails', 'Isn't this a lovely day?'

* winner of 9 Emmy Awards and Peabody Award

MAN ON A BICYCLE
3 September 1959, CBS, General Electric Theatre
Play with: Fred Astaire, Roxanne Berard, Ann Codee, Linda Watkins, Stanley Adams, David Hoffman, Jan Arvan / *Producer:* William Frye, MCA-Revue Productions / *Director:* Hershel Daugherty / *Writer:* Jameson Brewer, Victor Canning

ANOTHER EVENING WITH FRED ASTAIRE*
4 November 1959, NBC
With: Fred Astaire, Barrie Chase, Jonah Jones Quartet, Bill Thompson Singers / *Executive producer:* Fred Astaire, Ava Productions Inc. / *Producer, director:* Bud Yorkin / *Dance director:* Hermes Pan / *Assistants:* Gino Malbera, David Robel, Pat Denise / *Set designer:* Edward Stephenson / *Music director:* David Rose / *Choral director:* Bill Thompson / *including:* 'The Afterbeat', 'That face', 'Drum solo dance', 'Girl in calico', 'When the saints go marching in',

'Night train' (Jones), 'My baby', 'Waltzing Matilda', 'Sophisticated lady', medley: 'Fascinatin' rhythm', 'Dancing in the dark', 'The way you look tonight', 'Dearly beloved', 'Steppin' out with my baby', 'Let's face the music and dance', 'The Carioca', 'The Continental', 'One for my baby', 'By myself'

* winner of TV Guide Award

ASTAIRE TIME*
28 September 1960, NBC
With: Fred Astaire, Barrie Chase, Count Basie Orchestra, Joe Williams, Ruth and Jane Earl / *Producer:* Fred Astaire, Ava Productions Inc. / *Director:* Greg Garrison / *Dance director, associate producer:* Hermes Pan / *Set designer:* Edward Stephenson / *Music director:* David Rose / *including:* 'Romeo and Juliet' overture, 'Miss Otis regrets', 'Not now' (Basie), 'Sweet Georgia Brown' (with Basie), 'Valse Triste' (Chase), 'We have to dance', 'The Sheik of Araby' (with Earls), 'It's a wonderful world' (Williams, Basie), 'Blues', medley: 'Thank you so much', 'Mrs Lowsborough Goodby', 'Funny face', 'I love Louisa', 'Flying down to Rio', 'I'm putting all my eggs in one basket', 'They all laughed', 'Lovely to look at', 'Let's call the whole thing off', 'Easter Parade', 'A shine on your shoes'

* winner of 2 Emmy Awards

FRED ASTAIRE'S PREMIER THEATRE
Producer: ABC-Revue Productions
As host for two years (10 October 1961 to 12 September 1963) Astaire appeared in five plays

MR EASY
13 February 1962
With: Fred Astaire, Joanna Barnes, David White, George Petrie, Harold Fong, Fredd Wayne, Howard Wendell / *Director:* John Newland / *Writers:* Jameson Brewer, Matt Taylor, Claude Binyon

MOMENT OF DECISION
10 July 1962
With: Maureen O'Sullivan, Harry Townes, Oliver McGowan, Cathleen Cordell, Connie Gilchrist, Katherine Henryck / *Director:* John Newland / *Writer:* Larry Marcus, Peter Tewksbury, James Leighton

GUEST IN THE HOUSE
11 October 1962
With: Fred Astaire, Lloyd Bochner, Philip Abbott, Susan Gordon, Phyllis Avery / *Director:* Ted Post / *Writers:* James Dunn, Philip McDonald

MISTER LUCIFER
1 November 1962
With: Elizabeth Montgomery, Frank Aletter, George Petrie, Joyce Bulifant / *Director:* Alan Crosland Jr / *Writer:* Alfred Bester

BLUES FOR A HANGING
27 December 1962
With: Janis Paige, Richard Shannon, Lurene Tuttle, Lory Patrick, Tyler McDuff, Shelly Manne, Robert H Harris / *Director:* Bernard Girard / *Writers:* John and Ward Hawkins

THINK PRETTY
2 October 1964, NBC, Bob Hope's Chrysler Theatre
With: Fred Astaire, Barrie Chase, Roger Perry, Louis Nye, Reta Shaw, Linda Foster, Marilyn Wayne, Jack Bernardi / *Producer:* Richard Lewis / *Director:* Jack Arnold / *Dance director:* Hermes Pan / *Writer:* Gary Marshall, Jerry Belson, Bill Persky, Sam Denoff / *Music:* Tommy Wolf

DR KILDARE
22/23/29/30 November 1965, NBC
Fred Astaire appeared in a four-part episode of the series under the following titles: *Fathers and Daughters, A Gift of Love, The Tent Dwellers, Going Home*
With: Fred Astaire, Richard Chamberlain, Raymond Massey, Laura Devon, Audrey Totter, Spring Byington, Norman Fell, Harry Morgan / *Producer:* Douglas Benton / *Director:* Herschel Daugherty / *Writer:* William Fay

HOLLYWOOD PALACE
22 January 1966, ABC
With: Fred Astaire, Barrie Chase, Micky Rooney, Bobby Van, Petula Clark, The Nitwits, The Lenz Chimps, Ray Hastings / *Music Director:* Mitchell Ayres

HOLLYWOOD PALACE
12 March 1966, ABC (Repeat: 10 September 1966)
With: Fred Astaire, Ethel Merman, Jack Jones, Marcel Marceau, Pat Morita, The Hardy Family / *Music director:* Mitchell Ayres

HOLLYWOOD PALACE
30 April 1966, ABC
With: Fred Astaire, Barrie Chase, Herb Alpert and the Tijuana Brass, Louis Nye, Helen O'Connell, The Muppets, Bela Kremo, John Zerbini / *Music director:* Mitchell Ayres

THE FRED ASTAIRE SHOW
7 February 1968, NBC
With: Fred Astaire, Barrie Chase, Sergio Mendes and Brasil '66, Young-Holt Unlimited, The Gordian Knot, Simon and Garfunkel
Producers: Fred Astaire, Gil Rodin / *Director:* Robert Scheerer / *Dance director:* Herbert Ross / *Set designer:* James Trittipo / *Music director:* Neal Hefti / *Music coordinators:* Betty Walberg, Joseph Lipman / *including:* 'I've a shooting box in Scotland', 'I love to quarrel with you', 'Look to the rainbow', 'When the idle poor become the idle rich', 'Top hat, white tie and tails', with Chase: 'Oh, you beautiful doll', 'The look of love', 'Limehouse blues', 'Chinatown, my chinatown', 'Pinky's dilemma' (Simon and Garfunkel, Astaire)

TO CATCH A THIEF
Fred Astaire as guest star in four plays by Glen A Larsen in series starring Robert Wagner
Producer: Glen A Larsen / *Executive producer / director:* Jack Arnold

THE GREAT CASINO CAPER
16 October 1969, ABC (repeat: 16 February 1970)
Cast: Wagner, Astaire, Adolfo Celi, Edward Binns, Francesco Mule, Gerard Herter, Françoise Prevost

THREE VIRGINS OF ROME
6 November 1969, ABC (repeat: 20 April 1970)
Cast: Wagner, Astaire, Victor Buono, Edmund Purdom, Karin Dor, Massimo Serator

THE SECOND TIME AROUND
4 December 1969, ABC (repeat: 27 April 1970)
Cast: Wagner, Astaire, Malachi Throne, Adolfo Celi, Edward Binns, Alice Ghostley, Martin Kosleck

AN EVENING WITH ALISTAIR MUNDY
9 March 1970, ABC
Cast: Wagner, Astaire, Edward Binns, Francesco Mule, Lynn Kellogg, Logan Ramsey

THE DICK CAVETT SHOW
10 November 1970, ABC
with Fred Astaire as sole guest on 90-minute programme.

THE OVER-THE-HILL GANG RIDES AGAIN
17 November 1970, ABC
Cast: Walter Brennan, Fred Astaire, Edgar Buchanan, Andy Devine, Chill

[289]

Wills, Paul Richards, Lana Wood / *Executive producers:* Aaron Spelling, Danny Thomas / *Director:* George McCowan / *Writer:* Richard Carr / *Music:* David Raskin

SANTA CLAUS IS COMING TO TOWN
13 December 1970, ABC (repeats: 3 December 1971, 1 December 1972)
Animated cartoon with voices of: Fred Astaire, Mickey Rooney, Keenan Wynn, Paul Frees / *Writer:* Romeo Muller / *Songs:* Maury Laws, Jules Bass

THE DICK CAVETT SHOW
13 October 1971 ABC
with Fred Astaire again as sole guest on 90-minute programme.

'S WONDERFUL, 'S MARVELOUS, 'S GERSHWIN
17 January 1972, NBC
Cast: Jack Lemmon, Fred Astaire, Ethel Merman, Leslie Uggams, Peter Nero, Linda Bennett, Larry Kert, Robert Guillaume, Alan Johnson, Bell System Family Theatre / *Executive producer:* Joseph Cates / *Producer, writer; co-director:* Martin Charnin / *Co-director:* Walter C. Miller / *Dance director:* Alan Johnson / *Dance arrangements:* John Morris / *Music director:* Eliot Lawrence

MAKE MINE RED, WHITE AND BLUE
9 September 1972, NBC
With: Fred Astaire, Fifth Dimension, Michele Lee, Bob Crane, Jan Arvan, Irwin Charone, Jason Johnson, Iron Eyes Cody, Jimmy Joyce Singers, Tom Hansen Dancers / *Executive producers:* David L. Wolper, Warren V. Bush / *Producers:* Bill Hobin, George Sunga / *Director:* Bill Hobin / *Music Director:* David Rose / *Writers:* Ed Haas, Jack Lloyd

THE MAN IN THE SANTA CLAUS SUIT
1980
With: Fred Astaire, Gary Burghoff, John Byner, Bert Convy, Nanette Fabray, Harold Gould / *Producer:* Lee Miller / *Director:* Corey Allen / *Writer:* George Kirgo, story by Leonard Gershie / *Story:* Fred Astaire in title role and seven other parts in fantasy about the spirit of Christmas

BATTLESTAR GALACTICA
August 1979, ABC
Guest star Fred Astaire as Chameleon, intergalactic villain claiming to be father of Starbuck (Dirk Benedict)

KEY
Discography

1923 HMV with Adèle, George W Byng and his Orchestra: 'The whichness of the whatness and the whereness of the who' / 'Oh gee! oh gosh!'

1926 Columbia (UK): 'Fascinatin' rhythm' (with Adèle) / 'The half of it' / 'Dearie, blues' (piano, encouragement George Gershwin) / 'Hang on to me' (with Adèle) / 'I'd rather Charleston' (with Adèle, piano George Gershwin), 'Swiss Miss' (with Adèle, Empire Theatre Orchestra)

1928 Columbia (UK) with Julian Jones and his Orchestra: 'High Hat' / 'My one and only' / 'Funny face' (with Adèle) / 'The Babbitt and the Bromide' (with Adèle)

1929 Columbia (UK) with Al Starita and his Boyfriends: 'Not my girl' / 'Louisiana'

1930 Columbia (UK) with Columbia Studio Orchestra: 'Puttin' on the Ritz' / 'Crazy Feet'

1931 Victor with Lou Reisman and his Orchestra: 'I love Louisa' / 'New sun in the sky' / 'White heat' / 'Dancing in the dark instrumental' (piano Arthur Schwartz) / 'Hoops' (with Adèle) / 'Sweet Music' (with Adèle) (unreleased)

1932 RCA with Lou Reisman and his Orchestra: 'Night and day' / 'I've got you on my mind'

1933 RCA with Lou Reisman and his Orchestra: 'Maybe I love you too much' / 'Gold digger's song' / 'My temptation' / 'A heart of stone'

1933 Columbia (UK): 'Night and day' / 'After you'

1933 Columbia (UK): 'Flying down to Rio' / 'Music makes me'

1935 Brunswick with Lou Reisman and his Orchestra: 'Cheek to cheek' / 'No strings' / 'The Piccolino'

1935 Brunswick with Johnny Green and his Orchestra: 'Isn't this a lovely day?' / 'Top hat, white tie and tails'

1936 Brunswick with Johnny Green and his Orchestra: 'Let's face the music and dance' / 'Let yourself go' / 'I'm putting all my eggs in one basket' / 'We saw the sea' / 'I'd rather lead a band' / 'I'm building up to an awful let-down' / 'A fine romance' / 'The way you look tonight' / 'Never gonna dance' / 'Bojangles of Harlem'

[291]

1937 Brunswick with Johnny Green and his Orchestra: 'They can't take that away from me' / '(I've got) beginners luck' / 'They all laughed' / 'Slap that bass' / 'Let's call the whole thing off' / 'Shall we dance?'

1937 Brunswick with Ray Noble Orchestra: 'A foggy day' / 'I can't be bothered now' / 'Things are looking up' / 'Nice work if you can get it'

1938 Brunswick with Ray Noble Orchestra: 'Change partners' / 'I used to be colour blind' / 'The Yam' / 'The Yam step'

1940 Columbia with Benny Goodman Orchestra: 'Who cares?' / 'Just like taking candy from a baby'

1940 Columbia with Perry Botkin and his Orchestra: 'Love of my life' / 'Me and the ghost upstairs' / 'Poor Mr Chisholm' / '(I ain't hep to that step but) I'll Dig it'

1941 Decca with Delta Rhythm Boys: 'So near and yet so far' / 'Since I kissed my baby goodbye' / 'Dream dancing' / 'The wedding cake walk'

1942 Decca with Bob Crosby Orchestra: 'I'll capture your heart singing' (with Bing Crosby, Margaret Lenhart) / 'You're easy to dance with' / 'I can't tell a lie' / 'Let's say it with firecrackers' (unissued) / orchestra with John Scott Trotter (cond): 'You were never lovelier' / 'On the beam' / 'I'm old fashioned' / 'Wedding in the spring' / 'Dearly beloved' / 'The shorty George'

1944 Decca: 'This heart of mine' / 'If swing goes, I go too'

1945 Decca: 'One for my baby' / 'Oh, my achin' back'

1946 Decca with vocal Bing Crosby: 'Puttin' on the Ritz' / 'A couple of song and dance men' (with Bing Crosby)

1948 MGM with MGM Orchestra: 'Easter Parade' (with Judy Garland) / 'A couple of swells' (with Garland) / 'I love a piano' / 'Snooky ookums' / 'When the midnight choo-choo leaves for Alabam' / 'It only happens when I dance with you' / 'Steppin' out with my baby'

1949 MGM with MGM Orchestra: 'You'd be hard to replace' / 'My one and only highland fling' (with Ginger Rogers) / 'They can't take that away from me' / 'Shoes with wings on'

1950 MGM with MGM Orchestra: 'Where did you get that girl' (with Anita

Ellis) / 'Nevertheless' (with Anita Ellis, Red Skelton), 'My sunny Tennessee' / 'So long, oo-long' / 'Three little words' (with Red Skelton)

1951 MGM with MGM Orchestra: 'How could you believe me when I said I love you when you know I've been a liar all my life?' (with Jane Powell) / 'I left my hat in Haiti' / 'You're all the world to me' / 'Ev'ry night at seven'

1952 MGM with MGM Orchestra: 'Oops!' / 'Seein'g believing' / 'Bachelor dinner song' / 'I wanna be a dancin' man'

1952 Clef with Oscar Peterson Group: *The Astaire Story:* 'Isn't this a lovely day?' / 'Puttin' on the Ritz' / 'I used to be color blind' / 'The continental' / 'Let's call the whole thing off' / 'Change partners' / ''S wonderful' / 'Lovely to look at' / 'They all laughed' / 'Cheek to cheek' / 'Steppin' out with my baby' / 'The way you look tonight' / 'I've got my eyes on you' / 'Dancing in the dark' / 'The Carioca' / 'Nice work if you can get it' / 'New sun in the sky' / 'I won't dance' / 'Fast dance' / 'Top hat, white tie and tails' / 'No strings' / 'I concentrate on you' / 'I'm putting all my eggs in one basket' / 'A fine romance' / 'Night and day' / 'Fascinating rhythm' / 'I love Louisa' / 'Slow dance' / 'Medium dance' / 'They can't take that away from me' / 'You're easy to dance with' / 'A needle in a haystack' / 'So near and yet so far' / 'A foggy day' / 'Oh, Lady be good' / 'I'm building up to an awful let-down' / 'Not my girl'

1953 MGM with MGM Orchestra: 'A shine on your shoes' / 'I love Louisa' / 'By myself' / 'That's entertainment' (with Nanette Fabray, Jack Buchanan, Oscar Levant, India Adams) / 'Triplets' (with Nanette Fabray, Jack Buchanan) / 'I guess I'll have to change my plan' (with Jack Buchanan)

1953 MGM with MGM Orchestra (film soundtrack): *The Band Wagon,* The girl hunt ballet (narrated by Fred Astaire)

1955 RCA: 'Something's gotta give' / 'Sluefoot'

1956 Verve with Buddy Bregman Orchestra: 'Hello, baby' / 'There's no time like the present' / 'Sweet sorrow' / 'Just like taking candy from a baby'

1956 Verve with studio orchestra: *Funny Face:* 'Funny face' / 'Bonjour Paris!' (with Audrey Hepburn, Kay Thompson) / 'Clap yo' hands' (with Kay Thompson) / 'He loves and she loves' / 'Let's kiss and make up' / ''S wonderful' (with Audrey Hepburn)

1957 Verve with Buddy Bregman Orchestra: 'That face' / 'Calypso hooray'

1957 MGM with MGM Orchestra (film soundtrack): *Silk Stockings:* 'Too bad' (with Peter Lorre, Joseph Buloff, Julkes Munshin) / 'Paris loves lovers' (with Carol Richards) / 'Stereophonic sound' (with Janis Paige) / 'All of you' / 'Fated to be mated' / 'The Ritz roll and rock'

1959 Kapp with studio orchestra: *Now:* 'Change partners' / 'Isn't this a lovely day?' / 'A foggy day' / 'The girl on the magazine cover' / 'I love to quarrel with you' / 'Along came Ruth' / 'The afterbeat' / 'They can't take that away from me' / 'They all laughed' / 'I'll walk alone' / 'One for my baby' / 'Oh, Lady be good!' / 'Puttin' on the Ritz' / 'Top hat, white tie and tails' / 'Lady of the evening' / 'Something's gotta give'

1959 Choreo with studio orchestra: 'That face' / 'Thank you so much' / 'Mrs Lowsborough-Goodby'

1960 Choreo with studio orchestra (TV soundtrack): *Three Evenings with Fred Astaire:* 'Oh, Lady be good!' / 'Cheek to cheek' / 'A fine romance' / 'They can't take that away from me' / 'Nice work if you can get it' / 'A foggy day' / 'I won't dance' / 'Something's gotta give' / 'Night and day' / 'Top hat, white tie and tails' / 'Fascinatin' rhythm' / 'Dancing in the dark' / 'The way you look tonight' / 'Dearly beloved' / 'Steppin' out with my baby' / 'Let's face the music and dance' / 'The carioca' / 'The continental' / 'One for my baby' / 'By myself' / 'That face' / 'Miss Otis regrets' / 'Thank you so much' / 'Mrs Lowsborough Goodby' / 'Funny face' / 'I love Louisa' / 'Flying down to Rio' / 'I'm putting all my eggs in one basket' / 'They all laughed' / 'Lovely to look at' / 'Let's call the whole thing off' / 'Easter parade' / 'A shine on your shoes'

1962 Choreo with studio orchestra: 'The notorious landlady' / 'The Martini'

1962 Ava with studio orchestra: 'It happens every spring' / 'You worry me'

1966 RCA: *The band wagon:* original recordings from stage show *The Band Wagon* with 'Night and day' (from *Gay divorce*) / 'I've got you on my mind' (from *Gay divorce*) / 'Maybe I love you too much' / 'My temptation' / 'Heart of stone' / 'Gold diggers song'

1968 Warner with studio orchestra (film soundtrack): *Finian's Rainbow:* 'Look to the rainbow' (with Petula Clark) / 'If this isn't love' (with Petula Clark, Don Franks) / 'When the idle poor become the idle rich' (with Petula Clark)

1971 Daybreak with studio orchestra (TV soundtrack): *'S Wonderful, 'S Marvellous, 'S Gershwin:* ''S wonderful' / 'Oh, Lady be good!' / 'They all laughed' / 'Fascinatin' rhythm' / 'A foggy day' / 'Let's call the whole thing off' / 'They can't take that away from me'

1973 Columbia Special 3 record LP collection of all Brunswick releases 1935–1940: 'Cheek to cheek' / 'No strings' / 'Isn't this a lovely day' / 'Top hat, white tie and tails' / 'The Piccolino' / 'Let's face the music and dance' / 'I'm putting all my eggs in one basket' / 'We saw the sea' / 'Let yourself go' / 'I'd rather lead a band' / 'I'm building up to an awful let down' / 'A fine romance' / 'The way you look tonight' / 'Never gonna dance' / 'Pick yourself up' / 'Bojangles of Harlem' / 'The Waltz in swing time' / 'They can't take that away from me' / 'They all laughed' / '(I've got) beginner's luck' / 'Let's call the whole thing off' / 'Shall we dance?' / 'Slap that bass' / 'A foggy day' / 'Things are looking up' / 'Nice work if you can get it' / 'I can't be bothered now' / 'Change partners' / 'I used to be color blind' / 'The yam' / 'The yam steps' / 'Love of my life' / 'Poor Mr Chisholm' / 'Me and the ghost upstairs' / '(I ain't hep to that step but I'll) Dig it' / 'Who cares (so long as you care)' / 'Just like taking candy from a baby'

1973 CBS with Johnny Green, Ray Noble, Leo Reisman: *Starring Fred Astaire:* compilation double LP from Brunswick recordings of 'Top hat' / 'Follow the fleet' / 'Swing time' / 'Shall we dance' / 'A damsel in distress' / 'Carefree'

1975 United Artists with the Pete Moore Orchestra: *Attitude Dancing:* 'That face' / 'My eyes adored you' / 'I'm building up to an awful let down' / 'The wailing of the willow' / 'You worry me' / 'I love everybody but you' / 'Attitude dancing' / 'City of the angels' / 'The old-fashioned way' / 'Not my girl' / 'Life is beautiful' / 'Wonderful baby'

1975 United Artists with Bing Crosby, the Pete Moore Orchestra: *A couple of song and dance men:* 'Roxie' / 'Top Billing' / 'Sing' / 'It's easy to remember' / 'In the cool, cool, cool of the evening' / 'Pick yourself up' / 'How lucky can you get' / 'I've a shooting box in Scotland' / 'Change partners' / 'Mr Keyboard Man – The Entertainer' / 'Spring, spring, spring' / 'A couple of song and dance men' / 'Top billing'

1975 United Artists with the Pete Moore Orchestra: *They can't take these away from me:* 'Top hat, white tie and tails' / 'A fine romance' / 'Cheek to cheek' / 'I wanna be a dancin' man' / 'They can't take that away from me' / 'One for my baby (and one more for the road)' / 'Night and day' / 'Something's gotta give' / 'A foggy day' / 'Isn't this a lovely day?' / 'They all laughed' / 'That's entertainment'

1976 Sountrak: *Starring Fred Astaire & Ginger Rogers 1936–37, Volume 2:* soundtrack recordings from *Shall we dance* and *Swing time*

1976 Sountrak: soundtrack recordings from *Blue skies*

1978 Stet: *Funny Face:* soundtrack recordings from movie *Funny face* / *The Belle of New York:* soundtrack recordings from *The Belle of New York*, with 'There's no time like the present' / 'Just like taking candy from a baby' / 'Hello, baby' / 'Sweet sorrow' / 'The Martini' / 'It happens every spring' / 'You worry me' / 'The notorious landlady'

1978 Stet: *The Belle of New York* soundtrack rcording and 'There's no time like the present' / 'Just like taking candy from a baby' / 'Hello baby' / 'Sweet sorrow' / The Martini' / 'It happens every spring' / 'You worry me' / 'The notorious landlady'

1979 *The Astaire Story:* 1979 Hollywood Soundstage: *The Astaire Story: Soundtrack recording of Yolanda and the thief and You'll never get rich*

1979 Sountrak: *Holiday Inn:* soundtrack recording

1980 Classic International Filmusicals: *Broadway Melody of 1940*: soundtrack recording / *Flying down to Rio* and *Carefree:* soundtrack recordings / *Roberta:* soundtrack recording

1981 Sountrak:*The Barkleys of Broadway:* soundtrack recording

1982 MCA compilation: *Dancing, swinging, singing and romancing 1941–1946:* 'The wedding cake walk' / 'So near and yet so far' / 'Dream dancing' / 'Since I kissed my baby goodbye' / 'You were never lovelier' / 'The Short George' / 'Dearly beloved' / 'On the beam' / 'I'm old fashioned' / 'You're so easy' / 'I can't tell a lie' / 'Oh, my achin' back' / 'If swing goes, I go too' / 'Puttin on the Ritz'

1983 ASV Living Era: Fred Astaire / Crazy Feet: compilation LP of original recordings 1923–1930

Curtain calls – *Other undated recordings include:*

Silver Screen Soundtrack Series: *You were never lovelier:* soundtrack recording

Silver Screen Soundtrack Series: *Ziegfeld Follies of 1946:* Double LP soundtrack recording

Silver Screen Soundtrack Series: *A damsel in distress* and *The sky's the limit:* soundtrack recordings

Caliban

Soundtrack recording of *Let's dance*

Soundtrack recording of *The Story of Vernon and Irene Castle* and *Daddy Long Legs*

Hollywood Soundstage

Soundtrack recording of *Second Chorus*

World Records: *Lady, be good!*: original recordings from *Lady, be good!* with 'After you, who?' / 'Night and day' from *Gay Divorce* stage show, 'Flying down to Rio' / 'Music make me' from *Flying down to Rio* / *Funny face*: original recordings from stage show *Funny face*, also with Adèle (from *Stop flirting*) / 'Oh gee! Oh gosh!' / 'The whichness of the whatness'

Bibliography

Armitage, Merle, *George Gershwin, man and legend,* Books for Libraries Press, New York, 1958

Astaire, Fred, *Steps in time,* Harper, New York, 1959

Bacall, Lauren, *Bacall, by myself,* Cape, London, 1979

Barty-King, Hugh, *GSMD – A hundred years' performance,* Guildhall School of Music and Drama, London, 1980

Behlmer, Ruby (ed.), *Memo from David O. Selznik,* Viking, New York, 1972

Bookspan, Martin and Yockey, Ross, *André Previn,* Doubleday, New York, 1981

BBC, *The Fred Astaire story,* BBC, London, 1975

Cagney, James, *Cagney by Cagney,* Doubleday, New York, 1976

Carter, Randolph, *The world of Flo Ziegfeld,* Elek, London, 1974

Castle, Charles, *Noël,* W. H. Allen, London, 1972

Chaplin, Charles, *My autobiogrcphy,* Bodley Head, London, 1964

Connor, Jim *Ann Miller – Tops in taps,* Franklin Watts, New York, 1981

Cook, David, *A history of narrative film,* Norton, New York, 1981

Croce, Arlene *The Fred Astaire and Ginger Rogers Book,* Galahad, New York, 1972

Croce, Arlene, *Afterimages,* A & C Black, London, 1978

Crosby, Bing, *Call me lucky,* Muller, London, 1953

Crowther, Bosley, *The lion's share,* Dutton, New York, 1957

Dickens, Homer, *The films of Ginger Rogers,* Citadel Press, Secaucus, New Jersey, 1975

Devonshire, Duchess of, *The House,* Macmillan, London, 1982

Dietz, Howard, *Dancing in the dark,* Bantam, Illinois, 1974

Eames, John Douglas, *The MGM story,* Octopus, London, 1975

Eells, George, *Cole Porter – the life that late he led,* Putnam, New York, 1967

Eells, George, *Ginger, Loretta and Irene who?* Putnam, New York, 1976

Ellis, Mary, *The dancing years,* John Murray, London, 1982

Ewen, David, *The story of Irving Berlin,* Holt, New York, 1950

Ewen, David, *George Gershwin: his journey to greatness,* Prentice-Hall, Englewood Cliffs, New Jersey, 1970

Freedland, Michael, *Irving Berlin*, Stein and Day, New York, 1974

Freedland, Michael, *Fred Astaire: an illustrated biography*, Grosset and Dunlap, New York, 1976

Freedland, Michael, *Jerome Kerne*, Robson, London, 1978

Friedrich, Otto, *City of nets*, Headline, London, 1987

Goldstein, Malcolm, *George S. Kaufman: His life, his theatre*, Oxford University Press, New York, 1979

Green, Benny, *Fred Astaire*, Hamlyn, London, 1979

Green, Stanley and Goldblatt Bert, *Starring Fred Astaire*, Doubleday, New York, 1977

Gregg, Hubert, *Thanks for the memory*, Gollancz, London, 1983

Haden-Guest, Anthony, *Bad dreams*, Macmillan, New York, 1981

Hirschhorn, Clive, *The Hollywood Musical*, Octopus, London, 1981

Hirschhorn, Clive, *Gene Kelly*, Regnery, London, 1974

Houseman, John, *Front and center*, Simon and Schuster, New York, 1979

Houseman, John, *Run through*, Simon and Schuster, New York, 1972

James, Edward, (ed. Melly, George), *Swans reflecting elephants*, Weidenfeld and Nicolson, London, 1982

Jewel, Richard B. (with Vernon Harbin), *The RKO story*, Octopus, London, 1982

Kael, Pauline, *Reeling*, Little, Brown, Boston, 1976

Kanin, Garson, *Together again!*, Doubleday, New York, 1981

Katz, Ephraim, *Film Encyclopaedia*, Macmillan, London, 1982

Kobal, John, *Rita Hayworth: the time, the place, the woman*, Norton, New York, 1977

Leach, Jack, *Riders in the stands*, Stanley Paul, London, 1970

Leach, Jack, *Sods I have cut on the turf*, Gollancz, London, 1961

Lerner, Alan Jay, *On the street where I live*, Norton, New York, 1978

Lesley, Cole, *The life of Noël Coward*, Cape, London, 1976

Martin, Tony and Charisse, Cyd, *The two of us*, Mason/Charter, New York, 1976

Marx, Arthur, *Red Skelton*, Dutton, New York, 1979

Meredith, Scott, *George S. Kaufman and his friends*, Doubleday, New York, 1974

Minnelli, Vincente, *I remember it well*, Doubleday, New York, 1974

Morley, Sheridan, *A biography of Noël Coward*, Pavilion, London, 1985

Mueller, John, *Astaire dancing*, Knopf, New York, 1985

Niven, David, *Bring on the empty horses*, Hamish Hamilton, London, 1975

Niven, David, *The moon's a balloon*, Hamish Hamilton, London, 1971

Payn, Graham and Morley, Sheridan (eds.), *The Noël Coward diaries*, Weidenfeld and Nicolson, London, 1982

Pearson, John, *Stags and serpents*, Macmillan, London, 1983

Rense, Paige (ed.), *Celebrity homes II*, Knapp Press, Los Angeles, 1980

Schwartz, Charles, *Gershwin: his life and music*, Da Capo, New York, 1979

Selznick, Irene Mayer, *A private view*, Knopf, New York, 1983

Shepherd, Donald and Slatzer, Robert F. , *Bing Crosby – the hollow man*, St Martin's Press, New York, 1981

Shipman, David, *The story of Cinema*, Vols. 1 and 2, Hodder and Stoughton, London, 1982 and 1984

Swanson, Gloria, *Swanson on Swanson*, Michael Joseph, London, 1981

Thomas, Bob, *Astaire – the man, the dancer*, Weidenfeld and Nicolson, London, 1985

Thompson, Charles, *Bob Hope*, Thames Methuen, London, 1981

Vickers, Hugo, *Cecil Beaton*, Weidenfeld and Nicolson, London, 1985

Winters, Shelley, *Shelley – also known as Shirley*, Granada, London, 1981

Zierold, Norman, *The Hollywood tycoons*, Hamish Hamilton, London, 1969

Index

Aarons, Alex A. 51, 52, 53, 64, 70, 71, 81, 93, 114, 116
Aarons, Alfred A. 51
Actors' Church Alliance 29
Adler, Larry 83, 89, 94, 171
Allen, Gracie 147
Altemus, Jimmy 48–9, 50, 65, 76, 85, 93, 185
Altemus, Liz 48–9, 50, 65, 66, 74, 76, 135, 136, 221, 246
   marriage to Jock Whitney 81, 159
Alvienne, Claude, Dancing School 15–16, 17–20
Aly Khan, Prince 78
Amato, Minnie 34
The Amazing Dobermans 221, 284
An Evening with Fred Astaire 205–10, 286
Apple Blossoms 47, 49, 50, 266
Ash, Paul 114
Ashley, Edwina *see* Mountbatten, Lady
Astaire, Adèle 73–89, 117–19, 130, 201–2, 212, 225–7, 229–31, 232, 245, 247, 250, 263
   affairs 61, 74–6, 77
   birth 11
   Broadway début 27–8, 42–3
   and Cecil Beaton 61, 75–6
   character 1, 22, 29, 31, 32, 36, 120, 141–2
   childhood 11–16
   children 116, 137–8
   choreography 82
   dancing schools 12, 15–16, 17–20, 25–6, 28

   and Duchess of Devonshire 91–2, 121, 178
   education 18, 22, 25, 30
   films 32–3, 138–40
   first fully professional routine 26, 27–8
   first marriage 1, 4, 78–81, 84–6, 89, 90–2, 120–1, 140–1, 160
   James divorce case 119–20
   London début 53–5
   memorabilia 226
   name 11, 19–20
   New York début 18–19
   presentation at Court 92
   Prince of Wales given tap dancing lessons 1, 69–70
   professional début 20
   relationship with Fred 36, 73–4
   retirement 3, 6, 89
   second marriage 177–8, 184, 223
   vaudeville circuits 15, 19–28, 30, 33–41, 37–8, 40
   World War II 157–60
Astaire, Ann 3, 25, 29, 38, 41, 48, 53, 56, 61, 62–3, 74, 86, 90–1, 98, 116, 117, 159, 160, 184, 195–6, 210, 212, 223
   albums compiled by 21
   character 20–1, 22
   childrens' education 15, 18, 22, 30
   costumes made by 12, 15, 19, 22
   death 231–2
   family 102
   marriage 9–11
   and Phyllis Astaire 96

Astaire, Fred 35, 36
  accidents 13, 221
  advertisement appearances 204
  attempts to retire 3, 203
  attitude towards Hollywood 122
  awards 181, 187, 209, 211, 220,
    229, 250, 255
  birth 8, 11
  Broadway début 27–8, 42–3
  character 1, 2, 3, 4, 22, 30–1, 36,
    46–7, 83–4, 124, 134, 154, 156
  childhood 3, 8–16
  choreography 5–6, 57, 82, 93, 98,
    114
  collaboration with Hermes Pan
    108–10
  dance studios 176, 217
  dancing schools 12, 15–16, 17–20,
    25–6, 28
  diet 145
  dress and on-stage persona 19,
    31, 36, 39, 45, 47, 58, 60–1,
    66–7, 70, 126, 128, 144–6, 173,
    232
  dropped by RKO 153
  education 18, 22, 25, 30
  English mannerisms and dress 47,
    145–6
  fascination with crime 197–8
  fees 5, 23, 30, 40, 53, 64–5, 81, 84,
    101, 128, 156, 163, 164
  film career 32–3, 100–53, 252,
    253, 262
  first fully professional routine 26,
    27–8
  first marriage 4, 94–7, 99–100,
    102–3, 115–16, 117, 136–7, 154,
    194
  first solo venture 97–99
  golf 31, 38, 44, 67, 76, 119, 148,
    174
  grandchildren 221, 229, 256
  honeymoon 104
  horse racing 45, 46, 50, 59, 67–8,
    95, 119, 121, 133–4, 174–6, 196,
    200, 224–5, 233–4
  houses 155, 196–7
  influences on 4, 13
  London début 53–5
  money management 155–6
  motor cars 47, 64–5
  name 8, 19–20
  New York début 18–19
  Oscar award 181
  partnership with Rogers 1, 2–3,
    94, 107–8, 127–30, 131–2, 147,
    149, 162, 182–3, 250, 263
  perfectionism 1, 2, 4, 31, 36, 46–7,
    110, 111, 127, 255
  piano playing 18, 35, 50
  professional début 20
  promotion of Astaires as epitome
    of sophistication 39, 47
  relationship with Adèle 36, 73–4
  religion 28–30, 81, 170–1, 193
  riding attempted 68
  second marriage 4, 232–4, 236,
    244–50
  singing ability 185
  social dancing 48, 92, 216, 219
  song writer 184–6, 251
  Steps In Time 203–4
  straight acting 210–11, 215–21
  television début 204
  temper 83–4, 209, 210
  top hat and white tie 19
  vaudeville circuits 15, 19–28, 30–
    41, 37–8, 40
  women friends 45–6, 93, 205–14
Astaire, Fred Jr. 4, 138, 164, 191,
    192–3, 221, 229, 250, 256
Astaire, Phyllis 95–7, 98, 99, 102–3,
    105, 115–16, 117, 122, 129, 134,
    136–7, 148, 153, 154, 174,
    191–7
  and Ann Astaire 96
  death 192–5
  film studios 105
  first marriage 96, 99–100
Astaire, Phyllis Ava 4, 164, 173,
    191, 195–7, 199–200, 212,
    227–8, 245, 247, 250, 256
  marriages 228
Astaire, Robyn 4, 232, 233–50, 255,
    256

childhood 237–8
Hollywood 238–9
racing career 233–6, 239–45, 250
Atkinson, Brooks 88, 99, 114
Austerlitz, Frederic (Fritz) 3, 8, 12, 14, 21, 22, 31, 34, 49, 50
arrival in America 8
death 62
employment 9, 10, 11, 13
marriage 10–11
Austerlitz, Johanna see Astaire, Ann
Avedon, Richard 199
Ayres, Lew 133

'The Babbitt and The Bromide' 70, 71, 167
Ball, Lucille 115, 166, 168
The Band Wagon 87–9, 90, 92, 95, 96, 268
film version 144, 189–90, 192, 280
stage turntable 88
Bankhead, Tallulah 55
The Barkleys of Broadway 182–3, 278
Barnes, T. Roy 42, 44
Barrie, Sir James 63
The Baseball Act 26, 27–8, 29, 34
Battlestar Galactica 222, 290
Beaton, Cecil 61, 74, 158, 159, 223, 227
affair with Adèle Astaire 61, 75–6
'Beggar Waltz' 88
The Belle of New York 188, 280
Benchley, Robert 52, 70, 81, 82, 85, 105, 135
Berkeley, Busby 106
Berlin, Irving 47, 124, 126, 138, 185, 186, 250–1
Blue Skies 171–3
Carefree 125, 147–9, 150
Easter Parade 179–83
Follow the Fleet 125, 131
'I Love to Quarrel with You' 35
'Putting on the Ritz' 6–7, 173
Top Hat 125–31
'White Christmas' 164
Berman, Pandro 115, 118, 122–3, 124–5, 127, 151–2

Black Bottom 69, 109
Black Eyed Susan see Lady, Be Good!
Blore, Eric 98, 117, 124
Blue Skies 6–7, 171–3, 176, 179, 277
Bolton, Guy 64
Borne, Hal 4, 251–2
Bostwick, Lillian 93
Bowes-Lyon, Lady Elizabeth see York, Duchess of
Break the News 138–40
Bremer, Lucille 166, 168, 171, 264
Brice, Fanny 45
Broadway 27, 42–3, 42–55, 65, 273–4
Broadway Melody of 1940 162, 172
Brock, Louis 100–1, 110–11
Broderick, Helen 87, 107
Brown, Morris 38
Bruce, Virginia 84
Buchanan, Jack 54, 138, 139–40, 144, 189
Bull, Henry 95, 96, 102, 122, 136, 175
Bull, Maud 95, 96, 122, 136, 146
The Bunch and Judy 53, 267
Burns, George 145, 147
Butler, Josephine 113
Butt, Alfred 53, 55, 57, 59, 62, 69

Cabaret 64–5
Campus Sweethearts 114
Cansino, Eduardo and Elisa 38, 163
Carefree 125, 147–9, 150, 162, 272–3
Carioca routine 110, 118, 123, 124, 253
Carmen, Margarita 38
Carnarvon, Countess of see Losch, Tilly
Carnarvon, Earl of 152–3, 159
Caron, Leslie 193–5, 196, 205, 265
Carslake, Brownie 67–8
Carson, Jack 115
Carter, Desmond 64
Casanave, Charlie 176
Castle, Vernon and Irene 47, 150–1
Castlerosse, Doris 75–6
Cavendish, Lady Charles see Astaire, Adèle

Cavendish, Lord Charles 78–81, 117–18, 140–1, 157–9
  career 84, 79, 80
  death 160
  marriage to Adèle Astaire 84–6, 120–1
Cavendish family 121, 157, 160, 161–2, 178 see also Devonshire, Duke and Duchess
Cavett, Dick 218, 289, 290
Cawton, Joe 53
Chambers, Willard E., Dancing Academy 12, 15
Channon, Chips 119–20
Chaplin, Charlie 5, 135, 163
Charisse, Cyd 180, 189, 190, 200, 206, 250, 265
Chase, Barrie 205–8, 211–13, 250, 265
Chatsworth 78–9, 85–6, 90–1
'Cheek to Cheek' 6
Chevalier, Maurice 5, 65, 104, 139, 194
Church of the Transfiguration 29–30, 81, 170
Church of Zion and St Timothy 28
Churchill, Sarah 187
Citizen Kane 152
Clair, René 139
Coats, Mrs Dudley 60, 61, 65, 87, 93, 119
Coccia, Aurelia 34–5
Colbert, Claudette 97
Cole, Jack 206–7
Colman, Ronald 104
Comden, Betty 181, 182, 189
Continental routine 123
Cooper, Gary 104
Cooper, Mervyn C. 106–7
Coppola, Francis Ford 217
Coward, Noël 82, 100, 202, 203, 223
  friendship with Astaire 51–2, 54, 55, 57–8
  London Calling 57
  on movie making 77
Crawford, Joan 101, 104, 106, 119, 154, 172, 181, 263

Crosby, B[i]ng 39, 133, 156, 164, 169, 170, 171–2, 179–80, 205, 231
Curzon, Lady Alexandra see Metcalfe, Baba

Dale, Alan 52
Dale, Virginia 264
Daly, Bill 52, 53–5
A Damsel in Distress 125, 145, 147, 149, 150, 181, 272
'Dancing in the Dark' 88
Dancing Lady 52, 104–6, 118–19, 172, 269
Daddy Long Legs 193–5, 205–6, 207, 281
Delaware Water Gap 31, 34, 62
Depression, the 77–8, 80, 81, 84, 102, 106
Derby, Lord 117
Devonshire, Duchess of 85–6
  relationship with Adèle Astaire 91–2, 121, 178
Devonshire, ninth Duke 79–80, 91, 157
Devonshire, tenth Duke 79, 90, 91, 121, 157, 161
Dietz, Howard 87–9, 185, 189, 190
Dillingham, Charles B. 47, 49, 50, 52, 53
Dix, Richard 104
Dixon, Dorothy 40
Dolly Sisters 65
Donaldson, Walter 82
Donen, Stanley 188
Dooley, Johnny and Ray 53
Douglass, Kingman 178, 184, 223
Dr Kildare 217–18, 288
Dunne, Irene 125

Easter Parade 179–83, 277–8
Edens, Roger 199
Elizabeth II 67, 200
'Embraceable You' 94
Engel, Sam 194–5
Ephraim, Lee 117
Episcopal Actor's Guild of America (Actors' Church Alliance) 29
Erlanger, Abe 42

Fabray, Nanette 190, 219
Fairbanks, Douglas Jr. 167, 248
Fairbanks, Douglas Sr. 27, 62, 114, 119, 197
A Family Upside Down 220
Fanchon the Cricket 32–3, 62, 69, 269
'Fascinatin' Rhythm' 64, 65
Field, Marshall 93
Fields, Dorothy 125, 149, 185
Finian's Rainbow 217, 283
Flying Down to Rio, 106, 107–11, 115, 118–19, 122, 124, 269
Follow the Fleet 125, 131, 136, 147, 271
Fontaine, Joan 147, 181, 263
For Goodness Sake 52, 53–7, 59, 61, 63, 73, 266–7
Ford, Betty 219–20
42nd Street 107, 115, 101, 106, 107, 115
Fox, William 78
Foy, Eddie 82
Freed, Arthur 38, 166, 171, 179, 180–3, 186–9, 198–9
Freedley, Vinton 52, 64, 70, 71, 81, 93, 114, 116
Freeland, Thornton 107, 110
'Funny Face' 6
Funny Face 6, 70–2, 74, 76–8, 107, 118, 254, 267–8
film version 199–200, 210, 281

Gable, Clark 4, 101, 104, 119, 162, 172
Galen Hall, Pennsylvania 47–9, 50
Garland, Judy 166–7, 168, 179–83, 186, 187, 190, 219, 224, 264
The Gay Divorce (show) 97–100, 102, 116, 117–18, 121, 122, 123–4, 268
The Gay Divorcee (film) 123–4, 125, 127, 162, 270
Geilus, Johanna *see* Astaire, Ann
Genèe, Adeline 18
General Strike 69
George, Prince 56, 57, 59, 61, 117, 119

George V 67, 92, 139
Gerry Society 21, 24–5
Gershwin, George 39–40, 49, 134, 185, 197
  Damsel in Distress 125
  Funny Face 77, 254
  George White's Scandals of 1922 52
  Girl Crazy 93
  'I Got Rhythm' 83, 101
  La, La, Lucille 40, 51
  Lady, Be Good! 64, 65
  'Nobody But You' 40
  Shall We Dance? 125, 147
Gershwin, Ira 70, 185, 197
  Damsel in Distress 125
  Lady, Be Good! 64
  Shall We Dance? 125, 147
Ghost Story 248–50, 285
Girl Crazy 93–4, 107, 114
The Girl from Utah 38
Goddard, Paulette 163, 264
Gold Diggers of 1933 100, 106, 108, 115
Golder, Lew 36, 38
Goldwyn, Samuel 81, 87, 122–3, 135
Gone with the Wind 135, 162
Gordon, Max 87, 88
Gotlieb, Dr Howard 225–6
Gould, Dave 108
Grable, Betty 124
Grant, Cary 133, 156
Gratoit, Adèle 12
Green, Adolph 181, 182, 189
Griffin, George 59, 68, 117, 133
Guildhall School of Music 58

'The Half of It, Dearie, Blues' 64, 65
'Hang on to me' 65
Harbach, Otto 125
Hartington, Edward, Marquess of *see* Devonshire, tenth Duke
Hat Check Girl 114
Hayes, Max 40
Hays, Will H. 123
Hayworth, Rita 163–4, 166, 168, 264

Hearst, William Randolph 152
Henson, Leslie 77
Hepburn, Audrey 199–200, 250, 265
Here Comes the Bride 97
'High Hat' 71
Highwood Park School 25
Hoctor, Harriet 263
Holiday Inn 164, 165, 274–5
Holtzmann, Fanny 100, 102
Hope, Bob 82, 125, 156
'Hot and Bothered' 114
House UnAmerican Activities
    Committee 115
Houseman, John 248–9
Huffman, J. C. 44–5
Hughes, Howard 125, 133, 175
Hutton, Betty 186–7, 190, 205, 265

'I Got Rhythm' 83, 94, 101
'I Love Louisa' 88
'I Love to Quarrel With You' 35,
    126
'I Won't Dance' 125
'I'd Rather Charleston' 65
'If Not For Me' 94
'If You Would Always Be Good To
    Me' 83
'I'll be Hard to Handle' 125
Imp on a Cobweb Leash 204
'I've Got a Sweet Tooth' 126
'I've a Shooting Box in Scotland' 39

James, Audrey *see* Coats, Mrs Dudley
James, Edward 87
    divorce case 119–20
The Jazz Singer 106, 126
Johnstone, Justine 42, 43
Jolson, Al 45, 104, 106, 126

Kaufman, George F. 87–9
Kearns, Allen 93, 114
Keaton, Buster 4
Kelly, Gene 5, 144, 155, 166, 167,
    179, 180, 186, 188, 189, 199,
    201, 205, 219, 221
Kennedy family 161, 202
Kern, Jerome 134, 185, 251

Roberta 124, 125
Swing Time 125, 134, 140
The Bunch and Judy 53
'They Didn't Believe Me' 38
Kidd, Michael 189
Kilgour, French and Stanbury 92,
    255
Kirkwood, James 33
Klaw and Erlanger 51
Knights of Ak-Sar-Ben 14–15
Kreisler, Fritz 49, 50

La, La, Lucille 40, 51
Lady, Be Good! 64–5, 69, 73, 105,
    130, 185, 223, 267
Lane, Burton 185
Lannin, Phil 52, 53–5
Latham, Fred 49
Lathom, Earl of 54
Lawrence, Gertrude 55, 57, 100
Leach, Earl 113
Leach, Gillian Adèle 68
Leach, Jack 59, 67–8, 174, 225
Leader, Harvey 68
Lee, Sammy 105
Leeds, Billy 71, 75
Lejeune, Caroline 143–4
Lerner, Alan Jay 185, 187
LeRoy, Mervyn 100, 106, 115
Leslie, Joan 165, 264
Let's Dance 186, 186–7, 279
'Let's Face the Music and Dance'
    131
Lismore Castle 1, 86, 91, 98, 116,
    118, 137, 140–2, 160, 178, 184,
    200, 231, 256
London 65–70, 77–8, 56–64
London Calling 57
Losch, Tilly 87–8, 119–20, 142, 149,
    152–3, 227, 263
'Love Made Me a Wonderful
    Detective' 35
'Lovely to Look At' 125
The Love Letter 50–1, 52, 266
Luce, Claire 97–8, 99, 117, 118, 123,
    263
Lynley, Carol 213–14, 224

MacDonald, Gertrude 71
McDowall, Roddy 225–6
McGuire, William 82
McKenzie, Richard Clayton 228–9, 250
McMath, Virginia *see* Rogers, Ginger
Macmillan, Harold 177
Mamoulian, Rouben 200
Manners, J. Hartley 97
'The Man I Love' 70–1
Marlborough, Duke of 85, 94
Marsh, Vera 89, 90
Marx Brothers 76, 168
Mary, Queen 67, 86, 92
Maugham, Somerset 55
Mayer, Louis B. 100, 101, 162, 182, 186, 190
Mellon, Paul 202
Melly, George 120
Mercer, Johnny 165, 185, 186
Merkel, Una 107–108
Merman, Ethel 94
Metcalfe, Baba 60, 65
Metcalfe, Major Edward (Fruity) 59–60
Metro-Goldwyn-Mayer 69, 87, 101, 106, 162, 171, 173, 198, 218
Meyrick, Kate 57, 77, 86
Midas Run 216, 225, 283
Miller, Ann 180, 205, 264
Miller, Marilyn 81, 82, 84
Minnelli, Liza 180, 190, 218–19
Minnelli, Vincente 166–7, 168, 171, 180–1, 189–90, 211
Mistinguett 65
Mitford family 158–9
Morgan, Frank 87
Morgan, J. Pierpont 79, 84, 85
Motion Picture Producers and Distributors of America 123
Mountbatten, Lady 62, 65, 71
Mountbatten, Lord Louis 60, 61–2
Movies 32–3, 69, 76, 99, 100–53, 252, 253
  Astaire's attitude towards Hollywood 122

Astaire's shooting plan 122
the Big White Set 106
colour 135, 148, 162, 166
musicals 106
studio system 101–2
tap dancing sound tracks 3, 111, 125
Murphy, George 162
'My One and Only' 71

Nathan, George Jean 74
'New Songs and Smart Dances' routine 35
New York, Astaires' arrival in 15–16, 17
Night clubs 51–2, 57, 66, 77
'Night and Day' 98, 117, 118, 124
The Nine O'Clock Revue 42
Niven, David 122, 129, 136, 146, 151, 159, 167, 191–2, 193, 194, 203, 250
Nixon, Pat 254
'Nobody But You' 40
The Notorious Landlady 216, 282–3

Oelricht, Marjorie 61, 75
'Oh Gee! oh Gosh! oh Golly! I Love You' 56, 62
Olivieri, Mike 168–9
Omaha 8–16, 23, 204, 217
On The Beach 145, 210, 282
'One More for the Road' 165
'Oompah Trot' 50–1, 52, 54, 56, 64, 71
Orpheum Circuit 23, 37, 38, 40, 100
Osborne, Baby Marie 112
Over the Top 42–4, 149, 265

Palmer, Lilli 215–16, 192
Pan, Hermes 2, 3, 4, 124, 125, 127, 128, 129, 132, 136, 149, 151, 162, 163, 171, 172–3, 180, 181, 182, 186, 188, 193, 194, 199, 205, 208, 217, 248, 252
  Broadway début 114
  choreography 5–6
  collaboration with Astaire 108–10

early career 109
Pan, Maria 109
Paramount Decision 151
Paramount Pictures 76, 162–3
Parkinson, Michael 231–2
The Passing Show of 1918 44–6, 129, 266
Peck, Gregory 197, 225, 248
Pennies From Heaven 251
Phipps, Ogden 93
'Pick Yourself Up' 6
Pickford, Jack 32
Pickford, Mary 32–3, 62
The Pleasure of his Company 215–16, 282
Polglase, Van Nest 106, 133
Porter, Cole 134, 185, 197
　Broadway Melody of 1940 162
　Gay Divorce 97–100, 102, 116, 117–18, 122, 123–4, 125
　'I've a Shooting Box in Scotland' 39
　'Night and Day' 98
Potter, Eliphalet Nott IV (Peter) 95, 96, 99–100, 102, 104, 116, 117, 191, 229
Potter, Phyllis Baker *see* Astaire, Phyllis
Powell, Eleanor 162, 250, 264
Powell, Jane 187–8, 265
Professional Sweetheart 108, 115
Puttin' on the Ritz 6
'Puttin' on the Ritz' 6–7, 173

Rampling, Charlotte 221
Ray, Rev. Randolph 28–30, 81, 170
Raymond, Gene 108
Reagan, Ronald 204, 254, 256
Recordings 35, 62, 252, 291–7
Reed, Jesse 45
Reynolds, Debbie 215
Reynolds, Marjorie 164, 264
Rhodes, Erik 98, 117, 124
Riggs, T. Lawrason 39
Rio, Dolores del 108, 263
Riviera Club 59–60
RKO Studios 100, 106–8, 122–5, 130, 131, 148, 149, 151–2, 164–5

Citizen Kane 152
Robel, Dave 173, 195
Roberta 124–5, 136, 270
Robinson, Bill 38
Robinson, Edward G. 156
Rogers, Ginger 145, 153, 216, 223–4, 254–5
　blonde hair 113, 114
　'Charleston Champion of Texas' 113
　childhood 111–13
　Christian Science 132–3, 254
　dress, 128–30, 131
　marriages 114, 133, 154
　movie career 94
　Oscar award 181
　partnership with Astaire 1, 2–3, 94, 107–8, 124, 127–30, 131–2, 147–49, 162, 182–3, 250, 263
　screen début 112
　signed by RKO studios 108
　vaudeville act 113
Rogers, Lela 94, 111–15, 124, 129, 224
Rolls-Royces 47, 64–5, 66, 70, 76, 146
Roulien, Paul 108
Royal Wedding 187–8, 279
Royce, Teddy 50–1
A Run on Gold see *Midas Run*

' 'S Wonderful, 'S Marvellous' 71
Sandrich, Mark 100–1, 123, 124-5, 126-7, 128, 129, 147, 149, 164, 171, 172
The Sap from Syracuse 94
Schwartz, Arthur 87–9, 185, 189, 192
Scott, Randolph 125, 136, 156, 174, 175, 203, 212, 248
Second Chorus 162–3, 274
Seiter, William 124
Selznick, David O. 100–1, 106, 135, 162, 216
Shall We Dance? 125, 147, 272
Shaw, George Bernard 63
Shubert, Lee and Jake 40–1, 42, 42–4, 44–6

Shuffle Off To Buffalo 108
Silk Stockings 200, 206, 207, 281–2
Simpson, Wallis, 139
Sinatra, Tina 213
The Sky's the Limit 52, 165, 275–6
Smarty see *Funny Face*
Smiles 81–4, 87, 114, 268
Smith, Paul Gerard 70
Smith, Robyn *see* Astaire, Robyn
'Smoke Gets in your Eyes' 125
Snyder, Ted 35
The Soul Kiss 18
Steele, Tommy 217
Stevens, George 125, 149, 183
Stop Flirting see For Goodness Sake
The Story of Vernon and Irene Castle
 149–51, 153, 162, 273
Sullivan, Ed 204
Swing Time 125, 134, 140, 147, 149,
 271
'Swiss Miss' 64

Tap dancing sound tracks 3, 111,
 125
Un Taxi Mauve 221, 284–5
Taylor, Dwight 126
Television 204–5, 211, 217–18,
 286–90
 production companies 205, 209–
 10, 227
Tender Comrade 115
Thalberg, Irving 136
That's Dancing 285
That's Entertainment I and II 218–19,
 283–4
'They Didn't Believe Me' 38
Thomas, John Charles 50
Thompson, Fred 64, 70
Three Little Words 186, 278–9
To Catch a Thief 218
Tom, Dick and Harry see *Smiles*
Top Hat 125, 126–31, 127–31, 270–1
'Top Hat' 6, 127
Top Speed 109, 114
The Towering Inferno 221, 229, 284
Tree, Lady Anne 76
Trocadero cabaret 64–5

Twiggy 218, 254

Ustinov, Peter 221

Vallee, Rudy 114
Vanderbilt, Alfred Gwynne 133, 134
Vanderbilt, Alfred Gwynne II 233–
 6, 237, 243, 244, 245, 246
Vanderbilt, Consuelo 85, 94
Vanderbilt, Virginia 94–5
Vaudeville circuit 15, 19–28, 30,
 34–41, 37–8, 40
 'White Rats' strike 37
Vera-Ellen 186, 264
Vincent, Frank 23

Wagner, Robert 218, 221
Wales, Prince of 1, 57, 59–61, 63,
 65, 66, 67, 69, 77, 81, 87, 93,
 139
 taught tap dancing by Adèle
 Astaire 1, 69–70
Walker, James T. 75
Wall Street Crash 77–8, 81
Wallace, Edgar 67–8
Walsh, George 112
Walsh, Raoul 112
Walter, (dresser) 71, 83, 105
Walters, Charles (Chuck) 187
Wanger, Walter 76
Warren, Harry 185
Wayburn, Ned 25–6, 27, 28, 82
Weatherly, Tom 97, 98
Wedding Bells see *Royal Wedding*
Weehawken, New Jersey 25, 28
Welles, Orson 152, 163
'We're in the Money' 108
'The Whichness of the Whatness
 and the Whereness of the Who'
 52, 54, 62
Whitney, John Hay (Jock) 65–6, 69,
 75, 76, 97–8, 104, 134, 135,
 156, 166, 167
 marriage to Liz Altemus 81, 159
Wilman, Dwight 97
Winchell, Walter 99
The Wizard of Oz 162

Wodehouse, P. G. 147
Wolf, Tommy 186, 251
Woolcott, Alexander 49, 83
World War I 42
World War II 153, 156–60, 167–9
Yolanda and the Thief 171, 179, 276–7
York, Duchess of 61, 67
York, Duke of (George VI) 61, 66, 70, 79, 139
You Said a Mouthful 114
You Were Never Lovelier 163–4, 275

You'll Never Get Rich 52, 163–4, 274
Youmans, Vincent 82, 108, 185
'Young Man of Manhattan' 82–3, 84
Young Man of Manhattan 94, 109, 114
'You're Driving Me Crazy' 82

Zanuck, Darryl 122, 193–4
Ziegfeld, Florenz 42, 81–4
Ziegfeld Follies 166–7, 171, 173, 179, 186, 189, 276